SOVIET AGRICULTURE

BY ZHORES A. MEDVEDEV

The Rise and Fall of T. D. Lysenko
The Medvedev Papers
Ten Years after Ivan Denisovich
Soviet Science
Nuclear Disaster in the Urals
Andropov
Gorbachev

WITH ROY A. MEDVEDEV

A Question of Madness
Khrushchev: The Years in Power

SOVIET AGRICULTURE

Zhores A. Medvedev

W·W·NORTON & COMPANY
NEW YORK · LONDON

Copyright © 1987 by W. W. Norton & Company, Inc.
All rights reserved.

Published simultaneously in Canada by Penguin Books Canada Ltd.,
2801 John Street, Markham, Ontario L3R 1B4.
Printed in the United States of America.

The text of this book is composed in Primer, with
display type set in Weiss. Composition by PennSet, Inc.

Book design by Jacques Chazaud.

Library of Congress Cataloging-in-Publication Data

Medvedev, Zhores A., 1925–
    Soviet agriculture.

    Bibliography: p.
    Includes index.
    1. Agriculture—Economic aspects—Soviet Union—
History. 2. Agriculture and state—Soviet Union—
History. I. Title.
HD1992.M385   1987   338.1'0947   86–31119

ISBN 0-393-02472-5

W. W. Norton & Company, Inc., 500 Fifth Avenue, New York, N.Y. 10110
W. W. Norton & Company Ltd., 37 Great Russell Street, London WC1B 3NU

 2 3 4 5 6 7 8 9 0

Contents

Preface

This book is the result of my life-long involvement in studying and discussing the problems of Soviet agriculture and agricultural sciences. It has taken many years to write. The initial outline was far more optimistic than this final product, a result of extensive research and analysis.

As a biologist and geneticist who had participated in the controversy in Soviet genetics and agronomy since 1946, I believed that the main difficulties in agriculture arose during the decades in which the pseudoscientific ideas of T. D. Lysenko dominated Soviet biology, and other agricultural geneticists and selectionists were purged. I did not challenge the main dogmas of Soviet history, which maintain, first, that the October 1917 decree which nationalized land was a progressive measure taken on behalf of the peasants and, second, that the collectivization of agriculture was essential—except I thought collectivization would have brought more benefits if it had been done more gradually and without excesses. I expected that my book would concentrate on the problems of agricultural science, and that I would describe how the situation began to improve as soon as the Lysenko era ended in 1965. To my surprise, I was unable to follow that plan. I found that it was not only in the 1940s and 1950s that Soviet agricultural science and agricultural economy had little to do with real life—the same thing was true for the 1920s, 1930s, 1970s, and 1980s. Spontaneously, I moved from my intended analysis of science to a study of Soviet political history. This change reflected a gradual and surprising realization that it was not revolution, industrialization, or progress in science and technology that made Russia a unique case in modern history. It was specifically the controversial changes in rural areas that led the Soviet Union to develop outside the traditional pattern of Western civilization.

Lysenko's fall and the obvious improvement in Soviet science in the late 1960s and early 1970s did not have a visible impact on agricultural performance. Production was rising very slowly, but the economic cost of the growth was enormous and increasing. The growth of production based on new scientific methods normally should not follow this unhealthy pattern. It was obvious that poor agricultural performance was linked to bad management and the bureaucratization of the whole government apparatus. When a grain embargo was declared by President Carter early in 1980 as a punishment for Soviet intervention in Afghanistan, I felt sure that it would stimulate the Soviet leadership to reform the system. The Soviet economy had become too heavily dependent on food imports, and it was clear that the dependence had to be broken. The only rational response to the humiliation of the Soviet economic system in 1980 was to reform the system, reduce losses and waste, and release the potential of the land and the people. Amongst Western experts on the Soviet Union it had become a truism, based on the example of the Soviet war economy, that the Soviet system performed better under stress. I started writing this book in 1980, and I thought it would be interesting to observe and analyze the process of reform and improvement that might extend from the agricultural sector to other branches of the economy, and even lead to the liberalization of the whole Soviet system.

In fact, the situation deteriorated year after year, rather than improving. The response of the Soviet leadership was directed not at repairing and improving an obviously outdated and irrational system, but at forcing it to move faster and to operate under duress. The result was predictable. The whole system began to fall apart, and one disastrous harvest has followed another, without a single good year. Acute food shortages and considerable social tension, together with a shortage of foreign exchange for importing food, finally produced a modest political reform at the end of 1986—the legalization of a few forms of private enterprise, directed essentially at revitalizing rural life and rural trade, and the small towns that are directly involved in the rural economy. It will be several years before this reform makes any difference, and possibly the changes will prove to be too modest and too late. But the 1986 reform is the only interesting economic experiment in agriculture that the Soviets have tried in the post-Khrushchev era.

Despite its failures, Soviet agriculture is an interesting area of study for the historian and sociologist, because it is filled with dramatic developments that are closely linked to domestic and foreign policy. Agricultural problems have always played a key role in Russian history, and the Soviet period is no exception. The Revolution of 1917, in Marxist theory a proletarian revolution, was essentially an agrarian revolution. It was a spontaneous uprising of a peasantry determined to solve the land problem and redistribute the land. The main social conflict in Russia at the beginning of the twentieth century was not the class struggle between industrial workers and capitalists. Industrial development was a recent phenomenon, and workers' parties and trade unions were still weak. The conflict between archaic peasant communes and the *pomeshchiki* (the landowning class) was older and more desperate, the result of long delays in rural development. In the rest of Europe, which shared with Russia the tradition of a folk culture shaped by agriculture, the consolidation of farm plots and the division of communal land mainly took place in the eighteenth and nineteenth centuries. One to two hundred years had been needed to transform the archaic communal system of stripped agriculture, with peasant families owning from twenty to a hundred small plots outward from the villages. Peasant communes had resisted the change. Legislation, urban development, and local conflict gradually turned most peasants into independent family farmers who owned, leased, or rented their consolidated fields, and were free to introduce modern agricultural methods and innovations. They began to compete, to use new seed, fertilizers, and new machinery. (In North America free farming came into existence in an entirely different way.)

Communal agriculture and stripped fields remained intact in Russia at the beginning of the twentieth century. The first reforms following the common European pattern were introduced in 1906. Although they were progressive, they created many types of tension and conflict. However, these reforms stimulated agricultural production, and at the outset of the First World War Russia had become the largest exporter of high-quality grain, technical crops, and livestock products. Peasant communes were backward as productive units, but they reflected ancient traditions, genuine socialist principles, and common interests. The main trends in the Russian socialist movements of the nineteenth century were shaped by rural problems rather than by Marxist theories. The Socialist Revolutionaries, the strongest political party, represented the interests of the peasant communes. They thought that the *obshchina*—the traditional commune—was potentially the natural unit of a future socialist republic. The Bolshevik section of the Russian Social Democratic Workers' Party, however, strenuously opposed this view. The Bolshevik position contributed to Lenin's mistaken and almost fatal policy of "War Communism" in 1918–1921, which treated the peasants as a capitalist class and legalized the requisition of food from the villages by force and without compensation. The New Economic Policy of 1921 was a retreat, restoring communal agriculture in its traditional form. At the same time, it was an attempt to induce differentiation in the communes in order to stimulate agricultural production through individual competition. The process was suddenly and brutally interrupted by forced collectivization in 1930–1934. That unnatural and disruptive interference in spontaneous social development brought about many subsequent problems.

From being the food basket of Europe and the largest exporter of grain, the Soviet Union eventually became the world's largest importer of grain and livestock products—purchasing from more than sixty countries and sending cargo ships as far as Australia, Argentina, and New Zealand to bring back grain, meat, butter, and sugar. This book considers the historical, political, economic, and agronomic aspects of that vast change.

But the book not only describes and explains the failures of Soviet agriculture. What happened in the Soviet Union is only part of the story. Similar grand experiments in agriculture have been carried out in all the countries of Eastern Europe; as well as in China, Vietnam, North Korea, and several African countries. Although the comparative analysis of agricultural developments in various countries is too large a task for a book of this scope, readers will probably realize that many of the current problems of the world's food balance are closely linked to developments in socialist agriculture. My intention was to describe events, explain them, and indicate the alternatives that were rejected, whether by chance, deliberately, or through ignorance. I did not want to portray the history of Soviet agriculture as a sequence of efforts and errors, achievements and tragedies. I wanted to present it as a political, economic, and scientific experiment in which the final results differed from those originally expected. Soviet agricultural history provides a great lesson for the world at large—for rich and poor countries alike. Agriculture remains, and will always remain, the basis of human existence. Despite rapid urbanization we all need to know how much is left of the earth's agricultural potential. If a large, historically agricultural country like the Soviet Union is in a state of almost perennial food crisis, it is not a local political, social, or economic problem. It is a general problem. It must be studied, its causes must be discovered, and solutions suggested. My hope is that this book will prove interesting not only to Soviet specialists, but to more general readers, particularly those who have not cut their links with the land and who preserve their love of nature.

I would like to thank my brother, Roy, who assisted me greatly by sending dozens of books and journals and hundreds of newspaper clippings on agriculture over many years, and made it possible for me to follow developments within the Soviet Union. I am also grateful to my Western colleagues, with whom I have discussed problems of Soviet agriculture and who made their books and papers on the subject available to me. The help and advice of Dr. L. R. Brown, Professor R. W. Davis, Professor D. Joravsky, Professor A. Nove, Professor R. L. Paarlberg, and Dr. S. G. Wheatcroft was particularly valuable. I would also like to express my gratitude to Dr. Margot Light of the University of Surrey for her linguistic and editorial assistance during the book's writing. But most of all I would like to thank my teachers in agriculture, Professor P. M. Zhukovsky, Professor D. N. Prianishnikov, Professor N. A. Maisurian, and Professor B. A. Golubev—who tried to prove, in the most difficult period of 1944–1950, that if the Soviet Union followed the right policy it would have a great future in the world food balance. They did not live long enough to witness their prophecies come true. But their hopes live on in many of their students.

Zhores A. Medvedev
London

Part One

POLITICAL TRANSFORMATIONS, 1900-1964

Chapter 1

Agriculture
before the Revolution

Many current problems of Soviet agriculture can only be understood by examining the history of the traditional Russian rural community. A unique and extreme form of feudalism survived in Russia until the middle of the nineteenth century. Serfs were treated little better than slaves and when they were finally emancipated on February 19, 1861, they were burdened with such high "redemption payments" for freedom and for land that it was envisaged that repayment would extend over forty years. Many other problems inherited from the feudal system had not been resolved by the time the Revolution occurred in 1917.

Before the sixteenth century the Russian *knyaz* (prince) or *boyar* (count) was usually a very wealthy landowner whose power extended over whole principalities or provinces. He descended from the nobles who had founded Kiev Rus and later Muscovy in the ninth to eleventh centuries. Like the feudal nobility elsewhere, the Russian nobility was a military caste. The private armies of the nobles prevented the grand prince from enjoying the absolute power which the kings of France, Spain, and England already possessed in the fourteenth to fifteenth centuries. The monarchs of Western Europe were assisted in their acquisition of absolute power by the decline in the power of the nobility as towns developed and a new burgess class emerged. In Russia it was the czar's attempt to deal with the power of the nobility which finally resulted in the introduction of a particularly severe form of serfdom in 1581. Ivan IV (Ivan the Terrible) was the first grand duke to be crowned czar (derived from *Caesar*) of all Russia, a country inhabited by 3 or 4 million people, rather less than the population of Ireland, Poland, or Lithuania in the sixteenth century.

1. *The Rise and Fall of Russian Serfdom*

Ivan IV divided his territory into two parts. In one part the boyars continued to govern. In the other Ivan IV ruled with the help of a special corps of loyal bodyguards. Called the *oprichniki*, these 2,000 to 6,000 men were given land in return for their service. By the time the system was abolished in 1572 the *oprichniki* had become a new landowning aristocracy, called the *pomeshchiki* (from the the Russian word for "estate"—*pomestye*). Unlike the princes and boyars, this new landowning nobility was neither rich nor powerful. The czar had purposefully undermined the influence of the old aristocracy by fragmenting the previous system of land ownership. The new *pomeshchiki* owned a few villages, or perhaps only one, and the local peasants worked the land for them rather than fighting in their private armies. Part of the land and a substantial part of the peasant population (known as "state peasants") became the property of the throne.

The decree of 1581, which prohibited the free movement of the peasant tenants of the *pomeshchiki*, is usually considered as initiating Russia's strict system of serfdom. But this was only the beginning. The peasants were tied to the land, but it was land which belonged to the nobility, not the people. More than a century later, Peter the Great turned the peasants into the property of the landowners. *Pomeshchiki* could now sell peasants without land, arrange their marriages, and act as their supreme judge and executioner. Serfs and their families could be bought and sold, transferred from one place to another, or used as slave labor for Peter the Great's many building projects and factories. Subsequent monarchs extended the system: the ultimate form of Russian serfdom occurred at the end of the eighteenth century in the reign of Catherine the Great. Catherine extended serfdom into the Ukraine and passed decrees which made it possible for landlords to treat their serfs in a manner which had previously only been possible for the czar. Serfs became little different from slaves. It was not until Napoleon invaded Russia in 1812 that the system began to crack. The first sign of change was a decree by Alexander I which prohibited the sale of peasants without land.

The extreme form of serfdom extended over Russia and the northern part of Ukraine. The Cossack regions of the North Caucasus, the South Urals, and Siberia were areas of free farming, where there were neither *pomeshchiki* nor serfs. By 1861 about one-third of the population of the country lived in these areas. Landlord-peasant relations in Central Asia, Transcaucasia, Poland, and the Baltic provinces differed from area to area, depending on local tradition and religion. But since these areas played a minor part in the land and peasant problems which influenced developments in Russia in the first part of the twentieth century, these relations will not be examined here.

The Emancipation Act of 1861 was intended to preserve the viability of the *pomeshchiki*, the staunch allies of the monarchy. Peasants received their personal freedom, but the land was considered to be the property of the *pomeshchiki*. Arable land was divided between the landowners and the peasant *obshchiny* (communes), but the peasants had to buy their communal land from the *pomeshchiki*. Since the communes had no money, the state paid the landowners who received large sums of money to invest into the development of their estates and to employ agricultural workers. The peasant communes received their *nadely* (plots) and became indebted to the state. Their redemption payments for the land were to extend over forty-nine years, until 1910. The poorer communes were allowed to make payments in kind or by labor, but the intention was that they would convert to cash payments in time.

The amount of land given over to the peasants under the terms of the Emancipation Edict was less than they had cultivated for their own needs when they were serfs. Thus there was constant pressure for the redistribution of land. Moreover, under the terms of the emancipation, the forests remained the property of the landlords, to be used for hunting or for commercial purposes. Peasants now had to buy their timber for building and their firewood for heating and cooking from the *pomeshchiki*. "Illegal" tree felling, clashes between peasants and forest guards, and constant litigation became permanent features of rural life. The obligation to make redemption payments prevented the communes from investing in agricultural development. The expectation that the repayments could be completed by 1900 proved to be wildly optimistic. In most provinces the repayments had still not been completed by the 1905 Revolution and the redemption debts inherited by the generation of peasants born free after 1861 were a permanent source of hostility between the peasants and the *pomeshchiki*. It was not until after the 1905 Revolution that the government cancelled the remaining debts. All these circumstances served to encourage revolutionary tendencies amongst the Russian peasantry.

The peasants were represented by the *Narodnik* party, which soon became an influential part of the "Socialist-Revolutionaries" (SRs). Their influence was particularly strong in central Russia, from St. Petersburg in the North and Perm and Orenburg in the east; to Kursk, Orel, Kharkov, and Kiev in the south; and Minsk, Smolensk, and Brest in the west. It was here that communes were poorest, peasant plots smallest, and tensions between the *pomeshchiki* and *muzhiki* (peasants) strongest. It was also the most densely populated part of the country which could not produce any surplus grain for the market. Peasants could only support their dependents by supplementing their incomes: they worked for the local *pomeshchiki* or in the primitive rural industries (engaging in carpentry, producing agricultural tools, homemade flax and woollen cloth, carts, and other equipment for horses or trade) or they worked in the towns and cities in winter. The surplus grain and other foodstuffs sold on the urban markets and exported abroad was produced primarily in the more prosperous *chernozem* ("black-soil") provinces of the Ukraine, Don basin, North Caucasus, and Siberia.

2. *The Crisis in the Rural* Obshchina *at the Turn of the Nineteenth Century*

Cooperation between peasant families living in isolated villages under severe climatic conditions is a natural phenomenon. But the Russian peasant communes grew out of the feudal system rather than as a form of voluntary mutual assistance. The *pomeshchiki* found it more convenient to deal with a village commune via an elected or appointed chairman than with individual families. The communes became a compulsory institution from the middle of the eighteenth century, when serfdom was at its most exploitative. They were retained and incorporated into the Emancipation Act since the state mortgaged the land to the commune rather than to individual households. The reason for retaining the communal system was to prevent the formation of a class of free farmers. Neither the *pomeshchiki* nor the government wanted the village settlements to dissolve as peasants migrated from their plots. The only way to ensure that the redemption payments were made and that the landlords retained a work force was to make sure that the peasants remained the lowest social group, still attached to their land.

As a legal entity, the *obshchina* (the term is derived from the word *obshchii*, meaning "joint" or "common") was based on the socialist principle of equality: the standard of living of individual households was equalized by distributing land in proportion to the size of individual households or to the number of adult members in the household. Although the Stolypin reforms from 1906 to 1916 weakened the system, they were revived during the 1917 Revolution and the communes were an essential part of the New Economic Policy introduced by Lenin in 1921. It was collectivization which destroyed the system. Although communal land ownership and work was a positive social phenomenon, it was inflexible and it proved to be an obstacle to increasing agricultural productivity and introducing new, complex systems of crop rotation.

The main productive defect of the commune was the attempt to divide everything equally and to retain equality despite changes in the number of members or families in the commune. All the fields belonging to a village were divided into groups according to their quality and their convenience in terms of distance, water supply, and so on. Each field was then divided into sections (called *kliny*) according to a simple system of crop rotation— winter rye or wheat, barley or oats, and fallow land. This was the traditional Russian three-field rotation. It was considered unjust to give each household a consolidated piece of land. Each household should own a small piece of every field, so the *kliny* were divided into strips which were distributed to the households. This gave the communal fields their characteristic and peculiar striped appearance. The borders between strips were not cultivated. This was not only a waste of land, but also a constant source of weeds. A village might own several fields of various sizes, miles apart, separated by forests, rivers, or hills. Thus a family could have as many as fifty or sixty individual scattered strips and a great deal of time would be wasted, particularly at the height of the agricultural season, moving from one strip to another. Death, marriage, childbirth, and so on changed the size of the various families and made it necessary to redistribute the strips every ten years or so. The rural population grew rapidly, particularly in the second half of the nineteenth century, and the inevitable result was that individual households received fewer and fewer strips with each redistribution, and the strips gradually became smaller and smaller. Thus the productivity of the communal land remained very low, while that of the *pomeshchiki* increased as better crop-rotation methods and agricultural machinery were introduced and qualified agricultural advice became available.

Until the end of the century there were about 100,000 estates belonging to *pomeshchiki*. Although this was only 1 percent of the number of peasant households, these estates constituted about 50 percent of the arable land and most of forests and pastures. In the central provinces alone the peasant population more than doubled between 1861 and 1900, rising from 30 million to 70 million, but there was hardly any increase in the amount of land available for cultivation. Thus in economic terms (measured in food consumption and per capita income) the 100 million peasants in the Russian Empire were worse off in 1900 than the 40 million peasants had been in 1800. In 1800 there had been about 2 *desyatin* (5.4 acres) of grain-producing land per person, whereas in 1900 there was only 0.8 *desyatin* (2 acres) per person. Although emancipation had granted mobility to the peasants, the conditions were so strict that it did little to alleviate the overpopulation of the central provinces. Under article 130 of the Emancipation Edict, if a peasant wanted to leave his village to settle elsewhere he had to be free of conscription obligations, renounce forever his rights to a communal *nadel* (the sum total of all the strips to which he was entitled), and pay all his state, local, communal, and private debts (this was the most difficult obstacle to overcome). He also had to get the permission both of his parents and of the *mir* (the meeting of all members of the commune), and he had to have papers proving an offer of employment in town or, in the case of intervillage marriages, the agreement of the commune to which he was moving to accept a new member. Only when all these conditions had been fulfilled could he get a temporary internal passport from the police. The peasants were the only social group without an automatic right to internal passports. This was clearly a device to keep them at the bottom of the social ladder. Without temporary passports, they were liable to arrest and forcible return to their villages.

The periodic redistribution of strips was a just principle (indeed, it may even be called communist), but it seriously hampered the introduction of better farming methods. When the average size of the strips began to be reduced and more productive varieties of crops were introduced, many *obshchiny* in the central non-*chernozem* provinces ceased to redistribute the land. The soil in these areas required labor-intensive improvements like fertilization with manure, chalking, or drainage. Peasants were less likely to make the necessary investment if they expected to lose those strips at the next redistribution. On the other hand, without redistribution it became difficult to give land to new families. Adult children with their own families often had to continue living with their parents. Thus the large, extended Russian family with several generations living under one roof was a product of the rules of the commune. In the more fertile *chernozem* provinces, such as the Ukraine, Rostov, Voronezh, and Saratov, the system of redistribution was retained. These areas had rich, black topsoil as much as a meter deep. Good harvests were produced without intensive fertilization and most of the available manure was used as fuel or for growing vegetables and technical crops in the small plots attached to the peasants' houses.

One of the results of the emancipation was an immediate increase in the rural birthrate. This was not the product of an improved standard of living, but merely the result of the freedom to choose one's spouse and the knowledge that children would be born free and that they would work for themselves rather than for the enrichment of the *pomeshchiki*. In the European part of Russia the peasant population grew from 55 million in 1863 to 81 million in 1897.[1] In the thirty-four years following emancipation the population in the European provinces grew approximately as much as it had in that area in the hundred years before emancipation. But at the same time the limited opportunities for increasing the amount of communal land and the strict communal rules meant that the total acreage of communal holding remained virtually unchanged. About 3 million peasants moved to towns and cities and the total urban population grew from 6 million to 12 million by 1897.

The rapid growth in the rural population made it more and more difficult to preserve traditional communal principles. Reforms were urgently required, at the very least to encourage migration to the underpopulated eastern parts of the country. As the individual *nadely* became smaller and smaller in the central provinces, proper land cultivation became impossible. Individual strips were often only about 3 feet wide and 600 to 900 feet long and some were as narrow as 28 inches. It was difficult to use horses on such narrow strips. The same system of crop rotation had to be used by all the members of the *obshchina*. Similarly, mowing and haymaking had to be done jointly by all households, after which the fields would usually be turned over to communal pasture. In the nineteenth century the rest of Europe was already using more productive multi-rotation systems using soil-enriching leguminous crops. There is no doubt that the *obshchina* was an extremely backward agricultural system, but it was the only way to keep and feed about 100 million peasants at the end of the nineteenth century when Russian industry was not yet sufficiently developed to absorb the surplus population. Attempts were made to buy or rent land from the *pomeshchiki*, but the process of increasing communal land was extremely slow. Between 1877 and 1905 the average size of each peasant household's *nadel* in the European part of Russia was reduced from 8.9 *desyatin* to 6.7 *desyatin* (or from 24.1 acres to 18.1 acres) compared to 36.9 *desyatin* per household in the Baltic provinces and 53 *desyatin* of very fertile land per family in the Cossack villages of the North Caucasus. But the most acute land shortage occurred in central, northern, and western Russia.[2]

By the end of the nineteenth century and the beginning of the twentieth, the rapid development of capitalism began to attract peasants to the cities. Moreover, the smaller *pomeshchiki*, particularly in the central and western provinces, found themselves unable to compete with the more productive estates in the *chernozem* areas in selling their produce in Moscow, St. Petersburg, and the other large northern cities. As a result they began to sell, lease, or mortgage their land and move to the towns. The amount of arable land in communal ownership gradually began to increase. In 1861 more than half of all arable land belonged to the *pomeshchiki*. By 1905 their share had fallen to 36.2 percent of the agricultural land in European Russia (see Table 1).

Despite the increase of communal arable land, the problem of rural overpopulation remained acute. There was no real land problem in the eastern part of Russia. But in the rest of the country the 20 million *desyatin* of land which had been pur-

TABLE 1

Land Distribution in European Russia, 1905[3]

	Number	Land (*desyatin*)
Pomeshchiki and large landowners	133,918	79,318,000
Peasant households	11,998,705	139,715,000 (communal land)

chased from the *pomeshchiki* consisted of less productive or inconveniently located fields or forest clearings. In 1905 the *pomeshchiki* possessed less land than the peasants, but it was the best land. The total value of their land was higher than that of the communal land[3] and it was the *pomeshchiki* who produced most of the marketable grain. In 1905 they employed about 5 million agricultural workers.

The obsolete methods and low productivity of the communal land contrasted sharply with the modern mechanized techniques used on the large estates. In 1905 the average communal grain yield was about 45 to 48 *pud* per *desyatin* (7.5 centners per hectare), about a third of the level then usual in France or Germany. The discovery that leguminous plants assimilated atmospheric nitrogen (the nitrogen-fixation process) had revolutionized European agriculture in the nineteenth century and the use of clover and other leguminous plants in the seven- or eight-field rotation system had doubled the yield. But these discoveries were irrelevant to strip farming. The traditional three-field rotation system left 33 percent of all arable land fallow each year. Introducing a multi-rotation system with clover as a one- or two-year crop would have reduced the fallow fields to 12 percent and increased the fertility of the soil. The advantages were obvious to many peasants, but the cultivation of many small strips in different places and the periodic redistribution made the multi-rotation system almost impossible. A few *obshchiny* introduced a four-field rotation with clover, but only about 10 to 12 percent had begun to cultivate leguminous crops by the beginning of the twentieth century.

The humiliating defeat in the Russo-Japanese War of 1904–1905 resulted in many uprisings in the Russian Empire, particularly in the large industrial centers like Moscow and St. Petersburg. Although the 1905 Revolution did not begin as a peasant revolution, it rapidly spread to the countryside, and the estates of thousands of *pomeshchiki* were burned and looted. The Revolution was ruthlessly suppressed, but the monarchy finally realized that something had to be done about the overpopulation and political radicalism of the impoverished *obshchiny*. The combination of the urban proletariat and the peasant masses in the surrounding rural areas made an explosive union. The Stolypin reforms were intended to prevent this explosion. Their main aim was to increase the migration of the peasants from the overpopulated central provinces to the Urals and the east and to break up the communal system in order to create a new class of independent farmers.

3. *Stolypin's Reforms*

The immediate cause of the 1905 Revolution was the brutal gunning down of hundreds of St. Petersburg workers by the army on Sunday, January 9, 1905. A peaceful demonstration, led by the priest, Father Gapon, was marching to the Winter Palace to deliver a petition to Czar Nicholas II. It is not known whether the czar was in the palace at the time, but the populace held him directly responsible for the fateful events. This Sunday, subsequently known as "Bloody Sunday," was a turning point in Russian history. The immediate reaction to the shooting was a general strike in St. Petersburg, followed by spontaneous uprisings in January and February in other cities and in rural areas. In 1905 and 1906 peasant revolts occurred in half of all the provinces of European Russia. The most serious uprisings occurred in February 1905 in the Kursk, Orel, and Chernigov provinces. The regular army and the special Cossack units remained loyal to the throne and, together with the police and the gendarmerie, had little difficulty in suppressing these spontaneous and ill-coordinated uprisings. But the turmoil in the rural areas strengthened the left-wing faction of the SRs and transformed the party into a mass movement. A terrorist faction carried out a number of political assassinations of which the most significant was the murder of the governor-general of Moscow, the Grand Duke Sergei, uncle of the czar.

Towards the end of 1905 the czar's resolve to crush the uprisings weakened. On October 17 he issued a manifesto, promising reforms, including some civil liberties and a constitution which would reduce his absolute power. It was important to have a strong and able figure as head of the government. In July 1906 the czar appointed Pyotr Arkadyevich Stolypin as chairman of the Council of Ministers. Stolypin retained the post he had held since April 1906 as minister of the interior. He had previously served as governor of Saratov province, where he was renowned for his brutal and efficient suppression of peasant rebellions. His first act as chairman of the Council of Ministers was to dismiss the *Duma*, the legislative body which had been elected in fulfillment of the October Manifesto. He began to rule by executive decree and it was these decrees which later became known as the "Stolypin reforms." Stolypin also became notorious for his decisive measures to prevent the development of revolutionary processes in the provinces. He instituted special court-martials, which carried out more than a thousand death sentences in 1906–1907. He also later suspended the second *Duma* when it failed to approve his agrarian reforms.

The decree which initiated the Stolypin reforms was issued on November 9, 1906. The outstanding redemption debts were cancelled and peasant households were permitted to consolidate their communal strips, claim individual ownership of their *nadely*, and withdraw from the communes. The intention was to break up the communal system and to encourage the more prosperous peasants to become independent farmers. But the decree was not radical enough to change the traditions of village life. Although many peasants tried to consolidate their strips and build farms separate from the village, the process was extremely slow. Consolidation required the approval of a two-thirds majority of the commune, and few peasants were offered good land for their farms. Although the reform created the legal basis for individual farming, it did nothing to reduce the resistance of most communes to the process.

Stolypin's second reform, of June 14, 1910, was more radical, but it also was not very effective. It dissolved all the communes which had not redistributed land since the emancipation. These were mostly in the central, northern, and western parts of the country, where the villages were small and poor and the soil required substantial investment to increase its fertility. Although these peasants could now consolidate their strips, consolidation was almost impossible, since large areas of this part of the country were covered by forests and the fields were small. Few peasants wanted consolidated fields located far from the villages and roads. A year later, on May 29, 1911, Stolypin passed a new decree, which simplified consolidation and leaving the commune in any part of the country. Peasants who were leaving the communes could register their *nadely* as their own private property even if it was still fragmented into strips. They could sell part or all of it if they wished to move. Banks could offer large credits and the state offered grants to peasants who wanted to settle in the Urals, Siberia, or the Far East. The new Trans-Siberian railway which had been completed at the end of the nineteenth century made the colonization of Siberia much easier. This decree (approved by the conservative third *Duma*, elected on the basis of new election laws) was the first to make a real impact, since it extended to the more prosperous *chernozem* areas of the steppe where many peasants wished to get the title to their land and consolidate their scattered strips.

Stolypin expected that the *obshchina* would disappear entirely within fifteen to twenty years and that individual farmers would become the dominant class in rural Russia. By 1915 about half of all the households in Russia had become private owners of their *nadely*. Land titles had been given to 6 to 7 million owners (the head of each household was considered the sole property owner). However, most of this land was still in strips and only about 1.2 million peasants had been able to consolidate their holdings into separate farms. The problem was that consolidation affected every other household in the commune. Not only was their consent required, but the land distribution experts had to advise and the final decision had to be made by professional land commissions. The latter were established by decree, but they had to be set up by the local administration which also had to provide the services of the experts on land distribution. This was a slow and difficult task. Stolypin himself did not live to see the results of his reform. He was assassinated on September 1, 1911.

Most of the peasants who left the communes to start their own farms formed that section of the peasantry which was known as the *serednyaks*, or middle peasants. But Stolypin's hope was fulfilled that a class of wealthy peasants, or kulaks, would become established without damaging the interests of the *pomeshchiki*. By 1913 the kulaks were already producing more marketable grain than the *pomeshchiki*.[4] Agricultural production as a whole began to grow rapidly, and the differentiation of peasants into classes became more visible. Although most of the kulak farms were family based, some kulaks began to employ agricultural workers. Poor peasants often preferred to sell or rent their *nadely* and enter employment.Thus the formation of a rural bourgeoisie was accompanied by an increase in the rural proletariat. The term *kulak* did not, at first, have a negative meaning. Better-off members of the communes had been known as kulaks, which merely meant strong, hardworking, or efficient peasants who were better than the rest at cultivating their land. Between 1906 and 1916 the kulaks achieved a higher agricultural productivity than either the communal peasants or the *pomeshchiki*.

The *obshchiny* did not disappear without resistance. They often obstructed consolidation and there were innumerable local conflicts and lawsuits against kulaks for illegal use of land. Kulaks were not allowed to graze their farm animals on communal meadows. The competition between the communes and the kulaks was desperate, but it was clear that the victory of the kulaks was

TABLE 2

Grain Production by Social Group, 1909–1913
(as a Percentage of Total Production)

	Production	Consumption	Marketable surplus
Middle and poor peasants	50.0	42.6	7.4
Kulaks	38.0	25.0	13.0
Pomeshchiki	12.0*	6.4	5.6
Total	100.0	74.0	26.0

Source: Nemchinov (1945).[4]

* The reduced production of the *pomeshchiki* (compared to the situation in the nineteenth century) reflects the fact that they leased, rented, or sold a considerable amount of land in 1906–1913, particularly to kulaks.

inevitable. The communal form of agriculture with its strip farming and steadily decreasing size of *nadel* was obsolete, unproductive, and unsuited to the needs of a rapidly developing capitalist society.

Stolypin's reforms accelerated the agricultural colonization of eastern Russia. The peak years of migration eastward were 1907–1909, and about 3 million peasants settled in Siberia during the Stolypin period. After 1910 the newly cultivated virgin lands in the Urals, Siberia, and Central Asia began to produce significant amounts of grain, cotton, and other crops for internal and external trade. By average Russian standards most of the Siberian peasants were kulaks, but the establishment of prosperous individual farmers took place here without the kind of communal conflict that was typical in other areas. There was plenty of land available and no problem of overpopulation.

The results of Stolypin's reforms are well demonstrated in Table 2, which compares the amount of grain produced and consumed by various social groups in the period 1909–1913.

When the First World War began in August 1914, agricultural production was not significantly impaired, despite the mobilization of about 15 million peasants for military service. There was still a surplus work force in rural areas. The first two years of the war served to stimulate agricultural and industrial production. But the picture began to change in 1916 when the many defeats of the Russian army and the continuous retreat of the front deeper and deeper into the countryside started to disrupt the long communication lines between the agricultural south and the industrial north.

4. *The Agrarian Base of the 1917 Revolution*

Shocked by the first defeats in the war in August 1914, the government of Nicholas II reacted with a mobilization of unprecedented size, calling up about 15 million men to active military service. The Russian army became the largest in world history, but its technical level remained very low. More than 90 percent of the soldiers were former peasants with poor military training. The only exceptions were the Cossack divisions, since the Cossacks were traditionally half peasants and half soldiers. Losses in the Russian army were extremely high—by 1915 more than 5 million soldiers had been killed, wounded, or captured. Towards the end of 1915 the Austro-German army drove the Russian army out of the Polish provinces and occupied parts of the Ukraine, Byelorussia, and the Baltic provinces.

The number of peasant soldiers, the extended front, and the rapid expansion of military industries put tremendous new pressures on agricultural production. Although the overpopulation of rural Russia meant that the loss of manpower could be sustained, agricultural production could not be expanded sufficiently to feed the huge army and the swollen cities. Moreover, the loss of Poland, Western Ukraine, and parts of the Baltic provinces—areas where agriculture was better developed than in central Russia— had a severe impact on the balance of food in the country. The army "mobilized" several million horses from rural areas and this further reduced agricultural productivity. But the most serious problems were caused by the underdeveloped transport system. The railway network was inadequate to cope with the sharply increased procurement of grain and other food products. Food shortages were soon aggravated by shortages of fuel, textiles, tobacco, and hundreds of other commodities and goods. The industrial base was too weak to keep the army and the industrial centers supplied. Prices began to rise and by 1916 inflation was high. The government refused to raise the procurement prices for agricultural products and, as a result, the peasants were reluctant to sell their produce. The rural provinces around St. Potoroburg, the moot crucial industrial center (now renamed Petrograd'), and Moscow were barely able to feed themselves, and they were too far from the main granaries of the south to be supplied easily from there. During the late autumn of 1916 the first disturbances and strikes relating to food began to occur in many industrial cities. The government introduced rationing, but long lines of people waiting to buy bread became a common sight. The population of Petrograd had almost doubled since 1914, partly because of the growth of industries and partly because of the stream of refugees from the Baltic provinces. By 1917 Petrograd was the second largest city in continental Europe, with a population of 2.5 million. The only railway line that supplied Petrograd came from Moscow, itself a consumer city with a population of about 2 million. Although Petrograd was the capital, Moscow was the center of the railway. Food arrived in Moscow from the south and was divided and sent to Petrograd and to the industrial cities in the Urals, which were equally important to the war effort. And despite the acute food shortages in Petrograd, food had to be supplied from there to the province of Pskov, where the headquarters of the Russian army was situated, and to the northwestern section of the front, where a large concentration of troops protected Petrograd's vulnerable military position. The food shortages could have been alleviated had the transport system been more efficient. The war had halted the export of grain (between 1910 and 1913 Russia exported more than 10 million metric tons of grain annually) and there was a considerable amount in store in the south. The grain stocks in the south continued to grow, but not enough of it could be transported to Moscow, Petrograd, and the other industrial cities. Petrograd was in the worst position, since the approaches by sea were blocked by the German fleet.

At this critical stage of Russian history Stolypin's reforms began to misfire. Although the *obshchina* was an obsolete, unproductive method of farming, it was the ideal system in times of crisis, when mutual sacrifice and working for the common cause were required. It had always helped widows and the families of soldiers to cultivate their strips and to meet their obligations to the state. For centuries the Russian army had been a conscripted army. The commune had helped to decide who should be sent for military service. However, by 1916 the *obshchiny* had been mortally wounded by the reforms and they were extremely poor, rarely producing any surplus food. The peasant bourgeoisie—the kulaks—had become the main producer of marketable grain and other food products. But as a new rural capitalist class they reacted on the basis of capitalist principles—the increased demand for their products should have created a proportional increase in procurement prices, but the government had refused to increase the prices. The kulaks therefore sold their surpluses to speculators at high prices and the state had not yet instituted a system for procuring food from individual households which bypassed market rules. The productivity of the *pomeshchik* estates had deteriorated badly during the war, since conscription had deprived them of cheap labor. Many of their large fields were underused or completely idle. This encouraged the local communes, always hungry for extra land, to think about more radical means of land redistribution. Although the situation in the villages became more and more tense, there was no organization to produce coordinated action. In 1914, exploiting the patriotic and nationalistic sentiments provoked by the war, the government had swiftly arrested and exiled almost all the known members of the revolutionary parties—SRs, Bolsheviks, and Mensheviks—as well as their representatives in the *Duma* and members of smaller left-wing groups. Many of the leaders of these parties emigrated.

The February 1917 Revolution was a genuinely spontaneous, popular uprising which developed without the organizational in-

fluence of any political party or group. It was simply the culmi-
nation of innumerable independent strikes, meetings, and demonstrations, and mutinies within the army units stationed in
Petrograd and the naval units of the Baltic Fleet. Most of the
demonstrations were related to the shortage of food. The slogans
"Bread!," "Down with the war," and "Down with the monarchy"
were the natural result of the general anger with a government
which was incapable of providing food. The only city in which
there were serious disturbances was Petrograd, yet the monarchy
collapsed and the czar abdicated. Other cities and towns followed
the example of the capital without any struggle or fighting. The
Russian Empire had ceased to exist. The revolutionary parties
were as surprised as the czar had been, since the February Revolution was, as Harrison Salisbury points out:

> A revolution in which not a single revolutionary had yet
> played any role. It had been made by ordinary citizens, par-
> ticularly angry women, housewives sick and tired of standing
> in freezing queues before empty shops . . ."[5]

Once the czar had abdicated, the only remaining symbol of a
united Russian state was the *Duma*, or what was left of it after
the arrest of its radical members at the beginning of the war. It
had retained a purely consultative role during the war and although it had no constitutional power to form a government, it
was the only body capable of doing so. The public accepted the
first "Provisional Government" by default—there was no other
alternative. But the only way in which it could hope to survive
was by acknowledging military defeat and signing a separate
peace treaty. This was something the parties still represented in
the *Duma* could not bring themselves to do. Their decision to
continue the war was a fatal miscalculation.

In the cities the populace responded to the new government
with hope and excitement. Petrograd and Moscow quietened down,
civil rights and freedoms were granted, political processes were
instituted, and attempts were made to create order by building a

new infrastructure. The arrested members of the *Duma* were released and many of them joined the Provisional Government, in which the main influence was exerted by the Constitutional Democrats (Kadets), the Mensheviks, and the right-wing SRs. New locally elected councils, called Soviets, sprang up in Petrograd and other cities and assumed authority for problems that had previously been within the competence of the bureaucratic government hierarchy that had collapsed with the monarchy. The left-wing SRs and the Bolsheviks werc heavily represented in the Soviets. But, despite the rapid growth of the urban population during the war, Russia was still a predominantly rural country. In 1917 there were 29 million people living in cities in the unoccupied territories and 135 million in rural areas. In the countryside the Revolution was only in its initial phase, and it was spreading rapidly.

The peasants expected the new government to begin redistributing the land immediately. Land redistribution in favor of the peasant communes was the main platform of the SR party, which split over the issue. The left-wing SRs were committed to the immediate confiscation of land from the *pomeshchiki*, and they broke with the right-wing SRs to form an independent party. The government was reluctant to initiate land reform while it was still "provisional." But in any case, the war was continuing and 15 million peasants were in the army. Russia's allies failed to understand the acute danger of an internal explosion in the former Russian Empire and pressed the Provisional Government to continue the war effort. The rumors and expectation of redistribution had already provoked mass desertions, a trend which was almost impossible to reverse in such a vast and disorganized country.

It was not the storming of the Winter Palace in October, but the beginning of the sowing season in the spring of 1917, which was to change the course of Russian history. Had the Provisional Government begun to introduce agrarian reforms during that spring, it may well have been able to hold power until well into the following year. The decision to wait until the election of the Constituent Assembly in 1918 proved fatal. Frightened by the collapse of the monarchy and the absence of law and order, most of the *pomeshchiki* had fled to the towns, deserting their estates without preparing their land for the spring sowing season. The governement created local agricultural committees, but they had no power and no idea of how to deal with the situation. The peasant communes wanted them to start redistributing the land, while the *pomeshchiki* wanted them to guarantee the safety of their estates and their property. The inability of the *pomeshchiki* to start sowing aggravated the already acute food shortages in the cities. Bread queues were still the dominant sight in the capital. A Food Commission was set up, but it did not know where to begin. An unpredicted problem was caused by the financial reform. Banknotes bearing pictures of the czars were still circulating, but their value was dubious. The new banknotes issued by the Provisional Government were not taken seriously. Peasants refused to sell anything to anyone for paper money.

A less visible, but more profound revolution began in the spring of 1917, moving from south to north following the sowing season. Like the *Duma* in Petrograd, the *obshchina* was the only organizational unit in the countryside from the old regime which was capable of functioning in the countryside. It assumed power over local problems simply because there was no one else to do so. Impoverished by Stolypin's reforms, the *obshchiny* found the sight of the unused land of the *pomeshchiki* intolerable. Attempts by the *pomeshchiki* to sell their estates before the agricultural season began served merely to whet the peasants' appetite for the forced confiscation of land, an idea which they had nurtured ever since emancipation. Reports of the appropriation of unsown land by the communes began to arrive in the capital from all over the country. Since most of the soldiers were peasants, the local army garrisons made no attempt to defend the landlords' property. And since there was no one to give instructions to the police and gendarmerie to intervene, they kept a low profile or disappeared altogether. Army deserters had brought their rifles and ammunition with them and used them to deal with the private guards of the *pomeshchik* estates who tried to interfere. Many estates were razed, and peasants mowed the meadows of the *pomeshchiki* and used their pastures. The sudden rise in authority of the *obshchiny* in local affairs frightened the kulaks too. In any case, many of them returned to the communes in order to participate in the redistribution of the *pomeshchik* land.

The revolution in the countryside contributed significantly to the first crisis of the Provisional Government. In July 1917 Alexander Kerensky, a member of the SR party, became prime minister. But there was nothing he could do. In May the SR Congress had decided that land redistribution should be postponed "until the end of the war" and had condemned the forced confiscations which were taking place. This was a retreat from the official SR program and it alienated the radical communal peasants in whose hands the real power in the villages lay. The *pomeshchik* land that survived the spring and was left idle would not survive the winter crop sowing season in August and September.

Even after Lenin's return to Russia in April, the Bolshevik party remained a minor actor in the Russian political drama. The nationalization of industry and the dictatorship of the proletariat, the major pillars of the Bolshevik program, were not slogans likely to lead to a new revolution and the official party program did not contain a definite agrarian policy. When the Bolsheviks began to promise peace and the immediate confiscation of the *pomeshchik* land, their influence began to increase dramatically, although they still lacked a proper base in the rural communities. The promise was left rather vague since the Bolsheviks were reluctant to change their image from the party of the proletariat and had no wish to associate themselves with the interests of small individual farmers. Lenin had always believed that the peasant communes were reactionary institutions. The Bolsheviks were ready to find common cause with the rural proletariat, the *batraki*, and they tried to form *Batrak* Councils. Their plans failed because the *batraki* preferred land redistribution to the agricultural cooperatives or state farms which, according to Lenin, would be the most productive way of using the landlords' estates. Although the Bolshevik idea of turning the *pomeshchik* mansions into schools or hospitals was certainly better than simply burning them down, the peasants were afraid that if the estates were not destroyed, the *pomeshchiki* would simply return as they had done after the 1905 Revolution.

Meanwhile the food situation continued to deteriorate and food rations were declining. In spite of the sowing of confiscated land, the rural turmoil and the return of the kulaks to the communes led to a reduction in the area of cultivated land and a decrease in the amount of marketable grain. The financial situation was confused and inflation was very high. Peasants remained reluctant to sell their grain and few technical crops were sown. Shortages of flax and cotton forced many textile factories to close. By the summer there was serious malnutrition in Petrograd. The Provisional Government granted the workers' demands for an eight-hour day and the right to organize free trade unions, but these rights did nothing to improve the food crisis. In July the bread ration was reduced to half a pound per person in Petrograd and Moscow. There was danger of famine in the big industrial centers. Moreover, the army food deteriorated and that reduced the morale of even the most loyal units.

The Provisional Government finally began to discuss the nationalization and redistribution of land, but it immediately became clear that financial compensation presented a problem. In 1906–1913 more than half a million *pomeshshiki* and kulaks had mortgaged their estates—about 61 million *desyatin* (65 million hectares) were mortgaged. If the land was to be nationalized, the banks and insurance companies would have to be paid rather than the landowners. It was calculated that the banks stood to lose about 4 billion "gold" rubles. The government simply did not have enough money to cover this and it did not want to bankrupt the banking system. So if the land reform was to be implemented, the banks would have to be nationalized as well.

By September the transport system had deteriorated still further. The rivers, for centuries an important supply route in the summer before the rivers and lakes became covered by ice in October, could not be used because the villages in about 90 percent of the districts in the central provinces were in a state of revolt. The peasants had brought in the harvest and had time to intensify their burning and looting of *pomeshchik* estates. Random vandalism was replaced by systematic demolition as iron from the roofs and timber and bricks from the walls of architectural gems of the eighteenth and nineteenth centuries were distributed amongst the local peasants. Old scores were paid off and the dark hate which had accumulated over centuries was released in an attempt to destroy the old order. The peasants had never forgiven the *pomeshchiki* for the redemption payments which they had paid over a period of fifty years for land which they believed had been their own from ancient times. Although there were few peasants alive in 1917 who remembered serfdom, most of them knew only too well about the debts and obligations incurred during emancipation which they had inherited. They resented the restrictions on their movement and the injustices they suffered as the lowest, "passport-less" class of society. The differentiation brought about by the Stolypin reforms had created many local conflicts. The state authorities had usually been on the side of the kulaks rather than the communal peasants in these conflicts. With local justice now in their own hands, the communes were free to reverse the decisions previously made by the land distribution committees and experts. In some districts the communes forcibly expropriated the private, consolidated land of the kulaks.

Shortages and the difficulties caused by the disruption of transport, communications, and trade were not restricted to the industrial centers. The villages were deprived of badly needed manufactured goods and commodities. There was a shortage of salt, a vital ingredient in the traditional recipes for preserving food for the winter. The Provisional Government did not cancel the wartime freeze on procurement prices and there was no local authority with the power to force the peasants to sell food to the state. In the autumn the shortages of salt and kerosene, used for the lamps which were the only source of light in rural areas, caused serious disturbances in rural areas. Revolutionary activity in the countryside increased, where an often underestimated, very fierce civil war was occurring between the peasants and the landlords.

Most histories of the October Revolution concentrate on the

events in Petrograd. In fact the weakness of the Provisional Government and the easy success of the Bolshevik uprising on October 25, 1917, was brought about by the events in the countryside in September and October. Even Trotsky, in what is probably the best-known history of the October Revolution, described these events in a few paragraphs without attempting any serious analysis.

During September and October the possessing classes were awaiting the outcome as a hopelessly sick man awaits his death. Autumn with muzhiks is the time for politics. The fields are mowed, illusions are scattered, patience is exhausted. Time to finish things up! The movement now overflows its banks, invades all districts, wipes out local peculiarities, draws in all the strata of the villages, washes away all considerations of law and prudence, becomes aggressive, fierce, furious, a raging thing, arms itself with steel and fire, revolvers and hand-grenades, demolishes and burns up the manorial dwellings, drives out the landlords, cleanses the earth and in some places waters it with blood.[6]

But Trotsky was accurate in the way he attributed the events in the Russian countryside in 1917 to historic causes.

. . . The old Russia has gone up in smoke. The liberal press is a collection of groans and outcries about the destruction of English gardens, of paintings from the brushes of serfs, of patrimonial libraries, the parthenons of Tombov, the riding horses, the ancient engravings, the breeding bulls. Bourgeois historians have tried to put the responsibility upon the Bolsheviks for the vandalism of the peasant's mode of settling accounts with the "culture" of his lords. In reality the Russian muzhik was completing a business entered upon many centuries before the Bolsheviks appeared in the world. He was fulfilling his progressive historic task with the only means at his disposal. With revolutionary barbarism he was wiping out the barbarism of the middle ages. Moreover, neither he himself, nor his grandfather, nor his great grandfather before him ever saw any mercy or indulgence.[7]

In 1917 Russia was ready for a peasant revolution and when it occurred, it was as spontaneous as the February Revolution in Petrograd. No political party played a significant role. It would appear that Russia was much less ready for a Marxist type of proletarian revolution. The Bolsheviks took power in a palace coup rather than a mass revolution. The liberal Provisional Government was weak and in a state of crisis. The "storming" of the Winter Palace during the early hours of October 25, later named the "Great October Proletarian Revolution," was a very minor military action in which about fifteen people died on both sides. Soviet historians usually claim that Lenin's decree on the nationalization of land promulgated by the Congress of Soviets on October 26 gave the *pomeshchik* land to the peasants. In fact, by the end of October the *pomeshchik* land had ceased to exist. The land decree was not greeted with much enthusiasm in the *obshchiny*. It transformed communal ownership of land into the leasing of land which now belonged to the state. The leases had no time limit and there was no guarantee that the peasant would retain the full ownership of the products of his labor. Nonetheless, the decree did at least make it certain that the *pomeshchiki* would not be able to claim back their property. And the communes did generally improve their position after the forced appropriation of the *pomeshchik* land in 1917. Living standards began to rise after the Civil War and in the middle and late 1920s the Russian villages lived much better than in the 1900–1917 period.

If the main aim of a socialist revolution is to redistribute wealth amongst social groups, then it is clear that a successful socialist revolution took place in Russia in 1917. But the workers, on whose behalf the October Revolution took place, got nothing in terms of material benefits. In fact, the average standard of living of workers continued to decline for more than twenty years after the "Proletarian Revolution." There was only one social group which improved its material position and that was the communal peasantry. About 150 million hectares of arable land, pastures, and forests were confiscated and distributed amongst 25 million individual communal households. But it was not Lenin's decree on land which accomplished this redistribution. It was done by the peasants themselves well before the decree was passed.

Chapter 2

Agriculture
after the Revolution, 1918-1929

The arrest of the Provisional Government in October 1917 did not create a power vacuum in Russia. The Soviets represented a separate line of authority in the country and the Revolution had been planned to take place while the Second All-Russian Congress of Soviets was in session. News about the coup and the proclamations which were put on the walls of the houses in Petrograd, declaring that state power had passed into the hands of the Petrograd Soviet of Workers and Soldiers, split the deputies to the Congress. Those delegates who belonged to the political parties which formed the deposed Provisional Government walked out of the meeting, leaving the Bolsheviks and the left-wing SRs free to act. Lenin was the first speaker. He proposed the formation of a new government called the Council of People's Commissars (usually abbreviated to *Sovnarkom*, from the first syllables of the Russian words). The proposal was accepted and Lenin became the first chairman of *Sovnarkom*. He then proposed two decrees to the Congress—one on peace, which envisaged an immediate three-month armistice and peace negotiations, and the other on land. He had drafted the land decree the previous day. All private property rights were abolished and the land became the property of the state. The land of the *pomeshchiki* was to be confiscated and distributed to the poor peasants and the *batraki*. This was a compromise on the part of the Bolsheviks, who had "borrowed" their program from the SRs. Lenin had no wish to divide the large estates amongst members of the commune, believing that communal agriculture was unproductive and backward. The Bolshevik's own land program favored transforming these estates into state or collective farms which would form the nuclei of a future scientific, productive agricultural system. But Lenin understood that the necessary conditions for this program did not exist in 1917. Most of the land belonging to the *pomeshchiki*, and the crown and church land, had already been distributed amongst the peasant communes. The villages accepted the new decree as de facto approval of their own earlier confiscations. But the implementation of a new food procurement policy known as "War Communism" led to a rapid deterioration in the relations between the peasants and the Bolsheviks. The serious, protracted crisis which ensued almost cost the Bolsheviks the power they had assumed so easily in October 1917.

1. *The Agrarian Base of the Civil War*

In fact, the Decree on Land did not entail legal approval of the peasants' redistribution of the land. All private land and large estates were placed under the jurisdiction of district land committees and rural Soviets of Peasants' Deputies, which were to be a network of Soviet power in the villages. But Peasant Soviets did not yet exist and the decree had the opposite effect to what was intended. In November and December 1917 the destruction of private estates and the redistribution of the *pomeshchiki* land was rapidly completed. No entity, apart from the communes, possessed the authority and power to control events in the countryside.

Soviet historians usually claim that the events in the countryside of 1917–1920 reflected the Leninist policy as expressed in the land decree.[1] In reality, the decree expressed the intentions of the new government, but the agrarian revolution had started several months before the decree and it continued on its own course for several months after the decree was promulgated. Neither the Decree on Land nor the subsequent, more detailed, Law on the Socialization of Land[2] resolved the problem of private kulak land ownership. Their land was neither to be confiscated nor redistributed, although there were rules which made it possible for communes to put pressure on the kulaks to return to the *obshchina*. For the most part the kulaks successfully resisted this pressure. Once the large estates had been confiscated, they were responsible for an even larger share of the overall agricultural production. Although they did not get much new land in the process of redistribution, they tended to be the only peasants interested in confiscating the modern agricultural equipment which had escaped destruction when the *pomeshchiki* estates were looted. The poorer communal peasants could not use the sophisticated and complex machinery on their strips. The kulaks also took their share of the farm animals which had belonged to the *pomeshchiki*.

Towards the end of 1917 the food situation in Moscow and Petrograd improved slightly. This was not, however, due to better management of the transport and procurement problems. The new government was simply more thorough in confiscating the food stocks accumulated by private dealers and speculators. Special detachments of revolutionary sailors, soldiers, and workers were given authority to search warehouses and stores along the railroads and at the ports. Large quantities of grain, flour, and other products were found and included in the general rations. A new commissariat, the People's Commissariat for Food Supplies (known as *Narkomprod*), was set up and given almost dictatorial powers. Its task was to centralize food deliveries. But domestic food resources were too scarce and by the beginning of 1918 the food crisis had reappeared. Once again, Petrograd suffered most.

The October Revolution contributed to the already existing financial anarchy. All the banks were nationalized, new banknotes were issued, and old banknotes could not be exchanged for new. Paper currency was discredited almost entirely, particularly in the rural areas. As a result, the state could not procure food in return for money. There were only two alternatives: manufactured goods could be offered in exchange for produce, or coercion could be used. The new government tried both techniques. Although Soviet power was established rather quickly in almost all the provinces of the former Russian Empire, many local Soviets were too weak to implement forcible confiscation of food. Special Food Detachments would have to be used. Bolsheviks who, a few months previously, had proudly declared that their revolution gave immediate and obvious benefits to the peasantry now found themselves facing the painful task of forcibly confiscating food from that peasantry. The first Detachments were composed of revolutionary workers and sailors from the Baltic Fleet and they were equipped with consumer goods, which they planned to exchange for food. The villages were in desperate need of basic manufactured goods like matches, nails, sewing needles, textiles, kerosene, tobacco, and hundreds of other items. But it was quickly discovered that there were insignificant quantities of grain in the central and northern provinces. The only grain and food surpluses were in the Ukraine, the North Caucasus, the Don basin, and other southern areas, extremely far from Petrograd and Moscow. Since Moscow was closer to food supplies and a government in the Kremlin would be less vulnerable to the German army than it was in the Smolny Institute in Petrograd, there were sound strategic reasons for restoring Moscow to its former status of capital of Russia.

Lenin was desperate to sign a peace treaty with Germany as soon as possible and at any price. This would at least remove the burden of feeding the army. The Brest-Litovsk Treaty was signed on March 3, 1918, but it made the situation worse rather than better. Finland had already declared its independence. Under the terms of the Brest-Litovsk Treaty Russia was forced to recognize the independence of the Ukraine and Georgia. Poland, the Baltic states, and part of Byelorussia were ceded to Germany and Austro-Hungary. (Some, but not all, of these territories were recovered after the defeat of the Central Powers in November 1918). German and Austrian troops occupied the Ukraine and disrupted the main lines of communication between central Russia and the fertile south. The demobilization of the Russian army and the exchange of German and Austrian prisoners of war from camps in Siberia and the Urals created enormous traffic jams on the railways all over the country. The number of trains arriving in Moscow and Petrograd from other provinces dropped to about 10 to 15 percent of the 1917 level and only about 7 percent of the projected grain deliveries reached these cities at the beginning of 1918.[3] Once again there was famine in the industrial centers. Many peasants who had been mobilized into the military industries during the war began to return to their villages and became extra mouths for the villages to feed, leaving even less produce available for the towns. The population of the large cities began to decline and the rural population to rise as people moved out in search of food.

Spring is the busiest agricultural season. Peasants need quiet to plough and sow their land. In the spring of 1918 there were vast areas of newly acquired land to be cultivated. But the villages were still in a state of turmoil and there were many local conflicts which had to be settled. The government, however, pressed on with its food requisitioning policy. The drastic measures taken against the private food trade by introducing a grain monopoly and using terror against speculators only served to aggravate the urban food situation. The Food Detachments were turned into a Food Army and operations were extended into the Don and Volga basins, the North Caucasus, and Siberia. Many demobilized soldiers had taken their arms home with them to the villages and armed clashes between the Food Detachments and organized groups of peasants became common. In the Cossack areas Food Army units were often defeated and destroyed.

As a result of the famine and the migration of workers back to the villages there was a sharp decline in industrial production. Hastily nationalized and expropriated industrial facilities were, in any case, not necessarily efficient. *Narkomprod* became the most important commissariat and it tried to establish a direct exchange of goods for food products. But one *pood* (16 kilograms) of grain was priced at one horseshoe or 200 grams of nails, and few peasants were prepared to exchange food at that rate. On May 13, 1918, the government published a harsh decree granting extraordinary powers to *Narkomprod* to deal with what was called "the greedy stubbornness of the village kulaks and rich peasants" who had accumulated enormous sums of money in their cash boxes. Since these rich peasants remained indifferent to the groans of the starving workers and poor peasants,

Only one way out remains—to answer the violence of the grain owners against the starving poor with violence against the grain hoarders. Not one pood of grain should remain in the hands of the peasants beyond the amount required for the sowing of their fields and the feeding of their families until the next harvest.[4]

This decree was unrealistic and incompetent. In the drought-prone provinces of the south, peasant families always required grain reserves far in excess of the amount required for sowing, since the prospect of a poor harvest was always present. In May 1918 the quality and quantity of the next harvest could not be predicted. It would be impossible to confiscate all but a three- to four-month supply of grain without widespread violence. And as for the enormous sums of money accumulated in cash boxes—there probably were many such boxes, but they were filled with banknotes which had very little real value.

On June 1, 1918, *Sovnarkom* published a new directive signed by Lenin, Trotsky, Lunacharsky, and other prominent Bolshevik leaders. The newly formed Red Army was charged with the same tasks as the Food Army, but they were phrased in a more radical way.

The detachments you form, together with the disciplined units of the Red Army, led by experienced and tested revolutionaries and specialists in food procurement, will march out to win the grain from the village bourgeoisie.
Merciless war against the kulaks!
Thus and only thus, comrades, workers and starving peas-

ants, will you conquer famine and march on to further victories on the road to socialism.[5]

Within a few weeks the countryside was full of roadblocks, military food detachments, army units, and military tribunals which did not hesitate to exercise their power. Many provinces in the south were in open rebellion against Soviet power. The Cossack provinces of the Don basin declared their "independence" and the rich agricultural provinces of the North Caucasus were cut off from the Soviet Republic by a small but professional "Volunteer Army" created by czarist officers. A few months later there was a rebellion in Omsk. Admiral Kolchak's army took power in Siberia.

The Civil War which raged over an already devastated Russia from 1918 to 1921 was prolonged and bloody because the Bolshevik government had lost the confidence not only of the better-off peasants, but also of the middle peasants. But the White armies and their local government organs did not receive much support from the peasants of the central provinces either. They also needed food and they too confiscated produce and forcibly mobilized peasants into their armies. Moreover, the agricultural policy of the Whites envisaged restoring the estates of the *pomeshchiki*. In essence the peasants had to choose between two hostile forces, between the Red terror and the White terror, and there were many peasant revolts and conflicts in the areas controlled by the Whites. What had been gained during the Revolution was lost during the Civil War. The normal pattern of rural life was finally destroyed. Human losses during the Civil War were extremely heavy, but the resulting great famine of 1921–1922 was even more tragic. It was of epic proportions, unprecedented in the entire history of Russia.

The policy of War Communism was not an inevitable part of postrevolutionary change and the continuing war with Germany. It was the result of the incompetence of the new Soviet government. The government had very little understanding of the basic problems of agriculture in general, and of Russian agriculture in particular. The men who formed the Bolshevik leadership (in

March 1919 a Politburo was appointed with supreme power, consisting of Lenin, Trotsky, Sverdlov, Kamenev, Zinoviev, Stalin, Krestinsky, and Bukharin) were intellectuals and seasoned revolutionaries. None of them had a peasant background. Kalinin, a candidate member of the Politburo and the first chairman of the Central Executive Committee of the Russian Republic (VTsIK), was the only nonintellectual. He was a peasant by birth, but he had left his village at the age of seventeen to become an industrial worker. Lenin and his colleagues sincerely believed that most of the peasants would be as receptive to their proclamations and appeals for help as the workers, soldiers, and sailors were. They did not realize that two separate revolutions were taking place, a proletarian revolution and a rural revolution, with different objectives. The peasants did not believe that the Bolshevik Party represented their interests, and they were right.

The policies of confiscating surplus grain, using organized violence and terror against the kulaks, and transferring power in rural areas to special, revolutionary Committees of Poor Peasants (called *kombedy*) simply inhibited the peasants from increasing the sown area in 1918, despite their expropriation of the estates of the *pomeshchiki*. They knew that any surplus they produced would be confiscated. Thus the results of War Communism were predictable. The harvest of 1918 was very poor. The grain harvest of 1919, the most critical year of the Civil War, was also extremely low. The harvest of 1920 was only 45 million metric tons. It was not only the cities that went hungry. There was insufficient food to feed the villages. Transport was destroyed, industry paralyzed, and trade almost nonexistent since there were no consumer goods. The country was in a state of complete devastation. Continuing War Communism would have caused the collapse of the regime despite its victories in the Civil War. The half-starved people migrated to the villages in search of food and the population of some cities almost halved. Epidemics of typhoid, cholera, dysentery, "Spanish" influenza, measles, diphtheria, and other diseases became widespread, causing more deaths than the Civil War. Although accurate statistics for the population losses of 1918–1921 are difficult to obtain, most Soviet and Western demographers believe that the decrease in the population of Soviet Russia was about 10 million from all causes, including famine. There were strikes in many industrial centers and the incidence of rural revolts was high in 1920 and 1921. Many demobilized Red Army soldiers and sailors who had returned to their villages joined the rebels. A "free peasant Republic" was declared in Tambov in August 1920. It survived for several months and offered serious resistance before being put down by special units of the Red Army.

The most serious revolt occurred at the main naval base of the Baltic Fleet, Kronstadt. It took place a week before the opening session of the Tenth Party Congress in Moscow and it shook the foundations of Bolshevik power. February 1921 was a critical month. There were mass demonstrations and strikes in Petrograd and other cities, demanding changes in the food policy of War Communism. It was not only the peasants who were protesting. The workers objected to the dictatorial methods of the Bolshevik Party. A mass revolution would have been inevitable if the government had not retreated and changed its policy fundamentally.

2. *The New Economic Policy*

The Tenth Party Congress, which took place in Moscow on March 8, 1921, was a turning point in the early history of Soviet Russia. The ruling Party now knew all too well that its power was at stake. Changing course was a matter of survival, not a question of wisdom. But there was a second reason this Congress was a turning point: it was the last Congress at which some degree of intraparty democracy could be manifested. On the last day the Congress approved a resolution, "On Party unity," which had been introduced by Lenin unexpectedly. All factions and opposition groups within the Party with their own political platforms were forbidden and the Central Committee and its Politburo were given dictatorial powers to deal with internal Party affairs.

Proposals for a new economic policy had been under discussion in the Central Committee since the beginning of February, but they had been strongly opposed by Trotsky and others. The Politburo had created a special commission to study the problem—although Lenin was the main initiator of the New Economic Policy (known later as NEP), he did not have the power to proceed without a consensus amongst his closest colleagues. However, the majority of the delegates to the Congress supported Lenin's position and several important resolutions were passed, which formed the foundations of NEP. The forcible requisition of food surpluses was replaced by a proportional tax, payable in kind. The state grain monopoly was abolished and free trade in food and consumer goods was legalized. Many of the decrees of 1917–1920 were suspended and free enterprise in food and light industry was encouraged.

Despite the earlier opposition, these resolutions were passed without discussion and almost unanimously. The Kronstadt rebellion was still threatening the position of the Party and the Red Army detachments which had been sent to put down the uprising refused to obey orders to storm the fortress. The rebellious Kronstadt soldiers and sailors formed a Revolutionary Committee and began to publish a newspaper in which they put forward a liberal socialist program. Their demands received sympathetic support from a significant number of peasant soldiers serving in the local Petrograd garrison. Since the well-armed naval base was situated on an island off Petrograd which could only be approached over miles of frozen sea, storming it was a difficult military operation and the outcome was uncertain. About two hundred Congress delegates were sent to act as military commissars with the military units who were to storm Kronstadt. Because the regular army was unreliable, the assault troops consisted of cadets from the Red Army training schools and *Chekists* (members of the security forces). A week after the Congress had ended, the uprising was finally brutally suppressed. Nonetheless, it had not been fruitless. Most independent historians of the Civil War agree that the Kronstadt rebellion was instrumental in forcing the Bolsheviks to introduce NEP.

The unstable situation in Petrograd and the uncertainty were important factors in giving the resolutions which introduced NEP an easy passage at the Congress. Although NEP was Lenin's idea, he would not have been able to get the measures approved so easily if the Party Congress had not been under the threat of the heavy guns of the Kronstadt fortress. It was particularly important that the NEP measures were introduced in March, at least a month before the sowing season. Although 1921 was a disastrous agricultural year, it might have been an even greater tragedy than it was if War Communism had been continued.

The food detachments were disbanded and the roadblocks were removed. Several hundred thousand traders and speculators were released from prisons and concentration camps. Kulaks were no longer treated as "enemies of the people," but instead were encouraged to increase their production of food. But compared to the prerevolutionary years, there were few real kulaks left in the villages and hardly any wealthy peasants. A financial decree introduced a new currency based on gold and other stable valuables, putting an end to the rampant inflation. Peace was restored to the rural areas, but it was too late to prevent the famine of 1921. Nonetheless, it is almost certain that without the liberal changes of NEP, international assistance for the starving Russian population would have been much more difficult to obtain.

The famine was the outcome not only of War Communism, but also of a severe drought in the Volga basin and other regions of the south. Periodic droughts are a common feature of this region, where at least one agricultural season out of three is affected by droughts accompanying the strong, dry winds from the Central Asian deserts. Reserve stocks of grain are a necessity of life in this area, but in 1921 there were no surpluses and rural hunger was prevalent well before the harvest season. The harvest yielded 36.2 million metric tons, only half the normal prewar level. Although Russia had experienced many famines, the famine of 1921 was unprecedented in severity. More than 5 million people died of malnutrition and starvation in the autumn and winter of 1921–1922, more than the fatalities during the Civil War from all causes.

The 1921 famine became an international affair. The Soviet government could offer no assistance to the famine-stricken areas and on July 11 issued a general appeal to the West for aid. A personal appeal by Maxim Gorky was published in most Western newspapers on July 23. An independent All-Russian Relief Commission was set up to coordinate the assistance and the country opened its doors to foreign relief agencies which saved millions of lives. The assistance came mainly from the International Red Cross, the Save the Children Fund, and the American Relief Administration. Fridtjof Nansen, the famous Norwegian arctic explorer and scientist, made enormous efforts to organize help for the famine-stricken areas and to change world public opinion about the tragedy. Herbert Hoover, who became president of the United States in 1928, was the director of the American Relief Administration, the assistance of which was on a scale greater than that of all the other foreign relief organizations combined. The international assistance given to Soviet Russia later generated a comparatively large literature in the West, but few Soviet books on history or agriculture properly acknowledge the role of Western aid. At the height of its operations the ARA was supplying enough food for more than 10 million meals per day.[6]

Despite this assistance, the mortality figures peaked during the spring of 1922. A recent study shows that the death rate from starvation and malnutrition-related diseases alone in 1922 was at the level of 150 deaths per 1,000 of population in Saratov province.[7] The famine was an important contributing factor to the general decrease in the population of Russia in 1914–1922. In 1913 the total population of the Russian Empire was 165.7 million. The loss of Poland, Finland, Estonia, Latvia, Lithuania, Bessarabia, and the western parts of the Ukraine and Byelorussia reduced this to 143.5 million, but this was more than the number of people who lived within these borders in 1913 (139.3 million). The birthrate in 1913–1917 was higher than the losses in the war and the population continued to grow. The decline only started after 1917. According to official Soviet sources the population of the country numbered 136.1 million in 1922, a net loss of 7.4 million despite the continuing rather high birthrate (31–37 per 1,000 in 1919–1922, higher than the 27.1 and 26.3 per 1,000 in 1916 and 1917 respectively reflecting the postwar demobilization of the main part of the Russian army and the return of several million prisoners of war). The mortality rate, however, which averaged about 30 per 1,000 in 1910–1913, jumped to 44 to 45 per 1,000 in 1919–1920. There are no reliable figures for the mortality rate in 1921–1922. Even the *Jubilee Statistical Yearbook 1922–1982*,[8] which compares all the statistical records of the Soviet Union between 1922, the year that the Soviet Union was formally established, and 1982, does not give birth or mortality figures for 1922. But the urban population declined from 25.8 million in 1917 to 22.0 million in 1922 and the rural population fell from 117.7 million in 1917 to 114.1 million in 1922 within the same borders.

The 1922 grain harvest of 50.3 million metric tons was well below the optimal level of 65.5 million metric tons for the same area in 1909–1913. In 1923 it reached 70 million metric tons. The general improvement in nutritional levels was obvious both in the villages and in the cities. The birthrate was increasing rapidly (up to 45 per 1,000 in 1923–1926), while the mortality rate dropped to 25.5 per 1,000 in 1923 and 20.3 per 1,000 in 1926. The country was entering a new period of revival. The prewar level of industrial production and of urban population was reached in 1926. But the main architect of the October Revolution and of NEP did not live long enough to see this revival. After a serious stroke in December 1922 Lenin was partially paralyzed and no longer able to function as leader of the Party and the government. He died in January 1924. The next three decades in the history of the Soviet Union were dominated by Stalin. The developments in Soviet agriculture reflected his attitudes and interference.

3. *The Revival of Communal Agriculture: Social Change in the Village, 1922–1929*

War Communism and the attempts by both sides in the Civil War to extract food from the peasants by coercive means caused a sharp reduction in the proportion of arable land formed by individual consolidated fields in 1918–1921. Kulaks were the most obvious target for food requisitions. As a result they returned to the communes which could give them some protection, preferring to share their land and their agricultural produce with their fellow villagers rather than face the terror of having the latter confiscated by the Red and White armies. In 1922–1923 the role of individual consolidated households in the total production of food was insignificant. The proportion of poor peasants and *batraki* was also reduced, since the redistribution of land had made it possible for these social groups to improve their position. Rural Russia was now dominated by the middle peasants. Redistribution had also allowed very large families to separate into individual households. Within the 1922 borders there were about 21 million individual households which had about 180 million hectares of land under cultivation and used another 150 million hectares as meadows and pastures. On average each household had 8 hectares of cultivated land, or 1.5 hectares per person. Thus peasant families now lived slightly better than in 1906–1913, but they produced far less surplus marketable food. Agricultural methods were so primitive that production remained at subsistence level and the peasants consumed most of what they produced. Although the total harvest of grain, cereals, and other crops was higher in 1923 than in 1909–1913, the amount of marketable grain was only about 30 percent of the prewar level.

This situation was clearly not acceptable to a government which wanted to transform Russia into a modern industrial society. Lenin's well-publicized "plan of cooperative development" was impossible in a country where most of the sowing and harvesting was done by hand. To be viable it required a mechanized agriculture. Although the agricultural tax in kind provided the government with enough food to supply the diminished urban population, it was insufficient to support any form of industrialization or to produce badly needed export revenues. What was required was "productive peasants" and that implied consolidation of the peasant *nadely* and the segregation of the more prosperous households. Inevitably the government turned to the approach which had been so successful in 1906–1910, introducing a new version of the Stolypin reforms.

The "Fundamental Law on the Utilization of Land by the Workers" was passed on May 22, 1922, and the more detailed "Agrarian Code of the RSFSR" on December 1, 1922 (other republics adopted similar codes later).[9] Both laws encouraged consolidation of strips and separation from the communes. The laws acknowledged that the land belonged to those who actually worked on it, calling this a socialist substitute for the private ownership of the past. The communes were no longer to be called *obshchiny*, but were to be known as "land societies" (*zemel'noye obshchestvo*). According to the Land Code, peasants could choose between communal and consolidated forms of agriculture. The land societies were much better off than the *obshchiny* in 1909–1913, since they assumed "working ownership" of forests, meadows, and pastures and they controlled some local industries and rural trade in things like timber and firewood. The large forests remained the property of the state or were distributed amongst special "forest societies."

The attempt to encourage consolidation of strips without the right to sell, buy, or rent land were not successful at first and few peasants opted for consolidation. The land societies opposed the trend. Consolidated fields remained more common in the poorer provinces of the non-*chernozem* zone of the north, where fields were smaller, divided by forests and rivers, and far apart. The peasants could see that consolidation of their *nadely* improved their productivity. But this area did not produce any food surpluses. Consolidated fields were almost nonexistent in the more prosperous *chernozem* provinces. In Samara province, for example, consolidated peasant *nadely* had formed 19 percent of all arable land in 1916, but in 1922 they formed only 0.1 percent, and in Stavropol province in the North Caucasus they had formed 25 percent of the land in 1916, and 0.4 percent in 1922.[10]

The Bolsheviks had always argued that communcal strip agriculture, with its compulsory simple rotations and the long distances between strips making mechanization and intensification impossible, was backward and conservative. But they had also been against the Stolypin reforms, because they encouraged capitalist development in rural Russia. It was ironic that in 1922 they were forced to support what was essentially a modern version of the Stolypin reforms. The new trends, however, were not adopted as official policy, but were encouraged through propaganda and local initiative. Nevertheless, the number of applications for consolidation grew sharply and by 1925 the proportion of land under individual consolidated agriculture had reached the prerevolutionary level in some provinces of the central regions. A selective statistical analysis shows that the productivity of consolidated fields was 15 to 20 percent higher per hectare than that of the fields belonging to the land societies.[11] Curiously, it was not kulaks who were applying to consolidate. The study of local archives and provincial statistics carried out in the comprehensive study of the pre-collectivization village by Danilov shows clearly that applications were more frequently made by poorer peasants than by the prosperous.[12]

The former kulaks who had consolidated their fields in 1906–1916 did not usually want to leave the commune. They remembered the official hostility they had experienced in 1918–1921 and were wary of taking a risk on something they probably felt was a temporary trend. They lived in the villages and were better off than their neighbors, but their relative prosperity did not violate the rules of the land societies or antagonize the rest of the commune. They had better houses and larger stocks of farm animals and they used some modern machinery and equipment. Because of their prosperity they usually had larger families and this gave them the right to wider strips. As a result, they used their better farming experience to produce more grain and meat for the markets. In most cases they used the labor of their own families, but some of them employed other peasants as well, especially during the busy season or to look after their cattle. It should be emphasized, however, that limited use of employed labor was permitted under NEP and the kulaks followed the rules of the land society and did nothing illegal. Moreover, although there were some old scores to settle between the kulaks and former members of the *kombedy* who had participated in confiscating food from them and from middle peasants, there was usually very little hostility between former kulaks and other members of the commune.

The official Party doctrine and the terminology of the agrarian discussions of that period used the term *kulak* very widely, trying to present the kulaks as a separate class of rural capitalists. In fact, there was no definition attaching any special form of property or privilege to kulaks. The usage and the doctrine has been challenged by contemporary Soviet historians, very few of whom acknowledge that the kulaks were, in fact, members of the land societies. In 1925–1926 the former kulaks were an integral part of the peasant class as a whole. With 96 percent of the peasants in communes, the economic disparities within the villages were now based on initiative, agricultural know-how, literacy, the ability to use machinery, and, often, plain hard work. Peasants who worked better lived better. The borderline between the middle peasants and the better off was vague and it differed from region to region. A middle peasant of the central province would have been considered rather poor by the standards of the Ukraine or the North Caucasus, whereas middle or even poor peasants in Stavropol or Kuban provinces were better off than kulaks in the Tula, Smolensk, or Vologda provinces of central Russia.

The state had a very positive attitude towards these peasants in 1922–1926. Their importance as a productive section of the peasant community was officially acknowledged. But there was a change in official attitudes in 1927, when the Central Committee started to prepare the drafts of the resolutions for the Fifteenth Party Congress due to convene in 1927. The draft resolutions envisaged the collectivization of agriculture, which was to be the main aim of socialism in the countryside. During 1927 the previous policy of "appeasing" the peasantry began to be considered a "right-wing deviation." Stalin and the majority of the members of the Central Committee were disappointed that the communist candidates had failed to secure a majority in the local rural Soviet *(selsovet)* elections in 1925. With the *selsovety* controlled by non-communist peasant representatives, collectivization would be very difficult. It thus became essential to reduce the power of the *selsovety* and increase the power of the Party apparatus.

The system of Soviets which emerged in 1917 had considerable democratic potential. In the early 1920s, before the Party apparatus became powerful at the provincial level, the post of chairman of the Executive Committee of the provincial Soviet was more influential and powerful than the post of secretary of the provincial Party Committee, and prominent Bolsheviks usually tried to get themselves elected as chairmen of the provincial Soviets. But once Stalin obtained control of the Party and began to rely on the Party and the security apparatus, the position changed. After the Fifteenth Party Congress prominent Bolsheviks moved from the provincial Soviets to the provincial Party committees. The slogan of the October Revolution, "All power to the Soviets," had lost any meaning.

At the Fifteenth Party Congress in December 1927 a graduated system of agricultural tax in kind, much higher for those classified as kulaks, was introduced. Some restrictions were placed on the liberal NEP provisions allowing wealthier peasants to rent extra land and to use employed labor. Since the official statistics presented to the Congress numbered the kulaks as 4 percent of all households with a share of slightly more than 10 percent of the overall agricultural production, this was clearly a political move, rather than sound economics. Attempts were also made to restrict the trend towards consolidation and separation of individual households from the land societies. It was clear that consolidation and free farming was not segregating the kulaks. It was popular with poor and middle peasants and, ironically, it was stimulated by the active propaganda of modern methods of agriculture, including better rotation systems, and the increased output of some unsophisticated agricultural machinery. Those who were in favor of collective agriculture realized that it would be more difficult to sell the idea of collectivization to individual consolidated farmers who had developed psychological links with their own land than to the land societies.

The initial ideas of collectivization envisaged transforming the land societies into peasant cooperatives. The few small collective and state farms which existed in 1927 (producing about 4 percent of the total agricultural output) showed that collective farms needed large consolidated fields in convenient positions to be efficient.

Local officials began receiving instructions from Moscow to prevent individual consolidation. In 1928 the practice was suspended and peasants whose applications were still in the pipeline were labeled kulaks. The term began to acquire political connotations. In some areas previously separated fields were reintegrated into the land societies. A number of very complex and controversial land legislation acts were introduced between 1926 and 1928 and they contributed to the problems of agricultural production which arose in 1928 and 1929. Government attempts to extract more food from the villages without allocating extra funds for the higher procurement quotas were a more serious contributory factor: cheap food was vital for the industrialization program. Predictably, the villages resisted and reacted in the same way that they had reacted to War Communism—by reducing their agricultural production.

The original collectivization program adopted by the Fifteenth Party Congress was not very optimistic about the speed with which peasants would participate in collective farms. It was expected that collective farms would coexist with private, individual farming for some years. The final stages would result from the successes of collective agriculture. The visible advantages of modern methods of production, mechanization, and electrification used by the collective farms and the better life they produced would generate mass support.

After the Congress in December 1927 a new campaign against the kulaks began to gather momentum. In many regions local officials were instructed to begin redistributing land in those communes which seemed, by local standards, to be dominated by kulaks. At the republican level, decrees were issued prescribing that the surplus land of the better-off peasants should be confiscated and distributed to the poor peasants and *batraki*. These decrees were enforced by special, newly established land-court commissions. The natural result was that the better-off peasants began to cultivate less land and produce less. Many small rural capitalists who owned mills, workshops, farrieries, and other rural industries (perfectly legal under the provisions of NEP), closed their enterprises and moved into the towns. They perceived that an anticapitalist crusade was approaching and did not wish to stay in a hostile and vulnerable environment. This tendency was officially labeled as "kulak resistance."

According to the first comprehensive census of 1926, there were 21,681,300 individual peasant households forming a total rural population of 120.7 million. The urban population was 26.3 million, only slightly higher than the 24.8 million in the same territory in 1913. Urban living standards had not yet been restored to the prewar level. Although Moscow and Petrograd (renamed Leningrad in 1924) were well supplied, food shortages were still common in other industrial cities. But rural living standards were higher than in 1909–1913. More food was consumed and the quality was better. The large estates and larger kulak holdings which had produced surpluses for export and for sale in the towns before the Revolution had been divided into strips and joined to the land societies' land. Nineteen twenty-six and nineteen twenty-seven were good agricultural years. Although the total procurement of marketable grain in these years was 11.9 million metric tons, double the level of 1920 (but still much less than the amount of marketable grain before 1913), most of the extra food was now consumed by the rural population rather than being sold to the towns. In 1926–1927 the rural consumption of farm animal products was twice as high as in 1909–1913. This meant that far more grain was being used as feed grain. The general picture of grain production and distribution in 1917–1927 is shown in Table 3.

The total amount of marketable grain also included the amount consumed in the villages by non-peasant families like those of teachers, doctors, rural Soviet officials, and traders. Thus the amount that was available for export, for sale in the towns, and for consumption in the poor rural areas was only about 11.9 million tons or 15 percent of the total production, well below the 1909–1913 level despite the increase in total production. Although the villages could provide the towns with sufficient food, the needs of the state for grain to promote industrial development and to export to earn foreign currency were not satisfied.

Although the intrinsic limitations of the archaic communal

TABLE 3

Distribution of the Grain Harvest of 1926[13]

Form of distribution	Tons (million)	Percentage of total
Total grain production	77.8	100
Export	2.6	3.3
Sale in towns (through the state trading system and available for state reserves and army)	6.2	8.0
Sale in towns (through private channels)	0.9	1.1
Supplies and sales to consuming rural northern and central regions	2.2	2.7

mode of agricultural production can be blamed for the low level of marketable grain, procurements and sales to the state could have been increased if there had been something to offer in exchange for the grain. It was not only the needs of the state which remained unsatisfied; rural needs were also far from fulfilled. Trade between the rural and industrial sectors was still at a very low level. According to official statistics, the general trade in consumer goods in 1926–1927 was only 25 rubles per rural inhabitant per annum, compared to 223 rubles per person in the towns— the average urban family thus bought nearly nine times more consumer goods than the average rural family.[14] By 1928–1929 the production of consumer goods had increased, but the consumption per urban dweller was 350 rubles, whereas in the villages it was as low as 38 rubles per person. Increasing this trade was an obvious way to increase procurement of grain and other food. But the industrial development envisaged by the first Five Year Plan was oriented towards heavy industry, which had little to offer the rural population in the short run. There was a shortage of the equipment and materials necessary for agricultural work. At the same time the small private enterprises and businesses which had grown during the first years of NEP to fill the gap in the development of light, consumer industries were subjected to intense pressure and excessive taxation. This effectively put a halt to their productive potential. As a result the villages once again began to experience shortages of essential consumer goods such as textiles, wool, footwear, kerosene (very few villages had electricity), soap, and sugar. The chronic scarcity of these consumer goods did nothing to stimulate the flow of agricultural products from the villages into the towns.

The households which were classified as middle peasants were rather small in comparison with farms in countries with a well-developed agriculture. They usually had from 5 to 10 hectares of land under cultivation. Poor peasant families formed 17.3 percent of all households in 1927 and they often only had 1 to 2 hectares under cultivation. The "rich" kulaks cultivated from 10 to 16 hectares and formed 3.7 percent of all households. About 1 percent of all households, most of them in the North Caucasus and Siberia, cultivated more than 16 hectares of land, which they owned and rented. In general there was an increase in the number of middle peasants in 1925–1927, rather than of kulaks. This contradicts the political claims that the rural capitalist class was growing—in the period from 1923 to 1929 the relative proportion of kulak households only increased from 3.3 percent to 3.9 percent, and the size of the average kulak household was much smaller in the late 1920s than in the post-Stolypin period. More objective Soviet historians like V. P. Danilov acknowledge that "kulak households became limited in size, limited in the means of production and less able to exploit the poorer groups of the village and restricted in all forms of their activity."[15] The main social change which took place in the villages in the late NEP period was a reduction in the number of poor households. Some poor peasants left the villages for the towns and about 4 percent of them moved up and became middle peasants.[16]

Improved methods of agriculture could have achieved some increase of production within the land society system. But industry could not even provide peasants with the means for small-scale mechanization. In 1928, 77.4 percent of all crops were still sown by hand and 44.4 percent of all harvesting was done by hand with scythes and sickles.[17] The rest was dependent on horse-drawn equipment and machinery. The statistical records available in the annual yearbooks of the Soviet economy show that the average grain yield in 1925–1928 was 7.6 centners per hectare. Although this was higher than the 6.9 centners per hectare in 1909–1913, it is extremely low by any other standards.

Economic incentives like higher sales of manufactured goods and agricultural equipment would certainly have increased the amount of marketable grain. But this solution required two to three years to become effective and the first Five Year Plan would need to be altered. Some Party theoreticians argued that the same increase could be achieved more quickly and easily by raising agricultural taxation, nationalizing all forms of grain trade, and increasing the price of manufactured goods. The tragic experience of War Communism should have made it clear that this would be counterproductive: raising the price of manufactured goods and increasing the level of the agricultural tax in kind would once again inhibit agricultural production. Nonetheless, this was the course that Stalin chose to follow. The introduction of new methods of forced procurement did not produce the desired results. Instead it precipitated the developments which became known in Soviet history as the Grain Crisis.

4. *The Grain Crisis*

The government wanted to use the tenth anniversary of the October Revolution in 1927 to demonstrate that the life of the workers had improved as much as that of the peasants. Although total industrial production was already higher than in 1913, the production of consumer goods was lower. To some extent this was the result of the problems in agriculture. Many branches of light industry depended on technical crops like cotton, flax, tobacco, sugar, vegetable oil, or livestock by-products like leather and wool. Although the amount of food crops sown in 1923–1926 had risen, the cultivation of technical crops had not reached the prewar level. In order to change the balance, the government decided to increase procurement prices of technical crops and the other raw materials required for light industry. But increasing the acreage for technical crops could only be done at the expense of grain. Moreover, with more cash in hand the peasants could afford to wait for the procurement price for grain to rise. Their need for manufactured consumer goods was increasing, but the production of consumer goods in 1927 was only about 2 percent higher than in 1926. The workers' wages had been increased. The higher purchasing power of the workers and the decreases in wholesale and retail prices on most manufactured goods to celebrate the jubilee increased consumption in the industrial centers, but it also had the effect of reducing the flow of consumer goods to the small provincial towns and rural areas. This piece of economic mismanagement left the peasants with extra cash that they could not spend and little incentive, therefore, to increase production.

The government decided to increase procurements by introducing a new system of tax in kind. Under the original NEP system the unit of agricultural tax was based on the size of the household's *nadel* and the number of horses and cattle it owned. The new method based tax on an assessment of the household's actual income in kind and cash. Making this assessment was an extremely difficult task, which lent itself to arbitrary decisions at the local level. The total tax figures were increased for 1927 and the tax policy was revised again at the beginning of 1928. New quotas were introduced from April 21, 1928, which sharply increased the tax rate for well-to-do middle peasants and kulaks.

In the autumn and winter of 1926–1927, before the tax increases were implemented, procurement proceeded without any conflict. The total state collection from the harvest of 1926 in 1926–1927 (in the 1920s the agricultural year was measured from harvest to harvest, from July to the end of June of the next year) was about 12 million metric tons, 20 percent higher than the previous year. This figure was close to the amount projected in the plan and the improvement in supplies to the towns and the amount for export helped Stalin to defeat the Trotsky-Zinoviev Left Opposition, which advocated a harsher policy towards the peasants. Trotsky lost his Politburo position at the end of October 1926 and was expelled from the Party on November 14, 1927. But as soon as he and his followers were removed from positions of power, Stalin's policy began to change. The total grain harvest was slightly lower in 1927 than in the previous year. With the dependence of agriculture on the weather, it was unrealistic to expect an increase for three successive years. But the plan envisaged a 6 percent increase in marketable grain, the minimum necessary for industrial development. At the beginning of the autumn the procurement figures were well below the level of the previous year. This was probably partly due to a natural tendency to keep back more grain in anticipation of a worse harvest to come. But an extremely hostile anti-kulak propaganda campaign during the spring and summer probably also contributed to the nervousness of the peasants. In October 1927 a "reinforced offensive against the kulak" was declared. Predictably, the villages responded negatively and the grain procurements, already below target in September, dropped even lower in October and November. In December, during the "Jubilee" Fifteenth Party Congress which was to approve the first Five Year Plan of industrialization, food shortages began to be experienced in the large cities. This was only the beginning of a long winter.

Although the Fifteenth Party Congress has become known as the Congress that announced the gradual collectivization of agriculture and the timetable for this radical change, it was made clear that collectivization was to be based on the principle of complete freedom of choice for individual peasants. And despite the limitations imposed on renting land and employing labor, the Congress confirmed the general policy of NEP. But this made no impact on the procurement of grain, and the state received only half the amount that had been procured in the same period the previous year, although the 1927 harvest was only slighter lower than that of 1926. The authorities knew that more grain was available and a number of theories were suggested to explain the reluctance of the peasants to sell. It was said to be a reaction to the hostile propaganda against well-to-do households, or an unwillingness to sell grain for cash when there were too few consumer commodities for purchase, particularly since the peasants had already accumulated unspent cash from previous harvests. It was admitted that there was a natural fear that the next harvest might be poor, since the great famine of 1921 and the near-starvation level of 1924 had not yet been forgotten. It was also thought to be the result of the slight reduction in the price paid for grain. In fact, all these factors contributed.

The only rational way to improve the situation immediately was by economic means, by raising the procurement price and redirecting manufactured goods to the villages from the towns. At the end of December the Commissariat of Trade began to take the necessary measures to increase the dispatch of consumer goods to the key grain-producing areas. But at the same time the Party leadership sent groups of activists to various regions to "assist" in the grain procurements. Several Politburo members left Moscow to supervise the work. Finally Stalin himself left Moscow on January 15, 1928, to take part in a meeting of the Bureau of the Siberian regional Party Committee and to address Party meetings in a number of Siberian towns. This was his last tour. For the rest of his life he was to rule the Soviet Union from the seclusion of his official residences.

Stalin's speeches at the local Party meetings were not published or reported in the central press, but they were later included in the eleventh volume of his collected works. He demanded that local authorities take "extraordinary measures" against the peasants, especially the kulaks who tried to hoard supplies of grain. A special article (107) had been added to the Criminal Code of the RSFSR (and to the codes of the other republics) in 1927, according to which hoarding for the purpose of speculation was a criminal offence punishable by the deprivation of freedom for up to three years and confiscation of property. Stalin recommended that article 107 be used against the kulaks who refused to sell their surpluses. Similar directives had been sent to other areas of the country. These drastic administrative and legal methods increased procurements and the state received about 300 million *poods* of grain (about 4.6 million metric tons) during the winter. This was enough to supply the towns for several months, but not enough to fulfill the total quota planned for 1927–1928. As spring approached, the peasants' resistance to the extraordinary measures increased and not even the threat of repression could force them to sell their grain. Stalin continued to insist on the use of coercion and confiscation. Later he tried to justify his use of arbitrary and illegal methods, arguing that the government simply had no other choice.

> Whereas we had succeeded in January–March in securing nearly 300,000,000 poods affecting only the peasants' *manoeuvring* stocks, in April–June we failed to secure even a hundred million poods, owing to the fact that we had to encroach on the peasants' *emergency* stocks, and at a time, moreover, when the harvest prospected were not yet clear. Nevertheless, grain had to be secured. Hence the renewed recourse to emergency measures, administrative measures, the infringements of revolutionary law, the house-to-house visitations, the unlawful searches and so on, which worsened the political situation in the country and created a threat to the bond.[18]

Violations of legality were widespread. Special army detachments were used in many places to terrorize the peasants. The official press kept insisting that "extraordinary measures" were only being employed against the kulaks, but in practice they were used against the middle peasants as well. By themselves the kulaks could not have provided the state with all the necessary grain. Besides, it was impossible to approach peasants individually. In most regions the local authorities demanded fixed quantities of grain from every village or land society. This had been the practice during the War Communism period, and the political situation in the countryside became extremely tense once again. Arbitrary confiscations and declarations about the legal limits of grain reserves had a negative effect on the spring sowing campaign. Economic incentives to sow more and work harder had disappeared. Since the amount of extra land that kulaks could rent had been restricted, they had begun to sell off their machinery and curtail their production of agricultural equipment. The poorer peasants who had earned some money from leasing their land to kulaks were unable to sow their *nadely* properly. Many strips belonging to widows, invalids, and families with many small children remained unsown.

Stalin retreated in the face of the obvious signs that serious trouble lay ahead. Reports about the reduced acreage which had been sown made even those who knew very little about agriculture realize that a confrontation with the peasantry would be useless. Some people suggested the unsown land could still be used for winter crops which would be sown in August. Although this would not improve the 1928 harvest, it would increase the chances for a better year in 1929. At the beginning of June, Stalin sent new instructions to all local Party organizations cancelling the "extraordinary measures" and confiscations. In July 1928 a special Plenum of the Central Committee passed a resolution to publicize the new policies widely. The Plenum recommended that economic means should be used in dealing with the peasants and that strict legality should be reintroduced. Urgent measures were taken to increase the deliveries of consumer goods to the countryside and to raise the procurement price for grain. But it was too late.

The decree passed by *Sovnarkom* to raise the procurement price was published in August. The 15 percent increase was too modest to make much difference. In any case, the damage which had been done by the confiscations and repression could not be repaired that quickly. Many peasants had been arrested in the spring under article 107 of the Criminal Code and they were not released immediately. In some districts the "extraordinary measures" had left peasants with insufficient seed grain, and this shortage was one cause of the smaller sown acreage. The government failed to understand the difficulties of sowing winter crops in the unused strips between the fields of spring cereals. The essence of communal agriculture is the synchronization of essential work. These bare strips were like small islands among the growing spring wheat and rye. It would be impossible to harvest in September without damaging the weak, new winter crop seedlings. Most of the unsown land had previously been sown by kulaks and middle peasants under lease arrangements and they did not trust the change in government policy. They preferred to sow more intensive technical crops like sugar beets, sunflowers, potatoes and other vegetables, and tobacco or flax, which were not subjected to the "extraordinary measures" and were a better source of cash. Technical crops were now preferred to cultivating grain for the markets. The peasants also left more land to grow hay for feeding their livestock. Nobody had tried to confiscate hay and it seemed a safe investment for their labor. Many younger kulaks began a process of "self-liquidation," selling their livestock and machinery for cash and leaving the villages for good. Their elders continued living in the villages, but young, able-bodied people could find new jobs in the developing towns and cities. Previously it had usually been the poorest peasants who had left the village. Now the more prosperous migrated, their instinct for self-preservation driving them out of a dangerous environment.

The winter of 1927–1928 was unusually cold and there were late frosts. The grain-producing regions of the North Caucasus suffered significant losses of winter crops (mostly wheat) sown in the autumn of 1927. The fields required resowing, but there was no extra seed grain. During the second wave of confiscations of "surpluses" from March to May 1928 essential reserves and feed grain were often taken and many regions reported a shortage of feed grain and malnutrition of livestock in the spring and early summer of 1928.

It has been calculated (on the basis of many contradictory records) that the planting of technical crops increased by 17 to 18 percent in 1928, while the area under cereals decreased by 3 percent.[19] However, in the most important grain regions of the Ukraine, North Caucasus, and Lower Volga basin the decrease of acreage under grain crops was as much as 8 to 10 percent. And although the less important agricultural regions of northern, western, and central Russia increased their sowing of cereals, this had little to do with appeals from the Central Committee. The extra grain was not being produced for the market, but for local consumption. These areas had previously bought grain in the south in exchange for timber, firewood, flax, and locally produced industrial goods. In the winter of 1927–1928 they experienced an even more acute grain shortage than the towns and they were sowing in anticipation of another bad year.

After the severe winter, weather conditions improved in 1928 and the yields per hectare were slightly higher than in 1927. The total harvest of all crops was higher in 1928 than in 1927, but the production of the cereals required for human consumption (rye and wheat) was lower than in 1927, and much lower than in 1926. The peasants preferred to increase the acreage for barley, oats, and other feed cereals. In 1928 only 41.3 million metric tons of wheat and rye were harvested, compared to 45.9 million in 1927 and 48.6 million metric tons in 1926.[20] The rural areas could provide the towns with more sunflower oil and more potatoes, but it could not provide them with enough bread.

The procurement pattern in the 1920s before collectivization was quite different from the modern pattern. The agricultural tax in kind was not paid in full immediately and additional sales were spread out. The transport system was primitive and storage facilities were nonexistent. Thus procurements were collected over several months during the autumn, winter, and early spring. In 1928 the villages sold what was due in September and October, but in November the collections dropped sharply. The government was reluctant to reintroduce "extraordinary measures," since it was known that the villages were now much better prepared for resisting confiscations. Many peasants either had hidden their surpluses extremely well, or had quickly disposed of them through the private market or through the underground black market. Food shortages in the cities had raised the price on the black market to three to five times the official procurement price. A difference of such magnitude was bound to stimulate the private sector, which, although restricted, had not been suppressed entirely.

The restraint of the government did not last very long. As the winter approached, bread rationing was introduced in Moscow and Leningrad, to be followed by other cities a few months later. Although the peasants had retained much lower reserves of grain to avoid forced confiscations, a return to the arbitrary and illegal practice of "extraordinary measures" seemed inevitable. Nineteen twenty-nine was an extremely important year for the first Five Year Plan. The pace of industrialization was directly related to the ability of the state to feed the increasing industrial population. Influential experts and Party workers, later labelled the Right Opposition, proposed amending the plan to increase investment in the consumer-oriented industries, particularly those which provided goods for the rural areas. But Stalin rejected the proposals. In 1929 heavy industry (group A) was expected to increase output by 22.3 percent. About 30 percent of all investments had to be used to construct the requisite new plants and factories.

On September 30, 1928, N. I. Bukharin, the most senior member of the Politburo, published his famous "Notes of an Economist" in *Pravda*. He defended the case for a better balance of heavy and light industry as the only way to avoid a disruptive confrontation with the countryside. However, at the Central Committee meeting on November 19, 1928, Stalin supported the main targets of rapid industrialization, arguing that it was essential for the Soviet Union to catch up and surpass the capitalist industrial countries of the West. "Either we achieve this, or they will destroy us," he proclaimed. In 1928 his argument was very convincing. Great Britain had broken off diplomatic relations with the Soviet Union in 1927 (they were reestablished in 1929). The communist revolution in China had been defeated and relations between China and the Soviet union had deteriorated after police raids on the Soviet Embassy in Peking and consulates in other Chinese cities. Some diplomats had been arrested. In 1928 the Soviet leadership felt more than ever that the Soviet Union was isolated and threatened by the rising hostility of the capitalist countries. In an atmosphere of international tension the problem of preserving "strict socialist legality" did not have high priority. By 1929 a new offensive against the peasants seemed inevitable.

Chapter 3

Collectivization

The collectivization of Soviet agriculture in 1929–1933 was the most important social development in Russia after the two revolutions in 1917. Its effects on the rural community and on all aspects of life in the country were profound and enduring. The October Revolution had eliminated the two upper classes—the capitalists and the rural gentry—which had constituted a small minority of the population. "The revolution from above," as Stalin called collectivization, transformed the majority class in Russia, radically changing the lives of more than 80 percent of the population. The "proletarian" revolution of 1917 had changed the lives of the workers very little. They continued to use the same means of production and tools of trade, and they practiced the same professions and skills. Collectivization changed an entire way of life. It was not only the way in which peasants had worked for centuries that was changed. More than a million peasant families were displaced and the process was enforced by a campaign of terror, deportation, exile, and execution on a scale hitherto unknown in Russian history. And it was followed by a tragic famine in 1932–1933, during which more than 5 million people lost their lives. Nowadays, when people talk about Stalin's terror, they are referring to the purges of 1936–1938. But the terror which accompanied collectivization was directed against the grass roots of the population and it was equally savage. Moreover, it has never subsequently been repudiated.

Soviet official histories have continued to distort or omit the most important aspects and facts of this period of Soviet history. In 1965 a special research team at the Institute of History of the Academy of Sciences of the USSR completed a two-volume academic study of the history of collectivization, edited by V. P. Danilov. The Central Committee ordered the page proofs to be collected from the authors and destroyed. At an All-Union Ideological Conference in Moscow in October 1966 the study was criticized for being "a revision of the history of Soviet society."[1] The official view proclaims that collectivization was a success, a "victory of Marxist-Leninist theory on the socialist reconstruction of agriculture." In fact, it was far from successful. Based on a miscalculation of historic proportions, it was a complete failure. It did not solve the crisis in urban-rural relations which had been precipitated by the forced procurements of 1929. Instead the crisis became permanent. Moreover, it was not the product of carefully considered theory, but a sudden, ill-prepared measure, improvised by the leadership from beginning to end. It has been argued that there was no alternative way in which the Soviet Union could develop into a modern, industrial state. But that argument is untenable: there were several alternatives, any one of which would have been preferable to the drastic policy which Stalin initiated in 1929.

For the historian who aspires to objectivity, and for agricultural experts, the study of collectivization represents a major challenge. It has been the subject of innumerable studies by Western historians. In the single chapter that can be devoted to collectivization in this book it has been necessary to limit the account to the most important facts and concentrate on the economic and agronomic aspects of the process.

1. War against the Peasants

Nineteen twenty-nine was a critical year for the success of the first Five Year Plan. Industrial expansion and the many new construction projects entailed an increase in the urban population and in the amount of food required for the towns. But the procurement collections were going badly at the beginning of 1929 and "extraordinary measures" were considered useless, since there were no further surpluses. Moreover, the lessons of 1928 had not been wasted—it was recognized that confiscating essential stocks would further reduce the acreage of sown land. At first Stalin tried a new *kombedy* approach in Siberia, Kazakhstan, and the Urals, attempting to divide the village and organize the poor peasants against the more prosperous who would be expected to provide the major part of the quota which had been demanded from the commune as a whole. The "Ural-Siberian method" was presented as a local initiative. Local authorities set up commissions of poor and middle peasants empowered to decide individual levels of additional taxation on the basis of the known surpluses of grain in the better-off households. But the situation did not improve. In the late twenties poor peasants did not own horses, cattle, or agricultural equipment and they usually rented the horses and equipment they needed to do their work from the more prosperous households. In any case, there was a great deal of interdependence between peasants in the villages of Siberia and the Urals, where towns and shops were few and far between.

In March and April the state grain reserves began to run low. Without any formal announcement of "extraordinary measures," the state began to confiscate grain secretly. Local officials once again began to use article 107 of the Criminal Code, arresting thousands of kulaks and better-off middle peasants and confiscating their grain supplies. It was taken for granted that these were surplus supplies. Despite these measures, the total collection in the 1928–1929 procurement season was only 8.3 million metric tons, two million less than in 1927. Bread rations in the towns were reduced and rationing was introduced for other basic food products.

Although "extraordinary measures" were applied, procurement methods in 1929 were not as draconian as in 1928. The government was well aware that such measures were counterproductive and that it was essential to stimulate sowing rather than inhibit it. The total acreage of cereals sown in 1929 was 6 percent higher than in 1928 and the weather conditions were good. But for political reasons many local reports about the harvest were falsified and the planned procurement figure of 14 million metric tons, disclosed only at the end of the harvesting season, was based on this preliminary, overoptimistic estimate. In current statistical records, the total harvest of 1929 is shown to have been 1 percent lower than the 1928 harvest.

A new tactic to deal with the harvest was being planned secretly. It was decided to abandon the usual custom of extending procurement into the winter and spring. The targets were announced on September 1, 1929, as soon as harvesting had been completed in the main grain-producing regions of the south,[2] and the entire procurement was planned to be completed by the end of December. It was hoped that this would prevent peasants from selling their grain surpluses to private traders. At the same time economic incentives were introduced by increasing the supply of manufactured consumer goods to the rural areas, and the political campaign against the kulaks was intensified in the hope of softening the resistance of the middle peasants.

A new antireligious campaign exacerbated the tension. The previous major campaign against the Russian Orthodox Church in 1921–1922 had used the pretext of confiscating church valuables to help famine victims. Many rich churches and monasteries in the towns had been destroyed and their priests and monks exiled, imprisoned, or even executed. But there had been a revival of religious services in 1922–1927, particularly in the rural areas. In August 1928 the Central Committee closed down the remaining rural monasteries. The monks were deported to Siberia, the land was used to set up new collective or state farms, and the buildings were converted into workshops, garages, machine-tractor stations, and storage facilities for procured grain. The process continued until the summer of 1929, when an antireligious conference in Moscow sponsored a Congress of Militant Atheists. The antireligious campaign then developed into a real pogrom. Local Komsomol and Party activists and groups from the regional and national capitals raided village churches, looting them and stripping the walls of icons and other religious objects, which often were simply burned. Local priests and peasants who tried to intervene were arrested and deported. This vandalism was centrally coordinated and it had a purpose. The government had secretly prepared plans for collectivization on a massive scale. It was believed that the church would support peasant resistance: this potential obstacle had to be removed. Church services remained illegal until 1943, when the government began to understand that religion and the church were patriotic forces which could help the war effort.

The harvesting campaign of 1929 was not easy. There was an atmosphere of apprehension and hostility. There was no support for the government amongst the peasants and they were ready to resist pressure. The attitudes of the kulaks, middle peasants, and poor peasants amongst the permanent rural inhabitants towards the state did not differ much. The officials could only count on the poor newcomers, a sizable minority in some parts of the Ukraine, North Caucasus, Urals, and Volga and Don basins. In these traditionally Cossack regions there was often animosity between the local heredity Cossack familes and the households who had only recently settled in the more prosperous villages from the overpopulated poor provinces of central Russia and Byelorussia. The large southern villages often consisted of several hundred households divided into several land societies. The established households tended to be united into more prosperous communes which owned the best and most conveniently situated fields. The new settlers had worked in the villages as *batraki* and they were ready to support the drive against the rich peasants.

In September collectors and representatives of the various procurement systems arrived in the countryside. The local militia and *selsovety* were reinforced by large numbers of employees of the OGPU, as the state security apparatus was now called. Special corps of Party and Komsomol activists were sent to the countryside as well, some of them equipped with mandates signed by Stalin which gave them almost dictatorial powers. In addition to this formidable force, the Central Committee mobilized more than fifty thousand industrial workers (usually Party or Komsomol members) from Leningrad, Moscow, Kiev, and other industrial centers to assist the procurement. Many of them were armed (in the 1920s Party and Komsomol members were allowed to possess firearms, which were worn flamboyantly in special belts to make them visible. This Party privilege was cancelled in 1936 when some armed Party officials tried to resist arrest at the beginning of the Great Terror).

As in the previous year, the peasants tried to hide the harvested grain. Some was disposed of through private speculators and some was used as local currency, to pay off intervillage debts or for the salaries of the *batraki*, and so forth. But the "procurement army" was ready to deal with the situation, and those who were caught concealing grain or speculating were arrested immediately. The press was filled with stories of illegal speculators being intercepted, arrested, and their grain confiscated. Many kulaks whose wealth was not in land and grain, but in farm animals, hurriedly disposed of part of their livestock. Middle peasants followed suit and many more cattle and pigs were slaughtered than is normal for the autumn. "Self-liquidation" on the part of the kulaks became even more widespread. There were reports from all the grain-producing regions of direct confrontation and hostility and the official press usually attributed it to kulaks who, it was said, were trying to sabotage the procurements and terrorize the officials. Although many peasants still possessed the sawn-off rifles they had brought back with them from the Civil War, individually they were unable to resist the procurement brigades.

Central Committee members toured the countryside to supervise and instruct local officials. This procurement campaign was far more drastic than any of the "extraordinary measures" undertaken in previous years. The number of arrested and deported peasants was higher than ever before. Article 107 of the Criminal Code (including full or partial confiscation of property for failure to deliver grain) was used against about 6,000 households in the central Volga regions, 30,000 in the North Caucasus, 33,000 in the Ukraine, and 60,000 in Siberia and Kazakhstan. Across the country a total of 200,000 peasants are thought to have suffered under this law.[3] Fines, usually in kind, were levied even more widely. Although the press insisted that these measures were being used against the kulaks, it is clear that the middle peasants were affected as well. Any household that was slow in fulfilling its procurement quota was labeled as kulak. The term had begun to reflect political attitude rather than prosperity.

Coercion produced the desired result. Peasants brought their grain to the collection points and sold it to the state for a fixed price. Procurement brigades moved quickly from village to village. In some districts the speed of procurement was so high that local storage facilities became overloaded. There were shortages of space, sacks, and transport. The target figure—14 million metric tons—was reached well before the end of 1929. It was a record figure and was considered a great victory for Party policy. State stocks of grain were replenished and 1.3 million metric tons of grain were exported. Industrial development for 1929 and 1930 was secured. There was also an abundance of meat in the towns, since the confiscated property usually included livestock. In any case, households which owned two horses, or two or more cows and several pigs, were considered kulak, so it was safer to dispose of extra farm animals. Thus middle peasants and kulaks slaughtered their animals in the autumn of 1929 for political reasons, not because there was a shortage of feed grain and fodder. The result was an abundance of meat in 1929, followed by an acute shortage in 1930, when the production of meat fell by 30 percent.

The government won the battle against the peasants in 1929. But the approaching winter was a time for radical decisions. It would be impossible to mount a similar campaign every year. The peasants were unlikely to start the spring sowing season with the will to work hard. In 1930, 15 million metric tons of procured grain would be required to meet the demands of industry. It was extremely unlikely that it would be available.

There were two possible solutions. One was to revitalize NEP by raising the procurement prices for cereals and other food products and increasing the flow of consumer goods to the rural areas. It would mean ending the war against the kulaks and middle peasants and encouraging them to produce more. Rapid industrial growth could be beneficial to the villages. The market for agricultural products was growing, and more manufactured goods, machinery, and services could be offered to the peasants. The large excess labor reserves in the villages could be absorbed by industry. Although it was unlikely that the productivity of communal agriculture would rise sharply, there was significant room for improvement. A second possible solution was a gradual acceleration of the timetable for collectivization. The directives of the Fifteenth Party Congress and the Five Year Plan pointed in this direction, but made it clear that gradual collectivization must be supported by technical aid and agricultural machinery. Mechanization would make peasants understand the advantages of the new system. According to the plan, the rate of collectivization was expected to increase from 1931, when several newly constructed factories and plants would begin to produce tractors and other agricultural machinery. In the meanwhile, existing collective and state farms needed to be expanded and developed and buildings constructed to house the collective farm animals. It was not clear how the land would be divided between those households which joined the collective farms and those which remained in the communes or consolidated their land for individual farming. Nor was it known what the relationship would be between the remaining land societies and the collective farms. The existing collective and state farms offered no solutions, since they had either been created to cultivate virgin lands, or else they occupied the large estates and church lands which had not been distributed amongst the local communes in 1917. They were cooperatives, an intermediate form of collective farm in which the peasants cultivated the land in common and shared their machinery. Few of the members were middle peasants or even traditional communal peasants. Since their formation in 1918 these cooperatives had attracted landless and migrant peasants, agricultural laborers, former soldiers, and enthusiasts who had moved from the cities during the Civil War. Moreover, there were so few cooperatives that many villagers knew nothing about them and therefore could not see them as an alternative to the land societies. Nonetheless, it would have been rational to increase the scale of the cooperatives' operations and use them as the experimental ground for the more ambitious program which was planned. It would also have made sense to accelerate the establishment of state farms in the virgin areas of the Volga and Don steppes which had already proved to be productive.

There were 1,600 collective farms in Russia in 1918 and the number had increased to 10,000 in 1920.[4] Many of them were organized by demobilized peasant soldiers who were unwilling or unable to return to their homes which were in the territories lost by Russia after the First World War and Civil War. Others had fought for the Whites in the Civil War and, despite the amnesty, did not want to return to their native villages. The first All-Russian Congress of *Kolkhozy* (the term was formed from the first syllables of the words for "collective agriculture") took place in Moscow in December 1919. Lenin delivered a major speech to the Congress, which was later called "Lenin's plan for the socialist transformation of the village." He was very careful to stress the gradual and careful way in which any agricultural reforms would need to be introduced:

> . . . we can influence the millions of small peasant farms only gradually and cautiously and only by a successful practical example, for the peasants are far too practical and cling far too tenaciously to the old methods of farming to consent to any serious change merely on the basis of advice and book instructions.[5]

By the time the Second Congress of *Kolkhozy* was convened in Moscow in February 1921 there were 16,000 of them. The number increased very slowly to 18,000 in 1927. They tended to be much smaller than the average land society, consisting on average of fourteen to fifteen households which owned about 140 hectares of land and shared eleven working horses. But they farmed consolidated fields and introduced a multi-rotation system. Many of them received good-quality seed grain from the state and, in general, they demonstrated higher productivity than the land societies—in 1926–1927 their average cereal yield was 21 percent higher than that of the land societies and they produced comparatively more marketable grain per household. In 1928 active propaganda and the effects of the "extraordinary measures" produced a sharp rise in the number of collective farms. Most of the new members consisted of poor households who wanted to consolidate their *nadely* and who joined existing *kolkhozy* or, if there were none in the area, organized new ones. The new collective farms tended to be even smaller than the existing ones and they were organized as loose producer cooperatives rather than proper collective farms with collectivized machinery, implements, and livestock: the members held the land in common and shared some machinery, but the livestock was the private property of individual households.

In 1928 an All-Union Center was established in Moscow to coordinate the work and development of collective farms. The *Kolkhoztsentr* began to allocate virgin land in the Volga basin, the North Caucasus, Kazakhstan, and Siberia for establishing large, new collective farms. This was the first virgin land program. Some of the new *kolkhozy* received as much as from 2,000 to 20,000 hectares. (The largest collective farm established then, "*Stepnoi Gigant*," still exists in Kazakhstan). By 1929 the total acreage under collective farming had reached 1 million hectares and a special government decree envisaged increasing the acreage for new *kolkhozy* to 3.9 million hectares.[6]

The number of state farms or *sovkhozy* could also have been increased. Many *sovkhozy* had been organized after 1918 on the basis of very large estates which had not been distributed amongst the peasants. Often they were specialized farms, attached to food-producing industries such as sugar refineries, tobacco plantations, studs for horses or cattle and fruit farms. These *sovkhozy* and their associated plants and factories were united into trusts. In 1925 a special program of grain-producing state farms was introduced in the virgin land areas of the North Caucasus, Kazakhstan, and Siberia. Whereas the small collective farms relied on local resources and help, the state farms received substantial investments from the government. They were better mechanized than the *kolkhozy* since all the new, complex agricultural machinery and imported tractors were made available to them. The largest *sovkhoz* in the Soviet Union, *Gigant*, was established in the Salsk steppes of the North Caucasus in 1928 on 150,000 hectares of virgin steppe land which had always been unpopular with settlers because of frequent drought. Later it became the testing ground for a variety of agricultural drought-resistant systems. Its central settlement is now a medium-size town with a well-developed food and light industry.

In 1928 the total membership of the collective farms was about one million. Under strong pressure the membership rose to 1.9 million by October 1, 1929.[7] This level was already too high, but it would have been rational to maintain this level in 1930 and to try to increase the productivity of the collective and state farms by making generous assistance and funds available. The *kolkhozy* and *sovkhozy* could provide the state with 4 to 5 million metric tons of grain and thus reduce the procurement pressures on the land societies and the tension in the villages.

These are two realistic and rational ways in which the grain problem could have been solved in 1930–1931. Both methods had influential supporters within the Party (none of whom survived the Great Terror) and there were intensive discussions in Party and government circles in the autumn of 1929 about how to solve the grain problem. In the course of the discussions Stalin published an article in *Pravda* on November 7, 1929, the anniversary of the October Revolution. In this fateful article, "A Year of Great Breakthrough," Stalin favored neither of these approaches. He proclaimed a third, more radical way to solve the problem.

2. The Liquidation of the Kulaks

Although Stalin did not call for mass collectivization immediately, it was clear that this was his main objective. He declared the "determined *offensive* of socialism against the capitalist elements in town and country," (which signalled the end of NEP) and a "radical *change* in the development of our agriculture from small, backward, *individual* farming to large-scale, advanced *collective* agriculture," (which implied accelerated collectivization). He also made a prediction, which was rarely mentioned later.

> And if the development of collective farms and state farms is accelerated, there is no reason to doubt that in about three years' time our country will be one of the world's largest grain producers, if not the largest.

After the drastic measures of 1929 the number of peasants who had joined the *kolkhozy* had grown. In view of the campaign of terror against the kulaks, this reflected self-protection rather than a genuine social movement, but Stalin, perhaps intentionally, misinterpreted and exaggerated it, stating:

> The new and decisive feature of the present collective-farm movement is the fact that peasants are joining the collective farms not in separate groups as was formerly the case, but by whole villages, volosts, districts and even okrugs. And what does this mean? It means that *the middle peasant is joining the collective farm*. And that is the basis of the radical change in the development of agriculture that constitutes the most important achievement of the Soviet government during the past year.[8]

In fact, when Stalin wrote this article only 4 percent of peasant households were considered "collectivized," hardly sufficient to be considered a radical breakthrough or to be interpreted as a change in the attitude of the middle peasant.

A few days later, on November 10, 1929, a special Plenum of the Central Committee was devoted to the program of accelerated collectivization. Molotov, who had replaced Rykov as chairman of *Sovnarkom* when the latter resigned in 1928 in protest against the "extraordinary measures," presented the main report. The Plenum expelled Rykov and Bukharin from the Politburo, ending the careers of the Right Opposition, officially labelled as the "defenders of the kulaks." Although no specific figures or dates for collectivization were mentioned, it was made clear that at least 50 percent of marketable grain should be produced by collective farms. A "determined offensive against kulaks" was declared. Measures should be taken to prevent the kulaks from penetrating the *kolkhozy*. As a result of Stalin's article and the decisions of the Plenum, the Politburo set up a special Commission on Collectivization under the chairmanship of Y. A. Yakovlev, who also became people's commissar for agriculture. The Commissariat for Agriculture *(Narkomzem)*, the *Kolkhoztsentr*, and the Commission on Collectivization began to prepare quotas for collectivization in each region and rules by which the process should be carried out. The initial recommendations envisaged 30 to 40 percent collectivization in 1930 and 70 to 80 percent in 1931. The main grain-producing regions would be comprehensively collectivized, but the pace in the poor agricultural regions of the north and the non-Slav regions of Central Asia and Transcaucasia would be slower. A major part of the program was devoted to the problem of the elimination of the kulaks.

Despite the draconian measures taken against the kulaks in 1927 and 1928, *Narkomzem* experts and the agricultural department of the Central Committee knew that they represented the most efficient and professional part of the rural community. But the attitude of the Politburo was quite clear—the time had come for the "elimination of the kulaks as a class." This would require arrests and deportation. But even if the kulaks formed only 4 percent of the peasant households, 5 or 6 million people of different ages would have to be dealt with. Although the state already had an extensive prison and labor-camp system, it was not large enough to deal with the consequences of repressive measures on such an enormous scale.

Yakovlev was known for his militant attitudes towards the kulaks. Nonetheless, the plan prepared by the Special Commission was later said to be too modest. The plan proposed that kulaks should be divided into three main groups. The first group would include those who actively opposed collectivization and engaged in counterrevolutionary activity. Members of this group should be arrested and their families deported to distant regions of the country (a euphemism for Siberia and the North Urals). The second group would comprise the kulaks who opposed collectivization, but did not engage in active sabotage. They would be resettled in areas outside their own region (this implied the virgin lands and underdeveloped areas of European Russia or Kazakhstan). The third group would consist of kulaks who were generally loyal to Soviet power (judged by previous service in the Red Army, activity during the Civil War, and so on) and who were prepared to join the *kolkhozy*. It was recommended that they should be permitted to work in the collective farms for a probationary period of three to five years without voting rights. If they proved themselves, they could then become full members of the *kolkhozy*. The commission did not estimate the numbers of kulaks in each group, but it was made clear that the third would be the largest and that the first would consist of about 60,000 people. The recommendations were hotly debated at a special Politburo meeting in December and approved with some amendments. All that remained was for TsIK to turn them into a decree.

Before examining what really happened to these three groups in the winter of 1929–1930, it would be useful to consider who these people—described by official propaganda as a dark, reactionary force and symbolized in posters as terrorists with sawnoff shotguns in their hands—really were. Lenin made many contradictory statements about the political position of the peasants and these were often quoted in 1928 and 1929 to justify one measure or another. Sometimes he maintained that only those who exploit others or employ others should be classified as capitalist elements. The middle peasant household which lived from its small allotment did not belong to the capitalists.[9] However, Lenin often declared that all individual peasants represented "the last capitalist class"[10] or a kind of "primitive capitalism."[11] Another absurd idea was that even if a peasant did not employ and exploit labor, he exploited himself and his family.

In the 1920s, when the majority of peasants belonged to the land societies and received their *nadely* according to general rules, wealth did not depend on the size of *nadel*, but on the number of horses and cattle and agricultural implements owned and on the ability to work hard. In 1927 the State Central Statistical Bureau classified peasant households into three groups on the basis of the value of their means of production (horses, cattle, machines, implements). *Poor* households were those which normally did not possess a working horse. The total value of their means of production was less than 200 rubles. Of all rural families, 26.1 percent fell into this category. *Middle* households owned one or even two horses, and the total value of their means of production was between 201 and 1,600 rubles. They represented 70.7 percent of peasants. A small group, 3.2 percent of all peasants, were categorized as kulaks, owning means of production of a total value of more than 1,600 rubles.[12] Although 1,600 rubles does not seem very much now, the Soviet currency was strong in 1926–1927. The annual income of industrial workers was 600 to 700 rubles and the market price of a working horse in 1927 was 140 to 150 rubles. Nevertheless, possessing livestock and agricultural equipment of the value of 1,800 or 2,000 rubles did not really imply wealth. These households were "rich" only because they enjoyed a better diet and could produce extra food for sale. They made their profit from their own labor. It was often said that the kulaks exploited the poor peasants by lending them horses or equipment. In fact, this was perfectly legal and middle peasants were also involved in what was, essentially, the normal practice of offering communal assistance to the poor. It was calculated that the middle peasants made an annual profit of about 15 rubles from leasing out their instruments and horses, while the annual profit of the kulaks from the same practice was about 70 rubles, a modest sum by any standard.[13]

In 1922, after the general redistribution of land and a decline in wealth, only 0.2 percent of all peasant households were classified as kulaks. But the NEP system stimulated private initiative and rewarded hard work. The kulaks of 1929 had been actively encouraged by legislation to produce more in 1923–1926. They remained members of the land societies and worked entirely within the law. The official depiction of kulaks as criminals is entirely false. It was the policy of the state towards the kulaks and other peasants which was criminal and beyond the rule of law (even Soviet law).

At the end of December 1929 the First All-Union Conference of Marxist Students of Agrarian Questions was convened in Moscow. The topic which dominated the discussion was what to do with the kulaks. Elimination was not considered the best possible solution by everyone present, but at the closing session Stalin made a speech in support of militancy:

> . . . we have recently passed from the policy of *restricting* the exploiting tendencies of the kulaks of the policy of *eliminating the kulaks as a class*. . . . Dekulakisation . . . is now an integral part of the formation and development of the collective farms. . . . When the head is off one does not mourn for the hair.[14]

When the Politburo discussed the draft program of the Commission on Collectivization, Stalin objected to the idea that "loyal kulaks" would be permitted to join the kolkhozy. There were no "loyal kulaks" and he insisted that all kulaks should be debarred from the collective farms and resettled elsewhere. His insistence on these amendments to the draft program changed the scale of the "elimination" operation.

At the very beginning of 1930, Party instructions were sent to local officials. Collectivization and the confiscation of the property of kulaks and their deportation had already begun when TsIK and *Sovnarkom* jointly published a decree on February 4, 1930, containing specific recommendations. The heads of the 60,000 counterrevolutionary kulak households were to be arrested by the OGPU and sent to prison or camp without trial, their property was to be confiscated, and their families deported. Those who resisted should be sentenced to death. A second group of 150,000, who had been kulaks and owners of private plots before the Revolution and who had reentered the communes in 1917 or later, were to be listed by local groups of poor peasants and former *batraki*. Their property was also to be confiscated and they were to be exiled with their families to remote areas. Others, the 500,000 to 850,000 peasants who had acquired kulak status more recently and were loyal to Soviet power, should be denied entry to the *kolkhozy*, but they were to be resettled with their property within the borders of their native region, though away from their villages and the local *kolkhoz* land.

As cruel and unjust as this decree was, the way it was implemented was even more brutal. Time was short. The elimination of the kulaks as a class had to be completed before the spring sowing season. As a result, the recommendations of the decree were violated widely by the "army" of about a million armed men which was mobilized to eliminate the kulaks as a class. In February large OGPU units arrived in the rural areas to set up temporary prisons and transit camps. The militia was enlarged and local Party, Komsomol, and Soviet groups were militarized. Garrisons of the regular army could be called upon when necessary. The Central Committee instructed 25,000 veteran Party members and "progressive" workers from Leningrad, Moscow, and other industrial cities to assist collectivization. In fact, the number that went into the countryside was much larger. A large number of prosecutors was mobilized to give the operation some semblance of legality and the number of local courts and tribunals was increased. In every district a special Commission on De-kulakization was established to preside over a network of boards called *troikas*, consisting of a representative each from the local Party, Soviet, and poor peasantry. The troikas could set up special commissions to prepare lists of kulaks, dividing them into the three groups established by the *Sovnarkom* decree and listing the property, means of production, and livestock which was due to be confiscated. The troikas were empowered to take all the necessary measures to collectivize the area. Army, OGPU, and police units were attached to them to deal with possible resistance. The confiscated machinery, livestock, and buildings were to be transferred to the collective farms which were being set up while dekulakization took place.

It was, of course, impossible to carry out the program exactly. It was not only the kulaks who resisted collectivization. Many of them would, in fact, have joined the *kolkhozy* willingly, to protect themselves. But many middle and even poor peasants did not wish to join. This was attributed to kulak influence and propaganda and the unwilling peasants were called kulak sympathizers, or *podkulachniki*. They, too, became liable to arrest and deportation. Local traders, mill owners, priests, and other "parasitic" elements were also arrested and the scale of the campaign of terror grew rapidly. The families of the kulaks and *podkulachniki* were allowed to take with them only what they could carry. The places in which they were to be resettled were not ready. They were moved on foot or in freight cars to locations in the Urals, Siberia, Kazakhstan, the Far East, and the arctic regions of European Russia. The nightmare journey could take weeks and many old people and children died en route. When the survivors arrived at their destination there were often no houses or barracks. They had had to spend the most severe period of winter in the wilderness of the Ural forests, the Siberian taiga, or the steppes of Kazakhstan. Many died from cold, starvation, and disease. Nobody knows how many people died, but it is a miracle that anyone survived. In the spring the survivors tried to prepare land for sowing. They knew that no one would bring them food. In the summer they began to build new villages. Thousands of "special settlements" were established. Their inhabitants, men, women, old people, and children alike, were forbidden to travel beyond their own villages. It was only in December 1941 that this restriction was lifted, when troops from Siberia and the Far East were urgently needed for the Moscow winter offensive and the army required new conscripts. Men from the special settlements were permitted to serve in the Soviet army, although usually in penal battalions. After the war, when they returned to their families as war veterans and invalids, it was impossible to keep the settlements under police control. In 1946 the special settlements became ordinary *kolkhozy* and *sovkhozy*.

It is difficult to estimate how many kulaks of the first group were arrested and executed. The number certainly exceeded the estimated 60,000. Nor is it known exactly how many families were deported. Official Soviet sources give contradictory figures. At a Central Committee Plenum in January 1933 it was reported that 240,757 kulak households had been expropriated. In Danilov's more objective study 330,000 households from all three groups are said to have been expropriated, arrested, and resettled.[15] Thus a total number of 1,600,000 to 2,000,000 people were deported. But this includes only the first wave of de-kulakization and the real number was probably much higher. There were slightly more than 24 million individual households in rural Russia in 1929. A few years later it was reported that 17 million households had joined the collective farms and that this represented 90 percent collectivization. (In 1937 there were 18.4 million collectivized households). Thus 5 million households had disappeared. How many of them were deported, how many had fled to the cities, and how many perished in the famine of 1932–1933, nobody knows. But it is obvious that collectivization cost an enormous number of human lives.

The rate of collectivization was speeded up by the February de-kulakization campaign and in March many regions reported that 70 to 80 percent of all households had been collectivized. Peasants were required to offer their horses and cattle as a special entrance contribution. Their agricultural implements were collectivized. They demonstrated their resistance by slaughtering their livestock and their poultry. In February alone about 14 million head of cattle, a third of all pigs, and a quarter of all sheep and goats were slaughtered. This was a huge disaster. Several million horses were lost, and this was a serious setback for the approaching agricultural season.

In the general chaos the land commissions found it difficult to decide which land should be given to the new *kolkhozy* and which to those who did not want to join. It was still winter and the land was covered with snow. Nobody wanted to destroy the winter crops which covered about 40 million hectares of strips (about a fourth of all the land under cereals) belonging to different families. Collectivization and de-kulakization had effectively destroyed the infrastructure of the land societies. The *kolkhozy* usually allocated the best land to themselves, leaving the more distant fields to individual farmers. But land distribution was haphazard—the new *kolkhozy* did not have effective leaders or chairmen, there were no sowing plans or plans for organizing members into work brigades. Stalin suddenly came to his senses and realized that the agricultural year would be completely ruined unless there was a retreat from the instructions which had caused such anarchy.

On March 2, 1930, his famous article "Dizzy with Success" was published in *Pravda.* Stalin accused local officials of "leftist deviation." They had distorted the Party line, indulged in arbitrary repression, generalized the meaning of the term *kulak,* used threats, and violated socialist legality. The winter "breakthrough" was cancelled and the villages were instructed to carry on as before. Stalin assumed that the sowing season would be undertaken as if nothing had happened and that collectivization could be resumed in September after the harvest had been collected. He insisted that the voluntary principle should be restored.

> Collective farms must not be established by force. . . . Who benefits by these distortions, this bureaucratic decreeing of the collective farm movement, these unworthy threats against the peasants? Nobody, except our enemies![16]

He could not have expected his article to have the impact it did. He seriously thought that a fundamental turn of the countryside to socialism could be regarded as guaranteed and he regarded 50 percent collectivization in the main growing areas as a success. Soon after the publication of his article, the Central Committee adopted a resolution, "On the struggle against distortions of the Party line in the collective farm movement." The use of force was to cease and peasants were to be allowed to leave the collective farms if they so wished. The result was a mass exodus from the collective farms. By July 1, 1930, less than six million peasant households remained in the *kolkhozy,* about one-fourth of all poor and middle peasants and about 30 percent of the rural population. In some regions almost all the collective farms were dissolved.

But the policy change did not help those who were already in prison, camps, or on the way to deportation sites. The Central Committee resolution acknowledged that in some districts "de-kulakization sometimes includes part of the middle and even the poor peasants, and in some districts the percentage of peasants de-kulakized has risen to 15 percent and the percentage disenfranchised to 15 to 20 percent." Party organizations were instructed to correct their errors and to cease all action against the middle peasants, former Red Army soldiers, Red partisans, and their families. They were to be allowed to enter the *kolkhozy*. But those who had already been arrested or deported were not repatriated.

Inevitably there was a lot of confusion in implementing the new resolution. The redistribution of land in the southern regions had to be carried out when the sowing season was already under way. The families who remained in the *kolkhozy* did not wish to return the better fields to individual farmers. Those who were leaving demanded the return of their implements and livestock. They also wanted the seed they had contributed to the *kolkhoz*. Formal regulations were only published on April 12, 1930 (in a joint TsIK and *Sovnarkom* decree, "Measures to assist the extension of the sown area of individual households"), when the spring sowing season in the main grain regions would normally be in full swing. They merely contributed to the general chaos and the spring sowing season was severely damaged. Sowing was delayed almost everywhere and it was completed about a month later than usual. However, nature was unexpectedly generous— the spring of 1930 was very cold, and normal sowing weather was twenty to twenty-five days late. It was this that saved the harvest of 1930.

3. The Second Wave of Collectivization

A cold spring like the one that delayed the sowing season in 1930 is usually good for the winter crops, encouraging better vegetation and higher yields. The good harvest of winter crops sown in 1929 compensated a little for the spring sowing, which, given the forced deportation of hundreds of thousands of the more productive peasants and the disorientation of those who remained, was inevitably lower than in 1929. It may well be that the total harvest was normal, but there are no reliable figures to prove this. Local reports were usually falsified, to show that the newly established collective farms were more efficient and productive than individual farmers. Some official estimates put the level of the harvest at more than 85 million tons, others claimed that it was 77 million tons. Livestock production, however, was very low and there was a reduction in all kinds of farm animals. As a result, less feed grain was required and more grain could be sold to the state procurement system. To compensate for the shortages of meat, poultry, and dairy products, the government raised the procurement quotas for grain and other food crops to 23 million tons of marketable grain. This would be a difficult target to achieve.

It was expected that at least half of the quota would be provided by the collective and state farms which had been allocated the best fields. Individual households were put under strong pressure by a new "contract system" of delivery. The intention was to show that the peasants who had joined *kolkhozy* would benefit and be left with more food after they had fulfilled their procurement obligations. The land societies had disintegrated and the majority of individual peasants had consolidated their *nadely*, becoming individual small farmers. The government realized that it would become increasingly difficult to integrate them into the collective farms and was determined to demonstrate the disadvantages of remaining in the individual sector. In November 1930 the procurement quotas were changed: the target figure for collective and state farms was reduced to 7 million tons, while individual farmers were to provide 14 million tons—this was equivalent to the target for the entire country in 1929. "Extraordinary measures" were reintroduced on a small scale, de-kulakization continued, and with some difficulty, the plan was fulfilled. The state received about 22 million metric tons of grain, but there was an acute shortage of meat and other high-quality products. As soon as the harvesting season was over and the procurement quotas had been fulfilled, the collectivization drive was resumed.

According to the official plan, 50 percent collectivization was expected by the end of 1931. Measures were taken to make the process easier. The Five Year Plan had been amended to accelerate the completion of the Stalingrad Tractor Plant and the Rostov Agricultural Machinery Plant and it was expected that domestic production of tractors would begin in 1931. Prior to this, the only plant to produce tractors was the Putilov Works in Leningrad, where tractors formed only one part of the diversified goods produced by the factory. The annual output of tractors was only 3,000 in 1929. The number was doubled in 1930, and an additional 6,000 to 7,000 tractors were imported. In 1931 the imports were increased to compensate for the 3 million horses which had been slaughtered during the de-kulakization campaign. But there was still a shortage of draft power. Two further tractor plants were under construction at Kharkov and Cheliabinsk and it was hoped that the Rostov Agricultural Machinery Plant would begin producing combine-harvesters in 1931.

In order to silence the critics of forced collectivization, the campaign of terror was transferred from the villages to the town. On September 3, 1930, the major newspapers announced that the OGPU had discovered a counterrevolutionary organization called the Peasant Party. It was allegedly headed by a prominent agricultural scientist, Professor N. D. Kondratiev, assisted by L. N. Yurovsky, A. V. Chayanov, and A. G. Doyarenko, also agricultural scientists. The putative membership of the Peasant Party was between 100,000 and 200,000, and it was said to have an extensive network in various government organizations like *Narkomzem, Gosplan, Khlebotsentr,* and *Narkomtorg.* Thousands of officials and experts were arrested. This was a replica of the previously discovered counterrevolutionary "Industrial Party," which never really existed, but which, in spite of that, led to the trial and execution of dozens of "leaders." The Peasant Party was invented to provide scapegoats for the food shortages, particularly of meat products. The "confessions" of a large group of *Narkomtorg* officials were published on September 22, 1930: almost the entire department of food trade had been tried for organizing sabotage, intending to create famine, and being agents of imperialism. They had caused the decline in meat production. OGPU reported that some prominent *Narkomtorg* officials were former *pomeshchiki.* This group was said to be headed by Professor E. S. Karatygin, deputy chairman of the Scientific Council of the Food Industry, and Professor A. V. Ryasantsev. After a short trial, they were all found guilty and sentenced to death without the right of appeal. Forty-six other experts and scientists were executed almost immediately after the trial and their execution was reported in *Pravda* on September 25, 1930.

It is now well established that the Peasant Party never existed and that the confessions produced at the trials were extracted by torture or invented. Very few of the prominent agricultural scientists who were arrested in 1930 survived, but I knew one of the few. In the 1950s, while working in the Department of Agrochemistry and Biochemistry of the Timiriazev Agricultural Academy in Moscow, I met Professor Alexei Grigorievich Doyarenko. Before his arrest he had been one of the most eminent professors of the Academy, the author of many books on agriculture. He had joined the Academy in 1898 and had pioneered the establishment of experimental agricultural stations. In 1930 he was sentenced to five years in Suzdal prison and then exiled. After the war he was allowed to work in Saratov, but he was not permitted to teach until he was officially rehabilitated in 1955. His last book, *Iz agronomicheskogo proshlogo (Memoirs of an Agronomist)*, was published shortly after his death in 1958. He is now honored as a great scientist and his official biography was published in 1980 in the USSR Academy of Sciences series of biographies of prominent scientists.[17] There is a long, unexplained gap in his activities in this biography—it could not be explained, because the fact that the Peasant Party affair was invented has never been officially acknowledged.

The resumption of collectivization in the autumn of 1930 did not meet with a very good response in the villages. The "voluntary principle" did not produce the desired results, and coercion and various forms of pressure were resumed, including de-kulakization. The target figures were revised upwards at a Central Committee Plenum in December 1930, when "no less than 80 percent" collectivization was demanded in the Ukraine, North Caucasus, and the Volga basin and the completion of the elim-

TABLE 4
Horses and Livestock in the Soviet Union
(Millions)

	Horses	Cattle	Pigs	Sheep & goats
1928	33.2	66.8	22.0	107.0
1929	32.6	58.2	19.4	97.4
1930	30.2	50.6	14.2	93.3
1931	*	42.5	11.7	68.1
1932	*	38.3	10.9	47.6
1933	17.3	33.5	9.9	37.3

Source: Nar. khoz., 1956, p. 128; Nar. khoz., 1963, p. 311.[18]
* No reliable data available for these years.

ination of the kulaks was recommended in those areas. The target for the central *chernozem* areas, Kazakhstan, the Urals, and Siberia remained 50 percent. The non-*chernozem* areas of the north and west were treated more leniently. They mainly produced potatoes, other vegetables, and dairy products, and the government did not plan to send any new machinery to these areas.

According to official Soviet statistics, 37,900 tractors were produced in 1931 and 48,900 in 1932. Nonetheless, the shortage of horses was still felt acutely. Moreover, collectivization continued to damage the livestock population and the number of horses. On the other hand, the livestock losses probably made collectivization easier, since without a horse a peasant household had no choice but to join the local collective farm. The livestock losses during the years of collectivization are shown in Table 4. Two or three tractor plants could not compensate for the loss of about 15 million horses. The number of pigs was more than halved and the number of sheep and goats severely depleted. If the collectivization program had been limited to the land, rather than including the livestock, the damage to agriculture would have been far less severe. The newly organized collective farms were unable to deal with "collectivized" animals, and the program was extremely incompetent. In 1941, at the beginning of the war, the livestock level was still below the 1929 level. Livestock losses during the war were smaller than those during collectivization. The 1929 level was only regained in 1958, but if the population growth (both the natural growth and that caused by the incorporation of new territories after the war) is taken into account, the proportion of meat and dairy produce in the average diet did not reach the 1928–1929 level until 1961.

Official Soviet statistics normally give the proportion of collectivized households for 1927, 1928, 1929, 1930, 1931, and 1932 and then leave a gap until 1936. Nineteen thirty-seven is regarded as the year in which comprehensive collectivization was completed. There were still about one million private households, but the acreage of the collective and state farms had reached 99.1 percent of the total arable land. The gap from 1933 to 1935 reflects a period which official Soviet historians do not care to remember. These were the years of an extraordinary man-made famine, a ghastly disaster which cost the lives of 6 million people. The tragedy was directly caused by the errors, follies, contradictions, and miscalculations inherent in Stalin's policy of forced collectivization.

4. *The Famine of 1932–1933*

The 50 percent collectivization planned for 1931 was overfulfilled, but the pattern was very different from the one expected by the authorities. Peasants in the non-*chernozem* areas and in the large area between Moscow and Leningrad in the west and the Urals in the east did not resist collectivization. These were grain-consuming regions which did not produce any surplus for the market. The villages were overpopulated, there were very few kulaks, and the peasants were poor and dependent on temporary work in the surrounding towns. The "extraordinary measures" and the de-kulakization campaign had affected these areas far less than the more prosperous villages of the Ukraine and North Caucasus.

In the south and in Siberia the situation was very different. These peasants had been free settlers for generations and they were proud of their farming history. Middle peasants here were much wealthier than the kulaks in the non-*chernozem* areas. In 1931 more than 50 of the peasants in these areas joined the *kolkhozy*, but they tended to be poor or they were relative newcomers to the area. The older residents were reluctant to join for the simple reason that they lived quite well and they did not want to lose their freedom. Their independence became even more evident with the collapse of the land society system. Those who did not enter the *kolkhozy* consolidated their *nadely*. Many of the collective farms which were reported to have been established in 1932 were, in fact, "paper *kolkhozy*."

The 1932 harvest was at about the same level as that of 1931, but the urban population was growing rapidly and the government wanted to increase grain exports to pay for foreign technology and machinery. The targets were increased while the fixed procurement prices remained static. The priority given to heavy industry in the first Five Year Plan stimulated inflation which, by 1932, was as much as 30 percent per annum. Retail prices for grain and meat were at least ten times higher than procurement prices. In the areas where collectivization was reported to be as high as 60 or 70 percent, most of the procurements had to be obtained from the collective farms. However, the rules of collective farm work had begun to take shape in 1931 and they were extremely unpopular. According to the rules, the first obligation of the *kolkhoz* was to the state. As soon as harvesting began, the first priority was to deliver grain to the state in accordance with the procurement quotas, and the quotas were very high. The second priority was to create seed reserves, supplies of feed grain, and insurance reserves, and to pay the Machine Tractor Stations (MTS) in kind for any work that had been done. Only then could the rest of the harvest be distributed amongst the *kolkhoznik* families. The amount a family was paid depended upon the amount of work they had done on the collective farm. Work was measured

by working day, called *trudoden*. A small proportion of the grain
and other produce (10 to 15 percent of the total amount it was
estimated the family would earn) was distributed in advance, but
the final distribution would only be made in December. But the
state, afraid that the peasants would hide the harvest, demanded
deliveries as soon as the harvesting began. The system was extremely unpopular and the sight of the stream of grain moving
to the collection points slowed the harvesting down considerably.
In some districts as much as 60 percent of the total harvest had
been taken by the state in 1931 and this removed from the peasants any incentive to work hard. Many peasants did not have
enough food for their families in the spring and summer of 1932.
By July the harvesting and collections were already far behind
schedule and the sowing of winter crops in July and August was
seriously delayed. There were obvious signs of discontent, and
reports were published of delays in harvesting, absenteeism, delayed threshing, and general disorganization. This was once again
attributed to kulak resistance.

It was inevitable that new drastic measures would be introduced, but it was difficult to force the peasants to work. In many
areas they were simply hungry. Their resistance became known
as the "grain strikes": they refused to work unless their advance
payments in kind were substantially raised. The amount they
demanded varied from 30 to 50 percent, which was quite reasonable after a year of a very poor diet. The conflict was now no
longer with individual peasants, but between the state and the
collective farms. Collective farmers began to realize that far from
living better, they were actually worse off and totally dependent
upon the state. Previously they had been able to express their
dissatisfaction by refusing to sell grain. Now they refused to work.
They took heads of wheat and stalks for their own consumption
and they slaughtered the pigs and cattle for which, in any case,
they had no feed grain or fodder.

The main centers of resistance were in the Ukraine, the North
Caucasus, and parts of the Volga basin. The Politburo began to
consider taking measures not only against the collective farms,
but also against local officials, some of whom understood the food

problems and were sympathetic to peasant needs. In August Stalin personally drafted a decree, "On the protection of socialist (public) property," which began the special "grain protection" measures (which were, in fact, police, military and paramilitary, including cavalry units and Komsomol vigilantes, patrols in rural areas).[19] It was far stricter than the notorious article 107 of the Criminal Code. All socialist (i.e., *sovkhoz*) and public (i.e., *kolkhoz*) property was "sacred and inviolable" and those who took it were "enemies of the people." The plundering of *kolkhoz* property, including grain standing in the fields, was punishable by death or by the deprivation of freedom for a minimum period of ten years with confiscation of property. Kulaks and speculators would be sent to prison or to labor camp for a period of five to ten years. But the new law had little effect. The state could confiscate a harvest which had already been collected, but it could not force the peasants to work. Some local officials began to suggest that the *kolkhozy* should be suspended. Grain collections continued to be very low and the winter crops were threatened. In many collective farms the hungry *kolkhozniki* consumed the seed reserves from the winter crops during the spring and summer and there were many requests from local officials for help from the state.

There was some confusion in Moscow about what to do. The Central Committee decided to disband the *Kolkhoztsentr*, and a new Central Committee Department of Agriculture with very wide powers was established under the chairmanship of L. M. Kaganovich. Political departments were attached to the 2,000 MTS which had been set up, mostly in the grain-producing regions. They were staffed with cadres from the industrial centers and from the army. The MTS was not only to provide mechanical services, but also political power. Similar political departments were created in the state farms and transformed into bases from which the Central Committee could operate for both political and security activities. After 1932 the political departments in the *sovkhozy* and MTS became the real centers of power in the countryside. Trials and repressions were reported in the local press and some people were executed for hiding grain which belonged to the *kolkhoz*. Roadblocks were set up around many districts in the Ukraine, North Caucasus, and the Don region both to prevent private sales of grain and food and to delay the delivery of essential goods like salt, kerosene, and textiles until the procurement quotas had been met. State and cooperative shops were shut down in recalcitrant areas and it was made known that they would only be reopened if the procurement quotas were fulfilled. Extraordinary Commissions were sent into the villages in the south. But these measures had very little effect. Finally Stalin sent a special Politburo Commission headed by Kaganovich and including Yagoda, first deputy chairman of the OGPU, Kosarev, general secretary of the Komsomol, Mikoyan, the commissar for supplies, Gamarnik, head of the Political Directorate of the Army and Navy, and other high officials. The Commission set up headquarters in Rostov-on-Don and assumed full power in the grain-producing regions of the Ukraine, Don, and North Caucasus. In November 1932 the Bureau of the North Caucasus Party organization passed a resolution (Kaganovich was present at the meeting) to destroy all the saboteurs and counterrevolutionaries responsible for the failure of the grain collections and the sowing of the winter crops. As a result of this decision, the entire population (several hundred households in each) of sixteen large Cossack villages were interned and deported to various places in Siberia, Kazakhstan, and the Far East. Demobilized Red Army soldiers and families from the poor northern areas were brought in to replace the population of these villages.

Repressive measures were also directed against local officials, and hundreds of them were expelled from the Party or arrested. On November 19, 1932, *Pravda* reported the execution of purged Party officials who, it was said, had approved higher payments in kind to *kolkhozniki* to persuade them back to work. Despite the poor harvesting, pressure to meet the procurement quotas continued. The government still believed that both collective and individual farmers had kept some emergency reserves and that if they were confiscated, the resistance would be broken. As a young Komsomol member in 1932, Lev Kopelev took part in the collection campaign in the Kharkov region. He has described the methods used by the procurement brigades.[20] Each brigade included a member of the OGPU and of the local militia, as well as several armed Party activists and officials from *Narkomzem* and from the procurement agencies. It moved from village to village to carry out its task. The adult villagers were assembled in the largest house or in the local church and lectured on the internal and the international situation. The villagers were then told how much grain they had to bring to give to the state. No one was allowed to leave the meeting before giving a pledge to bring a specific amount of grain. Under this system of mass blackmail and torture, some peasants agreed quickly, others had to be threatened for as long as several days. In most cases they were parting with their essential supplies. As soon as the resistance of one village had been broken, the brigade moved on to the next one.

Party propaganda began to maintain that there were anti-Soviet elements within the collective farms which had been infiltrated by kulaks. At a Party conference in Moscow, Stalin advised against idealizing the *kolkhozy*.[21] The first unmistakable signs of widespread rural starvation and famine began to appear in December. The first victims were the farm animals. The Ukraine and North Caucasus, historically the richest agricultural areas of Russia and the granary of Europe, became famine-stricken. This famine was not caused by climate. It was precipitated by the forced confiscation of all available grain. Peasants began to move from the villages to the towns where the food situation was much better. Roadblocks and military cordons were set up to prevent the exodus, and the old czarist passport system, abolished after the Revolution, was reintroduced. The new system was even more restrictive than the prerevolutionary one. A resolution of TsIK and *Sovnarkom* on December 27, 1932, made passports available only to people who lived in the towns and they had to be registered with the local police immediately. It was a criminal offence to employ anyone without a passport. The peasant practice of finding temporary winter work in the towns was effectively prevented.

Kolkhozniki were forbidden to move from their villages and any movement of the population had to be registered with the local police.

But neither roadblocks, nor military cordons, nor the new law could prevent the starving population from reaching the towns. There are many eyewitness accounts of dying peasants reaching the cities only to be left there without food or help. All food products were rationed and no official attempt was made to save the starving peasants. It was not that the government did not have any grain in reserve. But it had no desire to move these reserves back to the famine-stricken areas. Soviet grain continued to be exported, while the peasants starved to death (but the volume available for export fell from 4.8 million tons in 1930 and 5.1 million tons in 1931, to 1.8 million tons in 1932 and 1 million tons in 1933[22]). Moreover, the government imposed a complete blackout on all information from the famine-stricken areas. Many people living in Moscow and Leningrad knew nothing about the famine, although the sight of malnourished corpses lying in the streets before being collected by special trucks became common not only in the smaller Ukrainian cities, but even in Kharkov and Kiev. In 1921 the government had issued an international appeal for aid. In 1933 it did everything possible to conceal the tragedy not only from the outside world, but also from its own population.

While hundreds of thousands of peasants were dying in the south, Stalin organized the first Congress of "Progressive *kolkhoznik* shock-workers" in Moscow. A new set of *kolkhoz* rules was approved. The aim of the Party, according to Stalin, was that all *kolkhozniki* should be well-to-do. He ignored the famine, refusing even to discuss it at Politburo meetings. It remained a forbidden topic until 1956, when Khrushchev mentioned it in his Secret Speech. But even after that, it was never acknowledged in any official Soviet history or account of collectivization. But there are many private memoirs, accidental remarks, and unofficial *samizdat* documents about the tragedy. The writer Tendryakov described the famine in his novel *Konchina (Death)*. It was published in the Soviet Union in the literary magazine *Moskva* in 1968 and is one of the very few descriptions which has slipped through the censors. Tendryakov describes the typical Ukrainian countryside in 1933:

> In Petrakovskaia cattle died for lack of fodder, people ate bread made from nettles, biscuits made from one weed, porridge made from another. And not only in Petrakovskaia. A year of hunger moved through the country, nineteen hundred and thirty-three. In Vokhrovo, the *raion* capital, in the little park by the station, dekulakized peasants expelled from the Ukraine lay down and died. You got used to seeing corpses there in the morning; a wagon would pull up and the hospital stable hand, Abram, would pile in the bodies. Not all died; many wandered through the dusty mean little streets, dragging bloodless blue legs, swollen from dropsy, feeling out each passer-by with doglike begging eyes. In Vokhrovo they got nothing; the residents themselves, to get bread on their ration cards, queued up the night before the store opened. Thirty-third.[23]

There are no official figures of the human cost of this famine, but unofficial estimates put it as high as 5 or 6 million lives. In fact, it is fairly easy to extract the figures from the ordinary demographic records, by comparing the official census of 1926 with that of January 1939, for example. The number of Ukrainians registered in 1926 was 31.2 million, whereas there were only 28.1 million in 1939. The number of Byelorussians increased during this period. The decline cannot be explained by more people registering their nationality as Russian. According to the official statistics, the Soviet population was 165.7 million in 1932 and there was an annual increase of about 3 million. Figures for 1934–1936 have not been published, but the census of 1939 registered a population of only 170.4 million, instead of the expected 180 million. Part of the loss can be explained by a decline in the birthrate, but most of it was a direct result of death caused by the famine. The annual statistical reports of 1934, 1935, and 1936 give the same population figure as the report for 1933 (165.7 million at January 1, 1933). In a speech at a conference of Combine Operators in December 1935, Stalin claimed that the annual population growth in the Soviet Union was about 3 million.[24] Although the birthrate might by then have returned to normal, it took some years to fill the demographic gap caused by the famine. Maksudov, in his unofficial calculations of population losses in the Soviet Union, considers it likely that 7 million people died from famine.[25] He found that the total population of the Soviet Union fell to 159.3 million in 1934. At least 3 million of those who died were children. The demographic gap of people born between 1932 and 1934 is easily recognizable in later censuses. The 1970 census gives the figure of persons born in 1929–1931 as 12.4 million, whereas the figure for those born between 1932 and 1934 is only 8.4 million. There were certainly more newborn in 1932 and 1933, but they were not born to live. Within the current borders of the Ukraine (the Western Ukraine was regained from Poland in 1939) there appears to be a deficit in the population of one million born in 1932–1934, if the figure is compared to those of the previous and subsequent years.[26] There is no similar gap in the population figures for Byelorussia. The losses cannot be related to the war, since the people born in 1932–1934 were too young to serve in the army.

As bad as the famine of 1932–1933 was, the following year threatened to be worse. The most fertile areas of the Soviet Union were not only starving, there was no seed grain for sowing in the approaching spring. Without government intervention the famine would have spread throughout the country. The 1932–1933 famine had been caused by the forced and brutal collection of all grain reserves from the south, but there would be nothing left to collect from the deserted villages in the autumn of 1933. Fear of the total decay of agriculture in these regions finally brought the government to its senses. Seed grain was sent to these areas and some aid was sent to the lower Volga and central *chernozem* regions. But even then, the seed was lent, not given, and the distribution was selective—villages suspected of "kulak sabotage" received very little or nothing. The sowing campaign was, of course, poorly prepared and it took much longer than usual. But there were fewer people left to feed and far fewer farm animals. Everybody, including children, was mobilized for the sowing campaign. The political departments of the MTS were given supreme power locally end the era in which locally elected Soviets enjoyed some influence ended. Direct Party rule was established in the countryside.

Conclusion

The elimination of the kulaks, the forced collectivization of the peasants, and the tragic famine of 1932–1933 made an enormous impact on the future history of the Soviet Union. This will be evident as further developments in agriculture are examined in this book. It will also be obvious that the impact was negative.

There is a persistent myth, sometimes repeated even in Western literature, that collectivization was inevitable, that it made the country strong and, therefore, that it was at least partially successful. In the *New Columbia Encyclopedia* one reads that collectivization "helped to modernize agriculture, to secure a reliable food supply, to free capital for industrial production and to release labor for heavy industry."[27] This is very close to the official Soviet point of view. According to this opinion, a heavy price was paid, but the benefits of the new system soon became obvious.

It is certainly true that agricultural reforms were necessary. But a more gradual and modest development of less disciplinarian, less "collectivized" forms of productive cooperative would have brought more benefit at the cost of less long-term damage to the countryside. It is useful to consider how long the most negative measures introduced during collectivization persisted. The very unpopular system of single annual payments in kind at the very end of the season continued until the end of the 1950s, when it was gradually supplemented and later replaced by monthly payments in cash. The arbitrary legal and police restrictions on the movement of peasants from one place to another and to the towns associated with the denial of internal passports to *kolkhozniki* survived until 1976–1978. The growth of productivity of arable land—slow but visible in 1906–1916 and in 1923–1928—stagnated, and the yields of the main cereal crops did not grow for the next twenty-five years. The total grain harvest, which was

86 million tons in 1913, remained at the same level until 1952–
1954 (fluctuating between 82 and 85 million tons), despite a
significant population growth. Grain production only began to
increase when Khrushchev introduced his Virgin Land Program.
The number of livestock was restored to the 1928 level only in
1956.

The political price of Stalin's collectivization was even higher.
The methods of terror used against millions of kulaks and other
peasants and against agricultural experts and the tragedy of the
famine of 1932–1933 created a serious rift in the relationship
between the government and the masses. The Party was dis-
oriented. An official purge of the whole Party began in December
1932, by which time the most able and moderate leaders had
been expelled. This purge created the foundation for the cult of
Stalin and his ultimate dictatorship. The terror of 1936–1938 has
many links with the terror of 1929–1933.

Even if the villages had been left as they were in 1928, the
creation of a network of MTS and the increase in machinery
would have brought about spontaneous changes in the old communal system and created extra grain and extra workers for industry. The continuation of NEP would have made industrial
development easier, since light consumer industries, services,
and trade would have developed to the appropriate level without
any investment from the state. The view that "capital" was extracted from the villages by collectivization to invest in industry
and offset against imports is an illusion. During the Great Depres-
sion of 1929–1933 the price of grain on the world market was
extremely low. Moreover, the collective farms remained in a continuous state of crisis, no matter what modifications and improvements were introduced and most of them always needed
credits which they could not repay. They operated only through
coercion. The process of replacing chronically insolvent and poor
kolkhozy with more disciplined and centralized *sovkhozy* has continued for decades. In 1940 about 93 percent of all arable land
in the country was cultivated by the *kolkhozy*. By 1985 their share
had fallen to 40 percent and they produced an even smaller proportion of grain. In financial terms, all the *kolkhozy* produced

less in the 1980s than the *sovkhozy*, and less than the private sector (the small individual plots left to the peasant families for their private needs). The reason *sovkhozy* have become the predominant form of agriculture in the last decade is not that they strengthen socialist agriculture. In fact, *kolkhozy* cost less and require less investment and would therefore be preferable. It is because the *kolkhoz* system cannot produce a viable agriculture. Despite enormous investments, *kolkhozy* have been declining rapidly. New *sovkhozy* usually replace totally impoverished and bankrupt *kolkhozy* which have lost their active population. Each year now, the *kolkhozy* require more investment just to survive than totals the amount of capital extracted from the villages (through very low procurement prices) during the two prewar five year plans. The myth that collectivization was harsh but effective does not withstand an examination of the performance of Soviet agriculture.

Chapter 4

Stalin's *Kolkhozy*,
1933-1941

The collectivization of agriculture changed almost everything in the countryside except for the kind of food crops and meat and dairy products that were cultivated. The peasants as a rural class based on the private ownership of the means of production and communal working ownership of the land disappeared. Individual small farmers with consolidated land and the comparative freedom to choose how to work and what to grow also vanished. They either joined the collective farms, or became workers on the state farms or in the MTS. The previous differentiation based on economic criteria, into poor, middle, and well-to-do peasants, was transformed into a new, professional differentiation. Most *kolkhozniki* were ordinary workers in field or livestock brigades. Above them were chairmen of sub-brigades (called *zveno*), the chairmen of brigades, and the chairman and deputy chairman of the *kolkhoz*. There were also those who specialized in using machinery. The everyday language acquired new terminology to describe the occupation and life of the *kolkhozniki*. If the transformation had come about more slowly and with better planning and foresight, it might have brought about a better life, larger harvests, and more food for both town and country. Mechanization could have improved the way the soil was cultivated and shortened the sowing and harvesting seasons. Consolidating the fields would have made it possible to introduce modern, highly productive rotation systems, which would have improved the fertility of the soil. Better planning with due regard for different climatic regions could have led to better seed grain and better varieties of technical crops. Under normal circumstances, the yields of the main grain crops could have been expected to grow from the very low average of 7 to 8 metric centners per hectare to the 14 to 15 centners per hectare obtained in many European countries at the end of the nineteenth century before chemical fertilizers became widely used. This is what the *Narkomzem* experts predicted for the collective farms within a few years. It was also the level expected by *Gosplan* in its projections of food production in the Soviet Union during the second and third five year plans. It was the level of agricultural output required to support the program of industrial construction, the rapidly growing urban population, and the creation of strategic reserves of grain and food for the war which was always considered possible. Stalin and some of his supporters expected even more spectacular results. They often repeated that collectivization and mechanization would rapidly make the Soviet Union the main producer and exporter of food in the world.

None of these expectations were fulfilled. Grain crop yields remained at the very low level of about 7.5 centners per hectare until 1953 (6.2 centners in Byelorussia, 7.0 centners in the RSFSR, and 10.7 centners in the Ukraine). The production of meat and other high-quality livestock products did not reach the pre-collectivization level until Stalin's death in 1953. The diet of the rural population and the rapidly increasing urban population did not improve for more than two decades. From the 1930s onward, potatoes formed an increasing proportion of the diet, replacing traditional products which were in short supply.

The slow growth of agricultural production in the 1920s had been caused by the organizational and economic limitations of the peasant communes. Collectivization was expected to remove these limitations and it may well have been able to do that. The disappointing performance of post-collectivization agriculture was mainly due to administrative mismanagement and incompetence. The man-made limitations of the collective farm structure and methods of work were inflexible and inhibited initiative even more than the strict rules of the traditional *obschina*. The enormous livestock losses in 1930–1933 reduced the level of natural, organic soil fertilization. The basic "law of return" of the elements of fertility was destroyed and the fertility of the topsoil declined even in large tracts of the rich, black earth in the south. A proper multi-rotation system may have been able to preserve the fertility of the soil for some time, but it takes a full cycle of seven to nine years for the benefits of rotation to become evident. In any case, the demand that more and more grain and technical crops be produced from the same acreage made it impossible to introduce an optimal system of crop rotation. Even in the 1960s more than half of the collective farms were unable to stabilize their rotation systems. Stripped agriculture may have been backward and primitive, but it did not cause soil erosion. The creation of poorly planned large fields led to rapid erosion. Streams were created by rain and they soon turned into ravines. About 10 percent of the arable land was lost within a few years of mass ploughing. Similarly, however primitive small strips and sowing and harvesting by hand had been, peasants had been able to care for their strips, weed them, sort the seed before sowing it, and remove heads of wheat, rye, or barley which showed signs of fungus disease (particularly smut and brand, *Tilletia caries, Fusarium*, and other species which contain strong toxins and make the grain inedible for humans and cattle alike). It was impossible to take this kind of care for large fields. With machine harvesting, nobody could predict or deal with problems effectively. Weeds, fungus diseases, and the infestation of fields soon became rampant and it was only in the late 1960s that herbicides and pesticides were more widely used. Collectivized farm animals also became vulnerable to infection and disease, which was hardly surprising given the hasty assembly of cattle and other farm animals into herds which were kept without any proper housing. But the worst effect on the efficiency of the collective farms was caused by the way in which they were ordered to operate by the collective farm statutes or *ustav*. The *ustav* was not designed to serve the interests of the *kolkhozniki*. The needs of the state were paramount, and the more than 100 million rural inhabitants who were producing the food were left with a very small residue after the huge appetite of the state had been satisfied. The result was predictable. The villages became poorer and poorer and the economic gap between the town and the countryside grew wider. The growing demand for food for the towns, which would have stimulated agricultural production in a normal economic system, in fact acted to inhibit production. The war with Germany in 1941 found the Soviet leadership unprepared not only in tactical military terms. The Soviet Union did not possess any strategic reserves of grain and food, and this made the Soviet war effort much more difficult.

1. *The Collective Farm Regulations*

When mass collectivization was launched in 1930–1931 there were no clearly defined rules about how the *kolkhozy* would operate. As a result there was a great deal of local improvization with consequent damage to the collectivized livestock and means of production. *Narkomzem* circulated a set of recommended regulations in 1930, but they were extremely vague about the distribution of the collective farm income, the obligations of the state, and other important details. The rules adopted locally were often far too radical, extending to the collectivization of poultry and the abolition of the small plots attached to the peasants' houses and used for growing vegetables and fruit. These plots had never belonged to the *obshchiny* or the land societies and the *Narkomzem* regulations permitted *kolkhozniki* to cultivate them (although the suggested size, 0.1 hectare, was far too small). But the regulations did not stipulate that households could own cattle

and in many *kolkhozy* peasants were told that their livestock had
to be presented to the collective farm as an entrance contribution.
They would receive milk and meat as part of their payment in
kind for their work.

In 1934 only 50 percent of households were collectivized. There
were still more than 9 million households who were farming
individually and it seemed unlikely that they would be tempted
to join the collective farms unless the regulations were clarified
and legalized in a more unified way. In May 1934 *Sovnarkom*
adopted a resolution[1] which was clearly a retreat from the previous policy of collectivizing cattle and other farm animals. Only
working horses were to remain the property of the *kolkhoz*. Previously collectivized cows, heifers, calves, pigs, sheep, and poultry
and the confiscated buildings in which they were kept were to
be returned to individual members. It had become clear that the
collective farms did not possess the fodder and feed grain to feed
the livestock and that the confiscated buildings (often the homes
of kulaks) were unsuitable for housing animals. Special purpose-
built buildings were required for farm animals and they could
not be built without state investment. In November 1934 the
Central Committee decided that the time had come to introduce
new guidelines for *kolkhoz* regulations. A draft *ustav* (statute)
was prepared by the Agricultural Department of the Central Committee and *Narkomzem* and, to give it a semblance of popular
democracy, it was submitted for discussion and approval to the
Second All-Union Congress of *Kolkhoz* Activists, which was convened in Moscow on February 11, 1935.

The delegates to this Congress had been selected in a rather
arbitrary manner. Officially 1,143 delegates had been elected at
meetings of the collective farms. But there were already more
than 200,000 collective farms in existence and no democratic
elections took place to reduce the number of delegates to 1,143.
Most of the delegates were chairmen of *kolkhozy*, local Party
officials (usually from the political departments of the MTS), and
there were a few local Soviet officials, chairmen of brigades, and
a sprinkling of *kolkhoz* activists. The Seventh Congress of Soviets

was completing its session in Moscow at the same time and about 300 Congress delegates took part in the *Kolkhoz* Congress.

Stalin was the most important speaker at the Congress, but the official report on the *ustav* was presented by Yakovlev, now head of the Agricultural Department of the Central Committee. The draft was approved with some small alterations. It was declared that the *ustav* was a "model" which should be adapted to local conditions. It was clearly impossible to construct a universal set of regulations, equally suitable for north and south, for the Ukraine and Tadzhikistan, for growers of technical crops and grain, and for the Kalmyk and Turkmen nomads. Each collective farm was therefore to alter the model in accordance with local conditions and then register it with the local Soviet. But in practice there were certain general rules which were not subject to alteration and which determined the future of collectivized agriculture. It is, therefore, important to examine the compulsory rules in the 1935 *ustav*.

THE LAND

The consolidated land of the households which formed the collective farm belonged to the state and was leased to the collective farm for permanent use. Each member family had the right to a small plot, attached to, or near, the family's dwelling. The recommended size of these private plots was 0.25 hectares, but in exceptional cases (for very large families if several members of the family worked on the collective farm or if the collective farm specialized in technical crops like sugar beets or cotton, which could not be consumed directly when received as payment in kind), the *kolkhoz* management could increase the size to 0.5 hectares. The individual plots did not belong to the household. They remained the property of the collective farm and if all members of the family stopped working on the collective farm, the plot would be taken away from the household.

The discussion about the size of individual plots was an important subject at the Congress. In 1930 *Narkomzem* had recommended a plot of 0.1 hectares for the private use of *kolkhoz-niki*. Workers on the *sovkhozy* were also allowed from 0.1 to 0.15 hectares each for private cultivation. Some delegates (mostly officials) argued that smaller plots would make the *kolkhozniki* give priority to working in the collective farm fields. Larger plots would make them more independent and encourage them to spend too much time working at home, particularly since enough could be earned from a plot of 0.25 or 0.5 hectares to keep a family. Others realized that if the individual plots were too small, the remaining (in 1935) 8 million individual farmers would not be encouraged to join the collective farms. Moreover, it had been found that vegetable cultivation on collective farm fields was a failure. These crops needed to be returned to the small fields where they had been grown before collectivization, together with fruit and other intensive crops. The private plots had received high levels of organic fertilizer from the privately owned farm animals and had been ideal for vegetable and fruit cultivation. In the communes and land societies individual plots had never been considered part of the communal land and their absorption by the collective farms had been a serious source of discontent.

LIVESTOCK

According to the *ustav*, working horses were considered part of the means of production and were, therefore, the property of the collective farm. Individuals could only own horses in a few regions where they were used for transport, or where the traditional way of life involved owning a horse, camel, or donkey (for example, in Central Asia and the steppe regions, where the traditional diet of the nomadic nations included horse milk and meat). In all other regions, horses could be hired from the collective farm for a daily fee to deliver produce to the markets, to transport timber and firewood, or to plough private plots.

As far as other livestock was concerned, it was recognized that the losses caused by the mass slaughtering of animals during the attempt to collectivize livestock could only be restored by lifting the restrictions on private ownership of farm animals.

Households were now permitted to own a limited number of animals for personal use. Each family could keep one milk cow, two calves or heifers, one sow with its piglets, and four sheep (raised to ten sheep in the steppe regions). The *ustav* also permitted an unlimited number of chickens. But the new rules did not solve the problem of feeding privately owned animals. The private plots were too small for fodder or grain crops and the meadows and pastures belonged to the *kolkhoz*. In theory, households were entitled to feed grain, fodder crops, hay, and straw as part of their payment in kind for work on the collective farms. But in practice the collective farms were under heavy pressure to fulfill ever-increasing plans for good grain and technical crops, as well as setting up collective livestock farms and feeding the collective horses. In comparison to these demands the production of fodder for privately owned animals was unimportant. Acquiring fodder and hay became a perennial problem for every family. *Kolkhozniki* began to mow clearings in the forest and unused land alongside the roads and railroads or to buy fodder from the *kolkhoz*. The problem has remained unsolved to this day.

The Organization of Agricultural Work

Every collective farm member was legally obliged to participate in the work of the *kolkhoz* according to a program drawn up by the management and under the direction of the chairmen of the brigades. The amount of labor contributed to ploughing, sowing, distributing manure, mowing, harvesting, threshing, haymaking, weeding, and dozens of other tasks was measured on a scale of "workday units" or *trudoden*, various tasks being accorded different values. Difficult manual work like ploughing or distributing manure was valued at two *trudodni* for one eight-hour working day. For lighter work like transporting food or water to the fields, the *kolkhoznik* would be credited with only 0.5 *trudoden* for the same number of hours of work. The chairmen of brigades (consisting of ten to twenty workers) shared the work load of their brigades and were rewarded with an extra *trudoden* for each day of their administrative duties. During the busy harvesting, sowing, or haymaking season, a *kolkhoznik* could earn two or three *trudodni* each working day, but in winter they earned little or nothing. In general a quota of about 120 to 150 *trudodni* per year was considered an average load.

Payment in kind was made in proportion to the number of *trudodni* registered by the brigade chairmen and the *kolkhoz* accountant. However, the actual income varied widely from one collective farm to another and depended upon the overall performance of the *kolkhoz*, the fulfillment of the plan, and many other factors. Successful *kolkhozy* could afford to pay their members generously in kind and cash, while less successful ones made the value of a *trudoden* very low. The poorest *kolkhozy* were often unable to provide their members with even the bare minimum necessary for survival. The *kolkhoz* regulations made the payment of members the last priority, after state and other obligations had been met. This "residual" principle of distributing the annual harvest and financial income was the most controversial aspect of the model *ustav* and it served to make the collective farms very unpopular with the peasants.

THE DISTRIBUTION OF THE COLLECTIVE FARM PRODUCTS

The distribution of harvested crops was organized to ensure the procurements of grain and other crops by the state at a minimal cost. The main law of socialist agriculture was that state obligations were paramount. Each collective farm was given a production plan for its main crops which prescribed how the land should be allocated for these crops. During the summer, agronomists and other experts working for the MTS or the local *Narkomzem* office estimated the "biological harvest," that is, the approximate expected yield from the fields which had not yet been harvested. In fact, it did not require an expert to make an approximate estimate of the harvest. Any experienced peasant could estimate the harvest by considering the density of the plants, the size of the wheat or rye heads, and the size of the grain. On the basis of the "biological harvest," the state estimated the level of the compulsory delivery from the *kolkhoz* to the state for which the state would pay a fixed procurement price, which was normally very low (much lower even than the production costs). The compulsory delivery was the first priority of the *kolkhoz* and it usually had to be delivered while the harvesting was in progress— "the first grain to the state" was the slogan commonly used at the beginning of the harvesting season after 1934. The compulsory delivery included all the varieties of grain crops (wheat, rye, barley, oats, corn, etc.) and technical crops. The *kolkhozy* were not permitted to distribute grain amongst their members until their procurement targets had been met, after which a small advance payment in kind could be made.

The *kolkhoz*'s second obligation was to pay the MTS in kind for work done on the collective farm. Tractors and other complex machinery belonged to the state and were held by the MTS. Any ploughing, sowing, cultivating, or harvesting which employed this machinery was evaluated in kind, irrespective of the level of the harvest. Work was measured in units of ploughing, and each unit was worth a specific amount of grain, depending on the kind of soil. Heavy and clay loam soil required more work and was accorded a higher value in kind than the light, fertile *chernozem*. Combine harvesting, threshing, and other work were evaluated in a similar way. The obligations to the MTS had to be met promptly. In 1935 these payments were still rather low, because the level of mechanization was modest and most of the work was done manually by the *kolkhozniki*, but over the years the proportion of the harvest paid to the MTS increased. Because the MTS belonged to the state, the payments which they received were considered part of the general procurement quotas and included in the total balance of marketable grain.

When the state obligations had been met (usually taking about 30 to 35 percent of the harvest), the *kolkhoz* had to create a seed reserve for the next sowing season. The scientific norm of sowing per hectare varies around 2 centners. Thus with harvests as low as about 8 centners per hectare, the seed reserve required about 25 percent of the harvest. After creating their seed funds, the fourth obligation of the *kolkhoz* was to create supplies of feed grain for the horses and the collective livestock. Then an insurance fund had to be established, in case of frost damage to winter crops causing a need to resow, and so on. The *ustav* also prescribed the creation of a small food fund (of not more than 2 percent of the harvest) as a food pension for village invalids, widows of Red Army soldiers, and wives and children of *kolkhozniki* who had been conscripted into the army. When all the payments had been made and the funds and reserves created, the remaining harvest was divided into two parts, one to be sold through the open market or to the state (as an excess) for higher procurement prices, and the other to be distributed amongst the *kolkhoz* members in proportion to their *trudodni*. The money earned from the former was required to buy goods for the *kolkhoz*, to pay the salaries of employed experts, and to pay for construction work. In some cases there was sufficient to supplement the payment in kind for *trudodni* with a cash payment.

The payment due to *kolkhoz* members was calculated and paid once a year, usually in November or December. Advance payments were deducted from what was owed. Payments in kind of farm animal products, for example milk and dairy products, could be made more often, but in practice neither dairy products nor meat were included in the payments in kind. The collective farms specializing in livestock used to sell all their produce to the state.

A system of payment in which the wages were the last stage in a long chain of compulsory distributions of the harvest could leave *kolkhoz* members with very little or nothing at all. Neither the state procurement quotas nor the payments in kind to the MTS were flexible enough to fluctuate with the weather and with other variables of the agricultural season. Moreover, the "biological harvest" was an inaccurate measure which made no allowances for inevitable losses, late droughts which could affect grain maturation, or rain during the harvesting season which could spoil the crop. In 1936, when weather conditions were very poor and the total harvest was smaller than average, most of the collective farms in the grain-producing areas could not even fulfill their procurement plans for seed grain. The government gave them seed grain, but it was considered a loan from the state—and the collective farms had to pay back their debts of the previous year in the procurements of the following year. Over the years many *kolkhozy* became perpetual debtors.

The cash income of the *kolkhozy* was very modest. Twenty percent of it had to be deposited as an investment fund. The rest was spent on replacing implements and simple horse-drawn machinery and paying the cash salaries of the chairmen and other employed experts. If anything remained thereafter, it could be distributed as part of the payment for members' *trudodni*.

The value of a *trudoden* and, consequently, the income of *kolkhozniki* varied greatly from one *kolkhoz* to another. In the poorer collective farms, members only received one to two kilograms of grain per *trudoden*, plus some fodder for their livestock. Successful collective farms (they were often set up as "model" *kolkhozy* and received state support) paid far more in food as well as a cash supplement of several rubles per *trudoden*.

THE MANAGEMENT OF THE COLLECTIVE FARMS

The *ustav* established that the average collective farm should elect a chairman and a deputy chairman at a general meeting of all members, and it was to employ an accountant. An agronomist could also be employed. Chairmen of brigades were to be appointed or elected by members of the brigade. Each brigade specialized in field work, livestock, or technical work. The chairman, deputy chairman, accountant, agronomist, and brigade chairmen formed the management committee of the *kolkhoz*. Problems were to be resolved collectively. Important decisions (for example, accepting new members, expelling members, resettlements, etc.) were to be decided by open vote at a general meeting of all members of the collective farm.

2. *The First Five Years of Comprehensive Collectivization*

Collectivization was completed in 1935–1937 through economic pressure, by taxing the remaining individual farmers very heavily. TsIK and *Sovnarkom* issued a decree in September 1934 that introduced a new, very high, progressive tax on individual farmers who did not want to join the *kolkhozy*.[2] The amount of grain and other products that they had to sell to the state for the same low procurement prices paid to the collective farms was doubled. The tax was calculated by an arbitrary advance estimate of expected income, rather than based on real income and, calculated on the acreage of land, it was 50 percent higher than the state obligations of collective farms. In practice the state was now entitled to take about 30 percent of the collective farm harvests for the needs of the state market, whereas individual farmers had to part with about half of their total harvest of grain and technical crops.[3] But the results were disappointing and a new resolution on March 3, 1935, raised the figures for the 1934 harvest and increased the agricultural tax. This was clearly unfair and many peasants had apparently already disposed of most of the previous year's harvest. It is not surprising that collectivization began to grow again and was almost completed during the second Five Year Plan.

By 1937, the jubilee year, more than 93 percent of all individual households had joined the collective farms and in the main grain-producing regions the figure was close to 99 percent. The total number of collective farms was now 245,126. The average number of households in each *kolkhoz* was 76 and the average *kolkhoz* acreage was 476 hectares.[4] In fact, these figures are rather deceptive. In the northwestern regions the *kolkhozy* were very small, consisting of about 30 to 50 households each, while in the main grain-producing regions of the south and the Ukraine they often contained 100 to 120 families or more and cultivated more than 1,000 hectares. Between 1935 and 1937 collectivization stimulated an increase in the number of households because it favored the segregation of large families so that each family could avail itself of the right to an individual plot. Nevertheless, the reduction in the total number of rural households from 24.5 million in 1929 before collectivization[5] to 18.4 million in 1937 is a clear indication of the high human costs of the "socialist transformation of the village." The decrease was not directly related to industrialization. A major part of it was registered in 1930–1933 and there was a slight increase in rural households in 1934–1937 as rural life became more stabilized.[6] (There is a discrepancy between the number of individual households reported in the 1926 census mentioned previously—21.7 million—and the figures for 1927 given in the annual reports of the Central Statistical Bureau—25.1 million. The census was carried out for demographic purposes and was based on verbal statements by individuals. There was a tendency to minimize the figure. The annual reports of the Central Statistical Bureau were carried out in the spring for tax purposes and tended to exaggerate the figures. The actual number of households probably lay somewhere between the two figures.)

By 1935 the technical base of collectivization had already become more established. The Stalingrad and Kharkov tractor plants were working at full capacity. The Rostov-on-Don agricultural machinery plant was producing several thousand combine-harvesters per year, as well as other types of agricultural machinery (for example, threshing and mowing machines, sowing equipment, tractor ploughs, cultivators, and so on). This plant, known since the early 1930s as *Rostselmash*, was the largest agricultural machinery plant in Europe. In 1936 its production was greater than that of the entire Russian agricultural industry in 1913. The Cheliabinsk tractor plant was nearing completion and was designed to produce more powerful 60 horsepower caterpillar tractors from 1936 onwards. The industrialization plan included the creation of an automobile industry and the production of trucks (1.5- and 3-ton trucks at first, and later 5-ton trucks as well) reached about 200,000 per year at the end of the second Five Year Plan. Although most of these trucks were for town use, about one-sixth of the production was sent to the MTS.

The number of MTS grew from 4,375 in 1935 to 5,818 in 1937. They had 365,800 tractors at their disposal and could service 78.3 percent of all collective farms.[7] In the grain-producing regions each MTS established a working agreement with thirty to thirty-three *kolkhozy* and their technical services extended over an area of about 18,000 to 19,000 hectares. In the Ukraine, North Caucasus, and Volga basin about 90 percent of all ploughing in 1938 was carried out by MTS. The MTS were state-owned and received free machinery and equipment from the state. But each item of mechanization had a certain value, which was returned to the state through the payments in kind from the collective farms. The people who worked in the MTS were considered state employees in the same group as farmers working on the *sovkhozy*. Collective farms could purchase simple horse-drawn machinery, but the ownership of tractors, combines, and other sophisticated machinery was a state monopoly.

The rapid mechanization of agriculture (it had to be rapid to replace the loss of draft horses and oxen) created new problems, which were often discussed in the press in the late 1930s. The main difficulty was the delay in organizing proper servicing and repairs. Although the production of machinery was part of the state industrial plan and thus centrally directed, the establishment of repair and servicing shops was decentralized and left to the regional authorities and the *Narkomzem* system. Inevitably there was little synchronization of the two processes. Repair workshops were set up far more slowly than the rate at which the centralized industry was growing. The result was a chronic shortage of spare parts, and about half of all tractors were out of service after only two years. More than 2,000 MTS did not have their own repair facilities in 1937.[8] In the end it was the collective farms that paid for the high rate of wear and tear on the agricultural machinery. Although the MTS were not required to make a profit, they were meant to balance their books (including paying their employees) from the payments in kind they received from the collective farms.

A second problem was a disproportion in the different types of machinery that were produced. The tractor industry was doing much better than other branches. The existence of a variety of tractors meant that other agricultural equipment had to be adapted accordingly. When the Cheliabinsk tractor plant began to supply MTS with 60-horsepower caterpillar tractors, their ploughs and other equipment were still only suitable for the smaller 15-horsepower model. Moreover, the *kolkhozy* had to pay more for work done by the Cheliabinsk caterpillars than for the same work done by smaller tractors. There were many conflicts about the annual contracts signed by the MTS and the *kolkhozy*. Theoretically, the MTS were organized to serve the *kolkhozy*, but in practice it was the MTS that decided the pattern and volume of agricultural work. They were staffed by the thousands of agronomists who were graduating annually both from older and from newly established agricultural colleges, and who felt superior to the *kolkhozniki* and considered the *kolkhozy* to be subordinate to the state-owned MTS.

Despite the enormous human losses in 1930–1933, there was still a labor surplus in the rural areas in 1937. The urban population had grown rapidly (from 28.7 million in 1929 to 46.6 million in 1937), but rural inhabitants still formed the larger proportion of the population (117.2 million in 1937). The average annual output of *trudodni* for a *kolkhoznik* was 181 in 1935 and 194 in 1937.[9] Until 1938 army service was compulsory for all men at the age of twenty-one. (In 1938 the age was lowered to eighteen.) After military service these men usually preferred to work in the MTS or in industry. Very few demobilized soldiers wanted to be ordinary *kolkhozniki*. But this constant drain of young men from the *kolkhozy* did not create a problem in the 1930s. The army was the main supplier of drivers and mechanics for socialist agriculture, but there were also thousands of short courses to train tractor drivers or combine-harvester operators. By 1937 there were 685,016 qualified tractor drivers and 82,413 combine operators, many more than the number of combines and tractors.[10] The mechanics and tractor drivers who did not join the MTS and remained members of the collective farms received higher salaries than ordinary *kolkhozniki*. Their work was also evaluated in *trudodni*, but they were calculated as *guaranteed trudodni*, and they were paid a minimum of 3 rubles in cash and 3 kilograms of grain per *trudoden* irrespective of the harvest, whereas the *trudoden* value of the ordinary *kolkhozniki* fluctuated. The value of the *guaranteed trudoden* was increased progressively for overtime to encourage tractor drivers and combine operators to work longer hours during the peak seasons. *Guaranteed trudodni* were also introduced for brigade chairmen, as well as for anyone doing more professional work on the *kolkhoz*, and the system soon became very complicated. A *kolkhoz* elite was created over the very poorly paid ordinary *kolkhozniki*, although the actual number of working-day units did not differ very much. The living standards of ordinary *kolkhozniki* were much lower in 1936–1940 than those of middle peasants in 1925–1928.

In official histories of the Soviet Union the period 1935–1940 is described as a great success in the socialist development of agriculture. It is true that the number of rural schools and hospitals grew and that the level of electrification and other indicators of social progress rose rapidly. Moreover, mechanization and the consolidation of the fields changed the methods of agricultural production. The transport system improved and the consumption of manufactured goods grew. The production of some technical crops, particularly cotton, grew enormously. It certainly became much easier for the state to make procurements of grain and other products and to obtain enough marketable grain both to feed the growing urban population and to export. In 1937 the ration card system was abolished. The food-processing industry grew significantly. All these changes were obvious. However, the main indicators of the level of agricultural production remained practically the same. The urban food situation improved at the expense of food consumption in the villages, not because there was an overall growth in agricultural production. There was a modest increase in the total acreage of cultivated land (partly due to the exiled "special settlements" and the *gulag* or prison camp *sovkhozy*), but the average yield of grain crops remained at the same low level of 7 to 8 centners per hectare. The average production of milk was about 1,000 liters per cow and the production of meat in 1940 was still below the 1928 level. Shortages of feed grain and fodder caused the collective farms to slaughter cattle and pigs which were below "normal" weight.

In 1936 the performance of the *kolkhozy* was very poor, partly because of the weather and partly because the new regulations and the way in which the harvest was distributed were very unpopular. It was also the year in which Stalin's Great Terror began. Local officials were terrified by the wave of arrests which began at all levels and they tried to press the *kolkhozniki* into impossible "achievements." In some regions the slogan "fulfill the state procurements in August" made the peasants so suspicious that they deliberately delayed starting to gather the harvest. They were afraid that all their grain would be taken by the state. In June 1936 a Central Committee Plenum recommended an increase in the rates of payment in kind for MTS work. This made the *kolkhozy* reluctant to employ the MTS services as much as they had previously. Attempts to fulfill the procurements at the height of the harvesting season disrupted normal working procedures, particularly since there was a great shortage of horses for transportation and grain was still delivered to the procurement sites by horse-drawn carts, rather than trucks. In many regions the procurement plans for August remained unfulfilled. But even worse was the fact that the harvesting, particularly in Siberia and Kazakhstan, was ruined. In these regions only about half of the fields had been mowed before the rains began in September and the rest of the harvest was destroyed.

In the general political atmosphere of the purges, these failures were attributed to acts to deliberate sabotage and thousands of local officials were arrested. In many regions the first secretary of the regional Party Committee was sentenced to death together with the whole bureau. A wave of arrests began in the *Narkomzem* and other state agricultural organizations. At the beginning of 1937 Ya. A. Yakovlev, the head of the Central Committee agricultural department and the main speaker at the *Kolkhoznik* Congress of 1935 (and at the Congress of Soviets in December 1936, which adopted the Stalin constitution), was dismissed. He was later arrested and executed as an "enemy of the people." The entire Right Opposition (Bukharin, Rykov, and colleagues) were arrested in February 1937. Many agricultural scientists and experts were arrested. This tragedy in Soviet agricultural science has been analyzed in detail elsewhere.[11]

The trials and executions of prominent Party members during the years of terror are well known and have been documented in many books. But the terror claimed an even higher cost in human lives at the local level. Almost the entire first generation of collectivization activists and a significant number of local agricultural experts were detained and many of them were shot. In practically all the districts which did not meet the procurement plans and payments in kind to the MTS in 1936 and 1937 there were local trials of "wreckers." *Kolkhoz* chairmen and *sovkhoz* directors, directors of MTS, chairmen of *Selsovety*, accountants, and tax inspectors were tried for being members of these "wrecking organizations." Every agricultural problem (such as livestock disease, shortages of fodder, poor ploughing, etc.) was classified as organized sabotage and followed by the arrest of thousands of *kolkhoz* chairmen, local agronomists, livestock experts, veterinary surgeons, and ordinary *kolkhozniki*. Many prison camps in Siberia, Kazakhstan, and the Far East were turned into special *gulag sovkhozy*. They were staffed by people from all walks of life who were arrested in 1936–1938, and there was no shortage of experts and agronomists to supervise their work. The *gulag sovkhozy* became the dumping ground for those who were too unfit and weak to work in the mines, timber plants, and other prison camp industries. There were dairy farms, chicken farms, and greenhouse complexes in the *gulag*, and needless to say, they produced food for the guards and the NKVD officials, not for the prisoners. My father, a philosopher and historian, died in one these *sovkhozy* in the Magadan region of the Far East in 1941. He had been transferred there in 1940, when he became too ill to work in the arctic copper mines nearby. By rare coincidence, the father of my school friend, I. P. Gavrilov, was an agronomist and the director of a large *sovkhoz*. He had also been arrested and he was working in the same prison greenhouse complex in 1941. He survived and told me the story in 1946. It is not surprising that the official statistics of agricultural production for 1937 and 1938 were much better than those for 1936. But it is clear that they are very unreliable.

At the Eighteenth Party Congress in March 1939 Stalin reported that the grain harvest had risen to 95.8 million metric tons. It is now acknowledged that this figure was falsified, and it is not reproduced in current statistical books.[12] The average grain production in 1936–1940 (within the borders of the Soviet

Union before September 1939) was still at the level of 77.4 million tons, the same as during the 1926–1928 period. The livestock level in 1939–1940 had not yet reached the pre-collectivization level. The average weight of livestock delivered for slaughter was 210 to 225 kilogram for cattle and 70 to 80 kilograms for pigs. These figures were very low and demonstrated that, rather than the fattening which normally takes place before slaughter, malnutrition was common in farm animals.

In 1939 the Soviet Union annexed the western parts of the Ukraine and Byelorussia, which had been part of Poland since 1921. In 1940 the Baltic states, part of Finland, and Bessarabia were taken over. The new western regions were primarily agricultural, with successful private farming. Most statistical records now compare current levels with the level of 1940, when the agricultural production of the new territories was put into the general balance. These figures are also compared with the production within the same borders in 1909–1913. The publication of more or less standardized statistical records only began in 1956 and the figures for the 1920s and 1930s are only to be found in more specialized works. They often vary, depending on the sources that have been used. The reports prepared for Party Congresses and conferences were often based on "biological estimates" or other arbitrary measures. However, more reliable sources can be found to draw up the balance sheet of collectivization. Tables 5, 6, and 7 show the main indicators of agricultural development in the 1930s within the borders of the Soviet Union prior to September 1939, and require some comment. A variety of figures are published in the yearbooks on the national economy *(Narodnoye Khozyaistvo)* and in the annual reports published in the 1930s. Other figures can be found in the newspapers of the time, in the documents of the Party Congresses and Conferences which took place in the 1930s, and in books on collectivization and the history of Soviet agriculture. Confusion is often caused by the use of artificial "biological" harvest estimates, particularly in the statistics of the period after collectivization. This method of generating statistics was only abandoned in 1953, when Khrushchev ruled that the amount of grain and other crops which had actually

TABLE 5
Average Annual Production of Grain, Meat, Milk, and Potatoes, and the Population Growth, 1909–1939[a]

	Population (millions)	Grain	Meat	Milk	Potatoes
		(million metric tons)			
1909–1913 annual average		*65.2*	*3.9*	*24.1*	*22.4*
1909	130.1				
1913	139.3	76.5	4.1	24.8	23.3
1924–1928 annual average		*69.3*	*4.2*	*28.8*	*41.1*
1924	141.1				
1928	154.4	73.3	4.3	32.3	46.4
1936–1939 annual average		*74.9*	*3.6*	*24.1*	*46.7*
1936	163.8[b]				
1939	170.6				

[a] *Sources for production figures: Nar. khoz.*, 1965, p. 258; 1972, p. 284; 1974, p. 304.

[b] The reduced rate at which the population grew between 1928 and 1936 is due to population losses during the famine of 1932–1933. The population figures are based on *Nar. khoz.* and the Census figures for 1926, 1937, and January 1939.

been harvested should be used. Thus, after 1953 grain which has been lost due to adverse weather conditions or for other reasons is not included in the production statistics, whereas until then it was recorded as part of the actual harvest. It is also the case that the agricultural production figures published in 1937 and 1938 were inflated, in 1937 because of the twentieth anniversary of the Revolution, and in 1938 in anticipation of the Eighteenth Party Congress. There is also some confusion in the way meat production was reported. In some statistical records for the 1930s, meat production is given in slaughter (carcass)

TABLE 6
Annual Production per Head of Population[13]
(Kilograms)

	Grain	Meat	Milk	Potatoes
1913	549	29	178	160
1928	474	27	208	301
1939	439	21	141	274

weight. However, to improve the figures meat is often indicated as "meat, animal fat and subproducts." As a result of the shortage of meat, many of the "subproducts" (hooves, heads, etc.) were used directly as food, rather than in the food-processing industry. It was also the custom to record all dairy products as milk. Moreover, the production from the collective and state farms and that from the private plots are lumped together in the statistics. In fact, most of the livestock growth between 1933 and 1938 was in privately owned livestock and more than 90 percent of the

TABLE 7
Number of Horses and Livestock, 1916–1938
(Millions)

	Horses	Cattle	Pigs	Sheep & Goats
1916	34.2	51.7	17.3	88.7
1926	28.4	63.3	21.1	123.5
1928	33.5	70.5	26.0	146.7
1933	17.3	33.5	9.9	37.3
1938	16.2	50.9	25.7	66.6

Source: Nar. khoz., 1956, p. 128; 1965, p. 367.

potatoes were grown on private plots. The private sector also dominated in the production of meat and milk. It is only the grain in Table 6 and the horses in Table 7 which reflect the socialist sector of agriculture.

The progress in the production of technical crops, particularly cotton, is often mentioned to prove the advantages of socialist agriculture. In fact, technical crops are a far less significant index of progress than food crops. Moreover, the success of crops like cotton put serious pressure on the production of food crops. In the densely populated areas of Uzbekistan and other parts of Central Asia where cotton became the dominant crop, agriculture became so specialized that most of the grain needed for local consumption had to be imported from the state reserves. As the number of specialized farms producing technical crops grew, so the pressure on the procurement of food crops increased and not only towns, but many rural areas had to be supplied with food from other regions.

There was an obvious deterioration in the average diet between 1928 and 1939 and it was more serious in the villages than in the towns. In a study analyzing the development of *kolkhozy* in 1933–1937, M. A. Vyzlan claims to have used archive materials to compare rural food consumption before the Revolution, in 1923–1924 and in 1937.[14] According to his figures before the Revolution a group of "working peasants" consumed 217 kilograms of bread and bread products, 97 kilograms of potatoes, 86 kilograms of milk and milk products, and 11.7 kilograms of meat and fat per annum per person. However, Vyzlan gives no indication of which year, how long before the Revolution, or how representative the group is. He selects 1937, the record harvest year of the 1930s, for his post-collectivization data and 1923–1924 (1924 was the worst harvest year after the famine of 1921–1922) for his NEP data. Nonetheless, even these artificially selected figures show that there was no growth in consumption (see Table 8) It can be seen that although the consumption of potatoes increased slightly after collectivization, the consumption of milk, butter, and other dairy products was halved. If the author had presented the figures for 1928, the decline in consumption in the 1930s would have

TABLE 8

Consumption per Person per Annum[15]

(Kilograms)

	1923–1924 (peasants)	1937 (*kolkhozniki*)
Bread & bread products	253.1	249.1
Potatoes	172.4	198.7
Milk & milk-related products	242.2	126.8
Meat and fat	18.2	15.8

been even more apparent. In 1928 the annual consumption of meat and fat in the rural areas was 25 kilograms per person.[16] Moreover, the per capita consumption of meat and fat in urban areas in 1937 was far higher than the rural consumption—Moscow residents were consuming 36 kilograms of meat and lard per person in 1937 and almost the same level of bread, 238 kilograms, as in the villages.[17] However, there were acute shortages of vegetables in the towns. The collective farms could not grow vegetables and the private plots were too small to produce a substantial surplus. And even if the peasants produced a surplus on their private plots, they no longer owned the horses to transport it to the town markets.

The countryside remained in turmoil for several years after collectivization. The harvest of 1936 was poor and most regions failed to fulfill their procurement plans. More than half of all *kolkhozy* became indebted. However, their debts were cancelled in the early spring of 1937 as a gesture to celebrate the twentieth anniversary of the Revolution. Although the harvest of 1937 was recorded as a success, the success was due more to the manipulation of statistics than to the actual level of the harvest. Procurements were difficult in 1938 and 1939, but by 1939 rural problems were of secondary importance. The Second World War had begun and the Soviet Union had regained territory in the west which almost restored the borders of the Russian Empire. In 1940 the population included 20 million people living in Eastern Poland and the Baltic states. The harvest of 1940 was excellent, a record in the twenty years of Soviet power. That year, 95.6 million metric tons of grain were produced in the old and new territories and 38 million metric tons were collected by the state as marketable grain. For the first time after many years of failure the state had enough grain for all purposes. Grain exports tripled. Most of the exports went to Germany. Trains and ships loaded with grain were still en route to Germany in the early hours of June 22, 1941, when German armies attacked the Soviet Union.

Chapter 5

The New Crisis
in Agriculture

The war and postwar periods were times of perennial crisis in Soviet agriculture. The enormous losses of human life, livestock, and machinery were followed by hot debates about agricultural systems and agricultural science and utopian attempts to "transform nature" born out of desperation at the inability of conventional methods to bring about the required improvement. It is particularly difficult to condense the events which are the subject of this chapter, since they are still very fresh in my memory. They occurred at the beginning of my professional career—from 1944 I was first an observer, and then an active participant in the many discussions that were taking place at the heart of the agricultural establishment, in the oldest and best institution of higher agricultural education in the Soviet Union, the K. A. Timiryazev Agricultural Academy in Moscow (called the Petrovskaya Academy from 1865 to 1890). When I was discharged from a military hospital as a war invalid early in 1944 I found that the doors of all institutes and universities were open to me. As a veteran I did not even need to pass an entrance examination. I had already decided that I would become a biologist, but I was not sure which branch of the biological sciences to choose. In Moscow I was interviewed at the Medical Institute, at Moscow State University, and at the Timiryazev Agricultural Academy. It was the human factor—the very warm welcome and the unusual charm of the beautiful campus—that made me become a student of agriculture, a decision I never later regretted. During the years described in this chapter I was a student at the Timiryazev Academy, where I graduated with a B.Sc. degree in agronomy and then a Ph.D. in plant physiology.

The Academy was named after the plant physiologist, K. A. Timiryazev, who was one of the very few scientists to support Bolshevik policy in 1918–1921. It is the largest and best center of agricultural education and research in the Soviet Union, producing most of the agricultural textbooks. Nonetheless, relations between the Academy and the government have almost always been strained. The Academy's professors and scientists have frequently opposed government agricultural policy. Although they have the expertise to improve Soviet agriculture, they have rarely been consulted about major decisions: their task has been to execute and explain policy, not to formulate it or even advise on it. The Academy has been closed twice by the government: first in 1890–1891, because of the revolutionary activity of the students (it was reopened in 1895 as a smaller institute); and second in 1962, because the staff disagreed with Lysenko's ideas and methods. (It was reopened again in 1964.) I left the Academy in 1962 to work in medical research, but I never lost contact with it or with agricultural science. It was this link and my continued interest in and dismay about Soviet agriculture which finally made me write this book.

The years 1942–1947 were the most difficult years in Soviet agriculture. Never before in Russian history had the rural areas suffered so severely from a shortage of able-bodied men. Never had so many villages been destroyed, forcing peasants to live in dugouts. Never before had the land been ploughed not by tractor power nor by horsepower, but by women. Women not only replaced men, they also replaced draft animals in many western regions and in the Ukraine. With the exception of the brief period from 1923 to 1926, when peasants were left in peace to make their lives as they wished, life in the Russian countryside has never been easy. But it had never before been quite as difficult as in the years 1942–1947. Of the 20 million people who perished during the war, 15 million were peasants. Of the 10 million who were deported to work in Germany, 7 million were peasants. Less than half of the former *kolkhozniki* who were demobilized in 1945–1947 returned to the village. Those who had survived preferred to settle in the towns. The Soviet countryside has never recovered from these losses.

1. *Wartime Agriculture*

A large part of the harvest of 1941 was lost. By the end of August 1941 the German army had occupied Byelorussia, the Ukraine, the Baltic republics, and a considerable area of Western Russia. At the beginning of September the front reached Rostov-on-Don, the center of the Russian grain-producing area. During the summer of 1942 the North Caucasus and most of the middle and lower Volga basin were lost to the German army. More than 70 percent of the arable land, an area in which about half the total population of the Soviet Union had lived before the war, was under German occupation. Sixty million Soviet citizens remained in these areas—about 30 million had managed to move eastward.[1]

Although the country was ill-prepared for the war, the reaction to the emergency was much more effective than in 1915–1916, when a smaller area had been lost to the enemy. Attempts were made to save the livestock and about 4 million cattle and horses and 4 million other farm animals were evacuated to the eastern regions of the country. All food was rationed throughout the country from August 1941. The emergency food aid which began to reach the Soviet Union under the U.S. Lend-Lease program from the beginning of 1943 was particularly useful in providing high-quality products like meat, dried milk, and egg powder. The city that suffered most from food shortages was Leningrad. It was cut off from the rest of the country by the siege, and more than a million people died of starvation. In July and August 1941 plans for sowing winter crops in the eastern regions were increased significantly and it was decided to extend the acreage under winter wheat by 2 million hectares in Central Asia, Bashkiriya, the South Urals, and the Far East to provide extra grain in 1942. The spring sowing was also increased in these areas and in Trans-caucasia.

Industrial workers had begun working harder, and the eight-hour working day (introduced by the Provisional Government in April 1917) had been replaced by an eleven-hour day. The *kolkhozniki* were soon also expected to work more. On April 13, 1942, a combined Central Committee and *Sovnarkom* decree raised the compulsory minimum of *trudodni* (i.e., the number of workday units required to qualify for membership of a *kolkhoz* and the right to a private plot) from 80 to between 120 and 150 in the main grain-producing regions and in Central Asia. Failure to meet this target became a criminal offence and the "compulsory minimum" was extended to younger people who had previously not been under a legal obligation to work. The working age in rural areas was lowered from sixteen to twelve, and these children were expected to work a minimum of 50 *trudodni* per year. The employment of children in towns (mostly in the light and food industries) was also legalized. In 1940 the average output of *trudodni* per *kolkhoznik* had been 254; in 1942 it increased to 352.[2] Most of the increase was due to the work of women, since the men had been mobilized. Qualified industrial workers were, as a rule, not called up into the army. They were evacuated with their factories to the east, or they served in temporary emergency military units defending towns near the front. But in rural areas the mobilization spared no one. Male tractor drivers and all those involved in mechanization were drafted as military drivers and tank and artillery crews. Whereas only 9 percent of all tractor drivers had been women in 1940, the proportion of female tractor drivers and combine operators had risen to 55 percent by 1943 and 81 percent by 1944.[3] Seventy percent of the *trudodni* worked in 1943 were worked by women, the rest by men over fifty and by young boys. In 1941–1942 the conscription age was seventeen to forty years, but in 1943 it was raised to fifty years to compensate for the heavy losses. The highest birthrate in Russia had been recorded in 1925. There were about 50 births per 1,000 population, or about 7 million births, in 1925. The men of this cohort were drafted into the army in 1943. Nonetheless there were too few soldiers for the decisive battles of that year.

One of the causes of the increase in the number of *trudodni* in 1942 was the involuntary decrease in mechanization. The army requisitioned most of the cars and trucks in the villages. Motorcycles and private bicycles were also taken and a large number of tractors, particularly caterpillar tractors, were taken over for artillery units and transport. About 5 million horses were mobilized for army use. Moreover, the agricultural machine plants were converted to produce military hardware. The tractor plants in Kharkov and Stalingrad and the agricultural machinery plant in Rostov were evacuated and reconstructed for military production. As a result, the number of new tractors received by the MTS declined from 20,000 per annum in 1937–1940 to 400 in 1942 and 500 in 1943. The production of simpler agricultural equipment (ploughs, cultivators, mowing machines, etc.) dropped to 1 percent of the prewar level in 1942.[4] In any case, there was very little gasoline available for the *kolkhozy*, *sovkhozy*, and MTS, and local workshops began to make special attachments to make it possible to run tractor engines on liquified fuels made from coal or wood.

The *kolkhozy* were unable to produce enough food to feed the cities and the army. In an attempt to cope with the problem, the government made allotments of land available around the towns for people who wished to grow their own vegetables and potatoes. Each factory and plant was directly attached to a particular *sovkhoz* or a number of *kolkhozy* and workers and their families were expected to help with agricultural work in their leisure time. Mobilizing the urban population to help with harvesting in return for payment in kind (one-tenth of the harvest) became common. The *sovkhozy* and *kolkhozy* were considered to be auxiliaries of the plant to which they were attached and could supply the plant directly without going through the state procurement system.

Work canteens became vital for the diet of the workers. The canteens sold some products, above the official ration level, to the workers, and so did the newly established departments for direct links between industry and the farms. Ironically, although the volume of food produced in the country dropped well below the 1918–1921 level, the system of distribution worked much better. A blind eye was turned to the much larger private plots which the *kolkhozniki* cultivated unofficially for their own needs. Since the state was taking almost the whole collective farm harvest, the peasants had to live entirely from their private plots. Private sales of food were encouraged and special markets where goods were exchanged for food became a normal feature of every town. There was a reversion to the NEP system. Many of the operations were conducted by war invalids. As a rule they were unable to do any other job and so their activities were tolerated. But there was very little surplus to reach these markets.

The Soviet offensive in 1943 and 1944 made the food situation even worse. The retreating German armies operated a scorched-earth policy, burning villages and destroying agricultural equipment. Farm animals and other food supplies were confiscated to feed the German troops or to send back to Germany. Able-bodied men and women were deported to work in Germany. Many of the areas liberated by the Soviet army were starving and required emergency food aid. The few cattle left in the villages were used as draft animals, rather than for meat or milk. More often, however, the ploughing was done by the women—a team of several women could move a horse plough just enough to scrape the soil. In the villages that had been destroyed in the fighting or by the retreating German army, people lived in primitive dugouts. It not only took several years to rebuild the village houses, but it was two to three years before many of the fields were safe enough to cultivate. In the Kursk, Orel, Kharkov, Kaluga, and other areas, where the main battles had taken place or where the front had been, the antipersonnel and antitank mines that had been laid had first to be found and deactivated.

At the end of the war the Soviet government prepared for official lists of the losses in agriculture as a direct result of fighting or of German occupation for the Nuremberg Trials.[5] Seventy thousand villages had been totally or partially destroyed. Ninety-eight thousand *kolkhozy*, 1,876 *sovkhozy*, and 2,890 MTS lost their machinery and equipment (137,000 tractors, 49,000 combine-harvesters, 46,000 sowing machines, etc.). The losses included 7 million horses, 17 million cattle, 20 million pigs, 27 million sheep and goats, and 110 million chickens and other poultry. In the occupied territories practically the entire livestock had been destroyed.

Stalin's repressive policies added to this destruction. In 1942 the predominantly agricultural Volga-German Autonomous Region was abolished and more than a million inhabitants were deported to Siberia and Kazakhstan. In 1943 the Kalmyks and several other Moslem national groups of the North Caucasus were also uprooted and deported. In 1944 more than half a million Crimean Tartars were accused of "collaboration with the enemy," summarily arrested, and deported to Uzbekistan. The deportation of several million members of the national minorities from the rural areas was brutal (more than half a million died in the process), criminal, unnecessary, and costly. These nationalities were only rehabilitated in the 1960s, but many of them were not allowed to return to their native lands. The Crimean Tartars and Volga Germans were forced to remain in the areas to which they had been deported and they still live in Central Asia and Kazakhstan.

The harvest of 1945 was very poor, partly because of drought (see Table 9). Taking the size of the country and the total population into account, it was worse than the harvest of 1921 (when the population was 134 million), the year of the great famine. Malnutrition was widespread in the western rural areas. The war left crops heavily infected and the fields full of weeds. The movement of cattle across the country caused animal diseases to spread and even anthrax, previously restricted to some parts of the Urals and Central Asia, became common in the Ukraine and Moldavia. In the early 1920s the postwar recovery in agriculture had been swift and spontaneous because of NEP and the large population resources in the rural areas. It cost the state very little. In 1946–

TABLE 9

Grain and Potato Production, 1940–1945[a]

| | Grain | Potato | Men | Women |
	(million tons)		(millions)	
			Population	
1940	95.6	76.1	93.0	101.1
1942	29.4	NA	—	—
1944	49.0	55.0	NA	NA
1945	47.3	58.0	NA	NA
1950[b]	—	—	78.3	100.2

Sources: [6,7,8].

[a] The Soviet Union received a total of 4.7 million tons of food products from the United States through the Lend-Lease program in 1942–1945. Because it was such a small proportion of the total domestic output, many Soviet historians have denigrated its importance. In fact, the lend-lease deliveries were a vital part of the diet, particularly for the army. They were mostly in concentrated forms of high-quality food (meat, dried milk, dried egg powder, sugar). The total production of meat in the Soviet Union in 1943–1944 was only 1 to 2 million tons per year (2.2 million in 1945[9]). American canned meat and other products supplied much needed animal protein.

[b] Soviet population statistics do not give demographic figures for 1942–1949. The figures for 1950–1953 (*Nar. khoz.*, 1963, p. 8) show that the population growth during 1950–1953 was 3 million per year. Because the ratio of males to females amongst the newborn is almost equal, the total approximate growth during 1945–1949 was (for a slightly reduced birthrate) probably 10 to 12 million. This means that there were approximately 73 million men and 95 million women in 1945, at the end of the war, a net loss of 26 to 27 million. Twenty million were killed or died during the war. The remaining loss of 7 to 8 million was caused by increased natural mortality and reduced birthrate during the war, as well as by death from the famine in 1946.

1950 postwar recovery was very difficult and painful. The human and material losses had been too high. A drought in 1946 made another tragedy inevitable. Soviet Russia suffered its third terrible famine.

2. *The Famine of 1946–1947*

In March 1946 the Supreme Soviet approved a new Five Year Plan for "Post-War Reconstruction and the Development of Industry and Agriculture." By 1950 total agricultural production was to be 27 percent higher than in 1940. Grain production was to reach 127 million metric tons in 1950 and similar increases were planned for other crops and for livestock products. The targets were unrealistically high, since the country possessed neither the manpower nor the resources to reach them. The only way to increase production to the planned levels would be to increase the acreage of sowing extensively, but the *kolkhozy* and *sovkhozy* possessed neither the manpower, nor the horses, equipment, or level of mechanization necessary to undertake any meaningful increase in the area of cultivated land. On the contrary, it would have been more prudent to reduce the acreage and leave more land fallow.

It did not make any agronomic sense to sow more in 1946. The increased plans of spring sowing consumed extra seed grain at a time when there was not enough grain to eat in the villages. Moreover, the shortage of tractors and horses made it impossible to complete the sowing in the shortest possible period when the soil has sufficient moisture from the spring thaw. The sowing season was extended and late sowing made the fields more prone to drought. Because of the shortage of seed grain, the amount of seed sowed per hectare was reduced, leading to a decrease in the density of cultivated cereals and leaving more space for weeds. There are well-established scientific norms of density for different crops. If the density is too high, the fields become overpopulated and plants compete for the limited resources of moisture and nutritional elements in the soil, becoming weaker. If the density is too low, individual plants grow better, but so do weeds. The density of seed grain per hectare should only be reduced after a year when the fields have been left fallow and cleared of weeds. Fallow fields accumulate nitrogen as ammonium through bacterial fixation of atmospheric nitrogen and make the other important minerals, phosphorus and potassium, more available through microbial processes in the soil. Where there are no herbicides (as in the Soviet Union in the 1940s), the only way to reduce contamination by weeds is to leave fields fallow. This is the best and cheapest way to restore soil fertility in the absence of organic or mineral fertilizers to compensate for the loss of nutritional elements through previous harvests. It was the only viable alternative after four years of war, but the planned targets made it an impossible option. Agriculture certainly entails risk, but it is not a game of chance. There are well-known and well-tested methods to reduce the occurrence of disasters.

The government pressure for the maximum increase in the acreage of sown land in 1946 was an incompetent and risky decision. Even a minor drought could cause serious damage. In fact the drought of 1946 was severe and widespread, affecting the southern and central regions of the country. The harvest was poor and the shortage of harvesting machinery meant that sickles had to be used. As a result the harvesting could not be carried out quickly enough to prevent grain losses from shedding and other causes. By July the scale of the disaster was already obvious. In spite of this, Stalin decided to increase grain exports to France, where there were acute grain shortages, making France heavily dependent on American aid. Stalin hoped to influence the outcome of the elections to the first postwar French parliament. The total Soviet grain harvest in 1946 was only 39.6 million metric tons, the lowest in a century. The grain harvest of 1921 had been 36.2 million tons, but the Soviet Union did not then include the western regions which had been recognized as an integral part of it at the Yalta and Potsdam conferences of 1945. In the 1890–1891 famine the harvest had been better than in 1946. In 1946 the urban population was 65 million and there were 8 to 9 million men in the half-demobilized army.

Strong government pressure and a new system of deliveries made it possible to procure 17.5 million tons of grain, just enough to prevent starvation in the towns. But 65 percent of the population living in the villages was left with 55 percent of the harvest with which to feed people and livestock, and to use as seed grain. The minimal amount of seed grain required for the autumn and spring sowing of the approximately 100 million hectares under grain crops was 15 million tons (the optimal amount would have been 20 million tons). Rural famine was inevitable under these conditions. In many regions which had been affected by the drought the entire harvest had been delivered to the state, including seed grain. The only food left was potatoes, but even the potato harvest was poor (55.6 million tons, less than in 1945).

By 1946 the Soviet Union was already isolated from the West. The "Iron Curtain" separated East from West and very little news filtered through to the West about the Soviet famine. There was hardly any mention of it in the Soviet Union either. When a description of the famine in the Ukraine (where it was most serious) was published in Khrushchev's memoirs in 1971 in the United States, it was considered a sensation.[10] Khrushchev made it clear how the famine developed and who was responsible. In 1046 he had been first secretary of the Ukrainian Communist Party and chairman of the Council of the People's Commissars of the Ukraine (renamed the Council of Ministers in 1946). He had not had much experience with agriculture before 1946. It was the famine in the Ukraine in 1946 which gave him his lifelong obsession to improve Soviet agriculture. His memoirs vividly describe the scale of the disaster.

We were supposed to supply the State first and ourselves second. We had been assigned an output plan of something like 400 million pood [7.2 million tons] for the year 1946. This quota was established arbitrarily, although it was dressed up in the press with supporting scientific data. It had been calculated not on the basis of how much we really could produce, but on the basis of how much the State thought it could beat out of us. The quota system was really a system of extortion. I saw that the year was threatened with catastrophe. It was difficult to predict how it would end. I was getting letters from collective farm workers and from their chairmen. These were heart-breaking letters. A typical one comes to mind. It was from the chairman of a collective farm, who wrote, "Well, Comrade Khrushchev, we have delivered our quota to the State. But we've given everything away. Nothing is left for us. We are sure the State and the Party won't forget us and that they will come to our aid." He must have thought their fate depended on me. I was Chairman of the Council of People's Commissars of the Ukraine and First Secretary of the Ukrainian Central Committee. He imagined that since I was head of the Ukrainian state, I could help him. Well, he was deceiving himself. There was nothing I could do once the grain had been turned over to the State receiving points. It was no longer in my power to dispose of it. I myself had to make a special request from the State for grain to feed our own people. . . .

However, I had no choice but to confront Stalin with the facts: famine was imminent, and something had to be done. I gave orders for a document to be prepared for the Council of Ministers of the USSR in which I asked that the State issue us ration cards so that we could supply the farm population with a certain quantity of products and organize the feeding of the hungry. I was doubtful of success . . .

In reply Stalin sent me the rudest, most insulting telegram. I was a dubious character, he said; I was writing memoranda to prove that the Ukraine was unable to take care of itself, and I was requesting an outrageous quantity of cards for feeding people. I can't express how murderously this telegram depressed me. I saw clearly the whole tragedy, which was hanging not only over me personally, but over the whole Ukrainian people. Famine was now inevitable; Stalin's response dashed our last hopes that it could be avoided . . . Soon I was receiving letters and official reports about deaths from starvation. Then cannibalism started. I received a report that a human head and the soles of feet had been found under a little bridge near Vasilkovov, a town outside Kiev. Apparently a corpse had been eaten . . .[11]

The Ukraine and the *chernozem* steppe regions of south Russia (Voronezh, Saratov, Stalingrad, Rostov-on-Don regions) were most seriously affected by the drought and the famine. There are no large forests in these areas and they are open to the dry winds from the Central Asian deserts. Although the drought extended into central Russia and Byelorussia, the people in these areas relied more on potatoes than on grain, and the large forests which cover more than 50 percent of the territory of Byelorussia and northwest Russia gave protection from the dry winds and provided natural food, as they had always done in years of hardship. In the remote villages of these regions peasant families collect large quantities of berries, edible mushrooms, and nuts. Starving cattle can be fed on "twig fodder" collected from the trees and bushes and pigs can be fed on acorns. The Russian and Byelorussian peasants are probably one of the few remaining groups in the world for whom natural forest food (mushrooms and berries) remains an important source of proteins and vitamins.

The winter of 1946–1947 was excruciatingly difficult for the rural population of the Ukraine, Byelorussia, and the western part of Russia. About half of the peasants were still living in roofed-over dugouts. As soon as spring arrived they began to dig up the few potatoes that had been left in the ground when the early winter frosts had set in. Frozen potatoes are usually used for pig fodder, but now they were welcome for human consumption. Hunting and fishing provided a little food and people collected normally inedible leaves and grass. The food cooked from these frozen and half-rotten potatoes and field grasses and leaves was hardly attractive, but it provided some sustenance for the people and their livestock. The dishes were given ironic, untranslatable names, for example, *pishchiki*, from *pishcha*, the Russian word for "food," and *toshnotiki*, from *toshnota*, from the Russian word for "nausea."

Russian peasants had never lived well, but they had the advantage of living in symbiosis with the greatest forest mass on earth, stretching from the Baltic Sea to the Pacific coast. In years of calamity the forest provided timber to build houses (as well as firewood to heat them and materials to seal them); it also provided food, and protection from the dry winds of the steppes and deserts. These benefits made scientists dream of extending the protective forests into the steppes of the south. After the drought of 1890 the conviction was born that if each field of the Ukraine, North Caucasus, and Volga steppes could be encircled by forest, drought would become impossible, the climate would become milder, and life would be easier. At the end of the nineteenth century some enthusiasts began trying to create man-made forests in the steppes, often on the estates of *pomeshchiki*. An extensive program was begun at the Nikitsky Botanical Garden in the Crimea to test varieties of trees from other parts of the world to find those most suitable for the various climates in Russia. These man-made forests were neglected in the 1920s and the 1930s and many of them were destroyed then or during the war. But neither the experience nor the dream were destroyed. The drought and famine of 1946 revived the idea that the afforestation of the steppes would be a universal cure for agriculture. It was discussed at a special agricultural Plenum of the Central Committee in February 1947 and finally developed into "Stalin's Great Program for the Transformation of Nature" in 1948.

3. The Disproportion between Industrial and Agricultural Development

The food procurement problems in the late 1920s and the 1930s were connected to rapid industrial growth which was not accompanied by a concomitant growth in agricultural production. Stalin's methods of resolving the problems were ruthless and incompetent. Other solutions might have been more successful, but they were never attempted. Before the war there had been large, underused labor reserves in the rural areas. Better ways to encourage these able-bodied people to increase their productivity might have been found. With time, experience, and greater flexibility, the *kolkhoz* system might have been reformed and become economically viable, particularly if the system of payment had been changed. After the war, however, the situation was quite different. The labor surplus had disappeared. There were millions of children, widows, single women, old people, and war invalids in the villages, but relatively few men of working age. In 1940 there had been 17 million able-bodied male members of the collective farms. At the beginning of 1946 the number had fallen to 6.5 million.[12] At the same time the Five Year Plan adopted in 1946 contained very high industrial targets: industry was to regain the prewar level of production and then double it. This pace of industrial development required a large increase in the number of industrial workers, an acceleration in the growth of the urban population, and an increase in food production well above the prewar level. The famine of 1946–1947 proved that the task was unrealistic and that the plan had to be amended. A special Central Committee Plenum was held to discuss the problem in February 1947.

A. A. Andreyev, the Politburo member responsible for agriculture, delivered the main report at the Plenum. This was the first Plenum on agricultural problems since the early 1930s, and its decisions were treated more seriously than the decisions of the Supreme Soviet on the Five Year Plan. The discussions were relatively open, since the problems could be blamed on the war and German occupation, rather than on Party policy. Some sensible decisions were taken: for example, state investments in agriculture were to be increased beyond the level provided by the Five Year Plan. Moreover, it was decided to give priority to restoring and reconstructing agricultural industry. As a result, the production of tractors, combine-harvesters, and other agricultural machinery reached the prewar level in 1949. Greater importance was accorded to the chemical industry and the production of chemical fertilizers. The human problems were much more difficult to resolve, however. Population losses could not be restored as quickly as losses of equipment and livestock. The Plenum attempted to tackle this problem and reached some decisions, which remained unpublished.

It was decided that most of the repatriated prisoners of war and deportees, many of whom were still in transition camps, should be sent to the *kolkhozy*, whether or not they came originally from rural areas. The Western literature on the repatriation of millions of Soviet prisoners of war and displaced persons usually focuses on documents about the forcible repatriation conducted by the British and American armies in Europe.[13] It is taken for granted that practically all these several million people spent the rest of their lives in concentration camps. It is true that those who were suspected of active collaboration with the Germans remained in prison camps. However, by 1946 significant numbers of repatriated ordinary soldiers (not officers) and deportees (both workers and peasants) were already being sent to *kolkhozy* rather than to prison camps. After the February Plenum many more were sent to work on the collective farms. They were rarely sent to their native villages and they lived under special restrictions, unable to leave the village to which they were attached. Many *kolkhozy* in the western parts of the country became places of forced exile. According to recently published Soviet sources, the number of working men on the *kolkhozy* was increased in this way by 25 percent in 1946 and by 17.6 percent in 1947.[14] Half of all the men and women repatriated from Germany and other parts of Europe were sent to work in agriculture. According to the state archives quoted by this source, some groups of repatriants were organized into special new collective farms— this must refer to collective farms in Siberia and North Kazakhstan and special regime *gulag* farms. In 1946, 1947, and 1948 the local Ukrainian press published many articles about the political education of the repatriants. This suggests that there was some discontent amongst these people who had seen a different, more prosperous agriculture in Germany and other parts of Europe.

The thirtieth anniversary of the October Revolution was celebrated in 1947. It was widely expected that rationing would be abolished if the harvest was normal. Although the weather was good in 1947, the villages were still too weak to perform normally. The harvest was not as low as in 1945 or 1946, but it was still well below target. The total grain harvest was only 65 million tons, 30 million tons less than in 1940. The number of farm animals was also still well below the prewar level. The number of milk cows had been restored (22.8 million in 1940, 23 million in 1947), but the number of goats and sheep had not reached the prewar level and the number of pigs (8.7 million) was less than half the 1940 level. More than 70 percent of the milk cows and pigs were privately owned by the *kolkhozniki*, *sovkhoz* workers, and the individual farmers of the Western Ukraine, Byelorussia, and the Baltic republics. Despite the shortages of agricultural products, the ration card system was cancelled in November 1947. It was essential to reduce consumption at the same time, and this was accomplished by introducing a new pricing system and reducing the amount of money in circulation.

Thus simultaneously with the abolition of rationing, retail food prices rose sharply and money was devalued.

These measures hit farmers particularly hard. Lower-paid urban workers were given special "bread bonuses" to compensate for the increase in food prices. For farmers the new pricing system meant a reduction in the prices they could charge on the free markets in the towns. These prices had been very high as long as there was rationing. They also lost almost all their savings. Banknotes were declared invalid if they had not been exchanged for new ones (at a ratio of 10 to 1) within ten days. The pretext for the drastic devaluation was that large amounts of counterfeit rubles, which had been printed in Germany and used in the occupied territories during the war, were still in circulation. The savings of the urban population were far less affected: money kept in savings banks was exchanged into new rubles at the rate of 3 old rubles to 1 new ruble. But there were no savings banks in the villages.

Given the chronic shortages of food it was difficult to supply all the towns and cities equally without a system of rationing. The government therefore introduced a special system, without ever making it public—some cities were to be more privileged than others. Urban consumers were divided into three main categories: Moscow and Leningrad were in the first category, and the food shops there were well supplied with all types of food. The other republican capitals and the cities that had earned the title "hero city" during the war were put into a second category. Other towns and cities fell into a third, less-privileged group. They were supplied with bread, potatoes, and some cereals; but meat, milk, and other high-quality products rarely reached them. This system of differentiated privilege has been retained to the present day. It creates many economic problems and a great deal of waste. Several million people commute daily to the big cities and capitals to buy better-quality food.

The financial reform not only affected the peasants individually; it was a blow for the *kolkhozy* as well. It was introduced in November, after the state procurements had been made. Procurement prices had been very low, but the modest income earned from sales to the state was suddenly reduced by two-thirds if the money had been put into savings banks, and more drastically if it had been kept in cash. The accounts of state organizations (factories, state farms, institutes, etc.) were not affected by the reforms. Workers continued to receive the same salaries in new banknotes. The aim of the reform was to reduce private savings and the amount of money in circulation, to stop the inflation caused by the war, and to limit consumption. The *kolkhozy* were cooperatives, not state organizations, and their finances were therefore more vulnerable.

Despite the price rise of 200 to 400 percent, the urban demand for food rose once rationing was abandoned. It was, in any case, inevitable that demands would grow, because of the postwar increase in urban population. Between 1945 and 1948 the number of urban consumers increased by 3 million per annum and this growth was expected to continue. Sixty-seven million people lived in towns and cities in 1947, several million more than in 1940. The rural population had been reduced by 25 million, and it did not have better means of production to increase the output of marketable food. Moreover, more than half of the people who lived in the countryside after the war were consumers rather than producers. The only method Stalin knew to increase the amount of food produced for the urban population was coercion.

The system of quotas for procurements that had been introduced during the war was cancelled at the Central Committee Plenum in February 1947. The new system was not much better. The quota system had not been entirely arbitrary. It was based on the acreage under cultivation and was intended to prevent the danger that fields would be left unused because of shortages of labor. The acreage system forced the *kolkhozy* to sow as much land as they could. If there were insufficient able-bodied *kolkhozniki* to bring in the harvest (harvesting is harder than sowing), the government and regional Party committees mobilized the urban population, including students and schoolchildren, to help. But after the rural famine of 1946 the quota system (which was partly responsible for the famine) could not be used. It was decided to return to the prewar system of assessing the "biological harvest" and making the procurement targets a proportion of this assessment. In 1937–1940, 30 to 35 percent of the "biological harvest" had been paid out in state procurements and payments in kind to the MTS. The new system was more flexible. The proportion for state deliveries was not specified in advance. Deliveries were linked progressively to the level of the harvest. The Ministry of Agriculture (the People's Commissariats had been renamed Ministries in 1946) established a network of "harvest inspectors." Tens of thousands of agronomists and students of agriculture were recruited every summer to do this wasteful work. They travelled from *kolkhoz* to *kolkhoz* in the late summer to assess the expected harvest from each individual field. Their assessments were usually arbitrary and inflated, but nonetheless they formed the basis for calculating the state quotas. State statistics once again began to be based on the theoretically possible harvest rather than the real one.

Disciplinary pressure was also increased. The wartime higher compulsory minimum of *trudodni* was extended indefinitely. At the same time the newly established Council of *Kolkhozy* chaired by Andreyev reconsidered and increased the work load of each *trudoden*. As a result, after 1947 the same compulsory minimum of 150 *trudodni* per annum required far more work than previously. Inability to meet the minimum was considered a crime, punishable by forced labor for 25 percent less pay in the same *kolkhoz* or elsewhere. Repeated failures to meet the minimum could lead to confiscation of private plots. Heavy penalties were introduced for stealing *kolkhoz* property—taking a few potatoes or a few pounds of grain or hay from the collective farm fields (a frequent occurrence in hungry villages) could mean that *kolkhoz-niki* were deprived of their freedom for up to ten years. Thousands of peasants sentenced under this draconian legislation began to arrive in the *gulag* system in 1947. According to official Soviet sources, about 20 percent of all *kolkhozniki* failed to meet the compulsory minimum in 1947–1948.[15] The culprits were usually women with children (the compulsory minimum was the same for women as for men). The laws pertaining to rural work did not recognize the needs of housewives—all women of working age had to work for the state or the *kolkhoz*.

While the urban population was growing, the rural population continued to decline, and the number of *kolkhozniki* declined particularly rapidly. Only 42 percent of the total rural population fell into the category of those able to work. The other 58 percent were children, old people, and invalids. The increase of the work load of each *trudoden* reduced the payments in kind. According to official statistics, the average payment in kind in 1947–1950 provided only 100 kilograms of grain (including both food and feed grain) per person per year.[16] This was less than the urban bread ration during the war. In 1947–1948 the state procured about 50 percent of the total harvest, a much higher proportion than before the war. Nonetheless, it was still insufficient to support the growing industry. Almost all the *kolkhozy* accumulated debts in 1948. They had no funds to buy new equipment, build animal farms, or pay cash for *trudodni*. Stalin tried administrative measures first and then introduced his long-term program to transform nature.

The first administrative measures involved moving peoples. Many villages in Byelorussia and the Smolensk area of the RSFSR had been entirely destroyed during the war. Government aid was needed to rebuild houses and restore livestock and equipment. At the same time there were empty villages and unused, fertile fields in extensive areas of the Crimea, the Volga German region, and parts of the North Caucasus. The population of these areas had been deported during the war. The decision was made to repopulate these villages with Byelorussian and Russian peasants from the poor western regions. In the summer of 1948 I was doing practical work in the Crimea when thousands of Byelorussian families arrived and settled into the typical Moslem villages of the area. When the natives of these areas were rehabilitated about two decades later it was practically impossible to return them to their homelands.

The second administrative measure undertaken was the forced collectivization of the individual farmers in the newly acquired territories of Bessarabia, Western Ukraine, and Byelorussia, Lithuania, Latvia, and Estonia. In 1945–1947 people in the Western Ukraine and the Baltic states resisted Sovietization with all their might. Thousands of nationalists fled to well-protected bases in the forests and mountains and launched partisan warfare against the Soviet Army. It took more than two years to defeat them and there was considerable loss of life on both sides. When the "pacification" had been completed (several hundred thousand nationalists and suspected sympathizers were sent to Siberia and the Far East), collectivization was begun. In 1948 the Central Committee passed a resolution to accelerate the collectivization of the western regions and the process was completed within a year. It was even more painful than it had been in Russia in the early 1930s. For one thing, the communal system had long disappeared and the peasants in the western regions owned their land individually. Although the settlements in Western Byelorussia and Western Ukraine remained much as they had been before the partition in 1921, in the Baltic states most peasants lived on individual scattered farms, a pattern which made the introduction of collective farms very difficult. Thirty-two thousand new *kolkhozy* were created in the west. Eastern Prussia (now called the Kaliningrad region) was repopulated and the native German population was deported to East and West Germany.

Although the weather was good in 1948, the harvest was very poor. The total grain production was only 67.2 million tons, still well below the 1940 level and even below the average level of 1909–1913. The production of meat was only 3.1 million tons, far less than the 4.7 million tons produced in 1940 and the 5 million tons in 1913. The potato harvest reached a record level of 95 million tons, but this in itself was an expression of peasant resistance—the state had no proper system for collecting potatoes. Moreover, the potato harvest is the last in the agricultural season to be collected. By the time it is brought in (in late October), only two or three weeks remain before the winter frosts. Unlike grain, potatoes cannot be taken from the villages during the winter, since frost kills the tubers. Less than 10 percent of the potato harvest normally reaches the towns through the state procurement system (7.2 million tons in 1948); the rest remains in the villages. After the famine of 1946, the farmers finally realized that they would have to abandon their reliance on bread. Potatoes became the most important staple food and could be used instead of feed grain for the livestock, particularly for pigs.

The state procurement (including payments in kind to the MTS) of grain in 1948 was 30.2 million tons, a very high proportion of the harvest. Since at least 20 million tons was required for reserves and for seed grain, the rural population and the livestock were left with starvation levels—17 million tons for both human and animal consumption, for a rural population of more than 100 million people. A new rural famine was avoided only because of the potato harvest. But potatoes, unlike grain, can only be preserved for a few months before damage and loss of quality occurs. Potatoes are also prone to disease, and in later years the potato fields suffered severely from Colorado beetle, unknown in Russia before the war.

The poor agricultural results of 1948 contrasted sharply with the successes of industry. Industrial output was significantly higher than before the war. Cities and towns were growing, and the demand for food was higher than ever. But no solution to this disproportion was in sight. The peasants were becoming poorer and poorer. It was in this situation that Stalin suddenly, without any preliminary scientific discussion, presented the country with his major project for the "transformation of nature."

4. *The Search for Miracles:*
The Plan for an Ecological Revolution

On October 20, 1948, the Central Committee of the CPSU and the Council of Ministers of the USSR adopted a joint decree, which introduced a monumental new program of agricultural development. The long title of the program and the accompanying decree speaks for itself: "The plan for shelter belt afforestation, the introduction of crop rotation and the building of ponds and reservoirs in order to ensure large and stable harvests in the steppe and forest steppe areas of the European part of the USSR."

It was the largest and most expensive agricultural program undertaken during Stalin's rule. Collectivization had become known as Stalin's "Revolution from Above"; the new plan was immediately labelled an ecological revolution, Stalin's "Plan for the Transformation of Nature." It was prepared in considerable haste, without being released for preliminary scientific and practical discussion, and it came as a surprise to farmers, local experts, and agricultural scientists alike. Although the team which prepared it has remained secret, it clearly included some agricultural and forestry experts as well as economists. Although Lysenko's influence in Soviet biology and agricultural science had just reached its peak, he was only partially involved, and he could not have been the main architect, since his theories are not reflected in the plan. It was a mixture of the ideas and practical recommendations of a number of scientists who had been forgotten by 1948: Vasilii V. Dokuchayev (1846–1903), who had made the first classification and map of Russian soils and had written the classical work *Russian Chernozem* (1883); Pavel A. Kostychev (1845–1895), a prominent soil scientist and the author of the theory that soil fertility was a biological process connected with the activity of soil microorganisms, and who had written the first textbook on soil science, *Pochvovedeniye* (1886); and Vasilii R. Williams (1863–1939), a professor at the Timiryazev Agricultural Academy, a soil scientist whose textbooks on the controversial theory of the unified dialectical development of the soil were still used in Soviet agricultural colleges in the 1940s and 1950s. Williams's theories of grassland agriculture were reflected in the agronomic part of Stalin's program, while Dokuchayev's and Kostychev's ideas were incorporated into the plan for the afforestation of the steppe areas to protect them against drought and the dry winds from the Central Asian deserts. The construction of pools and reservoirs was also a mixture of ideas, designed partly to improve irrigation and partly to create new fish-breeding facilities. By 1948 it was already known that the destruction and neglect of thousands of water mills and small dams during the Civil War and after the end of NEP had adversely affected water supplies, agriculture, fish reserves, and the climate. In some parts of Europe windmills were used to make flour from grain, but in Russia milling had been entirely dependent on water mills and small reservoirs dammed to create water pressure. The larger mills which replaced them were usually industrial and located in towns, and the water regime of the country had suffered as a consequence.

Although Lysenko and his supporters did not receive much credit for creating the new program, they were quick to join the bandwagon, offering methods of afforestation (dense planting) and crop rotation (increasing spring crops at the expense of winter crops) which proved to be expensive mistakes. I have discussed the scientific aspects of the Lysenko Affair in detail elsewhere,[17] but it is appropriate here to examine briefly some of the economic and agronomic aspects of the plan and why it failed. There was no opposition to the plan in 1948: it was greeted enthusiastically by Soviet scientists. It was revolutionary, and in purely scientific terms, it seemed to be rational. But from the practical and economic points of view, it was unrealistic. In 1948–1949 a project of such magnitude was beyond the capacity of the country as a whole, and, more particularly, of the peasantry, which would have to shoulder the main burden of labor.

The main problem of Russian agriculture has always been climate. The western and northern parts of the country have a good rainfall, but the soil there is the poor, acidic soil which normally develops under forest conditions. Moreover, the temperature balance is unfavorable for agriculture. There is a very short vegetation period: sowing can only be done in May (in April the fields are often still covered in snow) and the harvest must be completed in September, before the early winter, which sometimes begins in October. The best agricultural land is in the south, where there are great plains of rich black *chernozem*, but these plains are dry and prone to drought. Because of the shortage of rain (the average rainfall is 400 millimeters), the area is open steppe land, without any forests. It was certainly possible to plant forests in this area—there were some good forests along the rivers in the foothills and hills of the Caucasus and Crimean mountains and some man-made forests had been planted. There had been centuries of experience of growing trees on the estates of the *pomeshchiki* in the south, and in parks and along the main roads, where they had been planted from the time of Catherine the Great on, to protect the roads from snowstorms and winds. It was clear from this experience that many varieties of trees would grow if they were carefully tended for the first few years, until the root systems had reached the deep water table.

The afforestation of the steppes was an old idea, and Doku-chayev had carried out some experiments in the nineteenth cen-tury. It had been proved that forest belts protected fields from the dry winds and that fields which were encapsulated into forest belts were better able to retain moisture. It was also clear that planting trees and bushes in ravines would prevent further soil erosion and that earth dams and reservoirs preserved spring waters. Thus the individual measures were all sound and might have been successful if they had been introduced gradually, taking local conditions into account, rather than being directed from Moscow as a large, important campaign. Preliminary tests were required in each region and each climatic zone to select the most appropriate tree species, to measure the distance from the surface to the level of the water table, and so on. The afforestation of the steppes was a task that required several decades, rather than a crash national program carried out in haste.

However, the decree of October 20, 1948, envisaged a rapid program and it was extremely specific, stipulating the details of all the work involved. Some Party leaders went so far as to declare that the program was the plan for the transition from a socialist to a real communist society.[18] The program was divided into two parts, one relating to agronomy, the other to ecology. The agro-nomic section was concerned with the creation of forest belts around *kolkhoz* and *sovkhoz* fields, with local erosion protection measures (the afforestation of ravines and the building of small local dams and pools), and the introduction of stable crop rotation. Many additional agro-technical measures were recommended, including the use of organic and chemical fertilizers, irrigation, and land reclamation. Recognizing the acute shortage of man-power in the villages, the government promised to provide the necessary financial assistance for mechanization and the employment of experts to advise and supervise the work. It was also expected that the program would stimulate the enthusiasm of the peasants, who would be happy to work even harder to create a bright future for their children.

The state was entirely responsible for the second, ecological part of the program, since the plans were too grandiose for local resources. In the period from 1950 to 1965 eight wide and complex forest belts would be created to run from the middle of the mixed forest-steppe zone (about 300 kilometers south of Moscow) in the direction of the Caspian and Black Seas down the whole country. Some of these belts were expected to be about 1,000 kilometers long and to cross sixteen regions in the south. The total acreage under forest was planned to be 1.5 million hectares, and the belts would have a combined length of 5,320 kilometers. The work was to be carried out by the Ministry of Forestry of the USSR.

The afforestation of individual fields in the Ukraine, the Don and Volga basins, the North Caucasus, South Urals, and Crimea was also planned in great detail. The total acreage of these field-protecting forests was planned to be 4.2 million hectares. A special State Committee was established to supervise the work and provide technical, financial, and expert assistance. Various organizational problems were sorted out in the winter of 1948–1949 and the planting was begun in the autumn of 1949. Many regional officials declared their intention to overfulfill the plan. The first year of the program was not, however, easy. There was a shortage of manpower and the level of mechanization was still poor. Hundreds of thousands of town dwellers, including students and schoolchildren, were mobilized to help with the tree-planting. By the end of 1949 trees had been planted on 0.5 million hectares, rather more than expected by that stage in the plan. The construction of local dams and reservoirs was started briskly, often using German prisoner-of-war labor which had previously been used for urban reconstruction.

Studies of the routes of the eight main state forest belts was also begun in 1949 and land was allocated. Planting was to begin in 1950. But the enthusiasm that had led to overfulfillment of the plan in 1949 did not last into 1950, and the afforestation works of 1950 and 1951 were behind schedule. It was too difficult to use peasant labor for three years running, particularly when they were required to work outside the area of their own *kolkhozy*. The trees which had already been planted required careful tending and the kind of care which could not be provided by people who had been mobilized temporarily. Moreover, there was a shortage of water and the oak and pine trees that had been selected for their drought resistance and longevity were not easy to cultivate. The loss of planted trees was very high—27 percent on the *kolkhozy* and 11 percent on the *sovkhozy* in the first year after planting.[19] By 1951 about 50 percent, on average, of the trees planted in 1949 had died and the rate of planting declined.

After Stalin's death in 1953 most of the work connected with the program was halted and the State Committee was abolished. The great state forest belts were left incomplete and most of the trees that had already been planted died. The local forest belts fared better. They were more carefully tended and they played a limited positive role in future years. In all, about 0.5 million hectares of forest survived (10 percent of the plan) and there are about 25 million hectares of fields which are now considered protected by forest encapsulation. Experts who continue to study the affects of afforestation on agriculture agree that the possible influence on the climate was wildly overestimated, although forests do protect fields against erosion, particularly during the spring winds. The densely planted forest belts recommended by Lysenko proved to be ineffective, since the wind merely blows over them. Loosely planted trees (recommended by the forestry experts, but not endorsed officially) offer more protection. In 1969, when powerful eastern spring winds destroyed many fields in the North Caucasus, the fields that had been encapsulated into loose forest belts suffered far less.

In general, the ideas behind the afforestation program were quite sound, but the program was premature in 1948 and the results were modest, despite the very high investments. Inevitably, this caused great disappointment and contributed to the cancellation of the project in 1953. It would have made more sense to continue with a longer-term, smaller-scale project. What is certain is that the transformation of nature did not occur. Droughts and soil erosion remain the most serious agricultural problems in the grain-producing regions of the Soviet Union.

5. Stalin's Final Offensive against the Peasants

The harvest of 1949 was, once again, well below the 1913 and 1940 level. In 1949, 70.2 million tons of grain and 3.8 million tons of meat were produced (see Table 10), too little for the constantly growing urban population. State procurements continued to take extra food, which was badly needed for local consumption, from the villages. Stalin celebrated his seventieth birthday that year, and the press was forbidden to publish any bad news about the economy. The news blackout about the situation in the villages was almost total as newspapers, publishers, and film directors prepared reports, books, and films about the good, prosperous lives of workers and *kolkhoz* peasants. A new wave of terror in 1949 frightened people in the Party and state apparatus and removed from leadership (and often from life itself) some very able administrators and economists who had risen to prominence during the war. One of the victims was Nikolai A. Voznesensky, a member of the Politburo and the first deputy of the wartime Council of Defence, who had so successfully organized the rapid conversion to a war-oriented economy. After the war he served as chairman of Gosplan and first deputy prime minister. Because of his ability and experience he was considered Stalin's most likely successor, and this was the main cause of his disappearance (he was "tried" and executed in secret).

The plan of the afforestation of the steppes was a long-term project, designed as a monument to the future, rather than as a measure to solve urgent current problems. Other administrative and economic measures were introduced in 1948–1950 to raise the performance of agriculture more quickly. Some soon proved to be a failure and were abandoned. Others, like the amalgamation of small collective farms into larger ones, were irreversible. But none of the measures had any real impact on agricultural productivity.

In an effort to improve the administrative system, Stalin, who had retained his wartime position as chairman of the Council of Ministers of the USSR (a more convenient post for a dictator than merely being secretary of the Party), suddenly decided to create a number of specialized agricultural ministries. The Ministry of Agriculture was accordingly replaced by four new ministries: a ministry for general food crops, a ministry for technical crops, a ministry for livestock production, and a ministry to deal with the *sovkhozy*. This fragmentation resulted in the creation of several independent networks at the local level, which replaced the previous district departments of agriculture. Local experts who had been engaged in practical work moved into the new offices to fill the vacancies in the bureaucratic system and collective farms began to receive conflicting instructions. Within two years it was clear that the new structure was counterproductive, and the new ministries were amalgamated into a general Ministry of Agriculture. The Ministry for *Sovkhozy*, however, survived for many years.

In 1948 Stalin also decided to build an All-Union Exhibition of Achievements in Agriculture. The idea was to exhibit the experience of the best and most successful *kolkhozy* and *sovkhozy* in various branches of agriculture and from various republics. *Kolkhozniki* and directors of *kolkhozy* from all over the country would visit the exhibition and learn from it how to improve their own work. It was expected that at least 100,000 peasants per month would become educated by visiting the exhibition. Three hundred hectares of land was allocated in Ostankino, a Moscow suburb. The project included hotels and hostels and about thirty large pavilions. Some would be built by various ministries and would illustrate general agriculture, mechanization, agrochemistry, farm animals, field-protecting forestry, irrigation, technical crops, and so on. Individual Soviet republics would build other pavilions in their own national style. When construction was already under way, several new pavilions were added—for example, a display to glorify the achievements of the Michurin-Lysenko advances in agrobiology. There was something obscene about the construction of these spacious and expensive buildings, at a cost of several billion rubles, to demonstrate achievements in agriculture when the peasants in the western regions of the country were still living in difficult, primitive conditions and denied aid to help them restore the housing which had been destroyed during the war. Construction was finished in 1951, but the opening was postponed—it turned out that there were not many achievements to exhibit. In 1952 it was said that some reconstruction and modernization was required before the exhibition could be opened. It was finally opened by Khruschev in 1954. (He had recently been promoting modest building projects and an increase in dwelling houses rather than official buildings, and he had criticized "architectural excesses" like the exhibition buildings.) In fact, Khrushchev understood the uselessness of the exhibition, but it had been completed and it had to be used. Although it was launched as a permanent exhibition, it was closed a few years later. Finally it was converted into an exhibition of the achievements of the whole economy, science, and culture, rather than just of agriculture. It still exists, but serves as a tourist attraction rather than as the means to demonstrate and encourage progress in agriculture.

If the resources spent on building the mammoth exhibition had been used to raise the procurement prices for grain and animal products, a more positive effect on agriculture might have ensued. In 1952 the procurement price for grain was only 9 rubles per ton, several times less than the actual production cost. The government spent about 300 million rubles a year to buy grain for the whole country, less than the annual cost of constructing the exhibition. Another disastrous example of conspicuous expenditure at that time was the decision to build the "Great Turkmen Canal," to cross and irrigate the large Transcaspian Karakum desert. The project was abandoned in 1953 after enormous expenditure and several years of great effort.

A modestly successful reform was carried out in this period on the direct initiative of Khrushchev: the amalgamation of small *kolkhozy*. Khrushchev had spent a great deal of time from 1945 to 1949 touring the Ukraine and this made him familiar with the real problems of the *kolkhozy* and *sovkhozy*. He had made several practical concessions to the peasants and, as a result, the Ukraine did much better in agriculture in 1947–1949 than most other areas of the Soviet Union. This reestablished him as one of Stalin's favorites. At the very end of 1949 he was transferred back to Moscow and promoted to three important positions: first Secretary of the Moscow City Party Committee, first secretary of Moscow Regional Party Committee, and secretary of the Central Committee of the CPSU. In the winter of 1950 he visited rural districts in the Moscow region and was shocked by the poverty of the peasants and the impoverishment of their *kolkhozy* and their small villages, containing no more than twenty or thirty houses. They contrasted sharply with the larger, more prosperous villages in the Ukraine. Collective farms had been organized on the basis of existing villages and peasant communes. As a result, most *kolkhozy* in the poorer forest and mixed forest regions were small, cultivating between 100 and 200 hectares of arable land (26 percent of *kolkhozy* cultivated less than 100 hectares).

Khrushchev believed that amalgamating the small *kolkhozy* into larger ones would make it possible for more *kolkhozy* to have qualified chairmen and agronomists. The use of machinery would be more rational and the relations between the *kolkhozy*, the agricultural authorities, and local officials would be easier. He also thought that larger *kolkhozy* could become more specialized, oriented not towards the production of grain, but towards producing meat, dairy products, and vegetables for the big industrial centers situated in the same area. He also wanted to amalgamate the impoverished villages, destroying the small, ancient villages and building "agro-towns" instead, with good roads and modern facilities.

The amalgamation reform was carried out very quickly. Before the spring sowing season in 1950, 6,069 small collective farms in the Moscow region had been amalgamated into 1,541 larger *kolkhozy*, each cultivating an average of 770 hectares. At the end of May 1950 the Central Committee adopted a resolution to amalgamate small *kolkhozy* throughout the country. By the end of that year the 236,900 collective farms in the Soviet Union had been amalgamated to 123,700, and a few months later the number had fallen to 93,000. Some *kolkhozy* were converted into *sovkhozy*. The quality of leadership in the new, large *kolkhozy* improved as the Party mobilized more experienced organizers (often agronomists) and sent them to the newly established farms. But Khrushchev's agro-towns met with a cool reception from his fellow Politburo members. They would require time and substantial investments. All the money that was allocated to agriculture centrally was being absorbed by the giant "transformation of nature" program, the Exhibition of Agricultural Achievements, and the "Great Turkmen Canal."

Despite some positive effects, the amalgamation of the small *kolkhozy* did not really solve the problems of many of the impoverished farms. Throughout the central, western, and northern regions the debts of the *kolkhozy* continued to grow, and they were unable to meet the payments in kind for the services of the MTS. Bank credits remained unpaid and often there was nothing with which to pay the peasants for their *trudodni*, except promises. The peasants relied on their private plots for survival. Nineteen fifty-one was another bad year, and the total production of grain fell to 78 million tons, 3 million less than in 1950. The production of potatoes fell from 88 million tons in 1950 to 58 million tons in 1951, the same amount as the last year of the war. Despite their larger size, many *kolkhozy* were bankrupt, because the government forced them to sell more grain to the state in 1951 (33.6 million tons) than they had sold in 1950 (32.3 million tons). Meat and milk procurements were also higher, even though less was produced in 1951. Bankruptcy was not a new phenomenon in Soviet agriculture, but when the *kolkhozy* were very small it had been possible to wait for a better year. Sometimes the chairmen had been replaced and the debts reduced, but somehow or other the *kolkhozy* continued to exist as legal units. With larger *kolkhozy* it was more difficult to ignore the bankruptcies. It required economic assistance and investment in equipment, buildings, animal stock, as well as raising the income of the members to save a bankrupt *kolkhoz*. The state was reluctant to do this, since the *kolkhozy* were officially considered to be co-operatives, belonging to the farmers themselves. The natural solution seemed to be to transform the insolvent collective farms into *sovkhozy*, since state farms belonged legally to the state, and investment into their production was not a "gift" to the peasants.

The transformation of collective farms into *sovkhozy* was done by ministerial or local decree, not by a decision of the general meeting of *kolkhoz* members. Occasionally the peasants were rather glad to become state farm workers, but more often they were opposed to the change. The transformation did not give them any new rights. *Sovkhoz* workers living in rural areas did not have internal passports or the right to travel freely from place to place. They were under a stricter system of discipline and were entitled to smaller private plots. Their work was counted in daily hours, rather than in *trudodni*, and they received very low wages. As a rule, several impoverished and bankrupt *kolkhozy* were transformed into one larger *sovkhoz*. The number of collective farms began to decline and the number of state farms grew without any obvious benefit to agricultural production. The trend was invisible during Stalin's lifetime. Since he was reluctant to acknowledge the failure of collectivization, *kolkhozy* that had been converted de facto into *sovkhozy* remained registered as collective farms. After his death the transformation reached dramatic proportions. In 1955 the number of *kolkhozy* fell from 93,300 to 87,000, while the number of *sovkhozy* rose from 4,857 to 5,134. Within the next five years the number of *kolkhozy* halved to 44,600, while the number of *sovkhozy* almost doubled.

Of all the postwar reforms, the one that angered and alienated the peasants most was the decree in 1948 that introduced a tax in kind on individual households and on production from private plots. The forced procurements from the *kolkhozy* produced bread for the urban population and technical crops, but the situation with vegetables, meat, milk, and eggs was far more complicated. The collective farms were unable to cultivate these crops or to build new animal farms and the main source of this high-quality food remained the small peasant allotments. The original *kolkhoz ustav* had specified that the plots were intended to satisfy the personal needs of peasant households for products like eggs, milk, meat, vegetables, and fruit, which were unavailable from their collective farms. In fact, the peasants sold part of their produce through the free markets and it was to tap this source of production for its own needs that the government introduced substantial taxes in kind on the products of the private plots. Each household had to feed itself and deliver to the state a certain proportion of the food produced on its tiny, quarter-hectare plots. The quotas varied from region to region, but everywhere they caused dismay. A set tax in kind or in money was established for each fruit tree, without any account being taken of the periodicity of the fruit harvests and the fact that fruit trees sometimes produced very little. Often the peasants had to pay more in "fruit tax" than they could possibly earn from selling their fruit. As a result, in many villages old fruit gardens were simply destroyed by their owners—it was more economic to use the land for potatoes than to declare ownership of taxable fruit trees.

The plight of the villagers became almost unbearable. The peasants had been ruthlessly exploited for years and the legendary patience of the Russian *muzhik* was tried beyond endurance. Continuous hard work was impossible on a diet of potatoes. Young people approaching working age did not want to enter the *kolkhozy* and conscripted soldiers refused to return to them after completing their army service. Imprisonment or forced labor for refusal to work on the *kolkhoz* was deliberately courted as a means of getting out of the village. More and more peasant families retained only one person (usually one of the grandparents) as a *kolkhoz* member as a pretext to qualify for an allotment. The other members of the family went on living in the village, but tried to find work elsewhere. Passport restrictions made it difficult for people to leave the village to settle in the towns, but they could not prevent people from leaving the *kolkhoz* and working elsewhere in the rural areas where passports were not required. Peasants worked in forestry, in timber production, on road, rail, and canal construction, on the river communications systems, in rural trade or rural transport. The result was that the rural population remained at a level of 108 to 110 million between 1947 and 1956, but the number of working *kolkhoz* members fell after 1948 by 0.5 million each year.

The taxation in kind on private plots and privately owned livestock was an extremely shortsighted measure. In the 1930s the *kolkhozniki* had been promised high-quality products in return for their *trudodni* as soon as the production of meat, milk, and eggs could be organized on *kolkhoz* animal farms. By 1950–1951 the collective farm production of milk and meat was still very low in comparison with private production. About 30 percent of milk and meat was produced in *kolkhozy* and 6 percent in *sovkhozy*. The remaining 65 percent was produced by private households. A special plan for the development of livestock in 1949–1951 had failed because of insufficient government investment. But the attempt to extract meat, milk, and eggs from individual households inhibited private production in the same way that the tax on fruit trees acted as a disincentive. Peasants reduced the number of milk cows they owned and turned to goats instead. Goats were easier and cheaper to feed and keep, and they produced 2 to 3 liters of milk per day, enough for the consumption of a peasant family. The state milk industry could not deal with goat milk and there was no tax on goat or sheep milk. In 1951 the number of goats rose to the record level of 16.4 million, twice the number of 1940 and three times the number of 1913. At the same time the number of milk cows in private ownership fell below the 1940 level, to 15.8 million. For the first time in Russian and Soviet history there were more privately owned goats than privately owned milk cows. The total number of milk cows in the country fell from 24.6 million in 1950 to 24.3 million in 1951.[20] After Stalin's death the tax in kind on private households was abolished and the trend reversed itself.

In October 1952 the Nineteenth Party Congress was held, the first Congress since 1939. The harvest in 1952 was, in general, better. The grain harvest was 92.2 million tons, only slightly below the 1940 level. But the final figures of the real harvest were not yet available when the official report of the Central Committee on the development of the national economy was being prepared, or when the Congress opened in Moscow on October 5, 1952. The report was delivered by Malenkov, the most senior figure after Stalin in the Party apparatus and the Politburo member then responsible for agriculture. In this official report the grain production figures were highly inflated, reflecting the "biological" harvest. The problems of agriculture were not given any prominence during the discussions at the Congress. Malenkov reported that agricultural production had increased to well above the 1940 level. He maintained that the annual production of grain had reached 130.4 million metric tons, whereas in fact, the actual production was 78.7 million tons in 1951 and 92.2 million tons in 1952. The difference between the reported figures and reality shows the scale of the official falsification of the situation in agriculture. To loud and prolonged applause Malenkov claimed that "the grain problem, previously considered the most acute and serious problem, has been successfully, finally and irreversibly resolved."[21]

Some confusion about official Party policy on agriculture was generated by the publication of Stalin's *Economic Problems of Socialism* just before the Congress convened.[22] Disappointed by the poor performance of the *kolkhozy* and by the evidence that the private sector was more viable and resilient, Stalin unexpectedly offered a new doctrine which could only lead to the complete alienation of the rural population and a further decline in agricultural production. He declared that in the future the free market for food products should be completely eliminated. The surplus produced on individual plots or by the *kolkhozy* should be made available for direct exchange with industry for goods. This would be the system under the future communist society. However, before any action could be taken and when the 1953 agricultural season had only just begun in the southernmost parts of the country, the Soviet Union was plunged into deep shock and grief. The creator of the *kolkhoz* system had died on March 5, 1953.

A general summary of agricultural performance in the postwar period, which shows the final results of Stalinism in agriculture, is given in Tables 10 and 11. Although the results were much

TABLE 10

Annual Production
of Grain, Potatoes, Vegetables, Meat, and Milk
in 1913, 1940, and 1946–1952
(Million Tons)

	Grain	Potatoes	Vegetables	Meat	Milk
1913*	86.0	31.9	5.5	5.0	29.4
1940	95.6	76.1	13.7	4.7	33.6
1946	39.6	55.6	8.9	3.1	27.7
1947	65.9	74.5	14.9	2.5	30.2
1948	67.2	95.0	13.2	3.1	33.4
1949	70.2	89.6	10.8	3.8	34.9
1950	81.2	88.6	9.3	4.9	35.3
1951	78.7	58.8	8.8	4.7	36.2
1952	92.2	69.2	9.8	5.2	35.7

Source: *Nar. khoz.*, 1974, p. 304.
 * The difference between the figures shown for food production in 1913 in this table and those in Table 5 is caused by territorial adjustments. Table 5 shows agricultural production within the borders of the Soviet Union before September 1939. This table shows production within the current borders of the Soviet Union, including the new territories acquired before and after the war. The 1913 figures are for the comparable area of the Russian Empire.

better for some technical crops like cotton and sugar beets, the production of flax and wool was also well below the 1913 level. The quality of the average diet was about the same in 1952 as it had been in 1940, but it was below the level of 1913. However, when the sharp increase in urban population is taken into account, it is clear that the rural areas were left with far too little food. The decline in the production and consumption of vegetables after 1947 is dramatic. The livestock population did not increase beyond the prewar level. It should be borne in mind that 1940 was the best prewar agricultural year and that 1952 was the best postwar year before Stalin's death. In all other years after the war, the main concern for most families was to get enough to eat. The yields of the grain crops were lower than in 1913 and

TABLE 11

Agriculture Production per Person[a]

	Population		Production per person		
	Total	Urban	Grain	Meat	Milk
	(millions)			(kilograms)	
1913[b]	159.2	28.5	540	31	184
1928	—	—	474	27	208
1940	194.1	63.1	492	24	173
1952	184.8	80.2	498	28.1	193

Sources: Population, Nar. khoz., 1965, p. 7. The production figures are calculated from Table 10 and Table 6 (for 1928).

[a] The figures for grain include feed and seed grain, as well as grain which was exported. All dairy products are calculated as milk.

[b] The production of meat and milk are higher per person for 1913 than those shown for the same year in Table 6. This indicates the higher-quality diet in the Baltic states and in the Western Ukraine than in the rest of the Russian Empire. These areas were not included in the calculations of food production in Table 6.

it was only possible to keep the production at a comparable level by increasing the acreage of sown land. Seventy percent of all meat and milk and 90 percent of eggs, potatoes, and vegetables were produced from the small, individual plots which formed 3 percent of the sown land. At the same time the number of private rural households began to decline after 1949, both because of industrial growth and because of the difficulties of rural life. The number of persons in each individual household was also declining.

Rapid industrial growth from 1928 to 1952 was supported not by an increase in the production of food, but by an increase in the forcible extraction of food from the villages to feed the rapidly expanding towns. Even if there had been a return to Stalin's drastic measures of terror and coercion, the country could not have continued in this way for much longer. There had been no real growth of crop yields or food production for forty years, despite the introduction of mechanization and the use of chemical fertilizers. The only event to give some hope that the crisis could be solved was Stalin's death.

Chapter 6

Khrushchev's Reforms:
Achievement and Failure, 1953-1964

Although Khrushchev played an active role in agricultural policy in the last few years of Stalin's rule, he had little real influence. Malenkov replaced Andreyev as the Politburo member responsible for agriculture in 1950. Although he knew very little about the subject, both he and Khrushchev were well aware that the situation required urgent attention. Immediately after Stalin's death, Malenkov became chairman of the Council of Ministers. Khrushchev remained a secretary of the Central Committee, adding agriculture to his other responsibilities within the Presidium (the Politburo had been renamed the Presidium in 1952).

Khrushchev knew more about agriculture than his colleagues in the Presidium, but his knowledge was superficial, based on a rural upbringing and his travels in the rural areas, where he enjoyed meeting people, discussing their problems, and listening to their complaints. This could not replace real experience in agriculture. Although he made very serious attempts to improve the rural situation, he had already made some foolish mistakes by 1953 which indicated his lack of expertise. The utopian idea of building modern agro-towns to replace the old villages was one example. Another was his attempt to persuade the peasants in the Moscow region to cultivate crops which were successful in the Ukraine (for example, sugar beets, Chinese millet, and corn): he seemed not to understand that the colder climate was unsuitable for these crops. He was often more enthusiastic than Stalin in his support for Lysenko's bizarre theory (based on the neo-Lamarkist theory that plants could inherit acquired characteristics) that plants could be made more cold-resistant by cultivating them in a colder environment. In 1950–1953 he assisted in the creation of melon plantations in one of the *sovkhozy* near Moscow, and he tried to introduce the cultivation of artichokes, pumpkins, and grapes in some of the *kolkhozy* in the Moscow region.

The first few months after Stalin's death were taken up by a power struggle. The first priority of Stalin's heirs was to remove Beria. Once Beria had fallen, he was declared responsible for the plight of the villages: a *Pravda* editorial on July 10, 1953, accused him of attempting to destroy and destabilize the *kolkhozy* and to create food shortages (the leadership was not yet ready to link Beria with Stalin's terror—too many of them had also been involved). But even at this stage, few people took this diagnosis of the ills of Soviet agriculture seriously. However, with Beria out of the way, steps could be taken to deal with some of the urgent needs of the countryside. By July it was clear that the south was suffering from drought and that 1953 would be a poor agricultural year. The grain harvest was 82.5 million tons, 10 million tons less than in 1952.

1. *The Change in Taxation and Procurement Policies*

The first policy changes were proposed by Malenkov in his report to a session of the Supreme Soviet in August 1953. The counterproductive tax on private plots was abolished and tax arrears and debts accumulated in respect to this tax were waived. A modest monetary tax was introduced instead. There was an immediate improvement in the economic plight of the countryside and in the morale of the peasants, who were left with more produce for their own use and for sale on the markets. It was the first genuinely popular government action in the villages for many years. There was an incentive to improve the quality of production on individual plots and to increase the number of farm animals. At the same time, procurement prices were increased for products supplied by collective farms over and above their quotas. However, this did not help the situation much in 1953, since the *kolkhozy* were finding it difficult to meet their quotas.

The rivalry between Malenkov and Khrushchev had already begun when Khrushchev prepared a special Plenum of the Central Committee for September to discuss agricultural problems. A new tone was introduced at this Plenum. The false speeches and policies characteristic of the Stalin era were replaced by an impressive open discussion of the real problems and shortcomings in agriculture. This Plenum reestablished the dominance of the Party over government institutions. It was also the first time an "open" Plenum had been held. Agricultural experts, *kolkhoz* chairmen, *sovkhoz* directors, and officials from the Ministry of Agriculture were invited to take part in the discussions on possible remedies. Khrushchev's report was widely publicized. Apart from reducing the monetary tax on private plots still further and removing the tax on privately owned animals, Khrushchev wanted to encourage rural and suburban workers to acquire allotments and to raise private livestock for their own consumption and for sale. The number of cattle and poultry had fallen too low and a limited NEP was required to reverse the trend. "We must abandon the preconceived idea that it's disgraceful for a blue-collar worker or a white-collar worker to have livestock of his own," Khrushchev declared to the applause of those present.[1] A few years later it became clear that this was an uneconomical way to increase meat production, and the practice was forbidden. By 1958 the number of livestock owned by urban workers had risen to 3.5 million and, since there was no fodder or hay in the towns, cheap, subsidized bread and other food products were used to feed the animals.

The main efforts of the Plenum were directed towards methods to increase the grain and meat production by *kolkhozy* and *sovkhozy*. The most important proposal (which rapidly became law) was a change in the procurement system. In announcing that this reform was long overdue, Khrushchev not only criticized Stalin, but also implicitly attacked Malenkov, who had presented a false, glossy picture of the agricultural situation at the Nineteenth Party Congress and supported Stalin's statement that the market should gradually be abolished in the countryside. Before 1953 it had been forbidden to discuss procurement prices openly. As a result, most people were unaware of the enormous differences between procurement and retail prices. The price paid by the state for most agricultural products in 1953 (with the exception of technical crops, for which prices had been increased after the war) was the same as it had been in 1929. Even in the early 1930s, when inflation was rather high, the stability of procurement prices had already had a negative effect. By the late 1930s the difference between procurement prices and retail prices had become unreasonably large. Retail food prices were frozen during the war, but they were raised substantially in 1947, while procurement prices remained at the 1929 level. This absurd situation made the cultivation of food crops uneconomical. The prices of the manufactured goods and implements required in the country had risen several times in the same period, and were often eight to ten times higher than in 1929. For the same type of equipment the *kolkhozy* had to pay about 300 percent more in kind in 1940 than in 1929, 400 percent more in 1947, and 800 percent more in 1949. The prices of industrial equipment (trucks or ploughs) increased less rapidly than the price of consumer goods, but they also rose.[2]

Although labor was very cheap, by 1952 the cost of producing most crops was at least six or seven times higher than the revenues earned by selling the crops to the state. The cost of producing meat products was even higher. In short, procurement prices had become a very large tax in kind on the countryside. It was difficult for the *kolkhozy* to develop and expand on the basis of these compulsory sales. The only profit they could make was by selling their surplus after fulfilling the procurement quotas, and very few of them could rely on producing surpluses.

After the September Plenum, procurement prices were raised approximately fivefold for most food crops and for meat. The procurement prices for milk and butter were increased by a more modest 200 percent, and for vegetables, an almost negligible 40 to 50 percent. After the poor performance of agriculture in 1954 (85 million tons of grain), they were raised again. The new prices helped the financial situation of the *kolkhozy* and *sovkhozy*, but could not affect the amount of grain and other products which they could sell in 1953 because the harvest was poor. However, the benefits of the price reform can be seen by comparing the amounts of various products which the state procured in 1953–1955. The state purchased 31.1 million tons of marketable grain in 1953, 34.6 million tons in 1954, and 36.9 million tons in 1955. The increase was even greater in other crops. The procurement of sugar beets rose from 22.9 to 30.7 million tons, of vegetables from 2.5 million to 3.9 million tons, of meat from 3.6 to 4.2 million tons, and of milk from 10.6 to 13.5 million tons. But even these increases were insufficient to satisfy the demands of the urban population and foreign trade. Procurement prices continued to rise for various products after 1955, particularly in 1962 and 1963. The changes are shown in Table 12.

The costs of production differed from region to region. In the Ukraine and the North Caucasus, for example, it cost about 40 rubles to produce a ton of grain. This made it uneconomical to sell grain at the procurement prices of 1952 and earlier, but in 1955–1958 and in 1962 a modest profit could be made. In the poorer grain-producing regions of central Russia where the yields are lower, however, the production costs were 95 to 100 rubles per ton of grain, 105 rubles per ton of potatoes, about 2,000 rubles per ton of live weight of cattle, and 250 to 300 rubles per ton of milk,[4] all much higher than the procurement prices. It is clear that state procurement prices should have reflected these differences and higher prices should have been paid where production costs were higher. But the government was still determined to

TABLE 12

State Procurement Prices for *Kolkhoz* Products
(New Rubles per Metric Ton)*

Product	1950–1952	1954–1958	1962–1963
Grain	8.4	62.0	83.0
Potatoes	5.3	41.0	49.0
Sunflower seeds	19.2	148.0	181.0
Sugar beets	10.5	22.5	24.3
Cotton (raw)	319.0	340.0	341.0
Cattle (live weight)	50.0	589.0	764.0
Milk	28.0	113.0	122.0

Source: [3].

* In 1960 there was a currency reform. Old rubles were exchanged for new in the ratio of 10 to 1 and salaries and prices were reduced accordingly.

keep the retail price of food down and had not yet begun to subsidize food prices, except for meat. The retail price of wheat flour in 1952–1958 was 400 to 500 rubles per ton (40 to 50 kopecks per kilogram), well above the procurement price. The retail price of milk was 300 rubles per ton (30 kopecks per liter) and of meat 1,500 rubles per ton, about the same as the price of "live weight" cattle delivered to the slaughterhouses. If one takes processing and sales costs into account, the state did not make any profit from the retail sale of meat, but neither did the livestock farms—the production costs of meat were more than double the procurement price. Despite the very significant increase in state procurement prices in 1953–1962 (more than twelve times the 1952 level), there was very little economic incentive to the collective and state farms to develop livestock production.

Khrushchev was right, of course, to abolish Stalin's arbitrary methods of requisitioning agricultural products through cheap compulsory procurements. He intended to make procurement prices an economic incentive which would act to stimulate agricultural development. He took a step in the right direction, but the problem was so serious that the effect of even a twelvefold increase in procurement prices was only to reduce some of the *kolkhoz* debts, rather than to generate profits. Amongst the food crops, it was only in the climatically favorable areas that grain production became profitable. He faced a difficult problem: he could continue increasing procurement prices by increasing retail food prices—this would make both the production and the retail sale of food profitable. But increasing the price of food is always unpopular. On the other hand, if he continued increasing procuremnet prices without raising retail prices, a direct subsidy of the food trade would be required with large investments to support the new price system. Both methods would stimulate agricultural production. There was, however, a third, more attractive solution—*reducing the cost of production*. A significant increase in productivity would be required, as well as new reserves of comparatively cheap food crops. It was clear to any economist that intensifying the exploitation of existing fields (using mechanization and chemical fertilizers) would not produce *cheap* grain. Grain that is obtained over and above average yields always costs more to produce than the grain of normal yields. The intensification of agriculture does not lead to cheaper harvests, but to higher harvests for higher prices. The only way to obtain cheap grain was through extensive development, by exploiting new, fertile, virgin lands for agriculture. In September 1953 Khrushchev decided to adopt this third solution.

2. The Virgin Land Program

The Virgin Land program was the boldest stroke in Khrushchev's attempts to solve the problems of Soviet agriculture. It has also proved to be his most enduring reform and one which is becoming more important as the years pass. There have been several years in which only the good harvest in the virgin land areas has raised the total production of marketable grain above starvation level. The Virgin Land Program was also a crucial event in Brezhnev's political career. If Khrushchev had not put him in charge of the program in Kazakhstan, he would probably have remained far from Moscow for much longer and would not have become a member of Khrushchev's coterie. Khrushchev's choice of Brezhnev as his representative to conduct a purge in Kazakhstan and to persuade the republic to sacrifice its nomadic tribes for the benefit of the whole Soviet Union was an important stepping stone in Brezhnev's ascent to power. In 1978 Brezhnev published a short book about his work in Kazakhstan in 1954–1956. By then Khrushchev had become a nonperson and Brezhnev did not even mention him as the initiator of the Virgin Land Program. He described how his own involvement in the program began:

> It all started on a frosty Moscow day at the end of January, 1954, when I was called to the CC CPSU. I was already aware of the problem itself; this was not the first time I heard about the virgin lands. What was news was that they wanted to entrust the vast scheme of ploughing the virgin lands to me. The work had to begin in Kazakstan in the coming spring. Time was short and the task would be difficult. I was not given any illusions about this, but I was also told that this was the Party's most important task at that time.[5]

It is perfectly clear that the person who was entrusting this task to Brezhnev (and whose name he is so reluctant to disclose) was Khrushchev.

The search for virgin lands was not entirely new in the history of Russian agriculture. However, there had been practically no increase in sown area of grain crops between 1913 (104.6 million hectares) and 1953 (106.7 million hectares). The total area of cultivated land had increased, but this was mostly due to technical and fodder crops and the introduction of grasses (mixed and clover) into the rotation system. At the same time the population had grown by 30 million (within the same borders) and the urban population had increased by more than 300 percent. Grain yields could have been increased, but the production of chemical fertilizers was still at a low level. They were only used for some technical crops and it would take many years to develop the requisite new capacities in the chemical industry (an option under consideration at the time). It was therefore logical to consider resuming the exploitation of the lands in the east which had been cultivated by evacuated peasants during the war and then abandoned. The sparsely populated plains of the southwest Urals, eastern Siberia, and Kazakhstan had good soil, but the climate was very bad. The most promising area was north Kazakhstan—it had already been tested by settlers before 1913, by deported kulaks in the 1930s, and by the evacuated peasants and the Volga Germans who had been deported to this region.

Kazakhstan is the largest constituent republic of the Soviet Union: its area, 1,050,000 square miles (2,719,500 square kilometers), is about five times the size of France and a third of the United States. In 1953 the population was only 7.5 million. Eastern Siberia and the north Kazakhstan steppes have a potentially very fertile thick *chernozem* with a good granular structure. The absence of leaching rains favors the formation of good soil, but restricts its agricultural exploitation. The annual rainfall varies from 200 to 400 millimeters (10 to 16 inches). In 1949 William Vogt (already worried about a world shortage of arable land and the need to reduce population growth) drew attention to the Siberian and Kazakhstan steppes.

> No people on earth has yet successfully come to terms with such an environment. . . . But this appears to be the region on which the Soviet government is depending to feed its rapidly growing population. If the gamble on the agricultural productivity of the chernozem soils should turn against Russia, there might well be in store for the world such trouble as it has not yet seen. . . . Basic to the whole future of the U.S.S.R. and its relationship with the other countries of the world is its ability to cope with agriculture in dry-farming areas.[6]

Vogt's prophecies began to come true at the beginning of 1954. The Central Committee Plenum in September 1953 accepted the principle that the land under cultivation should be increased. The press then began to publish articles discussing the alternatives and analyzing the potential of various regions. Kazakhstan featured prominently, but the leadership of the Kazakh republic was unhappy about the project. The first secretary of the local Party was a Kazakh, Zh. Shayakhmetov. The Republican Central Committee was dominated by Kazakhs who realized that the Virgin Land Program would entail an influx of non-Kazakh people and a consequent Russification of a large part of the republic. Moreover, the traditional life of the rural Kazakhs would be threatened: many were nomads who grazed their sheep and camel herds on the steppes. A Plenum of the Kazakhstan Communist Party Central Committee met in October 1953 and approved a plan that diverged from the line that had been adopted by the Central Committee Plenum of the CPSU in Moscow in September. The sown area in Kazakhstan would be increased by half a million hectares. Khrushchev was furious about this unprecedented challenge and decided to send Brezhnev to purge the Kazakh Party.

On January 22, 1954 Khrushchev published a memorandum to the Central Committee, "Ways of Solving the Grain Problem." He suggested that the only way to remedy the acute shortage of marketable grain was by urgently increasing the area of sown land by exploiting at least 13 million hectares of virgin land in Kazakhstan, eastern Siberia, and the Volga basin. At an average yield of 10 to 11 centners per hectare, this would produce about 13 million tons of grain for a capital investment (on new villages, roads, machinery, etc.) of 600 million new rubles in 1954–1955. Khrushchev's optimistic calculations expected profitable returns within a year (5 new kopecks on a kilogram of grain). He then launched a nationwide campaign, appealing particularly to the Young Communist League (Komsomol) to mobilize its members for agricultural work in the new areas.

Khrushchev later described the arbitrary measures taken to defeat the Kazakh resistance.

We decided to replace Shayakhmetov with Comrade Pono-marenko, who was an experienced and reliable administrator. He'd received his formal training as a railroad engineer, but he was well qualified in agricultural administration and political work. We also replaced Shayakhmetov's colleague Afonov, the Second Secretary of the Kazakh Central Committee. His post was taken over by Brezhnev, who'd had experience as First Secretary of the Moldavian Communist Party.[7]

Within a few months of the Plenum of the Central Committee of the Kazakhstan Party, an extraordinary Seventh Congress of the Kazakh Party was convened to "elect" Ponomarenko and Brezhnev onto the Central Committee and make them secretaries of the Committee. The Seventh Congress also adopted a resolution to begin the large-scale development of Kazakhstan virgin and idle lands.

A special Central Committee Plenum on the Virgin Land Program was held in Moscow from February 23 to March 2, 1954. Since the ploughing of the steppe would be a difficult process and would take the whole summer, the plan was not expected to yield much in the first year. Tractors, ploughs, and other machinery would need to be transported to the area; roads would have to be built, as well as temporary storage facilities and tent villages. The people who were to cultivate the land would have to be resettled. But the harvest was expected to yield enough seed grain in 1954 for sowing in 1955 and the harvest was expected to be approximately 20 million tons of grain by 1955.

During the spring and summer of 1954 a major national organizational effort began. Three hundred thousand volunteers, recruited by the Komsomol from towns and villages both, set out for northern Kazakhstan, the Altai, and the southern areas of Siberia and the Urals. Hundreds of huge new *sovkhozy* were established, some of them covering tens of thousands of hectares. About 50,000 tractors, 6,000 trucks, and other agricultural equipment (almost the entire production of the agricultural industry) were shipped to the *sovkhozy* and to the new MTS which would service the enlarged *kolkhozy* in these regions. Nineteen million hectares (more than envisaged by the plan) were ploughed in 1954 and another 14 million in 1955. A limited area was sown in the spring of 1954 while the ploughing continued in preparation for the 1955 sowing. The harvest in 1954 was only 3 percent better than in 1953 (85.6 million tons) and very little of it came from the new areas, more than half of which were in Kazakhstan. This must have been a disappointment to Khrushchev. Although it had been expected that it would take until 1955 for positive results, he was eager to demonstrate the success of his plan. Brezhnev claims that his instructions were "to get grain this autumn; certainly this autumn!"[8]

Unfortunately, 1955 was a very dry year in the eastern part of the country and there was no rain after May. Brezhnev called it a "year of despair for the virgin lands." Twenty million hectares had been sown, 10 million of them in Kazakhstan. Almost all the spring wheat perished. Living conditions in the winter were hard. Supplies of food and other goods were unreliable and inadequate. Thousands of people lost heart and began to leave the area. Khrushchev was bitterly disappointed and his position in the Central Committee became precarious as opposition hardened. Malenkov, Kaganovich, and Molotov criticized him openly for his rash venture and his "great leap" methods. It was suggested that if the enormous investments in the new areas had been directed instead towards the traditional agricultural areas, the results would have been very different. Central Committee members began to demand that the flow of equipment and manpower to the east be shifted to the west and south. The weather appeared to confirm their objections—the 1955 drought affected Kazakhstan particularly severely. The Ural regions, western Siberia, and the Altai suffered far less and the weather was extremely good in the traditional grain-producing areas of the Soviet Union. One million hectares of virgin land had been cultivated in the western areas as well, in the Volga basin and the North Caucasus. As a result the total grain harvest in 1955 was a record 103.7 million tons.

Despite the opposition, Khrushchev retained his enthusiasm

and demanded an even greater expansion of acreage in the virgin lands. Ponomarenko became the scapegoat. He was replaced by Brezhnev as first secretary of the Kazakhstan Communist Party. At the end of 1955 a conference of Party and state managerial officials was held at which Brezhnev made a promise on behalf of Kazakhstan—in 1956 the republic would produce 600 million puds (about 10 million tons) of grain. This was a bold undertaking.

Thus 1956 was a decisive year, both for the program and for Khrushchev himself. A poor harvest would almost certainly have resulted in his removal from office. In fact, luck was distinctly on his side in that year. He managed to withstand two major political crises (the Chinese attack on his secret speech at the Twentieth Party Congress and the international outcry produced by the military suppression of the Hungarian revolution) and the weather was favorable in the eastern part of the Soviet Union and dry in the west. About 2.9 million hectares of newly ploughed land had been added to the land under cultivation in 1956. The total acreage of cultivated virgin land was now 35.9 million hectares, of which 19.9 million hectares were in Kazakhstan. Since there were substantial reserves of nutritive elements in this soil, there was little need for fertilizers. The wheat yield was unprecedented in the history of Soviet agriculture—60 million tons of grain were harvested in the eastern regions alone, 20 million of them in Kazakhstan (more than the harvest in the entire Ukraine that year). The total grain harvest was 125 million tons, the largest in Soviet history. Since the local population in the virgin lands was small, almost the entire harvest represented marketable grain. The state purchased one billion puds of grain (about 16 million tons) in Kazakhstan—the magic figure which the government had been trying to attain as a procurement target from the whole country since the end of the 1920s. A victorious Khrushchev toured the area with a proud Brezhnev. The latter, however, was no longer first secretary of Kazakhstan. He had been promoted to become one of the secretaries of the Central Committee and a candidate member of the Party Presidium. In 1957 he became a full member of the Presidium, a dramatic rise from the comparatively modest position of second secretary of Kazakhstan in 1955.

In fact, the virgin land harvest in 1956 exceeded even the most optimistic forecasts and created a series of new problems. The combine-harvesters could not complete their task in time and some fields had not been reaped when the winter began. Moreover, there was a shortage of storage facilities and insufficient manpower, trucks, roads, and railroad wagons to move the grain. A substantial amount was lost. But these were the problems of success. The new *sovkhozy* made substantial profits from selling their grain and they could repay their state credits and begin making real investments.

The weather in the virgin land area was very dry again in 1957 and the total grain production for the country fell to 102.6 million tons. However, a sequence of good and bad years had been predicted, and in 1958 the weather improved and the total grain production reached a new record of 134.7 million tons. Khrushchev now had good reason to claim that the Soviet grain problem had been solved. It was a remarkable achievement, but it did not really resolve the problems of agriculture. Moreover, it was naive to expect that the *natural* fertility of the virgin lands would endlessly continue to produce record harvests. The fertility of virgin soil has certain limits, and a complex cultivation—with proper rotation, the introduction of farm animals to produce manure, and the use of chemical fertilizers—is required to ensure future fertility. Unfortunately, in the euphoria of success the necessary decisions and investments in the virgin land areas were postponed. Khrushchev had argued that a wheat monoculture in these areas would be a temporary measure, giving bread to the nation for several years, and allowing time to improve agriculture in the traditional agricultural regions and to increase the production of fertilizers. Later it would be possible to reduce the acreage under wheat in the virgin lands, and introduce more complex and intensive systems.

In fact, the cultivation of the virgin lands delayed mechanization in the western areas. The agricultural industry was simply unable to manufacture enough equipment to supply both new and old lands and the virgin lands received priority. The total acreage of sown land increased 23 percent, from 157.2 million hectares in 1953 to 194.7 million in 1956. However, the production of tractors and other agricultural machinery increased only 15 percent, and most of the new machinery was sent to the east. From 1953 to 1956 the number of tractors increased by 11 percent in the Ukraine, and by 4 percent in the North Caucasus. The number of combine-harvesters actually fell from 52,400 in 1953 to 43,500 in 1956 in the Ukraine, and from 27,300 in 1953 to 21,000 in 1956 in the North Caucasus. There was a similar trend in other types of agricultural machinery. The amount of mineral fertilizer produced in 1956 was 11 million tons (raw weight of salt). This was not even enough to restore the fertility of the soil under technical crops. The virgin land scheme had made it possible to increase the production of grain from 80–90 million tons to 130 million tons in a very short period of time. The state had been able to create some grain reserves. Now it was necessary to tackle the chronic problems of the western, more populated areas of the country and to work towards a more balanced agriculture. The grain problem seemed to be solved, but what was urgently required was an increase in the production of vegetables, technical crops, livestock, poultry, milk, wool, and so on. This could not be done by a crash program. Longer-term reforms and practical measures were required.

3. *Khrushchev's Failures*

The Virgin Land Program can be considered a lasting success, but some of Khrushchev's other initiatives after 1958 were less fortunate. By 1958 he had become chairman of the Council of Ministers of the USSR as well as first secretary of the Central Committee and thus had assumed nearly dictatorial powers. Almost all his suggestions were implemented without proper discussion or tests. His opponents (Malenkov, Molotov, Kaganovich, Bulganin) had been removed from the Party Presidium and Central Committee. His policy failures have been analyzed in detail elsewhere,[9] but their agricultural and economic aspects are relevant here.

THE ABOLITION OF THE MTS

The Machine Tractor Stations had developed in parallel with the collective farms and they had become familiar and well-established institutions. When collectivization began, it had not been feasible for small *kolkhozy* to purchase and service all the necessary agricultural equipment. Moreover, the government did not wish to put the equipment (and therefore the entire means of agricultural production) in the sole control of the *kolkhozy*. After the amalgamation of small *kolkhozy* in 1950, there were some MTS which serviced a single large *kolkhoz*. It seemed sensible to merge the two under a single administration. In the Stavropol region, where the large *kolkhozy* covered several thousand hectares, the merger was tried on an experimental basis in 1957 in twelve *kolkhozy*. The *kolkhoz* chairman became director of the MTS. The results indicated a more efficient use of equipment. The quality of labor improved and management was rationalized, since there was no longer any need for liaison between the *kolkhoz* and MTS at the district level. But the experiment did not test other ramifications of the project. What kind of reorganization of equipment, repair shops, and workers' housing would be required, for example, in the more common situation where an MTS serviced several medium-sized *kolkhozy*? Carried away by the success of the Stavropol experiment, Khrushchev expressed a number of random ideas on the feasibility of merger, all of which required careful thought and testing. He spoke of the necessity for a gradual and selective reorganization of the MTS system. It would not be universal and it would take place only where the *kolkhozy* were capable of using the equipment properly and where the MTS serviced only one, two, or at most three *kolkhozy*. In the central, western, and northern areas where the *kolkhozy* were smaller and less efficient, the transformation would not begin for several years.[10]

A special Central Committee Plenum was convened in February 1958 to discuss the future of the MTS. The general and professional press was encouraged to launch a preliminary discussion of possible reform. However, with Khrushchev's opinion already clear, editors were reluctant to publish critical views. The pre-Plenum discussion turned into a chorus of support for his views without any analysis of the economic, technical, and social implications. There was no mention of the simple fact that it would be difficult to reconcile the social differences between the MTS workers, who were state employees, and the *kolkhozniki*, who still had no right to passports, paid holidays, or state pensions and who certainly did not earn stable salaries. More than 3,000 people had been invited to participate in the Plenum and it was impossible to have a serious or businesslike discussion with so many participants. In any case, the atmosphere was conducive to reaching a quick decision, rather than to careful consideration and consultation. Khrushchev had forgotten his earlier caution and was ready for rapid transformation. This course of action was approved by the Plenum and the directives ordering the MTS to transfer their equipment to *kolkhozy* were issued by the Central Committee even before the reform had been approved by the Supreme Soviet and become law.

The real reason for the reform had to do with financial problems. The increased procurement prices in 1954–1957 had improved the financial position of the *kolkhozy*, but adversely affected the amount of the payment in kind received by the MTS. These payments formed part of the procurement deliveries. They were calculated in rubles, but paid in produce, the value of which was calculated on the basis of the official procurement prices. Thus when the procurement prices rose, the *kolkhozy* had to pay far less produce to the MTS to settle their accounts. For work for which the MTS had received ten tons of grain based on 1952 procurement prices, for example, they received only one ton based on 1957 prices. Thus as the economic indicators of the *kolkhozy* improved, the indicators of the MTS calculated in rubles remained stable, but they actually received far less in terms of payments in kind. It seemed more sensible to let the MTS share part of the harvest they helped to cultivate, rather than continuing to express the value of their services in rubles. MTS employees were paid by the state and the state also supplied the machinery. The result was that the state was now receiving far less agricultural produce for the same financial investment.

The budget allocations for agriculture were far higher in 1958 than they had been in 1952, but Khrushchev was badly in need of money for a number of expensive programs which he had launched (for example, an expensive space program, the building of the Akademgorodok research center and university in Siberia, a large housing program, and an ambitious foreign aid program). Moreover, the Virgin Land Program continued to absorb large investments, since permanent towns had to be built to house the workers who were predominantly of urban origin and who expected a reasonable standard of living. On the face of it, abolishing the MTS and selling the machinery to the *kolkhozy* seemed economically expedient. It would not only save the state the cost of maintaining the MTS, but also realize some capital from the *kolkhozy*. As a result, the decisions adopted by the Central Committee Plenum in February 1958 differed from the successful Stravropol experiment. In the experiment the MTS had been merged with the *kolkhozy* for the purposes of administration only. They remained intact as working units and the *kolkhozy* had not been required to purchase the machinery. The 1958 reform required that the *kolkhozy* should buy the MTS machinery from the government and envisaged that most MTS would be abolished by the end of the year.

By the end of 1958 more than 80 percent of all *kolkhozy*, rich and poor alike, had been forced to buy MTS equipment. The only allowance made was that credit was offered to the 20 percent of extremely poor farms which could not afford the purchase. By January 1959, only 345 MTS remained of the 8,000 which had existed at the beginning of the reform. By the end of 1959 the number had been reduced to 34.[11] The speed and cost of the reform inflicted grave economic and organizational damage on the *kolkhozy*. In theory the total value of the MTS equipment (based on the prices paid when the machinery came from the factories) was supposed to be only 17 percent of the amount the state paid the *kolkhozy* for their produce. It was, therefore, assumed that the compulsory purchase would not force any *kolkhozy* into bankruptcy. In practice the situation was far more complex. An arbitrary new price was set for the equipment and the price of fuel, lubricants, and spare parts was doubled. The collective farms had not only to pay for the equipment but also to construct buildings to house it, and build repair facilities and fuel-storage facilities. Furthermore, they became responsible for the wages of the MTS employees. And although it was easy enough to distribute the machinery to the *kolkhozy*, other MTS facilities were immovable. Many of the large and well-equipped repair shops were bought by local industry rather than by the collective farms. Few farms could afford to create proper repair facilities. Servicing of equipment became poor and, as a result, the life-span of the machinery was reduced. A more serious problem was the drain of qualified personnel from the countryside. Few MTS workers wanted to join the *kolkhozy*, which could not offer them the legal and social privileges they had enjoyed as MTS technicians. Approximately 50 percent of the better-qualified drivers and mechanics sought employment in the cities.

An unforeseen but devastating consequence of the reform was the chaos into which the agricultural machinery industry was suddenly thrown. Previously the factories producing agricultural equipment had turned out their equipment according to plan, and shipped it to the MTS as directed. After 1959 the *kolkhozy* were expected to do their own purchasing. But they had exhausted their funds in buying the used equipment and in any case, they did not have qualified buyers who could evaluate requirements and buy directly from the factories. Sales dropped alarmingly. To avoid a slowdown in production, equipment was sent to the virgin lands or exported. Nonetheless, the manufacture of equipment declined sharply as enormous stocks of unsold new machinery accumulated within the factories. In 1958–1961 the total volume of agricultural machinery decreased for the first time in peacetime Soviet history. The production of silage combines decreased by a factor of four in 1957–1960. The demand for tractor-mounted ploughs, sowers, cultivators, mowers, and binders had fallen and the delivery of some types of equipment virtually halted. In the RSFSR alone, there was a shortfall of 420,000 tractors, 76,000 trucks, and 136,000 combines, all essential for optimal agricultural production. The percentage of worn-out equipment increased. The *kolkhozy* had machinery for only 26 to 48 percent of their work. By 1961 the delivery of combines to agriculture was still two times below the 1957 level.[12]

Thus Khrushchev's abolition of the MTS had a prolonged negative effect. Agricultural productivity was reduced. The adverse consequences of the reform are now acknowledged.[13]

THE FAILURE OF KHRUSHCHEV'S "MEAT PROGRAM"

The dramatic increase in the production of grain brought about by the Virgin Land Program suddenly made it seem that there were significant reserves of grain. The next natural step in the development of agriculture was to increase livestock production. In general there are four main sectors in the agriculture of any large country: grain (or potatoes) provides the main source of energy in the population's diet; vegetables and fruit provide vitamins; meat (or fish) and milk products are the source of high-quality proteins; and technical crops provide the raw materials for the light and food industries (plant oil and sugar are important sources of energy). Of these four branches of agriculture, the production of meat and milk is the most labor- and cost-intensive. In the advanced industrial countries it is usual for more farming land to be used for the production of meat, poultry, and dairy products than for the production of all other agricultural crops combined. In the United States, for example, which enjoys the highest level of meat consumption in the world, the production of feed grain (corn, soybeans, etc.) represents more than 70 percent of the total grain production. More than half the arable land in the United States is given over to the livestock industry. In fact, other countries do not need to emulate this distribution of agricultural production, since there are many plant sources of high-quality proteins which are cheaper than animal protein. Nonetheless, Khrushchev conceived the ambition to raise the quality of the Soviet diet to the American level. This target required a sharp increase in the production of meat and milk.

There was a modest growth in the production of meat (including poultry), milk, and eggs in 1954–1956 and, helped by the good grain harvest in 1956, the rate improved in 1957. Meat production rose 12 percent, and milk production 6 percent. However, the production of meat per head of population was still only 32 kilograms per year, well below the American figures of 97 to 100 kilograms per person in 1956–1957. Khrushchev held discussions with experts about ways to accelerate production. In a speech made in Leningrad in May 1957 he acknowledged that the professional advice he had received seemed quite reasonable: a 10 to 12 percent annual increase in meat production was the most that could be expected from Soviet agriculture, taking factors like the required increase in feed grain and fodder and the construction of livestock farms into account. This meant that it would take twenty years to reach the American level of production.

Intoxicated by the success of the Virgin Land Program, however, Khrushchev was in no mood to heed this pessimistic advice. He dismissed it as bureaucratic caution. (In fact, it turned out to be wildly optimistic—twenty-five years later, in 1983, Soviet meat production was 58 kilograms per person, while American meat production had increased to 118 kilograms per person). He toured the country, exhorting the population to reach the American level of meat production in three or four years. Finally, at the end of May, he addressed a public meeting in Leningrad and proclaimed that the Soviet Union could soon rival the United States in meat and milk production—it could and should be done within four years, although it might take five years to reach the target of 100 kilograms of meat per person. This promise, proclaimed on behalf of the Central Committee, had never been discussed or authorized by either the Central Committee or the Presidium. Khrushchev's opponents in the Presidium (dubbed the anti-Party group), used it to initiate a political crisis.[14] Their attempt to unseat Khrushchev failed and served only to stiffen his determination to prove that he was right.

But no matter how hard Khrushchev pressed his targets for meat production, they could not be achieved. In 1958, 7.7 million tons were produced, a rise of only 4 percent. Livestock production in the Soviet Union was very backward. More than half of all animal products came from private plots. The *kolkhoz* and *sovkhoz* livestock farms were poorly mechanized and only 5 percent of the labor involved made use of machinery.[15] Most of the milking, for example, was done by hand. Procurement prices for meat were still below production costs. As a result, state purchases of meat did not generate a profit that could be invested in improving and developing this branch of agriculture. On the contrary, increasing their livestock would increase their financial losses. Thus there was no incentive for the *kolkhozy* to increase their cattle herds. The expectation that exhortation would produce a rapid growth of livestock products was simply unreasonable. On the contrary, the *kolkhozy* demanded state subsidies when they were ordered to increase their quotas for meat production.

In 1959 Khrushchev put enormous pressure on regional Party organizations to make meat production their first priority and to mobilize all possible resources to achieve a 60 to 70 percent increase. This caused some bizarre adventures, the most notorious of which became known as the "Ryazan fiasco." An increase in meat production in Ryazan was achieved by slaughtering more animals and buying livestock from other regions to replenish the local herds.[16] The slaughter of farm animals increased elsewhere, too, and as a result meat production rose to 8.9 million tons in 1959. This represented an increase of 14 percent, far short of Khrushchev's target. In any case, production could not be maintained at this level and in 1960 the number of cattle and pigs declined. Annual production fell to 8.7 million tons and it remained more or less at this level until the end of the Khrushchev era. In 1964 the per capita production of meat was 36 kilograms, very little more than the 1957 level. The annual consumption of milk and eggs was lower than in 1957 and the production of milk and eggs was stagnant between 1959 and 1964. In real terms this represented a decline in production, since the population increased by about 12 percent in that period and the urban population grew by 17 percent.

Khrushchev made a last desperate attempt to save his plan in 1962. He increased the procurement prices for meat and other animal products, while increasing the retail price of meat by 30 to 40 percent without allowing any compensation for low-paid workers. This was the first increase of food prices since 1947, and it caused such widespread dissatisfaction that there were some strikes. The most dramatic strike took place in Novocherkassk. It developed into a demonstration and confrontation which was suppressed by troops, with many casualties among the local population.[17]

THE NEW PAY POLICY

The unpredictable system whereby the *kolkhozniki* were paid for their *trudodni* only once a year, and then in products which were left over after the *kolkhoz* had met all its other obligations, had always been very unpopular. It was certainly not the way to stimulate higher productivity. After Stalin's death, when the political climate became more relaxed and the Stalinist criminal code had been suspended, there was a spontaneous reduction in the total number of *trudodni* which the *kolkhozniki* were prepared to work without knowing their real value. The increased procurement prices made more cash available to the collective farms and the Plenum held in September 1953 recommended that the system of advance payments should be improved. The practice was finally introduced of giving each *kolkhoz* member four modest advance payments per year (between 10 and 15 percent of the *trudodni* which had been worked in the previous three months). It was also recommended that summer payments should include fodder and hay for private livestock. In an effort to stimulate production of certain crops a joint Central Committee and Council of Ministers decree of September 21, 1953, recommended that 25 percent of the cash revenues from the sales of vegetables and potatoes should be paid in advance to those who worked in potato and vegetable production brigades. In 1954 a similar system was introduced for those involved in the cultivation of flax, hemp, other technical crops, melons, watermelons, and fruit. Soon the system of advance payments became very complex, while the payments themselves remained random. In 1956 an attempt was made to standardize the procedure: there were to be regular monthly advances in both cash and kind, and *kolkhozy* were to distribute 25 percent of their cash revenues from all crops, meat, and milk in advance payments. This was very close to a system of monthly salaries, although the cash advances remained modest and the payments in kind remained irregular and unpredictable.

It seemed rational to try to work out a system of monthly cash advances in the form of a stable, guaranteed sum which did not vary according to the revenue earned each month by the *kolkhoz*. It was calculated in 1958 that the total annual cash payments to the *kolkhozniki* should be 401 percent of the 1952 level.[18] In fact, this only came to 400 rubles per annum, a very modest sum (all current statistical records are expressed in new rubles, introduced in 1960 when old rubles were exchanged for new in the ratio of 10 to 1 and salaries and prices were reduced accordingly). The average income was higher in the south than in the north, where monthly cash payments were paid in only a quarter of the *kolkhozy*. When the poorer *kolkhozy* were pressed by local authorities to introduce regular cash payments, they reduced the payments in kind. Over the country as a whole, payments in kind did not increase between 1952 and 1958, and the distribution of grain in payment actually declined, despite the increase in production.

Ignoring the reduction of payments in kind, Khrushchev declared that the increase in the cash income earned by the *kolkhozniki* represented social progress and indicated that the differences between the rural and urban population were gradually being eliminated. Some of the richer *kolkhozy* cancelled the *trudoden* system entirely and replaced it with monthly cash wages. Although this would have been a progressive move in an economically developed country, it proved to be premature in the

Soviet Union. The decline of earnings in kind created a demand in rural areas for the same food products which were on sale in the cities and the trade system was insufficiently developed to undertake the universal distribution of food supplies. Rural retail shops were unable to satisfy the demands, and peasants began visiting the towns frequently to buy bread, meat, and dairy products and to spend their accumulated cash. The tradition of home-made and home-processed foods declined and the state food industry proved unable to cope with the increased demand.

THE REORGANIZATION BLUNDERS

The abolition of the MTS was not Khrushchev's only serious organizational blunder. The problem was that he was dynamic and energetic, but very impatient. He was constantly carried away by ideas of reorganization. His numerous trips around the country almost always resulted in the precipitous dismissal of various officials with whose work he was dissatisfied. In September 1959 he spent several weeks abroad, first in the United States and then in China, where he attended the tenth-anniversary celebrations of the Chinese Revolution. He returned by train, stopping off to visit the big Soviet cities en route. In Novosibirsk he visited Akademgorodok, the new science town and center of the Siberian branch of the Academy of Sciences of the USSR, which he had created in 1957. He was upset to discover that some of Lysenko's professional opponents were working there. He ordered their immediate dismissal. Professor N. P. Dubinin, the director of the Institute of Genetics, lost his position and the local Obkom secretary received a strict reprimand.

Although the virgin land harvest had been promising at the end of August, by October there was chaos in the area. There were very few grain elevators, and piles of grain had not been moved to safe storage facilities. Transport shortages, poor roads, and an early winter combined to damage much of the grain that had been stored in the open fields. Kirichenko, second in command after Khrushchev and in charge of the Party Presidium in Khrushchev's absence, was held responsible. When Khrushchev returned to Moscow, Kirichenko was demoted to the position of director of a *sovkhoz* in the Penza region, and in 1960 the Central Committee stripped him of his Party and state positions. The minister of agriculture, Matskevich, a man of great experience, was also dismissed and sent to work in the virgin land areas. He was replaced by M. A. Olshansky, one of Lysenko's disciples who had no practical agricultural experience. Khrushchev seemed determined to turn the Ministry of Agriculture from an administrative organ into a propaganda center for modern methods. Lysenko was reappointed president of the All-Union Lenin Academy of Agricultural Sciences and head of the vast network of agricultural research. He immediately began to dismiss the people who opposed his pseudoscientific theories and methods.

By the end of 1961 Olshansky had demonstrated his incompetence and been dismissed. He was replaced by a minor administrator, K. G. Pysin, but he also survived in the job for only a short period. In 1962 Khrushchev was so impressed by the results achieved by a successful *sovkhoz* in the Lipetsk region that he appointed the director, I. P. Volovchenko, minister of agriculture. Pysin was demoted to the position of deputy. But Volovchenko had no experience of working at governmental level, and the Ministry of Agriculture lost practical control over the country. When Khrushchev himself was dismissed in 1964, Matskevich was reinstated as minister of agriculture and soon promoted to become a deputy chairman of the Council of Ministers. But this rapid sequence of ministerial appointments and dismissals was not an exception. There was a similar turnover of administrators in the Ministry of State Farms, the State Planning Committee (particularly in its agricultural section), the State Committee for Procurements, and other government and Party organs.

In January 1961 Khrushchev presented a proposal to a Central Committee Plenum for the radical reorganization of the whole system of agricultural education and administration. It was decided that the All-Union and Union Republican Ministries of Agriculture and of State Farms should be relieved of the bureaucratic responsibility of financing the *kolkhozy* and *sovkhozy,* supplying them with machinery and cadres and supervising agricultural administration. They were to concentrate on scientific direction instead—giving examples and advice, and disseminating knowledge through literature and through experiments and research at the educational institutions which were to become part of the ministerial system. Agricultural colleges were transferred from the Ministry of Higher Education to the Ministries of Agriculture. To facilitate their new functions, the administrative offices of the All-Union Ministry of Agriculture were moved to Mikhailovskoye *sovkhoz*, 100 kilometers from Moscow. Those of the Ministry of Agriculture of the RSFSR were transferred to Iakhroma *sovkhoz*, 120 kilometers from Moscow and the ministries of the other constituent republics were similarly moved out of the capitals to various farms. They were charged with the task of setting up large model farms where official visitors from other parts of the country could observe the latest agricultural techniques and then imitate them.

As with Khrushchev's other reforms, the move took place overnight, without the necessary construction of office buildings or housing. The All-Union Ministry, for example, was housed in the Mikhailovskoye sanatorium. The staff had to commute daily from Moscow in special buses along poor roads. The journey took two to three hours each way. Visitors to the Ministry and delegates invited to the various conferences held by the Ministry also had to stay in hotels in Moscow and commute. The entire staff, from administrative personnel down to the canteen workers, was obliged to devote some time to working in the fields, testing new equipment, or performing basic chores like weeding or digging potatoes. Within a year more than 1,700 of a staff of 2,200 had resigned, and the most senior positions were filled by new, underqualified personnel. Contacts with other parts of the country deteriorated. In most cases it proved impossible to construct the kind of model farm envisaged by Khrushchev. By the time Khrushchev was dismissed in 1964, proper housing had not yet been completed.

The attempt to relocate agricultural institutes and technical schools on *sovkhozy* and teaching farms was a similar failure.

Khrushchev had wanted to create American-style college campuses, but he had not considered the financial outlay involved. He insisted that the transfer should be completed within two or three years, but neither the State Planning Committee (Gosplan) nor the Ministry of Finance had the funds to move more than a hundred educational establishments. The plan was later abandoned—it would have cost 50 billion rubles, more than the entire agricultural budget for several years. But in the meanwhile several billion rubles were spent on the scheme in 1961–1964 and the admission of students was reduced. Moreover, thousands of professors and teachers changed their jobs to avoid being transferred from the cities.

Nineteen sixty-one was a bad agricultural year, and for the third year in succession the targets of the plan were not reached. Production increased by only 2.5 percent and the increase in the collection of marketable grain was less than 1 percent. Instead of analyzing the causes of the failure (the weather was good in 1961), Khrushchev immediately began thinking of new reforms. At the March and November Central Committee Plenums he introduced plans for a radical change in the entire Party structure. These plans proved to be extremely unpopular.

Under the existing situation the oblast Party committee, together with the Executive Committee of the oblast Soviet, was in complete charge of the oblast. The first secretary of the Party committee was the undisputed master. Traditionally, the second secretary took responsibility for agriculture. Under Khrushchev's new scheme, every oblast Party committee was to be split into independent agricultural and industrial committees. The Executive Committee of the Soviet was to be split in the same way. Thus the principle of administration by territory was to be replaced by administration by category of production. The agricultural committees, however, had few financial and organizational resources. Moreover, the need for manpower from the cities increased, and the agricultural Party committees had no power to recruit urban factory or office workers for seasonal agricultural labor. The industrial committees, now free of responsibility for agricultural performance, no longer had any incentive to lend industrial workers. Without this traditional assistance, many crops simply rotted in the fields. The autumn potato harvest was particularly dependent on the manual labor of a mobilized work force. The grain harvest in 1962 was better than in 1961 (it was actually an all-time record of 140.2 million tons, although it still fell short of the planned target of 170 million tons), but the potato harvest was only 69.7 million tons, the level of Stalin's worst years (1946 and 1951), less than the 80.7 million tons average in 1946–1950 and about 15 million tons less than the 84.3 million tons harvested in 1061. The 1902 vegetable harvest also declined, and the decline continued in 1963 (although the weather was then partly responsible).

In 1962 Khrushchev also changed the geographic administrative units, which had been in existence for years. Each oblast had been divided into twenty or thirty districts (*raiony*), in which the district administration was centered in a small town or large village. Khrushchev decided to create larger districts, in the hope that this would reduce the district bureaucracy and allow the selection of more competent people. In fact, the new system created anarchy and disorder, and once again part of the problem was the speed with which the changes were to be introduced.

The abolition of many of the traditional functions of the agricultural ministries complicated the task of administration. The ministerial network at regional and district level was partially preserved in order to create the model farms. But the government required statistical information to follow developments in all the regions, and the Central Statistical Bureau was given the task of collecting statistics. It was forced to establish its own network, but it did not have the administrative power to take any action if the figures were poor or if immediate intervention was required to improve performance. Agricultural planning was taken over by Gosplan, but it could only set general targets. It had neither the personnel nor the expertise to plan current work for different seasons in different regions. Two new state committees were created: the State Committee for Agricultural Machinery, to deal with equipment, spares, and fertilizer; and the State Committee for Agricultural Procurement (which, in effect, reestablished the

Ministry of Procurement, which had been abolished in a ministerial reorganization in 1957). In 1962 the State Committee for Agricultural Procurement was given the power to undertake current agricultural planning. The agricultural departments of the Central Committee and of the Committee for State and Party Control were enlarged to deal with administrative problems. Khrushchev also proposed creating an All-Union Committee on Agriculture, but it did not become operational before his dismissal. In 1962 a new administrative network was created, called the Territorial Production Administration, to replace the ministerial network. About 1,000 units were set up over the country to supervise production and procurement. However, the units did not coincide with the geographic, regional, or district organizations.

Far from producing a reduction in the agricultural bureaucracy, Khrushchev's reforms instituted a vast proliferation, with a consequent deterioration in coordination and communication. The result was anarchy and chaos. The *kolkhozy* and *sovkhozy* continued their routine work, but the quality of their work did not improve and most of the state investments in agriculture were wasted. Khrushchev was incapable of admitting his mistakes. Instead he tried desperately to improve the situation by personal interference. He toured the country from early spring to the beginning of the winter, visiting *sovkhozy* and *kolkhozy* and making speeches about how to grow fruit and cotton in Uzbekistan and corn in the central regions, and what rotation system worked best. He crusaded against fallow fields, promised that the production of mineral fertilizer would be tripled within a few years, and advertised Lysenko's pseudoscientific innovations (such as the hybridization of traditional Russian cattle with British Jersey and Channel Islands breeds). In July 1962 he brought the whole Party Presidium to the Lysenko experimental station near Moscow and lectured them about the importance of Lysenko's achievements.

4. The Agricultural Crisis of 1963

Nineteen sixty-three was Khrushchev's last full year of tenure. In some ways it was also the worst year of the Khrushchev decade. His popularity had been declining steadily since 1959, but it reached its lowest ebb in 1963 when a disaster in agriculture led to food shortages and long queues for bread even in the grain-producing regions of the North Caucasus and the Ukraine. The shortages were only partly due to adverse weather conditions. In many ways they were self inflicted.

There was a mild drought in the virgin lands in 1963. However, the yields in Kazakhstan declined from the 9 to 10 centners per hectare that had been achieved in good years to only 4.4 centners per hectare. The total harvest in the virgin lands was the lowest since 1955. The land had been overexploited and had suffered a loss of natural fertility. The program had been introduced in 1954 as a temporary palliative, to utilize the natural fertility of idle land. But the shortage of manpower and the absence of an experienced local agricultural population had made it necessary to select a simple monoculture method of agriculture. It had been expected that the financial gains from the first good harvests would make it possible to create better-organized settlements and introduce a more complex agriculture with normal rotation and farm animals. Attention would then be turned to improving the more populated traditional agricultural regions of the North Caucasus, Volga basin, Ukraine, and central and western regions. In fact, the enormous fluctuations in the harvest in Kazakhstan and Eastern Siberia forced many of the first settlers to leave the land. They were replaced by newly recruited urban dwellers, who often had no intention of settling permanently. The exclusive cultivation of wheat continued, and more and more new land (42 million hectares at the beginning of the 1960s) was cultivated. The continued single-crop cultivation caused a heavy infestation of weeds, precluding any possibility of applying fertilizers or increasing yields.

Soviet industry was not yet producing sufficient agricultural machinery and equipment to supply both the virgin lands and the traditional agricultural areas. Priority was given to the newly developed lands, and technical and financial assistance to the established agricultural areas declined after 1958. As a result, the average grain harvest in these areas remained at the 1955 level, and in some regions it decreased. At the same time, after 1956 the virgin land harvest never again lived up to expectations. Throughout the entire Seven Year Plan (1959–1965), the grain quota for the virgin lands was met only once and the average yield per hectare for 1959–1964 was lower than for the previous five years. This meant that the unit cost of production rose. In the European part of the Soviet Union the annual production of grain per capita was lower in 1961–1964 than in 1913. The entire grain stock produced in a given year was consumed that year, so that the government had no surpluses with which to establish reserves. This made the economy of the country alarmingly vulnerable to weather conditions.

Another serious problem to manifest itself in the early 1960s was soil erosion. It quickly became an ecological disaster. Earlier scientific research had already pointed to the danger and folly of ploughing millions of hectares of open steppe land unprotected by forest zones. But the urgency of the drive to open up the virgin lands left no time to consider local soil conditions or topography or to employ measures to prevent erosion. Not only were fertile lands ploughed, but also saline areas and large expanses of light sandy loams, which were soon blown away by the wind. Hundreds of thousands of hectares were destroyed by winds as early as 1955 and 1957. But antierosion measures were expensive and Khrushchev was loath to invest in them. In their absence it would have been wiser to avoid increasing the cultivated area. Preserving long strips of natural steppe land between fields would have protected the fields from wind erosion. Moreover, different methods of ploughing and cultivation should have been tried, and autumn ploughing should have been avoided because it turned down the more protected stubble topsoil. Herbicides should have been used to deal with weeds. In fact, these measures were finally introduced much later. In the dry summer of 1963, however, wind erosion affected several million hectares. In Pavlodar oblast alone, 1.5 million hectares were "blown away."[19] But this was only the beginning. In the spring severe windstorms, with winds raging up to 95 miles an hour, lifted millions of tons of fertile soil from the virgin regions and carried it miles away to the foothills of the Sayan mountains and other mountain chains. A dust cloud hid the sun for several days, irrigation canals were choked, and drifts of soil more than two meters high were formed along some stands of trees. Towns and villages were covered with dirt. The arable layer was so completely removed from thousands of hectares that the underlying bedrock was exposed. Precise data on the damaged areas have never been published, but millions of hectares were involved. It was a substantial ecological disaster.

Thus, although the drought of 1963 was not particularly severe, its effects combined with those of the widespread erosion to reduce the harvest in the eastern parts of the Soviet Union seriously—the total harvest was 38 million tons, the smallest since 1955. In 1963, 10.6 million tons was produced in Kazakhstan, 2.5 times less than the target and far less than the procurement quota. The total harvest for the country was 107.5 million tons, 70 million tons less than the target and about the same level as in 1955. But by 1963 the urban population had increased by 30 million (from 86.3 million to 114.7 million). The amount of marketable grain (44.8 million tons) was greater than the 1955 level (36.5 million tons), but it was 14 million tons less than the 1962 level and it was inadequate for the needs of the country. The potato and vegetable harvest was also poor, reaching only the 1955 level. As a result there were food shortages, and they were not confined to the urban areas.

The primary reason for the rural shortages was that Khrushchev had launched an unjustified and arbitrary offensive against private plots and private farm animals in 1960. This was a complete reversal of his previous policy of encouraging private agriculture. In 1959 it had become clear that Soviet agriculture would not meet the highly inflated goals of the new Seven Year Plan. As so often before, the blame was put on the *kolkhozniki*. They were accused of spending too much time cultivating their private plots, and too little working on the *kolkhoz*. In 1961 and 1962

Khrushchev revived the policy of putting economic pressure on the *kolkhozniki* to force them to concentrate on their work on the *kolhoz*. A major press compaign was launched: private plots were said to be a relic of capitalism and *kolkhozniki* who sold their produce on the free market were branded as speculators. In fact, the country could ill afford to discourage private agriculture, since it contributed a substantial proportion of the country's total food output. In the late 1950s, the 20 percent of the produce grown on private plots which reached the markets comprised no less than 50 percent of the fresh vegetables and potatoes, and about 80 percent of the fruit available in the cities.

The harassment of the *kolkhozniki* led to a sharp drop in the output of foodstuff. The amount that reached the urban markets fell and market prices rose. The growing urban population became even more dependent on government food supplies and so did the *kolkhozniki*, whose drive and initiative had been discouraged. At the same time the meat quotas to be fulfilled by the *kolkhozy* were increased. *Kolkhoz* chairmen began to demand that private livestock be sold to the collective farms. In 1959 alone, more than 3 million cows were purchased in this way and by 1963 the number of privately owned cattle had fallen by several million. There was a similar decrease in the number of privately owned pigs, sheep, goats, and poultry.[20] More serious than this decline, the livestock that had been forcibly purchased and integrated into the *kolkhoz* herds was inadequately fed. In the Ukraine, for example, the herds were increased by 43 percent, while the amount of feed allocated for the livestock rose by only 1 percent.[21] As a result, the aggregate meat and milk production did not reflect the increased size of the collective herds. The average yield of milk per cow decreased throughout the country, and milk became scarce. Moreover, when 12 million privately owned cattle were transferred to collective ownership, the *kolkhozy*, far from selling supplies to the state, became dependent on the state for feed grain. Because of the scarcity, the promises that had been made to those who were forced to sell their livestock—that they would be supplied with milk, butter, and meat from the *kolkhoz* stocks—could not be kept. It would have been far wiser to increase the collective herds gradually, keeping pace with the increase in feed supplies.

Restrictions were placed on the previously encouraged practice of raising livestock in suburban areas. In 1953 Khrushchev had said that people living in the suburbs or in small towns could own their own livestock. The Supreme Soviet now passed a law forbidding the practice. The real reason for the law was the scarcity of feed grain: the government was reluctant to sell feed grain to individuals. Some suburban residents fed their livestock on bread and the purchase of bread for this purpose became a criminal offence. These measures were all extremely unpopular, particularly amongst the peasants. They certainly did not feel inspired to work longer and harder to increase output. In any case, even if the grain and other agricultural quotas were overfulfilled, they would still be insufficient to feed both the population and the livestock.

Several other planning and administrative errors contributed to the disaster of 1963. Khrushchev interfered with the rotation systems, which traditionally included fallow fields. He also insisted that the acreage under corn should be increased in areas where the climate was unsuitable for this intensive crop. These mistakes combined to transform the comparatively mild drought into a serious agricultural disaster. In October there were shortages of bread in vast areas of the south, the Ukraine, the North Caucasus, and Transcaucasia. People queued for hours to buy two or three kilos of bread and flour disappeared from the shops. The bread supplies in Moscow and Leningrad remained satisfactory, but people from nearby towns arrived in their thousands to buy food. It became apparent that there were no government grain reserves, and that the 1963 harvest was not large enough to feed the nation until the 1964 harvest became available. Rationing would have to be introduced. The situation was extremely embarrassing for Khrushchev. He realized that there were no easy remedies. Calamity could only be avoided by purchasing grain and other foodstuffs abroad. This would be the first time in Russian and Soviet history that such extensive emergency measures had been required. Moreover, there were insufficient hard currency reserves to pay for the purchases. Khrushchev was forced to make a drastic decision—to use the available hard currency reserves and to sell some of the Soviet stockpile of gold to raise more.

The first consignment of 500 tons of gold ingots were shipped to foreign gold market. Soviet trade delegations immediately began purchasing grain (mainly from Canada and Australia, but from many other countries as well, including West Germany, France, and the United States). A consignment of rye was purchased in Finland, meat was imported from Australia and South America, butter from New Zealand and Scandinavia. Canned meat was bought from China. The Soviet Union, the largest agricultural country in the world, had fallen into agricultural dependency on capitalist countries, a dependency from which it has not yet been able to extricate itself.

Instead of making a serious attempt to analyze the real causes of the failure, Khrushchev cast around for new, magical reorganizations. He circulated some notes to Party activists to stimulate discussion of radical measures. His new ideas were highly controversial. He recommended the creation of seventeen agricultural zones to replace the traditional regional pattern with a central city. In addition, he proposed the creation of twelve state committees to supervise and administer twelve individual specialized branches of agriculture (animal husbandry, poultry, grain, soul improvement, mechanization, chemical fertilizers, etc.), each with a staff of 500 to 600 specialists. A draft proposal was sent to the Central Committee Presidium and to all oblast committees. Khrushchev hoped that his proposals would be discussed and approved at the Central Committee Plenum in November. In August, frantic Party conferences were organized across the country. It was perfectly obvious to everyone except Khrushchev that his project was completely unworkable. It would lead not just to dual (agricultural/industrial) authority, but to a total fragmentation of management. Oblast Party secretaries, already unhappy about their reduced status caused by the split into agricultural and industrial committees, were now concerned at the idea of having twelve different superiors in Moscow.

In fact, Khrushchev's new plans did not come to fruition. Instead of the Central Committee Plenum planned for November, an extraordinary Plenum met in October and insisted on Khrushchev's retirement. Although the Party elite had any number of reasons to be dissatisfied with his performance as leader of Party and state, it is known that agriculture was an important factor in his dismissal. The materials of the Plenum, however, have never been published.

Conclusion

The balance sheet of Khrushchev's agricultural policy is very controversial. What is certain is that he introduced major changes and that some of them were positive. The total acreage of cultivated land increased very substantially and the incomes of the collective farms and of individual *kolkhozniki* grew. The production of chemical fertilizers, pesticides, and herbicides increased and there was a more equitable investment of the country's financial resources, with a rapid increase in the proportion devoted to agriculture. The average production of grain after 1953 grew more than the growth of the population as a whole. However, the rate at which industry was developing (9 to 11 percent per year) continued to attract qualified workers away from the rural areas. As a result, urbanization was too rapid and the problem of supplying high-quality food to the towns and cities was not solved. The fact that there were no signs of famine in any part of the country was certainly an achievement. Bread was cheap and easily available. But this was not enough for a modern industrial country. The main statistical indicators (see Tables 13–17) show clearly where Khrushchev's policies succeeded and where they failed. In general, agricultural production grew more than the increase in the population and at a comparable level to the growth in urban population. This reversed the trend of the post-collectivization and postwar period, when the per capita production actually declined. However, the positive developments of the Khrushchev era were more visible in 1953–1959. In 1960–1964 the growth of agricultural production, and of the other indicators

TABLE 13
Acreage under Grain Crops, Grain Production, and Average Yields

	Acreage (million hectares)	Production	State procurements	Average yields (centners/ha)
		(million tons)		
1913	104.6	86.0	—	8.2
1940	110.5	95.6	36.4	8.6
1954	108.4	85.6	34.6	8.2
1955	126.4	103.7	36.9	8.4
1956	128.3	125.0	54.1	9.8
1958	121.4	134.7	56.6	11.1
1960	115.5	125.5	46.7	10.9
1962	128.7	140.2	56.6	10.9
1963	130.0	107.5	44.8	8.3

Sources: Nar. khoz., 1956, p. 112; 1963, pp. 256, 275; 1974, pp. 304–305, 318, 354.

TABLE 14
Production of Potato, Vegetables, Meat, and Milk
(Million Tons)

	Potato	Vegetables	Meat	Milk
1913	31.9	5.5	5.0	29.4
1954	75.0	11.9	6.3	38.2
1958	86.5	14.9	7.7	58.7
1960	84.4	16.6	8.7	61.7
1962	69.7	16.0	9.5	63.9
1963	71.8	15.2	10.2	61.2

Source: Nar. khoz., 1974, p. 304.

TABLE 15
Population Growth and
Growth in Agricultural Production
(1953 = 100)

| | Population | | Food* | | | | |
	Total	Urban	Grain	Potato	Vegetables	Meat	Milk
1953	100	100	100	100	100	100	100
1964	121	149	158.0	112.9	148.4	155.9	166.5

* The production of food is calculated as an average for 1963 and 1964, based on statistical records. 1963 was a poor year, while 1964 was the best year for all products, with the exception of meat, which was reduced by the excessive slaughter in 1963.

of development (level of mechanization, financial income of the *kolkhozy* and *sovkhozy*), slowed down.

On the negative side of the balance sheet of Khrushchev's effect on Soviet agriculture, the production of grain was satisfactory, but the improvement was due to extensive methods of cultivation. Moreover, Khrushchev used Stalinist methods of coercion to force the villages to deliver more meat to the cities than they could afford without disrupting the normal pattern of rural life and work. In 1950 the proportional difference between the total production of meat and state purchases of meat was much higher than in 1960. Livestock production remained an unprofitable branch of agriculture, despite increased procurement prices. As a result, the substantial increase in the number of cattle and other farm animals which was noticeable until 1959 slowed down visibly in 1959–1964. The number of pigs declined from 53.4 million in 1960 to 40.9 million in 1964, reflecting Khrushchev's drive against privately owned livestock. The number of sheep also increased sharply to 136 million in 1960, but then began to decline, while the number of goats and horses declined throughout the Khrushchev era. In 1964 there were only 8.5 million horses, less than in 1946 (10.7 million).

TABLE 16

Deliveries of Chemical Fertilizers[a]

(Million Tons of Active Substance)[b]

	1950	1958	1960	1963
Total	1.26	2.46	2.62	3.60
Nitrogen	0.31	0.68	0.77	1.36
Phosphorus	0.53	1.03	1.09	1.33
Potassium	0.42	0.74	0.76	0.90

Source: Nar. khoz., 1963, p. 300.

[a] Soviet statistics give separate figures for production and for deliveries for agricultural purposes. The latter figures are usually lower, because part of the production of chemical fertilizers is utilized for purposes other than agriculture (in industry, for export, etc.). For our purposes, only the delivery figures for agriculture are relevant.

[b] It is usual to give statistics of fertilizers in what are called "standard units." In the Soviet Union the standard unit for nitrogen fertilizers is taken as ammonium sulphate (NH_4SO_4). Because there are many other fertilizers (for example, potassium nitrate, sodium nitrate, ammonium nitrate, etc.), it is more useful to give the amount of active substance delivered (NH_3 for nitrogen fertilizers, K_2O for potassium products, and P_2O_5 for phosphate fertilizers). In Soviet statistics the standard unit for potassium fertilizers is a product with 41.6 percent of active substance (K_2O). The standard unit for phosphates is less concentrated, containing 18.7 percent of active substance (P_2O_5). Many of the types of phosphate fertilizers which were still in use in the Soviet Union in 1950–1963 were of poor quality (for example, phosphorite powder with low concentrations of soluble phosphate).

The amalgamation and conversion of bankrupt *kolkhozy* into *sovkhozy* continued. Between 1958 and 1964 the number of *kolkhozy* dropped from 67,700 to 37,600, while the number of *sovkhozy* grew from 6,002 to 10,078. The tendency to merge several small *kolkhozy* into a large *sovkhoz* meant that the amount of arable *sovkhoz* land (105.6 million hectares) more or less equalled the area cultivated by the *kolkhozy* (111.5 million hectares). The state inherited the heavy debts (unpaid credits, money owed for the machinery bought from the MTS, many years of wages for *trudodni* owed to the workers, etc.) which led to the creation of the new *sovkhozy*. The process of transforming *kolkhozy* into *sovkhozy* was thus very expensive. In 1954–1959 the state paid 25.4 billion old rubles (2.5 billion post-1960 rubles) for this purpose.[22] Since the conversion process was highest in 1960–1961

TABLE 17

Number of Tractors (All Types) and
Combine-Harvesters in Agriculture, 1953–1964

	1953	1958	1960	1962	1963
Tractors	744,000	1,001,000	1,122,000	1,329,000	1,442,000
Combines*	317,600	502,000	497,000	520,000	517,000

Source: Nar. khoz., 1956, pp. 156–157; 1963, p. 332.

* The decline in the number of combines between 1958 and 1960 and the slow increase in later years reflects the negative effects of the abolition of the MTS. The number of combines in the main traditional grain-producing areas declined in these years. In the North Caucasus there were 34,300 combines in 1958, 32,200 in 1960, and 28,000 in 1963. In the Ukraine there were 66,800 combines in 1958, 64,800 in 1958, and 62,200 in 1963. In Kazakhstan, where the virgin lands were, for the most part, cultivated by *sovkhozy* independent of MTS, the picture was slightly different. There were 96,100 combines in 1958, 94,100 in 1960, and 105,100 in 1963. There was a similar trend in other sophisticated machinery. The production of tractors and other, less sophisticated agricultural equipment was less affected by the abolition of the MTS, but the servicing of machinery was poor and the work load per unit declined.

(7,970 *kolkhozy*), the total cost was probably as high as 10 billion new rubles between 1954 and 1964.

However, any overall evaluation of agriculture during the Khrushchev era must conclude that Khrushchev's imprint was positive. Rural living standards improved substantially, and there were sufficient food surpluses to support industrial growth. Nonetheless, the country was still unable to provide a balanced, healthy diet to the population. The average diet contained sufficient calories, but there was a shortage of animal proteins, vegetables, and fruit, particularly in the urban diet.

Martin McCauley, one of the most thoughtful researchers of Khrushchev's agricultural reforms, offers the following diagnosis of the "Khrushchev syndrome":

The thinking behind most of his reforms . . . was fundamentally correct. Where Khrushchev went wrong was to take everything to excess . . . A fervent believer in the virtues of socialist agriculture, Khrushchev sometimes undid with one hand the good he had done with the other.[23]

This is a fair assessment. By 1964 even Khrushchev had finally realized the need for more intensive development. Agriculture was receiving a far larger proportion of state resources than previously, but the returns on the investments were too modest.

However, the most important change of the Khrushchev era related to the human factor. Khrushchev's main contribution to history was to end Stalin's terror and to begin to rehabilitate millions of Stalin's victims. His contribution to Soviet agriculture is similar. He demolished the notion that the peasants are the enemies of the proletarian state and have to be treated with suspicion. He ended the grave injustice with which both Lenin and Stalin treated the people who produce food, society's most essential and valuable commodity. His rural childhood and early work as a miner made it possible for him to identify both with peasants and workers. If he had had the advantage of an education in agriculture, his reforms might have been more successful. But it is certain that none of the other contenders for power after Stalin's death would have done as well. Khrushchev failed to turn Soviet agriculture into the success story about which he dreamed, but if Malenkov, Molotov, Kaganovich, or Beria had become Party leader in 1953, the situation would have been much worse and the methods of terror and coercion would have taken much longer to be eradicated.

The leaders who replaced Khrushchev in 1964 were of a different caliber. They were bureaucrats, not revolutionaries. They were better educated. They relied on collective leadership and consensus rather than on impulse and intuition. The second part of this book will investigate whether they were any better able to resolve the chronic problems of Soviet agriculture.

Part Two

ECONOMIC SOLUTIONS, 1965-1986

The first part of this book has dealt with the period of Soviet history when most events, including the development of agriculture, were very strongly influenced by the personality of the leader, reflecting his political ideas and whims. It makes sense, therefore, to deal with Lenin's, Stalin's, and Khrushchev's eras in Soviet economic and agricultural development as discrete, chronological periods. It is much more difficult to call the period after 1965 "Brezhnev's era" and it is virtually impossible to think of the Andropov, Chernenko, or Gorbachev eras. In the latter case, all three leaders essentially continued the preceding policy with some modifications. The policy involved intensification and the use of economic mechanisms, the distinctive features of post-Khrushchev agricultural development.

At the Central Committee Plenum in October 1964, which dismissed Khrushchev, the decision was made to separate the positions of Party leader and chairman of the Council of Ministers permanently. Most of the excesses of the Khrushchev period had occurred after 1958, when he assumed both posts and became too powerful. A. N. Kosygin, a seasoned technocrat and administrator, was appointed prime minister. He had very little agricultural experience, but he was a good economist and a relatively independent man. The division of power meant that the Party leader had to work through a collective leadership. Brezhnev would have to win the consensus of his Politburo colleagues (the Party Presidium reverted to being called the Politburo in 1966) before any important decisions and reform could be implemented. In general this suited Brezhnev. He was a cautious leader and he preferred not to take risks.

A good indication of the difference between Brezhnev's approach and that of Khrushchev is provided by the way in which they made pronouncements about agriculture. Khrushchev often delivered spontaneous speeches without getting preliminary approval of his texts. There would then be an "editing" gap of a week or ten days before the speech could be published. Many of his more outrageous oral pronouncements failed to be printed. Brezhnev, on the other hand, spoke from texts carefully prepared by special groups and previously circulated to the relevant specialized Party and state departments for discussion and suggestions. Some of his initial ideas would be changed or delayed in the process, but the Party and state *apparatchiki* were delighted by his careful approach, which avoided the rush and impatience that had been typical of Khrushchev. Brezhnev never forced the decisions of his own advisors on his colleagues. The opinions of all Politburo and Secretariat members were considered important. There was a concomitant collective responsibility for failure. For a proper understanding of the changes which followed the end of the Khrushchev era, it is important to keep these changes in the decision-making process in mind.

Unlike Khrushchev, Brezhnev was the son of a steel worker. His first work experience was in a steel mill, although in the mid-1920s he enrolled in a land reclamation and surveying technical college in Kursk. After graduating he worked as a land surveyor in Byelorussia, in the Kursk region, and in the Urals. His job entailed allocating land to commune peasants whose strips were reorganized. In 1928–1929 he was in charge of the land department in a district of the Sverdlovsk region. In 1930 he returned to the Ukraine and enrolled in the Dneprodzerzhinsk Metallurgical Institute, graduating in 1935. By 1939 he had become a full-time professional Party official. When he was appointed first secretary of the Moldavian Central Committee in 1950, he became more involved in agricultural problems—Moldavia was primarily an agricultural area, producing fruit, vegetables, grapes, and tobacco. (It was there that he first met Konstantin Chernenko, the man he later designated as his successor). He became even more concerned with agriculture when Khrushchev selected him to lead the Virgin Land Program in Kazakhstan in 1954–1956. Brezhnev certainly knew far more about agriculture than his colleagues within the Party Presidium before and after the Twenty-second Party Congress in 1961. (It was only when Fyodr Kulakov, Central Committee secretary for agriculture, was elected to the Politburo in 1971 that a professional agricultural expert joined the top Party echelons. Gorbachev, who replaced Kulakov in 1978, also had a formal agricultural education.)

The first task facing Brezhnev and Kosygin in 1964 was urgent "de-Khrushchevization." The territorial oblast Party committees were restored and the bifurcation of the Party and governmental hierarchy into agricultural and industrial sectors was abolished. The Economic Councils and State Committees were replaced by traditional ministries with broad powers for directing particular branches of the economy. The All-Union Agricultural Ministry and the RSFSR Ministry of Agriculture were allowed to return from rural exile to their former premises in Moscow. The other Union Republican Ministries of Agriculture also returned to the capitals of their respective republics. Khrushchev's plan to move the agricultural institutes into the countryside was abandoned.

Agriculture remained an economic priority and a special Plenum was planned for March 1965 to introduce reforms. This Plenum (at which Brezhnev presented the main report) and the books and papers published after it are considered the turning point in Soviet agriculture and the beginning of a "scientific" approach to the problems. The main decisions reached by the Plenum restored some of the trends originally introduced by Khrushchev in 1953–1955. Procurement prices were increased significantly in the hope that this would both improve the financial situation of the *kolkhozy* and *sovkhozy* and act as a stimulus for production. There was to be a rational reorganization of agriculture in the virgin land areas to decrease the vulnerability to soil erosion. Private plots were restored to their former size and all restrictions on the private ownership of livestock were lifted. Farms were given more freedom to decide what crops to grow and this led to an immediate reduction of the acreage under corn. Various recommendations were made about increasing the production and use of chemical fertilizers, pesticides, and herbicides, raising the level of mechanization, changing the planning system, and so on. The changes all aimed to encourage intensification and specialization of agricultural production.

The decisions taken at the Central Committee Plenum in March 1965 remained in force for many years and formed the foundations of Soviet agriculture as it is at present, with its achievements and failures. Later Plenum, Party Congress, and Council of Ministers decisions from 1966 to 1986 developed and extended the process that was begun in 1965. For this reason, and because one-man leadership was absent, it is appropriate to abandon the chronological approach that we have followed up to now in this study of Soviet agriculture. Instead, individual branches of modern Soviet agriculture and agricultural economy will be examined in turn (although a certain historical perspective will be retained within each chapter).

Chapter 7

The Production of Food
and Technical Crops

In Soviet literature and statistics, agriculture is divided into two main areas: field (or soil) agriculture *(zemledeliye)* and livestock *(zhivotnovodstvo)*. Field agriculture includes the production of grain, potatoes, vegetables, fruit, and technical crops, while the production of fodder crops (hay and silage crops) is considered part of livestock farming. We will adhere to a similar division in the following discussion. In this chapter the most important food and technical crops—those which occupy at least a million hectares of cultivated land—will be considered.

1. The Grain Problem

When Khrushchev left for his holiday at the Black Sea resort of Pitsunda in October 1964, he felt reasonably confident that agriculture was once more doing well. It was a great relief after the disaster of 1963. Although he had good reason for optimism, the excellent harvest did not save him from the wrath of his colleagues. The production of grain reached a new record of 152 million tons in 1964. The virgin lands once again produced a good harvest and the production of marketable grain reached the highest-ever level of 68.3 million tons. There was a record harvest of other food and technical crops as well. Brezhnev was less fortunate in his first agricultural season. The organizational and economic measures adopted at the March 1965 Central Committee Plenum were sensible and necessary, but the weather was bad, with drought in the eastern regions. Antierosion and antidrought measures had not yet been implemented and the fields were still heavily contaminated by weeds. The average grain yield in Kazakhstan was only 3.1 centners per hectare. Total grain production declined to 121 million tons and state procurements were only 36.3 million tons, less than in 1963 and even less than in 1955. The total harvest was higher than in those years, but more grain was left in the villages to feed the increasing livestock population. Large quantities of wheat and corn had to be purchased abroad once more.

The Shortage of Food and Feed Grain

A new Five Year Plan was adopted at the Twenty-third Party Congress in 1966. The state planned to invest 41 billion rubles in agricultural projects in 1966–1971, considerably more than in the previous decade. A set of agro-technical measures including protective strips of uncultivated land, the more extensive use of herbicides against weeds, and the use of deep but "mild" ploughing (without turning over the topsoil) was recommended for the eastern drought- and erosion-prone regions. The "Mal'tsev" system of agriculture (named after Terentii Mal'tsev, an agronomist on an experimental farm in the Kurgan region) had been developed in the 1950s, and the system of ploughing had proved effective against drought, but only in combination with other measures.[1] To some extent the plowing system involved returning to the methods that had been used before the modern plough (with a moldboard to turn the furrow slice cut by the ploughshare) was designed in the eighteenth century. (The more advanced metal one-piece share and moldboard was invented in the United States in the nineteenth century.) The ability of the plough to turn the topsoil upside down was considered an important advance, allowing crop residues and weeds to be buried. Mal'tsev challenged the modern method on the grounds that it destroyed the soil and increased the loss of moisture. He recommended a method which combined deep-disc ploughing with turning over only a very thin layer of topsoil. In this way the optimal soil structure would be retained and erosion would be reduced. The system had its problems. It was difficult to use on fields that were heavily infested by weeds, and it wasn't very effective in years with good precipitation. It required mass production of new ploughs, and needed further testing on different types of soil. However, the use of herbicides, and the recurrence of drought, created conditions favorable to acceptance of the Mal'tsev system.

The implementation of a set of drought-protective measures (which were developed by the Research Institute of Grain Cultivation in Kazakhstan) made it impossible to lose a whole harvest. Even in very dry seasons, the new agronomy promised at least 6 to 8 centners per hectare, double the yield of the harvest in 1955 or 1965. The weather was as bad in 1967 and 1968 as it had been in 1965, but the harvests were much better. But the plans to develop livestock farming and to increase the production of poultry, milk, and eggs put continuing pressure on the grain sector. The growth of the population, particularly the urban population, also increased the demand for grain. Another factor which contributed to the rising demand for food crops was the demographic change taking place in rural areas. The birthrate in the western Slavonic regions was very low (15 to 16 per 1,000), but it remained high in the predominantly Moslem areas of Central Asia (30 to 40 per 1,000). Central Asia was not self-supporting in food. The local collective and state farms specialized in producing cotton and fruit. The acreage under cotton was so vast that, despite the higher proportion of the rural population, the urban population (including schoolchildren) was mobilized for two to three months every year to help collect the harvest. The combination of a high birthrate and the replacement of grain fields by cotton over the years had added another 20 million people to those who were dependent on the import of grain and other food products from the grain-producing areas. One hundred fifty million to one hundred seventy million metric tons of grain, an amount which would have seemed like an impossible dream to Khrushchev, now became the barc minimum, and continuing imports were required to supplement it.

The total production of grain increased and the average yields improved, but the production targets still could not be met. In 1970, for example, the total grain production set a new record (186.8 million tons), but this was well below the planned target. In 1971 the harvest fell to 181.6 million tons and in 1972 it was a disastrous 168.2 million tons. Grain shortages (particularly of feed grain) had become a chronic disease of Soviet agriculture. The record amount purchased from the United States and Canada in 1972 (40 million tons) became known as "the great grain robbery." It served to increase the world price of grain significantly and thus had a negative effect on poorer countries which also needed to import grain.

The total harvest for 1973 was an astonishing 222.5 million tons, almost double the average production of the Khrushchev decade. State purchases reached 90.5 million tons, more than the average total harvest during the Stalin period. If the harvest could be kept above the level of 200 million tons it would be unnecessary to purchase grain abroad. Soviet planners and experts became convinced that it was possible. Analyzing the factors which had made the 1973 harvest a success indicated that it was the result of *intensification*: improvements in mechanization, the use of chemicals, better organization of agricultural work, and increased productivity had produced a dramatic increase in the harvest without an increase in the total grain acreage. The figures given in Table 18 show that until 1965 the development of Soviet agriculture was extensive and the average grain harvest did not rise above a yield of 10 centners per hectares. It was only after 1965 that the new investments began to pay off and to be reflected in an increase in average yield per hectare. These figures do not, of course, reflect variations between geographic regions. Maximum yields (25 to 30 centners per hectare) were obtained in

TABLE 18

Average Grain Yields, 1940–1985[a]

(Centners per Hectare)

	All grain crops	Winter wheat	Spring wheat	Winter rye
1940	8.6	10.1	6.6	9.1
1951–1955	8.0	11.3	6.9	8.6
1956–1960	10.1	15.3	9.3	9.4
1961–1965	10.2	15.2	7.9	9.1
1966–1970	13.8	18.8	9.1	11.8
1971–1975	14.7	22.5	11.0	13.5
1976–1980	16.0	24.7	12.2	14.0
1981–1985	14.8	22.8	10.1	15.2

Source: Nar. khoz., 1975, p. 319; 1977, p. 203; 1922–1982, pp. 248–250; 1985, pp. 184, 210.

[a] The average yields include not only wheat, but also spring and winter rye, barley, oats, corn, other cereals, and grain-beans (soy, pea, haricot).

1970–1974 in the North Caucasus and the Ukraine. The non-chernozem and eastern regions continued to yield an average of 10 to 13 centners per hectare. In general, the yields of winter wheat were double those of spring wheat. However, attempts to increase the acreage under winter wheat were not very successful—each year the plan called for 40 million hectares of winter wheat and each year it remained unfulfilled. Winter wheat is best planted after leaving fields fallow. The best sowing time is in August and early September, when the harvesting of spring cereals and other crops is still in progress, absorbing most of the available human and technical resources.

The record harvest in 1973 was due to a rare combination of favorable weather conditions throughout the agricultural season across the whole country. The optimism of Soviet officials that the harvest would continue to be more than 200 million tons every year was disappointed the very next year, when the total

TABLE 19

Total Grain Production
and State Procurements, 1974–1986
(Million Tons)

	Total production	State procurements
1974	195.7	73.3
1975	140.1	50.2
1976	223.8	92.1
1977	195.7	68.0
1978	237.4	95.9
1979	179.3	62.8
1980	189.1	69.4
1981	158.0[a]	58.1
1982	186.8	69.7
1983	192.2	75.6
1984	172.6	56.2
1985	191.7	73.5
1986	210.0[b]	NA

Source: Nar. khoz., 1977, pp. 202, 210; 1980, pp. 202, 209; 1985, pp. 180, 193.

[a] The very low harvest of 1981 made the Soviet government to classify all the figures of grain production and procurement for 1981 and subsequent years. Only the U.S. Department of Agriculture estimates[2] were available for Western publications. Figures of grain production were "declassified" in 1986 in *Nar. khoz.* statistical yearbook for 1985. The U.S. estimates proved to be accurate (160 million tons for 1981, 180 for 1982, and so on). The average annual harvest projected in the Five Year Plan for 1981–1985 was 240 million tons.

[b] This figure was reported as preliminary in the Y. Ligachev's "October Revolution Anniversary Report," published in *Pravda* on November 7, 1986.

harvest dropped to 195.7 million tons (see Table 19). It was a disastrous 140 million tons in 1975, the lowest since 1965. Although 140 million tons had represented a record in 1962, by 1975 the total population had increased by 36 million (from 217 million in 1962 to 253 million in 1975). The urban population had increased by 44 million (from 108 million in 1962 to 152 million in 1957). Apart from the requirements of this growing population, extra grain was needed for the large state-owned poultry and livestock farms and the milk factories that had been created around the big industrial centers and capital cities (to supplement *kolkhoz* and *sovkhoz* livestock production, which was still inadequate for the rapidly growing cities). A new branch of the feed and fodder industry, the production of concentrated mixed feed granules, was expanding and consuming large amounts of marketable grain. The Soviet Union also had trade and aid obligations to deliver grain to Cuba, Vietnam, Czechoslovakia, and Poland. The production of beer and vodka also consumed several million tons of grain (the domestic consumption of alcohol and the export of vodka was increasing faster than the average harvests).

It was calculated in the 1970s that the Soviet Union required at least 100 million tons of marketable grain annually. This target was nearly reached three times, in 1973, 1976, and 1978. In every other year the shortfall had to be imported. If one considers the average grain production for the five-year periods 1965–1970 (167.6 million tons), 1971–1975 (181.6 million tons), and 1976–1980 (205.0 million tons), it is clear that there was an annual increase. But this trend was reversed in the 1981–1985 harvest. This was the main reason why grain production figures (and all other relevant data about grain crops) ceased to be published in the statistical records until 1986. In 1979–1984 state grain procurements averaged 60 million tons. The state has been unable to raise the procurement level above the amount procured in Khrushchev's best (and last) year—68.3 million tons. The situation has become no less serious than the grain crises of previous decades.

Soviet statistical yearbooks, textbooks, and the review books which are published periodically to commemorate important anniversaries[3] usually contain impressive graphs showing the growth in grain production and procurement. They are designed to demonstrate progress. However, they do not project the increases (normally shown as the average over a five-year period) against the population growth and the growth in urban population, nor do they show the different proportions of grain consumed by the population and by the livestock farms (an increasing amount). Even if one makes the optimistic assumption that the state procured an average of 70 million tons of marketable grain annually in 1979–1985, this figure only looks impressive if it is compared to the 15 to 16 million tons that Stalin extracted from the peasants by "extraordinary measures" in 1927–1929. But Stalin needed those 15 to 16 million tons for the army and an urban population which numbered 28.7 million. By 1986 the urban population had reached 184 million and a significant proportion of the rural population was normally dependent on state-procured grain. In other words, while grain procurements had grown by 450 percent, the urban population had risen even more, by 650 percent. At the same time, a larger proportion of the marketable grain was now consumed by various industries (for example, the complex feed industry and the alcohol industry) and by the rural population of Central Asia and the northwestern regions of the country. This is why it has become necessary to import from 30 to 50 million tons of grain (in addition to other food products) per annum. Without these imports the average Soviet diet in the cities would be worse than it was in the 1920s.

In the 1970s some articles were published arguing that it is perfectly natural for an industrial power to import food and that the exchange of oil and gas for grain makes economic sense. These arguments were shaken by the grain embargo imposed by President Carter in 1980. They had been weak arguments anyway, since it was clear that much of the grain and other food was being imported from the United States, Canada, France, and other EEC members, countries that were industrially more developed than the Soviet Union. Any lingering idea that importing food was a positive phenomenon finally disappeared in the face of the economic realities of the 1980s—food shortages in Poland, the foreign debt crisis in Eastern Europe, a decline in the production and export of oil in 1982–1985, the fall in oil prices in 1985–1986, and Soviet inability to give food aid to African allies, who were experiencing the worst famine in human history.

In fact, the grain crisis of the 1980s is even more critical than estimates of the amount produced and the procurement levels lead one to believe. It is not only that there are shortages in the total tonnage of marketable grain. There has also been a sub-stantial decline in the quality of grain products, a reduction in the quality and quantity of grain protein, and negative changes in the kind of grain crops which are cultivated. Some of the more serious of these problems will be examined next.

The Decrease in Acreage under Winter Crops

As Table 18 indicates, winter crops give a much higher yield than crops sown during the spring. This is a well-known fact for varieties of wheat, rye, barley, and other traditional grain crops. In every Five Year Plan and the accompanying annual plans, attempts are made to increase the acreage under winter crops. The usual target figure (calculated by scientists on the basis of proper rotation) is an acreage of 40 million hectares, close to the acreage of winter crops which was cultivated under the primitive three-field rotation system in prerevolutionary Russia. But, as Table 20 indicates, despite the obvious rationale of increasing the proportion of winter crops, there has been a steady absolute and proportional decrease in the acreage under winter crops since 1965 (as well as the total acreage of grain crops). This decrease has nothing to do with agronomic considerations. It is entirely due to organizational problems, shortages of manpower and ma-chinery, and, occasionally, shortages of seed grain.

The decline in the acreage of winter crops has, for the most part, been due to a reduction in the sowing of winter rye rather than winter wheat (see Table 21). Russia used to produce more rye bread than the rest of the world combined, and most of it was made from winter rye. It was the traditional crop of Russia and in prerevolutionary times the winter rye acreage was always larger than the spring wheat acreage. Rye not only yields a higher harvest than spring wheat, but it is also more frost resistant than winter wheat. It was the main winter crop in central, western, and northern areas where climatic conditions are too severe for winter wheat. In these areas winter rye has now been replaced by spring wheat, which has a lower yield. Scientists and agri-cultural experts have been arguing for years that the decline in

TABLE 20
Total Acreage under Grain Crops
(Million Hectares)

	1913	1940	1950	1965	1975	1980	1981	1985*
All grain crops	104.6	110.7	102.9	128.0	127.9	126.6	125.5	117.9
Winter crops	37.1	38.2	36.5	37.2	29.2	32.7	29.4	28.6
Spring crops	67.5	72.5	66.4	90.8	98.7	93.9	95.1	89.3

Source: Nar. khoz., 1963, p. 242; 1922–1982, p. 244; 1985, p. 206.

* The statistical reports for 1982, 1983, and 1984 do not give full information about the acreage of different grain crops, since by then all information about grain production except total acreage had become classified. However, general figures of the winter crop acreage can easily be found in the weekly newspaper reports about the progress in sowing and harvesting. Weekly reports of the harvest are published in *Izvestiya, Sel'skaya zhizn'*, and other papers. The 1984 annual plan provided for 40 million hectares of winter crops. In the weekly reports it was stated that by September 17, 1984, 27.9 million hectares (69 percent of the plan) had been sown.[4] Two weeks later, on October 1, 1984, the sowing of winter grain was said to have reached 29.4 million hectares.[5] It does not make sense to sow any later and no more figures were reported. However, in 1985 the sowing of winter crops continued until the end of October, probably under pressure or because a milder winter was expected. The second half of September is rather late for winter sowing, since the plants do not have sufficient time to develop good vegetation and they are vulnerable to winter frosts. Part of the winter crops can be lost in this way (significant damage was reported during the winter of 1984–1985 because of severe frosts) and the fields have to be resown in the spring. This is why the data extracted from the weekly reports are estimates and are not as reliable as the final official statistical records, which, when they were published in the annual yearbooks, included only the *harvested* winter crops.

the rye acreage is a negative phenomenon. There have been dozens of articles in newspapers, specialized agricultural journals, and even in literary magazines (for example, the brilliant essay by Yuri Chernichenko on rye bread[6]) which have maintained that rye is a more secure and a more economic crop for the whole area from Byelorussia and the Baltic states to Siberia. Rye bread (the traditional Russian black bread) has more nutritional value than white wheat bread. In the humid climate of Byelorussia and northern and central RSFSR rye grain contains

TABLE 21
Acreage under Rye
in Russia and the Soviet Union
(Million Hectares)

1913	1940	1950	1960	1970	1979[a]	1980	1981	1983	1985
28.2	23.3	23.7	16.2	10.2	6.5	8.6	7.5	10.3	9.4

Source: Nar. khoz., 1965, p. 298; 1975, p. 354; 1980, p. 224; 1985, p. 206.

[a] Table 18 shows that the average yields of the rye harvest are markedly higher than the yields of the spring wheat which is usually substituted for rye. It is also the case that winter rye is much more resistant to drought. In 1975, a disastrous year for Soviet agriculture, the average rye yields were only slightly reduced (11.3 centners per hectare), while the average yields of spring wheat fell to 7 centners per hectare. The difference was even more dramatic in 1965, another drought year, when the average yield for rye was 10.1 centners per hectare, while the average spring wheat yield was 5.5 centners per hectare.[8] It is clear that if the acreage under winter rye had not been so severely reduced since 1950, the overall performance of the grain sector during the drought years would have been much better.

more protein (17 to 18 percent) than spring wheat, particularly the soft wheat which is found in humid areas and which only contains 11 to 12 percent of protein. Moreover, the protein found in rye is of a higher quality than wheat protein, with a better proportion of amino acids. Wheat protein contains less of the important amino acids like lysine (2.8 percent compared to the 4.1 percent in rye protein), which makes it necessary to consume 30 percent more wheat bread than rye bread to satisfy the same protein requirements of the human body. Rye bread also contains more vitamins, phospholipids, and calcium. There is a high demand for rye bread in Western Europe and it costs more than wheat bread.

The decrease in the rye acreage has been a direct result both of poor planning in the intensification of Soviet agriculture and of inadequate selection work. The agricultural machinery industry has not yet invented suitable combine-harvesters for rye, which is a much taller crop than wheat. Until the war rye was usually harvested with sickles or with horse-driven mowing machines and sheafers. With the postwar decrease in rural manpower, these

methods have become difficult, but no machinery has been produced to replace them. Tall forms of wheat were also common
before the war. The main disadvantage was that tall wheat with-
stood rain badly, but the flattening of the fields by rain did not
present a serious problem until combine harvesting was introduced. In most countries, including the Soviet Union, combine
harvesting has encouraged the selection of shorter forms of wheat,
which are better protected against flattening (and use much higher
levels of fertilization). The worldwide increase of wheat yields
would have been impossible without these short varieties. Soviet
geneticists have used foreign genetic material (mostly from the
isolation of "shortness genes") to breed productive forms of wheat.
Unfortunately, a similar selection has not been achieved for rye.
The Soviet Union was the main rye producer in the world, but
the seleciton of new forms of rye has been seriously delayed by
the general neglect of proper genetic methods under Stalin and
Khrushchev. Poland is now the only country in the world where
the acreage under winter rye (3.4 million hectares) is higher than
the acreage under winter wheat (1.5 million hectares).

In the 1970s and 1980s the Soviet Union actually began to
import rye, primarily from Canada (342,415 tons in 1981 and
299,750 tons in 1982[7]). The import of feed grain and corn can
perhaps be justified in economic terms (the international price
for corn is very low and there are very few suitable places in the
Soviet Union for cultivating it), but there is no possible economic
justification for importing rye. Neither the weather nor the demands of livestock production explain the need. It indicates that
there is a real shortage of food grain which is entirely the result
of poor planning and incompetent administration.

The Decline in Quantity and Quality of Wheat Grain Protein

The reduced amounts of protein consumed as a result of the
decreased consumption of rye bread has been aggravated by a
decline in the quality of wheat grain. For many years the five
year plans have concentrated on wheat yields, rather than on the

quality of the grain. Inevitably, in attempting to increase the yields, *kolkhozy* and *sovkhozy* have changed to cultivating varieties of the more productive soft wheat. However, soft wheat contains less protein and is not very good for making bread or for producing the popular, wheat-based foods of the spaghetti and macaroni type. Moreover, it is particularly susceptible to fungus diseases.

Between 1958 and 1963 the protein content of the wheat cultivated in the southern Volga regions fell from 17.2 percent to 13.2 percent, while in the Ukraine it fell from 15.5 to 13 4 percent.[9] In 1939–1940 the protein content of the wheat grain in these areas was 18.9 and 18.5 percent respectively. Protein is the most valuable part of wheat flour: the commercial value of wheat grain is directly related to its protein content. Before 1913 Russian wheat was considered the best quality, superior to the hard wheats of southern Italy, Spain, and the other Mediterranean wheats. It was highly priced on the world market precisely because of its high protein content. The most valuable Russian wheat was of the very hard *Triticum durum* type, with a protein content of more than 20 percent.[10]

Attempts have been made to reverse the trend towards soft wheat in the main wheat-growing areas and to increase the production of hard and strong types. Procurement prices, for example, began to reflect the protein content. However, production plans continued to be calculated in metric tons and, as a result, the reintroduction of the *durum* type was very slow. The quality of Soviet bread and other wheat-based products has declined visibly over the last twenty years. Soviet-made macaroni and noodles (made from a mixture of soft wheat) are white, fragile, and starchy, easily losing their form and integrity when they are boiled. The suggestion that the real grain harvest should be calculated not on the basis of the net weight of grain, but on the basis of its protein content has a certain merit. As the production and consumption of rye has declined, so the quantity of wheat protein required has increased. A decrease in the percentage of even one essential amino acid in protein reduces the utilization of protein in the human body in direct proportion to the decrease. The reduction of the protein content of wheat has had an adverse effect on the protein balance in the average Soviet diet. It has made an increase in high-quality animal protein essential for the general health of the population, particularly for children. The modest increase in the per capita consumption of meat and dairy produce in the last twenty years has thus not improved the protein balance of the diet—it has merely gone some way towards replacing the protein lost from wheat and rye consumption. In order to increase the protein composition of bread, some bakeries have begun to mix flour with milk serum (the liquid which remains as a by-product in the production of butter and cream) rather than with water. Although the nutritional value of bread made in this way is higher, it cannot substitute for the protein specific to wheat, which is necessary for the normal structure and taste of bread.

In 1971–1978 the proportion of hard and strong wheat in the total harvest began to rise, but the poor grain harvests of 1979–1985 once again had an adverse effect. The quality of the grain in the Ukraine, North Caucasus, and the Volga basin, the traditional centers of hard and strong wheat, declined dramatically and it became necessary to import hard wheat from Kazakhstan and eastern Siberia into these areas to mix with the local wheat for making bread. A significant proportion of the local soft wheat was once again used as feed grain. In 1982–1983 Kazakhstan and the other virgin land areas produced about three quarters of all the hard and strong wheat used in the bakeries of the western part of the Soviet Union.[11] The *durum* type of wheat has almost become extinct. It has been calculated that the minimal requirement of this type of wheat for the food industry (for macaroni products) is a modest 3 million tons. But it has been many years since this level has been reached, and the production of *durum* fell again in 1979–1984, despite a procurement price 50 percent higher than that for soft wheat.

The amount of bread produced in the Soviet Union remained at the level of 34 million tons per year (for both rye and wheat bread) from 1972 to 1982.[12] Some authors have tried to explain this per capita decline in the production of bread (particularly in the towns) by maintaining that the proportion of vegetables and animal products in the public diet has increased. However, this explanation does not withstand examination. The decline of bread consumption is partly related to the lower quality of bread and to bread shortages in many regions. The per capita consumption of animal products has increased very modestly, and it did not increase at all in 1979–1985. The growth in the marketable production of vegetables, milk, and other dairy products was lower in 1970–1984 than the population growth (particularly the growth in urban population). The lower bread consumption can only be explained by an increase in the consumption of potatoes. This can hardly be interpreted as an improvement in the average diet.

The Reduction in Production of Groats and Leguminous Crops

For statistical purposes groats and leguminous crops are grouped with grain. Bread and porridge eaten with milk are the staple ingredients of the traditional Russian diet. Oatmeal, pearl-barley, or fine-ground barley figure prominently, but the most popular porridges are millet and buckwheat. Amongst the leguminous crops, peas are most common in the Ukraine, while kidney and haricot beans are more popular in the North Caucasus and Transcaucasia. It is the wide diversity of grain crops which has always made the Russian traditional diet rather attractive, even though it consists predominantly of grain. But, as Table 22 demonstrates, the production of these crops has not improved since 1964. If the growth of total and urban population is taken into account, there was a decline in the production of all these crops, with the exception of barley, which was used as a feed crop for livestock and for the production of beer. The production and procurement of high-protein leguminous crops (which also improve the soil by assimilating atmospheric nitrogen) declined quite sharply. Although the figures for 1981–1985 are classified, it is obvious from the general discussion in the press that the decline has neither been halted nor reversed.[13] The traditional meal of porridge is often unavailable in canteens and restaurants. The old saying

TABLE 22

Total Production of Various Grain Crops, 1940–1980

(Million Tons)

	Wheat	Rye	Corn	Barley	Oats	Millet	Buckwheat	Rice	Legumes
1940	31.8	21.1	5.2	12.0	16.8	4.4	1.3	0.3	2.2
1960	64.3	16.4	9.8	16.0	12.0	3.23	0.64	0.19	2.71
1964	74.4	13.6	13.8	28.6	5.5	3.5	0.7	0.5	11.1
1971–1975[a]	88.9	11.5	10.2	43.3	14.8	2.5	1.0	1.8	7.3
1976[a]–1980	99.7	10.9	9.6	55.1	17.2	2.2	0.9	2.3	6.9
1981–1985	77.9	14.3	13.1	43.4	17.5	2.3	1.0	2.6	7.7

State procurements

	Wheat	Rye	Corn	Barley	Oats	Millet	Buckwheat	Rice	Legumes
1940	15.6	8.0	0.6	4.3	4.9	1.6	0.4	0.3	0.4
1960	30.7	5.8	2.2	3.7	1.9	1.2	0.15	0.06	0.35
1964	38.7	4.9	3.5	12.2	0.6	1.5	0.2	0.2	4.8
1971–1975[a]	43.0	4.1	2.4	11.1	1.9	1.3	0.4	1.2	1.1
1976[a]–1980	47.9	3.6	2.2	15.2	2.7	1.1	0.4	1.6	1.0
1981–1985	33.7	5.9	3.8	12.4	3.6	1.3	0.4	1.8	0.9

Source: Nar. khoz., 1965, pp. 262, 340; 1980, p. 230; 1922–1982, pp. 249, 256; 1985, pp. 182, 194.

[a] Annual average.

"*shchi i kasha—pishcha nasha*" ("cabbage soup and porridge is our food") has almost become obsolete.

Agricultural experts and dieticians are clearly aware of the problems caused by the acute shortages of groats, peas, and haricot beans, particularly for those for whom they used to form the staple food. The government has made numerous attempts to encourage the production of these crops. The procurement prices are very generous (five times higher than the price for wheat). The problem is similar to that of cultivating rye. The agricultural machine industry has failed to design and produce machinery which is suitable for the mechanized cultivation of these crops. Machines of a more universal type, particularly those which already exist in the United States, Canada, and other grain-producing countries, are produced with ease. However, machinery for cultivating more specific "Russian" crops does not exist. The initial agricultural machinery plants were built in the 1930s on the basis of imported technology. The government was preoccupied with the need to mechanize the cultivation of large fields (wheat and barley) and there was sufficient manpower then to cultivate other cereals and beans which were more labor-intensive and which did not require large fields.

The reason for the comparative decline in the production of oats (considered to be a more valuable feed crop than barley) also concerns inadequate mechanization. Until 1940 more oats were produced than barley. But oats have a longer vegetation period and require earlier sowing than barley. Early sowing, when the soil is still very wet, cannot be done with heavy tractors. Before mechanization, when sowing was done by hand or with horse-drawn machinery, oats was the favored crop because it enabled an early start to the agricultural season. But the introduction of heavy machinery and the decline in manpower have removed the advantages of cultivating it.

The shortage of buckwheat probably causes the greatest disappointment to consumers, particularly those who remember the remarkable taste of buckwheat porridge. For centuries buckwheat was the most popular of the groats crops. From time immemorial until 1940 Russia was the main world producer of buckwheat. Some provinces (Chernigov, Vladimir, Yaroslavl, Smolensk) specialized in it. It has exceptionally good nutritional value and was once the staple food of peasants and workers. It is now rarely found outside the few regions which still produce it and the Moscow and Leningrad restaurants which serve foreign tourists. Its value extends beyond its nutritional qualities. It is an important source of valuable honey (buckwheat honey) and the leaves of the buckwheat plant are an important source for the industrial production of rutin (Vitamin P), which is widely used in pharmacology to make antiarteriosclerosis vitamins. In countries like Canada, buckwheat is cultivated not for the seeds, but for the leaves, to extract Vitamin P. Soviety industry has tried for many years to design machinery to mechanize buckwheat production. At the same time, geneticists have attempted to breed varieties which have compact heads and in which the seeds mature simultaneously. However, neither line of research has yet been successful.

2. Potatoes, Vegetables, and Fruit

Potatoes are now considered to be "second bread" for the population. They are also an important technical and fodder crop. However, before 1913 they were cultivated together with vegetables, and did not form part of the field-rotation system. The potato had arrived in Russia much later than in Western Europe and by the end of the eighteenth century peasants were still resisting pressure from the czars and the *pomeshchiki* to cultivate more potato. By the middle of the nineteenth century it had become a common food crop, but the acreage under potato was only about 1 percent of the cultivated land. The discovery that it could be used like grain for producing alcohol (mainly vodka) made it more popular, but its real value was only found after the Revolution. Indeed, the only agricultural success which can be attributed to the Soviet system is the increased production of potatoes.

Grain production in the Soviet Union remained approximately at the 1913 level for several decades (until 1956), whereas the production of potato grew dramatically. In 1909–1913 the average annual harvest was 30.6 million tons. In 1940 it had grown to 76.1 million tons and in 1948 it reached 95.0 million tons. During the postwar period (1945–1950) grain production fell below the 1909–1913 level, while potato production was triple the pre-revolutionary level. It was the cheapest food available and the easiest to produce. During the war the consumption of potato was higher in many areas than the consumption of bread. It has remained a very high proportion of the diet. It is also widely used for animal feed (particularly for pigs) and large amounts are used in the starch and alcohol industry, as well as in the production of synthetic rubber.

Production was more than 100 million tons in both 1968 and 1973. The reason this level was not maintained was not a decrease in demand; rather, it was due to organizational, technical, and transport problems. The urban population suffers from a shortage of potatoes from the middle of the winter until the middle of the summer. Over a period of years there has been constant discussion in the media and in specialized books about the need to improve production (particularly around large cities to make deliveries easier), increase state procurements, and create proper storage facilities.[14] State procurements are rather low (12 to 16 million tons) and have remained static over the last two decades. The acreage under potato has fluctuated from 7 to 8 million hectares.

As will be seen from the chapter on private agriculture (Chapter 11), more than 70 percent of the annual potato harvest is still produced on private plots. The urban population buys more potato from the free market than from state shops. The potatoes sold privately are of better quality and they represent what is probably the most important source of cash income for the rural population. Potato is a labor-intensive crop and its cultivation is poorly mechanized. In the *kolkhoz* and *sovkhoz* sector the harvest is heavily dependent on the mobilized urban population. The harvest takes place in the autumn and there is always a danger that many fields could be lost if there is an early winter. Despite high levels of production, the annual plans are almost always higher than the actual output.

The main problems in the production of potato are transport and storage—the late harvest leaves very little time for the crop to be transported before the winter frosts kill or damage the tuber. There are insufficient refrigerator trucks and railway cars (and many of the trucks that are available are not well enough insulated) to transport potato, vegetables, and fruit over long distances. The river system is still widely used to transport agricultural produce by barge, but as soon as the winter frosts set in, the whole transportation system of frost-sensitive cargoes comes to a halt. It is, therefore, important to transport sufficient supplies to storage facilities in the cities and towns. The potato crop is often very wet, and there are no facilities to dry the crop (which has usually been collected by hand because the "potato combines" cannot operate on wet soil and are notorious for leaving a large proportion of the crop in the ground). Even in Moscow the storage facilities are primitive and not equipped to dry or clean the potatoes. Diseased or frostbitten tubers are rarely sorted and it is difficult to keep potatoes in this condition for several months.

Attempts have been made to create specialized potato *kolkhozy* and *sovkhozy* in suitable areas (Byelorussia, the Baltic republics, and the Bryansk and Kalinin regions). Specialization makes better mechanization possible, as well as the selection of the best varieties for food and for technical use (the latter requires a high starch content). But concentrating production in these western areas exacerbates transport and storage problems. Moreover, the procurement price of potato has remained very low and the retail price (10 kopecks per kilograms or 10 rubles per ton) is subsidized. The price on the free market is five or six times higher than the state retail price in the autumn and it rises towards the spring.

The problems with other vegetables are similar. Since most vegetable crops are labor-intensive and need well-fertilized light soil, they are expensive to cultivate. This problem is not unique to the Soviet Union. In the United States, for example, the selection and cultivation of varieties of tomatoes suitable for mechanization (tomatoes that ripen simultaneously, have strong surfaces, and are a standard size) has led to a significant decline in the quality of the taste. In the Soviet Union few vegetables (with the exception of cabbages) are cultivated in *kolkhoz* or *sovkhoz* fields. The rural consumption of vegetables, the main source of vitamins in the normal Russian diet, is very high. Urban fruit and vegetable shops, on the other hand, tend not to stock any fresh vegetables during the winter and spring, offering instead the processed products of the food industry—marinated, salted products and juice. The free market is the only source of high-quality vegetables, at prices often ten to twenty times higher than state retail prices, which are subsidized. The total production of vegetables (including those cultivated on private plots) has risen very slowly. The average annual production increased from 19 million tons in 1966–1970 to 25 million tons 1976–1980. Less than half the total production was available for state purchases and more than 70 percent was produced on private plots. *Kolkhoz* and *sovkhoz* vegetable production occupies no more than 0.5 million hectares, and most of this is given over to cabbages.

The idea has often been mooted of creating specialized vegetable farms near large cities and industrial centers or combined with food-processing facilities, but this is still at an early stage of development. Some progress has been made in building large greenhouse complexes for cucumbers and early vegetables around Moscow and Leningrad, but they are part of a new form of agro-industrial agricultural production and do not fall within the traditional *kolkhoz* and *sovkhoz* system. They use industrial heating systems and depend upon large state investments. In spite of this program and attempts to create specialized farms for the mechanized production of vegetables, the virtual absence of fragile fresh crops like lettuce and spinach, shortages of other vegetables, and the sight of empty state vegetable shops for most of the year are symptoms of a chronic, seemingly insuperable condition.

The problem is partly caused by inadequate storage and refrigerator facilities in most cities. As a result the state is unable to purchase large amounts of fruit and vegetables in season and store them. They are, therefore, easily available in the autumn, but in short supply for the rest of the year. Railroad transportation of fruit and vegetables from the rural areas of the North Caucasus, Transcaucasia, Crimea, Moldavia, Central Asia, and southern Ukraine is virtually impossible in winter, since there is a shortage of railway cars and trucks insulated from the freezing temperatures. Farmers often charter special planes to take their fruit and

TABLE 23

Total Production of Fruit (Collective and Private)
(Million Tons)

1940	1950	1960	1965	1970	1975	1980	1982	1984
3.9	2.8	4.9	8.1	11.7	14.2	14.6	18.4	18.5

Source: Nar. khoz., 1982, p. 227; 1984, p. 260.

vegetables to the north and to Siberia and the cost is reflected in the very high prices for which the products are sold on the free market. During the winter and spring, tomatoes, apples, melons, grapes, mandarins, and so on, sell for as much as 8 to 10 rubles (8 dollars to 14 dollars) per kilogram. Very few families can afford to buy them and when they do, they are usually for the children. The adult diet is thus deficient in vegetables and fruit. Before 1947 health problems caused by vitamin deficiencies were quite common in Siberia, the Far East, and in northern regions. Later the vitamin industry and the production of tinned vegetables reduced the incidence of vitamin insufficiency, but the quality of the diet in winter and spring has deteriorated in the last two decades.

Fruit production is accorded low priority in the collective agricultural system. Most fruit is produced privately and will be discussed in Chapter 11. There are, however, some large collective and state fruit and grape plantations in Moldavia, the Crimea, and other traditional fruit-producing areas, particularly around the food-processing and wine-producing industries. The production of fruit, including grapes, grew rapidly between 1950 and 1965, but the growth slowed down and the level of current production is well below the target projected in the plan (see Table 23). About 40 percent of the total production shown in Table 23 consists of grapes produced for the wine industry (7.8 million tons in 1982).

Despite the severe shortages of fruit in the winter and spring, only about one million tons of fruit is imported annually. Both the consumer demand and the necessary currency reserves are available to import more, particularly citrus, bananas, and other fruit which cannot be grown in the Soviet Union. But the same obstacles which prevent the better distribution of home-grown fruit and vegetables militate against increasing the amount which is imported.

3. Technical Crops

Technical crops have been cultivated, on the whole, more successfully in the Soviet Union than have food crops. This reflects both the priority with which they have been treated in terms of allocating fertilizer and labor and a more rational pricing policy. Cotton is the most successful technical crop and it has become a major export.

COTTON

Cotton is only cultivated in irrigated fields in Central Asia, Kazakhstan, and Azerbaijan, but by dint of increasing both the acreage and the yields, the Soviet Union not only has become self-sufficient in cotton, but exports both raw cotton and cotton textiles. It is now the world's second largest producer, responsible for about 20 percent of the total world production. The steady increase in production is demonstrated in Table 24.

The impressive increase in cotton production was made possible by substantial investments in irrigation and new technology and by the priority accorded to the cotton-growing regions for fertilizers and machinery. In 1935 cotton became an exception to the government policy of paying low procurement prices. Procurement prices quadrupled and even higher prices were paid for raw cotton produced over and above the quota in the state plans. As a result, it became a very profitable crop. It became rational for many Central Asian and Azerbaijani *kolkhozy* to increase their production and sale of cotton and use part of the

TABLE 24

Cotton Production in Russia and the Soviet Union

	Yield (centners/ha)	Total production (million tons)
1909–1913*	10–11	0.74
1940	10.8	2.24
1965	20.1	5.66
1971–1975*	27.3	7.67
1976–1980*	29.3	8.93
1981–1985*	28.1	9.11

Source: Nar. khoz., 1965, pp. 258, 356; 1982, pp. 189–190, 216; 1984, pp. 224–225; SSSR v Tsifrakh, 1985, pp. 117, 119.
* Annual average.

profit to buy grain and other food crops from the state. The cotton-producing regions became very prosperous. In these areas the rural population remains larger than the urban population, because the incomes which can be earned in agriculture are often higher than those paid in industry. In Uzbekistan, for example, the rural population was 10.4 million in 1984, while the urban population numbered 7.5 million. This ratio of rural to urban population contrasts with the Ukraine, where 17.5 million people live in the countryside and 33.2 million in the towns, and the RSFSR, where only 27 percent of the population lives in rural areas.

State procurement prices for cotton have continued to rise in the last two decades. Nonetheless, cotton production has not become uneconomical for the state budget. State subsidies for food crops and meat, paid to ensure that retail food prices remain low (usually even lower than the cost of production), have become an extremely heavy burden on the budget. The consumer price of textiles, on the other hand, is not subsidized. Prices rise as production costs increase. Consequently the production of cotton not only remains profitable for the *kolkhozy* but also for the state. Until 1935 about 50 percent of the cotton textiles required in the country had to be imported. By 1955, cotton had begun to be exported. In 1982 exports of more than 95 million meters of cotton textile earned the state about 33 million "export" rubles. The export of raw and staple cotton was even more profitable. In 1976–1984 about a million tons were sold annually, bringing in more than a billion rubles.[15]

Unfortunately this progress has been achieved at a very high ecological and demographic cost. The irrigation has involved diverting water from two great rivers, the Syrdar'ya and the Amu-Dar'ya. Both feed the beautiful inland Aral Sea, the world's fourth-largest body of inland water (measuring 66,458 square kilometers or 25,659 square miles). By 1982 it had shrunk to about half its size and its population of freshwater fish had died off almost entirely. For centuries the Aral had been rich in freshwater fish like sturgeon, carp, and barbel. The two ports, Aralsk and Muynak, are now a considerable distance from the shore and the fishermen who live in dozens of fishing villages on the shores have been deprived of their traditional livelihood. The river flow, which accounts for about 90 percent of the inflow of water into the sea, continues to decline, despite the warnings of ecologists. Plans to bring water to the area from the Siberian Irtysh River have not materialized because the cost would be too high. The diversion of the waters of the Syrdar'ya and Amu-Dar'ya has doubled the concentration of salts in the Aral Sea and many thousands of kilometers of wasteland have been created. Some attempt has been made to cultivate saltwater fish such as Atlantic herring and mullet, but the continuing diversion of river water will make the complete drying up of this unique inland sea inevitable. Soviet ecologists are still arguing about the possible climatic effects of this development. The negative economic effect is inescapable, however, and can hardly be justified by the increasing exports of cotton. It would make better economic sense to restrict the growth of the cotton and textile industries to the level of internal requirements and to increase the production of grain (particularly corn) in Central Asia. To increase cotton exports to Europe while increasing grain imports from the United States and Canada to satisfy the demand for food and feed grain in Soviet Central Asia seems a wasteful exchange.

FLAX

In contrast to the production of cotton, the production of the traditional Russian textile crop, flax, has essentially been a failure. Russia was the world's largest flax producer and the Soviet Union is still the leading producer. Flax textile (called "the northern silk") continues to be very popular, but the acreage under flax is declining because it is a labor-intensive crop.

Historically, the cultivation of flax predates the cultivation of cotton. It was cultivated in India, Egypt, and Mesopotamia 4,000–5,000 B.C. and Egyptian mummies are wrapped in woollen and flax tissues. Flax cloth was used as sailcloth and canvas by the Greeks and Romans and in Spain it has been found in Bronze Age archeological sites. Slav tribes began cultivating flax in the sixth to seventh centuries A.D., well before the foundation of Kiev Rus. The flax industry began in the thirteenth century around Novgorod, Vologda, and Pskov, and flax ropes were exported to Western Europe. Russian flax differs from the Mediterranean varieties. It originated in Central Asia and is related to the varieties found in the Pamir, Kazakhstan, and Kashmir areas.[16] Flax linen is popular for its strength, durability, and ability to absorb moisture. In old Russian hospitals it was used to dress wounds and was thought to have special healing qualities, probably because it is more resistant to microorganisms than cotton cloth. It also offers better protection from cold and heat and its quality improves with age: older linen is softer, whiter, and more lustrous.

The unique character of flax tissue makes it far superior to either cotton or synthetic textiles. Its value continues to rise and the demand for the material grows. Nonetheless, both the acreage under flax and the total production is declining steadily in the Soviet Union (the decrease in acreage is partly compensated by increased yields). This decline can be seen in Table 25. The average annual production of flax in 1970–1985 was below the

TABLE 25

Flax Production and Export
in Russia and the Soviet Union

	Acreage (hectares)	Yield (centners/ha)	Total production (thousand tons)	Export (thousand tons)
1913	1,350,000	2.8	401.0	272.0
1940	2,100,000	1.7	349.0	18.0
1950	1,900,000	1.3	255.0	5.6
1960	1,620,000	3.0	425.0	29.0
1970	1,284,000	3.6	456.0	9.3
1980	1,116,000	2.5	291.0	2.1
1981	939,000	2.8	263.0	2.2
1982	1,012,000	4.1	415.0	7.6
1985	1,020,000	3.5	352.0	8.4

Source: *Nar. khoz.*, 1965, pp. 258, 262–263, 671; 1982, pp. 189–190, 217–218; *Vnesh. torg.*, 1983, p. 28; 1985, p. 28; *SSSR v Tsifrakh*, 1985, pp. 117, 119.

prerevolutionary level and the acreage was about half that of 1940 or 1950. If the population is taken into account (1913—165 million, 1986—280 million) the decline in production is even more striking. In the last decade, production has been about half the amount envisaged in the plan. But even so, the flax-processing industry is unable to process all the flax delivered to it. Many articles have been published in specialized journals and the press, criticizing the delays in completing new modern flax-processing plants, particularly in Byelorussia, where flax is the main technical crop. Those plants which are in operation suffer from a severe labor shortage—they are unmodernized and about 50 percent of the processing requires heavy manual labor.

Since flax textile is still very popular and its price on the world market is higher than the price of cotton textile, there is no rational economic reason for the decline in production. Moreover, it is a profitable crop, even when the yield is as low as 2 to 3 centners per hectare. The yield can be as high as 8 to 9 centners per hectare, giving a profit of about 200 percent. Several new technologies can be used a shift the primary treatment of the crop into specialized flax-fiber factories and make it more efficient and less reliant on manual labor. Although the Soviet Union remains the leading world producer of flax textile, exports have fallen. The average value of flax and flax textile exports has varied from 1 to 7 million rubles, less than 1 percent of the value of the export of cotton. Before the Revolution, when Russia had the virtual world monopoly of the flax trade, it represented 6.2 percent of the total Russian export. In 1928 it formed 3.1 percent of the total export. By 1955 it had fallen to an insignificant 0.2 percent of the total export (cotton formed 11.7 percent). Moreover, the Soviet Union imported more flax textile (from Poland and Romania) in 1981–1982 than the total export of fiber and textile (the value of the imports was 25 million rubles and 37 million rubles respectively, while the value of exports was about 1 million rubles).[17] Although Western Europe is an importer of flax, particularly high-quality flax for sheeting, lace, and clothing, domestic demand and reduced production makes it impossible for the Soviet Union to take advantage of this market.

SUGAR BEETS AND OILSEED CROPS

Although these crops are vital constituents of the food balance of the population, they are categorized as technical crops in the Soviet Union, because they require industrial or semi-industrial processing before they can be used as food. Table 26 gives a general picture of their production and the output of sugar and vegetable oil.

Although the total harvest of sugar beets grew in the 1960s and 1970s, the production of sugar did not increase (about 80 percent of Soviet sugar is processed from sugar beets, the rest is from raw sugar imported from Cuba). Measured against the population growth, there was therefore a relative decline in processed sugar. Until 1975 the amount of sugar produced from the total amount of sugar beets was published in the statistical yearbooks.

TABLE 26
Production of Sugar Beets, Sugar, and Vegetable Oil
(Million Tons)

Annual average	Sugar beets	Sugar[a]	Oilseeds	Vegetable oil[b]
1940	18.0	2.2	3.22	0.8
1956–1960	45.6	6.2	4.10	1.7
1961–1965	59.2	11.0	5.70	2.8
1966–1970	81.1	10.2	7.18	2.8
1971–1975	76.0	9.8	6.69	3.3
1976–1980	88.7	10.1	6.04	2.6
1981–1985	76.3	11.7	5.70	2.6

Source: Nar. khoz., 1982, pp. 184, 186, 189; 1983, pp. 191, 195, 207; 1985, pp. 180, 252.

[a] Production of sugar in 1961–1985 includes the processing of raw sugar imported from Cuba and other countries. The output of sugar per one metric ton of sugar beets actually diminished and the domestic production of sugar has not increased since 1962.

[b] The increase of the output of oil per one ton of seed reflects the successful selection of high-quality sunflower varieties.

The percentage decreased from 12.7 in 1940, to 12.1 in 1970, and 10.1 in 1974. The production of vegetable oil was also well below demand and there has been an absolute reduction in production between 1961 and 1980–1982. Sugar shortages are easily compensated by imports from Cuba, which has little else to sell in exchange for its vast imports of more than 250 different Soviet products. In 1981, 3 million tons was imported and the amount rose to 4.2 million tons in 1982.[18] Cuban raw sugar often requires additional processing in the Soviet Union and it is, therefore, included in the figures given for the overall production of processed sugar. But as far as vegetable oil is concerned, there is no reliable CMEA source from which it can be imported and increasing the domestic production is an important task. Both sugar plants and oil-processing factories produce large amounts of secondary residual products, which are used as fodder.

TEA

The production of tea, like the production of cotton, became an important part of collectivized agriculture. These two crops, and a few other minor technical crops, have been specially subsidized since the 1930s to make them profitable. Tea plantations are found mainly in Georgia, Abkhazia and Adzharia, the Krasnodar region near the Black Sea, and in some regions of Azerbaijan near the Caspian Sea, where there are high precipitation levels and a humid, subtropical climate, which make it possible to cultivate tea and other valuable crops. Although the tea plant was introduced into Georgia in the middle of the nineteenth century, tea plantations only occupied about 1,000 hectares in 1913. Tea was a popular drink in Russia, but most of it was imported from India, China, and Ceylon. The acreage under tea increased to 13,000 hectares in 1932, 55,000 hectares in 1940, and 78,000 hectares in 1980. Five hundred and thirty thousand tons of tea were produced in 1980. Although tea continued to be imported, the amount (84,521 tons in 1981 and 73,391 tons in 1982) was only a fraction of the domestic production.

Conclusion

Khrushchev's reforms had brought about an increase in grain production to an average level of 130 to 140 million tons per annum. In the next twenty years the increase was very modest, to a level of 170 to 190 million tons, despite very significant investments in the *kolkhozy* and *sovkhozy*, the agricultural machinery industry, the chemical fertilizer industry, road construction, and rural electrification. In the last Five Year Plan, 1981–1985, the shortfall between the target figure (240 million tons annually) and actual production was about 60 to 70 million tons, greater than it had been in the Seven Year Plan period under Khrushchev, from 1959 to 1965. Moreover, the increases in procurement prices and (as will be seen more clearly when mechanization, chemicalization, and irrigation are discussed) the costs of modernization have meant that the modest increase in the production of grain and other food crops has been extremely expensive. The purchase of grain abroad in 1963 was treated as a temporary emergency. In later years the government quietly dropped the idea of self-sufficiency in grain production and resigned itself to the necessity of importing vast amounts of food and feed grain annually from almost any country in the world that was prepared to export grain products. In 1909–1913 Russia was the world's largest exporter of grain, exporting 12 to 14 million tons per year. It has now become the largest grain importer, importing 30 to 50 million tons annually. The political costs of this reversal have been high. Western propaganda has scored many points from the inability of socialist agriculture to feed its own population.

But the imports are not enough to satisfy the demands of a growing industry and an expanding urban population for high-quality food. Soviet port facilities are inadequate to cope with importing more than the present 40 million tons per annum and, in any case, the amount of grain available for export in other countries is limited. Soviet planners have calculated that if the production of livestock (meat, poultry, milk, dairy products, and eggs) is to rise to an appropriate level and if the promise of a "scientifically balanced diet" is to be honored, grain production must increase to a level of 260 to 270 million metric tons. This does not seem an impossible task, since the total acreage under grain crops is now 126 to 127 million hectares (of a total of 215 to 217 million hectares of cultivated land). All that is required is to increase the grain yields to 20 to 22 centners per hectare, three times less than the average yields now obtained in Britain, France, or Sweden.

Amongst the CMEA countries, only Mongolia has a lower grain yield than the Soviet Union. But even the highest reported yields in 1976–1980 (an average of 16 centners per hectare) are lower than the yields reported in all other East European countries for the same period (35.4 centners per hectare in Bulgaria, 41.6 in Hungary, 35.4 in East Germany, 24.5 in Poland, 30.1 in Romania, and 36.9 in Czechoslovakia[19]). In those countries the yields continued to rise in 1981–1985, (with a maximum of 50.5 centners per hectare in Hungary), while they declined in the Soviet Union. The weather cannot be held solely responsible for Soviet agricultural performance. In 1976–1980, for example, weather conditions were generally quite good. Nonetheless, the average grain yield in the Ukraine was 26 centners per hectare, well below the level in Hungary or Romania, which have a similar climate and soil and where agriculture was collectivized on the Soviet model in the late 1940s and early 1950s. It is significant that the yield in Latvia and Estonia (23 to 25 centners per hectare), which have a very poor climate and poor soil, was higher than in the rest of the Soviet Union.

In the 1970s and 1980s enormous investments were put into Soviet agriculture: 130 billion rubles in 1970–1975, 171 billion rubles in 1976–1980, and about 200 billion rubles in 1981–1985. The returns were an insignificant annual increase of agricultural production of about 2 billion rubles until 1982 and no increase thereafter. To obtain an extra 30 to 40 million tons of grain from its own fields, the Soviet government spent much more capital than was required to buy the same amount abroad (12 billion rubles worth of foreign currency was spent annually on food imports in 1976–1980, of which about 6 to 7 billion rubles, or 10 billion dollars, per year was for grain). Although large amounts of food, particularly vegetables and fruit, are imported from Hungary, Bulgaria, and Romania and can be considered part of the mutual cooperation which is said to be the basis of CMEA, importing food from capitalist countries can hardly be explained in the same way. It is the source of great political and economic embarrassment for the Soviet government. The large grain purchases made in the United States, Canada, and Western Europe are never discussed in the press. In purely financial terms (if rubles were convertible), the cost of foreign grain is not excessively high. The procurement costs of purchasing the same amount of *kolkhoz* grain above the official quota would be higher. The problem, however, is that Soviet foreign currency is earned mainly by the sale of oil. In 1982–1985 Soviet oil production began to decline and the fall of oil prices in 1986 has made grain imports very difficult.

The critical situation with regard to proteins finally made it necessary to introduce a system of procurement prices in July 1985 which began to reflect the protein content of "soft" wheat (10 percent bonus above the basic price) and offered particularly high prices for high-quality "hard" wheat. The new price for hard wheat was 150 rubles per ton, but it could be raised by 70 to 100 percent for grain of the highest standard.[20] The best hard wheat could fetch as much as 250 to 300 rubles per ton or more in 1986 if it was in excess of the plan. On the official exchange rate this is much more than the market price of American or Canadian grain (in 1984 the Soviet Union purchased 8.6 million tons of Canadian wheat for 1.2 billion "convertible" rubles and 7.6 million tons of American wheat for 1 billion rubles, or about 130 to 140 rubles per ton[21]).

It is unlikely, however, that the new system of payments will make a difference in 1986 or 1987. The grain harvest in 1986 (210 million tons) is well below the target figures. The total yield is still a priority. The acreage under grain crops has continued to decline (from 127.9 million hectares in 1975 to 120.8 in 1983 and 117.9 in 1985) and the total acreage of sown land has also decreased during the last decade (from 217.7 in 1975 to 210.3 in 1985). The decrease is partly due to an increase in fallow fields (from 11 million hectares in 1975 to 21 million in 1985) and partly to the loss of land to various industrial and hydroelectric projects. Increasing fallow lands is, in general, a positive trend in Soviet conditions, but only if they receive proper attention and cultivation (which has not been the case). The decrease of land under cultivation (for all crops) has not yet been compensated by an improvement in the agricultural use of existing fields. The attempt to introduce so-called "intensive" technologies of grain production has increased the production costs of extra grain well above the bonus procurement payments. Because a significant part of the production costs is covered by state subsidies (irrigation schemes, chemical fertilizers, machinery, etc.), the actual expense to the state for the very modest increased production on some farms is much higher than the generous procurement payments.

The fact that the total harvest has stabilized at a level of 170 to 190 million metric tons in 1979–1986 despite increased investments has made the gap between the plan (reflecting official expectations) and reality grow even wider. However, at the Twenty-seventh Party Congress in February–March 1986 the leadership did not even try to reconsider the highly inflated and unrealistic targets of the "Food Program." Achieving self-sufficiency in the production of cereals (wheat, barley, rye, oats, and others) and ceasing to import grain were confirmed as the official goals of the Soviet government. The production figure of 250 million tons of grain or more for the period of 1986–1990 has also been confirmed as the target by many recent decisions and statements. But to discover how realistic the goals are, further analysis is required of the performance in other branches of Soviet agriculture and agricultural industry. The following chapters will investigate the problems in the other major agricultural sectors.

Chapter 8

The Livestock Problem

Farm animals are an essential part of any normal agricultural cycle. In a well-balanced food production chain they play the important role of assimilating the natural plant resources of the environment and transforming them into animal products for the human diet, raw materials for industry, and organic fertilizer for field crops. Thus in an ecologically balanced agricultural system animals both contribute to good, stable harvests and are important in the human diet. Herbivorous animals transform poor plant proteins and the indigestible cellulose of the leaves into high-quality animal proteins and fats. Part of the transformation is carried out by specialized bacterial processes in the animals' complex digestive system: microbial organisms use the cellulose and other insoluble carbohydrates as their source of energy and synthesize essential amino acids from simpler nitrogen compounds or nonessential amino acids.

The ability of some animals to utilize and transform available and reproducable plant materials from the environment made meat, milk, and fat the staple diet for the many nomadic tribes that lived in Russia east of the Volga, in the Urals, Siberia, and Central Asia. Although crop farming is an ancient tradition for the Slav nations, Russia (together with Mongolia, which, economically at least, can be considered part of the Soviet Union) is the largest natural habitat of nomadic ethnic groups in the world. There are vast stretches of land where field agriculture is impossible. The Kirgiz and Kalmyk steppes between the Volga and the South Urals and large parts of Turkemania and Kazakhstan are too dry, and the very thin, salty topsoil is unsuitable for irrigation. Natural vegetation can only grow there in winter and early spring. Large parts of the Siberian taiga and arctic tundra are covered by permafrost and cannot be cultivated. But both areas are suitable for livestock. Large herds of sheep migrate from the Caspian steppes to the Urals and the mountains of Central Asia every season. Until the twentieth century, the Kalmyks, Tartars, Kazakhs, Kirgiz, Turkmen, Yakut, Tungus, and many other small ethnic groups of the one-hundred-odd nationalities which inhabit the Soviet Union were pastoral nomads, migrating with their herds of horses, cattle, camels, sheep, reindeer, or whatever. Their traditional diet depended almost entirely on their livestock. Siberian stag and domesticated reindeer provided food for the Buryats and other Siberian and Far Eastern peoples, transforming the grass and lichen of the taiga and tundra into meat and fat and migrating hundreds of kilometers for food in the summer and winter. The severe climate has made many other animal products an important part of everyday life. Heavy sheepskin coats, woollen boots, and fur hats are essential for survival in the winter.

The livestock can only continue fulfilling these vital needs, however, as long as there is a balance between the human and animal populations and between the animal population and the plant environment. Once the balance changes, animals begin to destroy forests by damaging and consuming young trees. As a result, the forests cease to reproduce themselves. In the nineteenth and early twentieth centuries, when herds of sheep and cattle were normally moved from the Ukraine and central regions to southern pastures for the winter, large forests in the Crimea,

North Caucasus, and South Urals were systematically destroyed by the herds. The demands of a growing population and the expanding towns for meat, fat, and milk caused the destruction of so many forests and lands in the less-populated areas of the country that even Stalin's grandiose plan for the afforestation of the steppes would, if it had been successful, only have made a small dent in the problem.

Resources for developing Soviet livestock farming extensively were exhausted even before the resources for extensive field agriculture. The Virgin Land Program, for example, was launched at the expense of pastureland. The pressure for more and more meat and other animal products made it essential, therefore, to develop intensive methods of livestock production. A significant proportion of cultivated land had to be used to feed animals, rather than people. Traditionally, Russian peasants did not make silage or use grain to feed their cattle. Working horses were the only animals to be given feed grain in the busy season. This situation continued until the 1950s, but the growing demands of a rapidly expanding urban population for a higher-quality diet made it impossible to continue traditional practices in the 1960s and 1970s. Livestock farming became the most expensive and difficult branch of Soviet agriculture. Farm animals have absorbed most of the state investments in agriculture. Nonetheless, livestock farming still remains the weakest sector of the Soviet economy. This chapter will examine the development of animal farming and the formidable problems which have yet to be overcome.

1. *The Problem of Animal Proteins*

Proteins are the most essential part of the human diet. They are required to replace the proteins of the body that are destroyed during the metabolic process and they can also be used as a source of energy. In all organisms cellular proteins are in a permanent state of turnover. Part of this turnover represents irreversible degradation and must be replaced by the intake of amino acids with food. Although survival is possible without fats and carbohydrates, a protein-free diet cannot support life. My professional interest in proteins is long-standing. In the 1950s and 1960s I studied protein biosynthesis in relation to development and ageing. My last research position in the Soviet Union, in 1970–1972, was in the Protein Laboratory of the All-Union Research Institute of the Physiology, Biochemistry and Nutrition of Farm Animals in Borovsk, in the Kaluga region. This institute studied the most economic and rational way to feed farm animals and the effects of different types of feeding on the quality of farm produce. But science, as always, was far ahead of what the *kolkhozy* and *sovkhozy* could accomplish.

Meat, milk, and eggs are produced throughout the world to satisfy human requirements for proteins of animal origin, for vitamins D and B_{12}, which cannot be obtained from plants, and for a concentrated source of energy (in the form of animal fats and butter). Livestock and poultry farming is the most labor- and land-intensive, and therefore the most expensive, form of agriculture. As Table 28 indicates, many countries in Asia and Africa are unable to produce enough animal protein for human consumption. Human protein requirements depend on the way of life: the growing body requires a higher level of protein per kilogram, so younger people require more than adults. People engaged in active physical work need more than those with a sedentary way of life.

The proportion of protein of animal and plant origin available for human consumption is not, however, the only indication of a healthy diet. A great deal depends on the amino acid composition of the proteins which are consumed. All food proteins are degraded into amino acids in the digestive system and all human proteins are synthesized from amino acids circulating in the blood. There are twenty amino acids which are necessary for the synthesis of most proteins. Twelve of them, called *nonessential* amino acids, can be synthesized by human cells (and the cells of other mammals) from ammonium compounds and the products of carbohydrate metabolism. The other eight (valine, lysine, leucine, isoleucine, threonine, methionine, phenylalanine, and tryptophan) are *essential* amino acids, which cannot be synthesized by animal cells. Moreover, protein synthesis requires that they be available in the proportions in which they are actually present in animal cells. A deficiency in any one of them prevents protein biosynthesis. Thus the nutritional value of food proteins depends on the closeness of their essential amino acid composition to that of the proteins of the human or animal body. If the amount of any essential amino acids is reduced in the food protein, the consumption of that protein must be increased proportionally to compensate for the deficiency. Any extra amino acids consumed at the same time will be used for energy rather than for protein synthesis. Some mammals (for example, cattle, horses, sheep, goats, and other herbivores) can supplement their protein and amino acid requirements through bacterial protein synthesis in their complex and specialized digestive systems. Others, like pigs or fowl, cannot do this, since the passage of food through their digestive systems is too rapid. Like humans, they require higher-quality proteins to satisfy their metabolism.

The amino acid composition of various animal and plant products is shown in Table 27. It will be seen that wheat protein contains less lysine and valine than other cereals. It will also be noticed that some mixtures of plant proteins are a better source of essential amino acids than others. Rye and rice, for example, are closer to animal proteins than wheat and maize. Fine flour contains less protein and has less of some essential amino acids than grain. Removing the germ and the bran from flour makes bread less nutritious than grain.

The human body normally needs about 1.2 grams of protein per day per kilogram of weight. An average person weighing 65 to 70 kilograms thus needs about 90 grams of protein per day (calculated as protein with an appropriate aminoc acid composition). This figure rises to 130 grams for a person engaged in physical activity and to 160 grams for people doing heavy manual work, or for feeding or pregnant mothers. Medical and scientific specialists recommend that at least 60 percent of protein requirements should be provided by proteins of animal origin (meat, milk, eggs, fish). For many developing countries this is an impossible goal for the immediate future. Table 28 shows that the proportion of animal proteins in the diet in the United States and

TABLE 27

Essential Amino Acid Content
of Various Food Products[1]
(Grams per 100 Grams of Protein)

Amino acids*	Meat	Eggs	Milk	Wheat	Rye	Rice	Maize	Pea	Soybean
Lysine	8.5	6.9	7.4	2.7	4.1	3.8	2.7	6.1	6.9
Methionine	2.5	3.1	2.1	1.5	1.6	1.8	1.9	1.2	1.5
Threonine	4.6	5.0	4.6	2.9	3.8	3.6	4.1	3.9	3.7
Tryptophan	1.1	1.6	1.5	1.2	1.1	1.1	0.7	1.1	1.5
Isoleucine	4.7	6.6	6.4	4.3	4.3	4.7	4.9	5.6	5.9
Leucine	8.0	9.5	9.4	6.9	6.7	8.4	12.5	8.3	8.4
Phenylalanine	4.6	4.7	5.8	4.9	4.7	4.5	4.6	5.0	5.4
Valine	5.5	6.5	7.4	4.5	5.2	6.3	5.2	5.6	5.7

* A serious deficiency of any amino acid in a product is indicated by underscoring. Maize is seriously deficient in lysine and tryptophan, wheat in lysine, and pea in methionine. This means that as a source of essential amino acids 100 grams of meat protein has the same value as 300 grams of wheat and maize protein and 200 grams of pea protein. Rye and rice proteins have the same nutritional value as pea protein. Of the grain products, soybean proteins have the highest quality. One hundred fifty grams of soybean protein has the same value as 100 grams of meat protein, 110 grams of milk protein, or 130 grams of egg protein. The figures given in the table are, however, for whole grain. Flour contains less of some of the essential amino acids because the germ, which contains the amino acids with the highest nutritional value, has been removed. In high-quality wheat flour the lysine content is reduced from 2.7 grams per 100 grams of grain protein to 1.9 grams, and the tryptophan is reduced from 1.2 grams to 0.8 grams. Maize flour is particularly deficient since almost all the lysine is in the germ.

Canada is more than 60 percent of the total, a sign that there is an overproduction of meat. The populations of Asia and Africa, on the other hand, clearly suffer from protein deficiency, and this is partly responsible for the lower life expectancy, higher infant mortality, and poorer health of people in these areas. The Soviet Union does not publish figures to illustrate the proportion of animal proteins in the diet. However, by examining the consumption patterns of meat, milk, eggs, and plant products (available in the annual statistical reports), and comparing them to the pattern in Western Europe and the United States, it becomes

TABLE 28

Average World Protein Consumption, 1970–1980[2]

(Grams per Day)

	Protein consumption per person	Consumption of protein of animal origin
Asia (except Japan)	69	23
Africa[a]	66	21
Latin America	80	43
Western Europe	97	62
Eastern Europe (except Soviet Union)	93	60
United States & Canada	102	82
Australia, New Zealand	106	78
Soviet Union[b]	82	38

[a] Protein consumption and the general level of nutrition declined in Africa in 1980–1985, while the levels rose in Asia (mostly because of an improvement in Chinese agriculture).

[b] My estimate is based on the recommended scientifically balanced diet with optimal amounts of meat, milk, fish, and egg products for a daily consumption of 100 grams of protein [3] and the tables, published annually in the statistical yearbooks *Narodnoye khozyaistvo*, of the average consumption of the main food products by the Soviet population.[4]

apparent, first, that the average Soviet diet suffers from protein deficiency, and second, that the deficiency has been increasing in the last decade. This has made it particularly urgent to increase the production of proteins of animal origin.

The problem of the amount of proteins and animal proteins in the diet cannot be separated from the more general question of the proportion of the main food components (proteins, carbohydrates, fats, minerals, and vitamins). Carbohydrates and fats are important sources of energy, and their consumption is usually measured in calories. Men with sedentary occupations require an average of 2,700 calories per day and women need 2,300 to 2,200. Those engaged in physical work require 3,500 to 3,700 calories and men who do heavy manual labor (miners, peasants, dockers) need as much as 5,000 calories. Simple physical laws can be used to calculate the amount of calories required for certain types of physical work. But from the point of view of health, it is more important to satisfy the body's protein requirements first. As we have seen, animal products are important because they have much higher concentrations of proteins. If grain products or other plant sources (for example, potatoes) are used to satisfy the protein requirements, the consumption of carbohydrates will be higher than optimal, resulting in fat deposits in the human body.

Urbanization is usually accompanied by a decrease in the physical activity of the population. Thus food consumed by peasants should contain a higher proportion of carbohydrates as a source of energy than the diet of the urban population. A more sedentary, urban life-style requires a higher proportion of proteins. Thus the general effect of urbanization is to reduce the total amount of food necessary per person, but to increase the quality of the food and the proportion of protein required for a healthy diet. Most of humankind, however, still does not consume sufficient proteins with the best amino acid composition. There are three major ways in which this protein deficiency could be reduced. The first and most labor-intensive and expensive way is to increase the output of animal products—this is the American solution. The second solution is less expensive and more sensible: consumption of high-protein plant sources (peas, soybeans) can be increased. This is the best solution for countries with a very high population density, such as India, China, and Indonesia. A third way of compensating for a deficiency of certain amino acids (lysine, methionine) is by supplementing the diet with these amino acids in forms which have been synthesized or extracted from nonedible sources. This is the most economical way to reduce protein deficiency and it is widely used in feeding animals, particularly poultry. The continuing growth of the world population will eventually make it necessary to use critical amino acids as food additives in the same way that vitamins and some minerals are now often added.

Ever since Stalin's first postwar program of increasing the livestock in 1949–1951, the remedy adopted by the Soviet government to counteract protein deficiency has been the American solution. Khrushchev made reaching the American level of meat consumption a high-priority economic target. As we have already seen, he failed. But the target remained. Some slow progress has been made, but at a very high price. Moreover, the problem of feeding an increasing number of farm animals has proved as intractable as the problem of feeding the human population.

2. The Economy of Livestock Production

After the failure of Khrushchev's program of meat production the official targets were scaled down. The slogan of "catching up" with the American level of consumption of animal products was shelved indefinitely. Nonetheless, at the Central Committee Plenum in March 1965 and in later Party resolutions on agriculture it was stressed that the increase in production of meat, milk, and poultry should be higher than the population growth. It was also acknowledged that livestock farming was poorly mechanized and far too dependent upon manual labor.

The problem with livestock farming was partly due to the fact that feed grain, fodder, and the other ingredients of animal food were not subsidized. This made them expensive in comparison with food grain. The formation of more specialized livestock farms which would have to purchase feed grain and fodder from the state or from other farms was inhibited. The cost of meat production was high and the livestock sections of the *kolkhozy* and *sovkhozy* did not make any profit. To encourage livestock production procurement prices for all animal products, particularly meat, were increased. Later this was supplemented by a substantial rise in the procurement prices for feed grain and fodder products, as well as better salaries for workers on animal farms. Generous subsidies and credits were offered to the *sovkhozy* and *kolkhozy* for the technical reconstruction of their livestock sectors.

When Khrushchev's decentralized economic administration was dismantled, new ministries were created to share the tasks of the Ministry of Agriculture. In addition to the Ministry of Food Industry, a separate Ministry of the Meat and Dairy Industry was established. It was not directly involved in the affairs of the collective and state farms, rather it supervised a network of specialized industrial technology centers for meat production which were designed to introduce "fattening centers" for substandard cattle delivered for slaughter by the farms. It was also in charge of transporting cattle from the farms to the slaughterhouses and improving meat and milk processing. A special Ministry of Machine Building for Livestock Farming and Fodder Production was set up to deal with mechanization. In fact, these administrative measures increased the production costs of animal produce and made it necessary to continue increasing procurement prices. By the beginning of the 1970s the procurement price for "live weight" of cattle and pigs ("live weight" is normally about 50 percent higher than the slaughter weight of carcasses) was about the same as the retail price of meat in the state shops. Although large subsidies were paid to keep down retail prices of meat and other animal produce, many animal farms still could not make a profit. In 1964 the livestock branch of agriculture operated with a net loss of 17 percent. Despite an increase in procurement prices for "live weight" of cattle from 800 rubles per metric ton in 1964 to 1,712 rubles in 1976–1977, livestock *kolkhozy* only made a profit of 3.5 percent and *sovkhozy* of 7.4 percent.[5] Grain and other field crops, by contrast, produced profits of 41.4 percent for *kolkhozy* and 37.4 for *sovkhozy*.

The state subsidies required to cover the difference between animal produce procurement prices and the low retail prices became astronomical. In 1977 the state spent 20 billion rubles to keep food prices down and by 1980 the amount had reached 25 billion rubles.[6] This was more than the amount spent on the health service (14.8 billion rubles) or on state pensions and social security (24 billion rubles). It was even higher than the officially declared military budget (17.1 billion rubles in 1980). Nonetheless, by 1982 livestock production was again operating at a net loss and procurement prices were raised substantially from the beginning of 1983.

Tables 29, 30, 31, and 32 give a general picture of the perfor-

TABLE 29

Livestock and Horse Population, 1965–1986
(Millions)

	Cattle	(Cows)	Pigs	Sheep & Goats	Horses
1965	87.2	(38.8)	52.8	130.7	7.9
1970	95.2	(39.4)	56.1	135.8	7.5
1975	109.1	(41.9)	72.3	151.2	6.8
1980	115.1	(43.3)	73.9	149.4	5.6
1982	115.9	(43.7)	73.3	148.5	5.6
1984	119.6	(43.9)	78.7	151.8	5.7
1986	120.9	(42.9)	77.8	147.3	5.8

Source: Nar. khoz., 1965, p. 367; 1975, p. 391; 1982, p. 241; 1983, p. 258; 1985, p. 236.

TABLE 30

Comparison of the Numbers of Cattle and Pigs
Owned by the Socialist Sector and the Private Sector
(Millions)

	State and collective farms			Private households		
	Cattle	(Cows)	Pigs	Cattle	(Cows)	Pigs
1961	52.8	(19.5)	43.2	23.0	(16.3)	15.3
1966	62.1	(22.7)	38.3	25.1	(16.1)	14.5
1982	93.0	(30.3)	60.9	24.2	(13.5)	15.8
1984	95.0	(30.3)	63.1	24.6	(13.6)	15.6
1986	96.8	(29.7)	63.9	24.1	(13.1)	13.9

Source: Nar. khoz., 1963, pp. 312–313; 1975, p. 391; 1982, p. 241; 1983,p. 258; 1985, p. 236.

TABLE 31

Total Production of Meat, Milk, and Eggs
(on *Kolkhozy*, *Sovkhozy*, and by Individual Households)
(Million Tons)

	1965	1970	1975	1980	1983	1985
Meat (slaughter weight)	10.0	12.3	15.0	15.1	16.4	17.1
Milk & dairy products (as milk)	72.6	83.0	90.8	90.9	96.4	98.6
Eggs (billions)	29.1	40.7	57.4	67.9	75.1	77.3

Source: *Nar. khoz.*, 1974, p. 314; 1982, p. 245; 1983, p. 207; 1985, pp. 180–181.

mance of all types of animal farms (*kolkhozy*, *sovkhozy*, and individual households) for the two decades after Khrushchev. Table 33 gives the official figures for the average consumption of animal products. They are slightly lower than would be calculated by measuring the production figures against the population growth, despite the fact that they reflect not only domestic production,

TABLE 32

Population Growth
(Millions)

	1965	1970	1975	1980	1983	1984	1986
Total population	229.3	241.7	253.3	264.5	271.2	275.0	280.1
Urban population	121.7	136.0	153.1	166.2	174.6	178.5	184.0

Source: *Nar. khoz.*, 1983, p. 5; 1985, p. 5.

but also imported meat and dairy products. The difference reflects losses suffered in the food-processing cycle, partly natural (the use of bones and some animal fats in light industry), and partly because of the perishable nature of the products. Some milk and meat is also used for feeding animals.

The figures make it clear that the only improvement has been in the production and consumption of eggs. This increase, which will be discussed later, is entirely due to the creation of an independent state system of chicken factory farms which operates outside the *kolkhoz* and *sovkhoz* systems. Chicken production has also increased, but Soviet statistics usually include poultry in the total production of meat. Other statistics indicate that poultry constituted about 9 percent of the total meat production in 1913, 10 percent in 1974, 14 percent in 1980, and 16 percent in 1982. There has been no visible growth in the per capita production or consumption of animal products in the last thirteen years and the meat and milk situation has actually deteriorated for the urban population since 1975. State procurements of meat and milk per capita of urban population were 10 percent higher in 1974–1976 than in 1982–1984. This has created shortages of meat, milk, and dairy produce in towns. Despite the rise in imports of meat and butter (from as far afield as Argentina, Australia, and New Zealand), it has been necessary to ration meat and butter in most industrial centers (with the exception of Moscow, Leningrad, and some of the other republican capitals and "hero cities"). In the early 1980s shortages of animal products became very obvious and the price of meat sold in private and collective farm markets rose dramatically, often to four or five times more than the official retail price.

Comparing animal population figures with production shows that the low productivity of farm animals remains a serious problem. The average production of milk per cow in the Soviet Union is still only about half the European level and this cannot be explained by the climate. The climate in Norway and Finland is no better than the climate in the Ukraine, yet the average production of milk per cow was 2,238 kilograms in the Ukraine and 4,300 kilograms in Finland in 1979.[7] The main difficulty in in-

TABLE 33

Consumption of Farm Animal Products
in the Soviet Union and Eastern Europe

	Meat, chicken, animal fat, and related products (kg/person/year)				
	1970	1975	1980	1982	1984
Soviet Union	48	57	58	58	60
Bulgaria	44	61	65	73	75
Hungary[a]	58	68	71	76	78
Poland	61	78	82	65	64
Czechoslovakia[a]	71	81	86	81	84
East Germany[a]	66	83	89	92	94

	Milk and dairy products calculated as milk				
	1970	1975	1980	1982	1984
Soviet Union	307	316	314	295	317
Bulgaria	161	198	234	250	263
Hungary[b]	110	127	166	175	185
Poland	413	432	451	403	426
Czechoslovakia[b]	196	210	228	239	242
East Germany[c]	476	494	516	534	536

Source: [10d].

[a] Figures for meat consumption only. Animal fat is not included.

[b] Hungary and Czechoslovakia report only fresh milk and dairy products excluding butter. This explains the lower figures. In other countries butter consumption is calculated as the milk which has been used in the production of butter.

[c] The consumption of dairy products is so high in East Germany that the figures are not given in the Russian edition of the annual CMEA statistical yearbooks. They were published separately in *Vestnik statistiki*, No. 10, 1984, p. 51.

[d] Different figures are given for meat and milk consumption for some countries in 1982 in the CMEA yearbooks for 1983 and 1984. In the 1983 yearbook, for example, the consumption of meat in Poland is given as 58.5, while a higher figure is given in the 1984 yearbook. The assumption is made in this book that the latest figures are the most accurate. The differences are not explained in the yearbooks, but there is usually a statement in the introduction which indicates that the figures for the current year are preliminary and may be corrected later.

creasing the productivity of Soviet farm animals concerns the problems of animal feed, which will be discussed separately.

The tables clearly show two other major negative trends: a decrease in privately owned cows in the last two decades and a continuing and rapid decline in the number of horses. The fact that official alarm has been expressed about this state of affairs indicates that it is not a natural trend caused by an increase in the proportion of meat and milk produced by the socialist sector in the one case, and of mechanization in the other. Official propaganda and economic incentives have been used in recent years to encourage an increase in the number of privately owned cattle. At the same time, the failure to develop the "mini-mechanization" of agriculture and the campaign to economize on the use of gasoline and other fuels has made it necessary to make more rational use of horses and to renew the production of horse milk and *kumys*, the traditional food of many of the people who live in the steppe and semidesert areas. An active press campaign has also been launched to restore the use of camels for transport, milk, meat, and wool production in the traditional camel areas of Central Asia and Kazakhstan. In 1929 there were 1.7 million camels in these areas. By 1982 the number had fallen to 0.25 million.[8] The volume of sheep and goats milk, popular in the Ukraine, Transcausasia, Central Asia, and some other regions, has also fallen. The number of sheep has not decreased significantly, but the mechanization of milking sheep is difficult and the production of sheep's milk and cheese has almost been forgotten. Some attempts have been made to introduce a small, purpose-designed, mobile milking apparatus for sheep, and it is calculated that there is potential for producing about 0.5 million tons of sheep milk per year.[9] Horse's, camel's, and sheep's milk has a higher nutritional value than cow's milk.

The decrease in the number of privately owned farm animals reflects complex social and demographic developments in the rural areas. The older generation still has vivid memories of the famines of the 1930s and 1940s, but it is dying out. The younger generation is better educated and does not want to spend time taking care of animals. The private ownership of milk cows is still restricted to one per household, but even one cow requires at least two hand milkings per day. Private animal owners cannot use any form of mechanization, and their labor productivity is very low. There is a reverse correlation between the production of milk and meat in socialist and private sectors. There is no economic rationale behind the state's attempts to achieve growth in both sectors. The private production of meat and milk is still high, because the shortage of these commodities in the state shops means that there are very few supplies available for the rural population, and that causes the market price of meat and dairy products to remain very high. These are the only real incentives for the expensive, labor-intensive, and nonproductive private ownership of a few farm animals by individual households. The only way to keep the private sector at a reasonably high level while increasing the socialist sector is to remove all restrictions on private households and to permit small-scale mechanized private animal farms and small milking cooperatives. Some experimental approaches to this problem have been tested and will be discussed in the chapter on private agriculture (Chapter 11).

East Germany, as Table 33 indicates, enjoys the highest level of meat consumption in the CMEA countries (and a higher level than France or Great Britain). This reflects a German tradition of high meat production. It is more appropriate to compare Soviet consumption with that of two other Slav nations, Poland and Czechoslovakia. The level of consumption in Poland in 1982–1984 is lower than in 1980 and 1981 because of the agricultural and food crisis. Food rationing was introduced in Poland in 1982, and food donations were made by Western Europe and the United States. It is interesting, therefore, to note that the level of consumption in Poland in 1982 was higher than the average consumption in the Soviet Union. In 1981 and 1982 the Soviet Union sent significant amounts of meat to Poland to help defuse the political situation. These deliveries, widely publicized in Poland, were kept a secret in the Soviet Union and were not reported in the annual statistics of Soviet foreign trade.

The Soviet consumption of eggs has increased significantly (from 159 eggs per person in 1970 to 216 in 1975 and 249 in

1982). However, this was still well below the Hungarian and Czechoslovakian level (301 and 315 eggs per person respectively). If one examines patterns of food consumption more generally, the Soviet Union holds the record for bread consumption per person (137 kilograms in 1982), Poland leads in the consumption of potatoes per person (159 kilograms in 1982), and Bulgaria has the record for the consumption of fresh vegetables (147 kilograms per person in 1982).[11]

The number of cattle in the Soviet Union is comparable to the number in the United States (115.7 million in 1982)[12] and there are more milk cows and sheep in the Soviet Union than in the United States (but more horses, 9.9 million in 1982, in the United States). However, the productivity of U.S. livestock is much higher than the Soviet Union's. The U.S. average production of milk from one cow is 5,100 kilograms, whereas in the Soviet Union it is less than half that (2,258 kilograms in 1983). Comparing American and Soviet levels of meat production is difficult. It is known that the average consumption of meat in the United States was 111 kilograms per person in 1979,[13] double the amount consumed in the Soviet Union. But American "statistical" meat is different from Soviet "statistical" meat. Meat, pork, chicken and rabbit meat, animal fat, and other subproducts are not combined into a single group in American statistics. Various kinds of meat are listed separately, and not in slaughter weights. Separate figures are given for milk, butter, and eggs. Western countries report the production of eggs in metric tons, rather than actual eggs, because eggs vary in size (which in turn depends on the nutrition of the poultry).

It would clearly be much more economical for the Soviet Union to decrease the number of farm animals and increase their productivity. This would reduce the requirements for feed grain and fodder. The planning organizations rightly see the solution to the problems of productivity in the introduction of industrial technology or intensification, based on complex and comprehensive mechanization and a scientific approach to the feeding of farm animals. The total investments in livestock farming and milk production have been very high and have increased annually from

1970 to 1985. Nonetheless, the average production of milk per cow was only 2,110 kilograms in 1970, 2,204 in 1975, 2,134 in 1982, and 2,322 in 1985.[14] In other words, there has hardly been any increase. The reasons for this need to be examined.

3. The Technical and Organizational Problems of Livestock and Milk Production

In almost every region of the Soviet Union there is a highly productive model animal farm where cows (of the same breed as elsewhere in the region) each produce 5,000 kilograms of milk per year and where beef cattle grow faster, and have reached a much higher weight when they are delivered for slaughter, than the average for the area. The propaganda apparatus and the press try to disseminate the experience of these farms and to convince others to follow their methods. In fact, there are no secret or special methods involved. The model farms simply have better supplies of feed grain and fodder, sufficient workers, modern, purpose-built buildings, and well-qualified mechanics to keep the milking and other equipment in good working order. Moreover, they follow the well-organized sequence of operations which is set out in any elementary textbook on livestock production. Most other collective and state farms simply do not enjoy similar conditions. In the vastness of the Soviet Union, where the rural road system is often very poorly developed, the distance of an animal farm from the nearest industrial center is a key factor in its success or failure. If the farm is close to an industrial milk or meat production plant and to a good motorway or railway, the economics of animal farming are much easier. Milk can be delivered to the processing plant quickly and cheaply. Cattle can be transported in the shortest possible time without any loss of weight. Many feed products are processed and distributed from towns and cities. Technical assistance is more easily obtained if the farm is close to a town. Yet few *kolkhozy* and *sovkhozy* enjoy the advantages of this proximity.

Twenty or thirty years ago there were many small rural facilities for making butter and dairy products. Sometimes they were attached to the animal farms and it was normal procedure for the state to accept milk procurements in the form of butter, smetana, cheese, and other dairy products, calculated according to the amount of milk used to make the products. The remaining "milk serum" was used on the farms as a nutritional drink for calves and other animals. The gradual extinction of these local small-scale food-processing plants was probably the inevitable result of rapid urbanization and rural labor shortages, but nothing was done to ensure that it took place in a coordinated way.

Very rapid urbanization (the urban population has increased from 60 million to 184 million in the postwar period alone) and industrialization were not accompanied by the development of a well-organized rural distribution network or a transport infrastructure. The modernization of rural settlements was delayed. Meat- and milk-processing plants were usually located in regional centers and larger towns, often some distance from the actual centers of agricultural production. The government favored the building of fewer and larger highly mechanized processing plants, neglecting the alternative of smaller, but better-distributed processing facilities. It soon became clear that there was a serious disproportion between the capacity of the processing plants and their ability to collect the raw products. Milk is an easily perishable commodity and needs fast processing. It must be cooled very quickly (within an hour or two after milking) and maintained at a low temperature. But the specialized milk transport system is neither refrigerated nor insulated. Milk is transported in tanker trucks or simply in cans. As a result, speed of transportation is vital, particularly between May and September, when the temperature is high, and between December and February, when it is very low.

Until very recently, farms were responsible for their own transport. But only one type of milk tanker is produced in the Soviet Union and it has a capacity of 3,300 kilograms, far more than most farms produce in a single milking. As a result, the tankers either have to collect milk from several farms en route to the processing plant, or they have to wait for the second milking of the day to fill up and make the delivery economically viable. Not surprisingly, an enormous amount of milk is lost at this stage. Only recently has the task of collecting and transporting milk been transferred to the processing plants. For years the press has reported the advantages of this new "centralized collection" system, as it is called. But as late as 1984 "centralized collection" of milk and cattle was used for less than 30 percent of the milk and cattle delivered from the farms to the processing plants.[15] The processing industry simply did not possess sufficient milk tankers and specialized cattle trucks. Only one type of cattle truck is produced in the Soviet Union (capable of carrying 6 tons of weight). This lack of diversity of trucks and milk tankers means that transport facilities are not flexible enough for local road conditions. There are no specialized facilities for poultry, and the new state chicken factory farms have chronic transport problems.

The gradual disappearance of small local processing plants in favor of larger ones has made the task of collecting or delivering products from the farms formidable. In a recent description of the daily work of one of the most modern milk-processing plants in Novocherkassk, which employs 530 workers and is equipped with modern technology, the centralized delivery system used by the plant is highly praised. But the description indicates the problem, not the solution.

> . . . 60 drivers are employed for collection. They have to drive to *kolkhozy* and *sovkhozy* situated very far away (often a hundred, two hundred, sometimes even three hundred kilometers) from the plant. And they have to make these trips daily, during the winter frosts and blizzards and during the summer heat.[16]

Novocherkassk is in the Rostov region, a well-developed agricultural area with a dense population of 4.2 million people and rich, rather large villages. It is senseless to transport milk 200 to 300 kilometers for processing. It is as if all the milk in a country like Denmark or Holland were collected for processing in a single central plant. The road system is so poor in rural areas of the Soviet Union that it is unlikely that milk tankers can make the journey in less than three to five hours. And if the problem is serious in the Rostov region, it is even worse in the eastern parts of the country. The Novosibirsk milk-processing plant, for example, collects milk from a region which is probably as large as England and from districts "where there are practically no good roads with hard surfaces. During the spring and autumn rainy seasons, these roads are almost unpassable."[17]

It seems clear that the disappearance of local small processing facilities and the construction of large modern food-processing plants (part of the agro-industrial complexes which were to solve the problems of agriculture) has actually aggravated many problems. It is acknowledged that the quality of dairy products has deteriorated in the last decade and that many famous and popular local brands of butter and cheese have disappeared. In a country as large and diverse in agricultural and cultural traditions as the Soviet Union, it would be better if the modernization program was used to supplement, rather than to replace, local practices and traditions. Recommendations about restoring small-scale processing facilities were made at the Twenty-seventh Party Congress in 1986, but practical measures have not yet been initiated.

State procurements of cattle, pigs, and poultry are made according to "live weight," and this is the basis of payment for livestock. During the war, when the calories of animal fat were as important as the protein of the meat, this made sense. But for years since then meat-processing plants have been arguing that they should pay different rates for meat and for fat. However, the system remains unchanged. It is easier for animal farms to fatten the livestock on high-carbohydrate diets than on high-protein diets, which are more expensive. The meat production figures given in the state statistics include animal fat and subproducts and usually consist of 50 percent fat and bones.

Attempts have been made to adopt progressive livestock technology by creating giant, specialized livestock farms around the large cities. Like the more widely tested system of chicken factory farms (some containing up to a million chickens), this branch of meat and milk production is outside the collective and state farm system. Together with the huge greenhouse using the waste heat from the towns and cities to grow fresh vegetables, these animal farms represent a new branch of the agricultural industry employing urban workers. However, they are heavily subsidized and highly uneconomical. Each farm is stocked with 3,000 to 10,000 cows and beef cattle, and instructed to use scientifically designed diets to produce the maximum amount of meat and milk. The high concentration of animals makes it impossible to use meadows and pastures in the normal way. As a result the animals need a permanent supply of feed and fodder and most of the farms are dependent on centralized state deliveries of feed grain, complex feed, and fodder. The *kolkhozy* and *sovkhozy* around these farms specialize in the production of cattle food (silage, hay, and seed grain). But it was quickly found that traditional breeds of cattle need pasture and exercise for normal growth and development. Moreover, keeping them in barns has led to an increase in the incidence of various kinds of disease. Although some of these "industrial farms" are successful, producing up to 2,000 metric tons of meat and 10,000 tons of milk per year, they do not represent a solution for agriculture as a whole. There is no proper balance between elements of the agricultural cycle in this kind of farming and the organic fertilizer produced by the cattle is wasted. Traditional rural life is disrupted and, in any case, the problems of mechanizing all the work on such large farms still remain to be solved.

In 1970 only 10 percent of all *kolkhoz* and *sovkhoz* animal farms enjoyed "complex mechanization" (the term refers to the mechanization of most of the work on an animal farm, including the preparation and distribution of food and drinking water, removal of waste, milking, etc.). By 1978 complex mechanization had been extended to 36 percent of cattle and milk farms, 60 percent of pig farms, and 67 percent of poultry farms.[18] The level of mechanization of the various operations in animal farms ceased to be reported in later statistics, but this did not mean that mechanization had been completed. The productivity of labor (measured in the Soviet Union by the number of "human-hours" per 100 kilograms of production) increased rapidly from 1965 to 1975 and then stopped rising. Increases in productivity are usually

TABLE 34
Productivity of Livestock Farms
(Human-Hours per 100 Kilogams of Production)

| | Kolkhozy | | | |
	1966–1970	1971–1975	1976–1980	1981–1985
Milk	14	11	10	9
Weight Increase				
(growth & fattening)				
Cattle	71	61	53	51
Pigs	60	44	37	38
Sheep	64	58	57	58
Eggs (per 1000)	44	26	21	19

| | Sovkhozy | | | |
	1966–1970	1971–1975	1976–1980	1981–1984
Milk	10	9	8	8
Weight increase				
(growth & fattening)				
Cattle	48	45	41	41
Pigs	30	23	19	19
Sheep	42	41	41	44
Eggs (per 1,000)	12	7	4	3

Source: Nar. khoz., 1979, p. 310; 1984, p. 324; 1985, p. 320.

registered in Soviet statistics by taking the level of a certain period as the base and calling it 100, and then comparing subsequent levels. Between 1970 and 1976 livestock farming productivity grew from 100 to 126. But in subsequent years, from 1976 to 1983 no increases was registered.[19]

Table 34 shows the direct expenditure of labor hours per 100 kilograms of production in 1971–1984. The only real improvement was in the egg industry. Compared to the standards of agricultural production in Europe, Canada, and the United States, Soviet agricultural production shows very low productivity. It is also clear from the table that although the productivity on the *sovkhozy* is by no means high, it is well above *kolkhoz* performance. The difference is particularly evident for the production of pork and eggs. There was no significant increase in the productivity of wool between 1970 and 1985. In 1966–1970 the production of 100 kilograms of wool normally consumed 197 human-hours on the *sovkhozy* and 294 human-hours on the *kolkhozy*. In 1980–1984 the figures were 223 and 276 hours. The general performance of the *kolkhozy* was very poor in 1970–1984. If the index of all types of animal production in *kolkhozy* was 100 in 1970, it rose to 109 in 1975 and then fell to 99.7 in 1980 and 99.5 in 1982.[20] The increase in 1975 reflects the slaughter of cattle because of a very poor harvest of grain and other crops. The fall in production between 1970 and 1985 occurred despite an increase in the total number of cattle (from 41 million to 50 million) on the *kolhozy*, including an increase in milk cows.

The productivity of the large specialized animal farms which have been created outside the collective and state farm system (called *mezhkhozyaistvennye predpriyatiya*, or "interfarm enterprises") is also rather low. The number of such enterprises grew from 315 in 1970 to 1,018 in 1983 (and dropped to 989 in 1984), but they do not yet contribute a great deal to overall livestock production. Most specialize in the intensive growth and fattening of cattle and pigs purchased from the *kolkhozy* and *sovkhozy*. In 1984 they owned about 1.3 million cattle and 1.7 million pigs,[21] less than 2 percent of the total livestock population. Since their function is to fatten up substandard cattle and pigs, they report the "extra weight" which they have achieved by using a more intensive feeding technology. Between 1980 and 1984 the number of enterprises did not increase and their production of "extra weight" has declined (280,200 metric tons of cattle meat in 1980 and 260,200 tons in 1984). Thus each plant produces an average of 620 metric tons of meat per year, very little compared to the investments and their total cost.

The growth of productivity has been well below the increase

of machinery for animal farming supplied by the state industry. The introduction of machinery sharply increased production costs of animal produce, and this was the main problem in the 1970s and 1980s. To offset these costs, procurement prices were increased several times, but with very little effect. Initial calculations of the effects of mechanization had shown that it would enable a reduction of the work force by at least 3 million in the last decade. However, the directors of *sovkhozy* and chairmen of *kolkhozy* have been reluctant to reduce their work force, since they have wanted to be able to cover the many emergencies which occur when the equipment malfunctions. In any case, most farms are still incompletely mechanized. Nonetheless, although the number of registered workers per 100 animals is rather high on Soviet farms compared to modern farms in Western Europe and the United States, most livestock farms suffer from an acute shortage of qualified personnel. The labor situation is so serious that a special decision was taken by the Politburo at the beginning of 1984 to mobilize 50,000 Komsomol members to work on the animal farms.[22]

The performance of the animal farms differs, of course, from one region to another. The best performance, however, is not found in the climatically most favorable areas of the Ukraine and North Caucasus, but in Latvia and, particularly, Estonia. For the most part this is due to better organization and higher-quality agricultural labor. Livestock and milk farms are reasonably sized and many farm brigades are based on family units. Milk production in Estonia was as high as 3,600 to 3,700 kilograms per cow in 1981–1982, 60 percent higher than in the Ukraine. Estonia also produces more wool per sheep and more eggs per hen than any other republic of the Soviet Union. It has the highest productivity of meat per head of cattle and the highest level of overall livestock production per 100 hectares of cultivated land. The average "live weight" of cattle delivered for slaughter in the Soviet Union was 309 kilograms in 1970 and 340 kilograms in 1982. In the Baltic republics the figure varied from 400 to 500 kilograms, well above the average. Similarly, all other indicators of productivity (milk and meat per unit of nutrition and per human-hour of labor, production costs, etc.) were much better in Latvia and Estonia than in all other regions of the Soviet Union, despite poor soil and a cold climate. One hundred twenty-five kilograms of meat (slaughter weight), 800 kilograms of milk, and 330 eggs were produced per head of the 1.5 million population in Estonia in 1980, more than in Finland or the other Scandinavian countries.[23] The productivity of the livestock industry is seven times higher in Estonia and Latvia than in Uzbekistan. This indicates how large the regional differences of performance are in the Soviet Union.

The only branch of farm animal production that can be considered relatively successful is poultry. But even this is not because of improvements in the *kolkhozy* and *sovkhozy*. In fact, *kolkhoz* poultry production declined between 1970 and 1983. Most of the chickens and eggs consumed by the urban population were produced by private households and by special state chicken factories. The factories are combined into a specialized industrial system called *Ptitseprom* ("poultry industry"), which is separate from both the Ministry of Agriculture and the Ministry of the Meat and Dairy Industry. Economically independent, *Ptitseprom* was created during the last year of Khrushchev's rule as part of his program of dividing agriculture up into twelve individual specialized branches (see page 196). The rest of the program was abandoned after Khrushchev's downfall, but *Ptitseprom* survived and did quite well after 1964. The number of poultry factories grew steadily, to about 1,400 in 1981. In 1982 the *Ptitseprom* network produced 40 billion eggs, compared to 22 billion pro duced by private households and 4.9 billion produced by the *kolkhozy*.[24] *Ptitseprom* is now responsible for about half the total production of eggs, chicken, turkey, geese, and other farm poultry. But the system is heavily dependent on centralized supplies of special feed from the state and it consumes a significant proportion of imported grain. It would now be impossible to preserve this branch of the agricultural industry at its present level without importing grain and special complex mixed chicken feed. A large proportion of the machinery used in the chicken factories is also imported. The most efficient methods of battery farming (including breeding broilers, which require special genetic methods of inbreeding, linebreeding, and crossbreeding) are only at the planning stage.

The commonest complaints about the state of the poultry industry have to do with shortages of essential food supplements (lysine and methionine), antibiotics, packing materials for eggs, and the inability of modern plants to deliver their produce in the best possible form for retail sale. More than 60 percent of the battery chickens are sent for retail sale (in frozen or cooled form) without the removal of internal organs. This loss of a very useful by-product (which could be used to make high-quality feed) is a typical feature of Soviet milk, meat, and poultry farming. It is ironic that a country in which the main agricultural problem is the acute shortage of all types of feed for farm animals suffers from such unnecessary large losses and waste of potentially high-quality feed products due to poor planning, incomplete mechanization, lack of transport facilities, and general mismanagement or, as it is called in Russian, *bezkhozyaistvennost'* (a word which defies translation, since it includes poor and shoddy work as well as poor coordination between different branches of the economy).

4. The Feeding of Farm Animals

The single most serious and intractable problem of Soviet agriculture is clearly the feeding of farm animals. In developed industrial countries, farm animals consume more grain and larger amounts of cultivated crops (feed potato, turnips, corn for silage, clover, alfalfa, mixed sown grass) than do people. A larger part of the arable land is therefore cultivated for animal feed. In addition, meadows and pastures covering a significant area of land are required. For a human population of 280.1 million on July 1, 1986, 126.7 million cattle and horses, 225 million pigs, sheep, and goats, and more than 1 billion fowl of various kinds had to be fed in the Soviet Union. For every 1,000 calories of human diet, Soviet agriculture has to produce at least 5,000 calories of farm animal diet (for the sake of simplicity, the metabolic rate of all mammals and birds is taken to be the same) if animal produce is consumed as a source of high-quality proteins. If the produce is considered as an energy source as well, for every 1,000 calories of human diet, the animals need to be fed about 12,000 calories of feed grain, fodder, and various feed supplements. In China, with a population of more than one billion, the total number of large-size farm animals is 112 million, while the number of pigs, goats, and sheep is 480 million.[25] In general, farm animals in China consume only slightly more calories than the human population does. The situation in the United States is quite different. With a population of 234 million in 1982, agriculture must produce at least ten times more plant food for animals than for people. In 1982, 300 million metric tons of feed grain (corn, barley, oats, soybeans, cotton seed) was produced in the United States and only 85 million tons of grain for local human consumption and export (wheat, rice, rye).[26] The level of production of feed grain in the United States in 1982 was about twice as high as the total amount of grain for all purposes (170 million tons) produced in the Soviet Union for a larger population.

It is not suggested here that the Soviet Union should follow the American example in proportion of arable land used to feed livestock. There is considerable overproduction in the United States, which damages the topsoil and entails a high ecological price. One hectare of arable land can produce twenty times more calories and ten times more proteins in the form of grain than in the form of meat and milk. Even the Soviet level of agriculture is damaging the ecological balance, and the fertility and substance of the topsoil is steadily being lost, particularly in the *chernozem* areas. But most of the agricultural problems in the Soviet Union are caused by poor organization and planning, not by overproduction. There are unnecessarily high losses of nutritional materials in the normal cycle of livestock production. The production costs of one ton of coarse fodder is about the same in many regions of the Soviet Union as the production costs of one ton of feed grain. This is an absurd situation, which is partially caused by labor shortages. In the haymaking season millions of urban dwellers with no training in agricultural work are mobilized and sent to help with the work.

Preparing supplies of animal food is a national problem from early spring until late autumn. The Central Statistical Bureau publishes weekly reports in central newspapers like *Izvestiya* and *Pravda* of the production of all types of fodder. Regional statistical reports are published in regional and district newspapers. Every week millions of newspaper readers are told how much grass has been mowed and how much has been dried and made into hay or "grass flour." Later in the summer there are reports on the production of silage and *senazh* (haylage, a more concentrated form of low-moisture silage, made from slightly dry wilted grass that is tightly packed into trenches). Then straw products are added to the reports. Finally the maize for silage and turnips and other special fodder crops are listed and the newspapers begin to report the figures as a percentage of the plan. The plan usually covers the amount of feed required to ensure a proper diet for the livestock until the beginning of the following summer. But I cannot remember ever reading a report which indicated that the target figures had been reached. If 80 percent of the target tonnage of fodder has been reached in the second half of October, the output is usually considered successful.

The weekly statistical reports deal mostly with fodder supplies for cattle and horses. Pigs and poultry require more concentrated and complex feed made from feed grain, feed vegetables, and special-made, highly nutritional fodder granules. For cattle, horses, sheep, and goats coarse fodder (grass, hay, silage, straw) is more important than grain. In fact, cattle cannot survive without coarse fodder, since they need not only to consume certain amounts of proteins, carbohydrates, and fats, but also to fill their large and complex stomachs and long intestines with cellulose fiber from plants and other coarse products. Grain improves the productivity of cattle, but is not essential for life. Concentrated feed can only be used by cattle if their digestive systems are filled with coarse fodder. A significant proportion of coarse fodder (maize, silage, clover, mixed grass, turnip, straw) is produced as part of the field rotation system on the cultivated lands. The rest is consumed directly from meadows and pastures in the summer (from May until the beginning of October) and then prepared from those areas (as hay and haylage) for the winter. There are large areas classified as meadows and pastures in the Soviet Union, but most of them are situated in Kazakhstan and the eastern parts of the country, which support large numbers of sheep (the traditional multipurpose animal for these rather dry regions). As Table 35 shows, the European parts of the country, and particularly those parts with a large cattle population (the Ukraine, Byelorussia, and the Baltic Republics), have a rather limited acreage of pasture compared to the acreage of cultivated land.

Many attempts have been made to improve the productivity of meadows, pastures, and hay-mowing land by using fertilizers and irrigation or introducing a more rational system of grazing. However, they have remained small-scale measures and they have not really improved the general output of hay and grass. The farm animal population has grown much more rapidly than the productivity of pasture and haymaking land.

The difference between pastures and meadows is simply that land which is unsuitable for mowing (because of bushes, ravines, bits of forest, etc.) is classified as pastureland. The pastures in Kazakhstan are often rather arid, but this is not the case in the Ukraine or Latvia. It is clear from the table that there is a shortage of meadows and hay-mowing land in the traditional agricultural areas, which are also the most populated areas. The reason why the acreage of meadows as a whole has declined by as much as about 8 million hectares from 1965 to 1984 without a concomitant increase of sown land has mostly to do with industrial development, and particularly the construction of hydroelectric projects. The building of power stations like the Volga, Don, and Dnieper cascades, the Dnieser power station, and others has created large water reservoirs which permanently cover some 10 million hectares of very productive flood meadowland, as well as cultivated land and some forests.[27] Many thousands of villages and settlements in theses areas were abandoned or relocated. Lately agricultural experts have been arguing that the dams and hydroelectric projects should have been built by the Dutch method, with parallel dams which would have protected the valuable fields from flooding. This would have increased the cost of the projects,

TABLE 35

Distribution of Land between Cultivated Crops
and Meadows and Pastures
(Million Hectares)

	Food and technical crops		Meadows & haymaking land		Pastures	
	1965	1984	1965	1984	1965	1984
Soviet Union	223.4	227.0	42.23	34.3	266.3	291.0
Kazakhstan	35.2	35.6	5.7	5.1	147.7	156.1
Ukraine	34.1	34.2	2.5	2.1	4.5	4.6
Byelorussia	6.3	6.2	2.1	1.4	1.3	1.9
Latvia	1.8	1.7	0.65	0.20	0.4	0.5
Estonia	0.8	1.0	0.47	0.30	0.2	0.2

Source: Nar. khoz., 1965, pp. 277, 278; 1984, p. 244.

but it would have preserved fields and villages as well as meadows. It would also have made irrigation systems much easier.

It is also clear from Table 35 that although the livestock population grew rapidly between 1965 and 1984, there was a decline in the acreage of pastures and meadows in the European part of the Soviet Union. Every effort should have been made to increase the productivity of existing meadows and pastures and to transform into what agricultural science calls "cultural" meadows and pastures. Simple methods of regulating varieties of grass species and selecting the best possible time for mowing (when the grass contains the maximum concentration of proteins) can double or triple the nutritional value of meadow- and pastureland. This was not done and the nutritional value of these lands increased more slowly than the livestock population, as the figures in Table 36 indicate. The proportion of natural grazing in the general balance of available fodder also declined, and the amount of feed and fodder per "cattle unit" remained roughly at the same level as in

TABLE 36

Production and Consumption of
Feed Grain, Fodder, and Pasture Grass
(Million Tons)

	1965	1970	1975	1980	1982	1984
Concentrated feed (grain & complex feed granules)	65.3	103.2	118.9	143.9	141.3	143.5
Rich fodder (silage, haylage, feed potato, etc.)	416.6	447.1	501.6	580.0	596.3	679.1
Coarse fodder (hay, straw, etc.)	164.0	173.1	237.6	231.7	239.8	266.2
Production of feeding units per livestock unit	22.5	24.8	25.1	27.3	25.6	26.5

Source: Nar. khoz., 1978, p. 258; 1982, p. 254; 1984, p. 292.

1970 when calculated in nutritional or "feeding units." These units indicate the actual amount of useful elements in fodder or feed grain which is assimilated from a particular kind of nutrition. They are important indicators of the quality of the feed. The amount of hay could be increasing, for example, while the nutritional value actually decreased (if the mowing was done too late, when the grass had grown beyond the stage when the concentration of protein is at its maximum). Different methods of preparing silage produce different nutritional values. In the scientific literature the feeding units are specific for different animals. Straw and hay have nutritional value for cattle, for example, but not for poultry or pigs. However, in general statistics such as those given in Table 36, feeding units are given as an artificial average for all farm animals.

The figures given for "concentrated feed" (which also includes special complex feed granules) in Table 36 reflect both domestic production and the import of feed grain. This figure has been kept above 100 million tons by purchasing feed grain (and sometimes complex feed as well) abroad. Many experts argue that the Soviet Union would be able to reduce the amount of grain it imports if active measures were taken to increase the nutritional value of domestic fodder and if better use were made of the meadows and other sources of animal food. It has been known for years that more proteins, soluble carbohydrates, and vitamins are preserved when hay is dried as quickly as possible and kept in specially pressed brickettes. In 1982 only 12 million tons of hay, less than a fifth of the total, was preserved in this way.[28] Brickettes of hay or straw are also more convenient for transport and storage. However, special machines for producing them were only designed in the Soviet Union after a long delay.

Soviet pastures and meadows tend to be used in an archaic fashion. Fields are not divided into sectors and there is no pattern of using pasture grass. The grass composition of the natural meadows and pastures could be improved—with even a modest use of fertilizers, the hay harvest could be increased three- or fivefold from the current extremely low level of about 8 centners per hectare. Although many articles have been published advocating the wider introduction of "improved meadows and pastures," these measures have been adopted for a very small proportion of the natural pastures. It was not until Brezhnev's Food Program in 1982 that the government finally accepted the need to improve pastures and meadows, setting a target of 27 to 29 million hectares of "improved meadow fields." But even that was less the result of rational argument than a consequence of the further deterioration of existing meadows and pastures in the traditional agricultural areas. The search for new land to cultivate grain and other crops had reduced the acreage available for cattle grazing. Many collective and state farms restricted their grazing to land that was difficult to cultivate. As a result these areas became overgrazed and their productivity declined. Although a significant number of cattle is maintained indoors during the summer as well as the winter (this is the "industrial method" of livestock production), it is important that milk cows and pedigree cattle graze in the spring and summer. The indoor maintenance of sheep and goats is very uneconomical. In any case, grazing is important in the Soviet Union because of the chronic shortage of feed grain and fodder, particularly in the late spring. On many farms the cattle suffer from malnutrition after the long winter, and grazing is essential until the grass is long enough for mowing. Many meadows have been so overgrazed and neglected that they need more than improvement: "rejuvenation" is required, by means of ploughing, repeated cultivation, fertilization, and sowing with special mixtures of grass crops. It is a costly method, but important in many regions with a high concentration of livestock.

Even traditional work like hay mowing has become heavily dependent on the seasonal mobilization of the urban work force. Every year millions of industrial workers, local officials, scientists, students, and schoolchildren are sent to help with the animal fodder campaigns. They usually use primitive instruments like scythes, rakes, and pitchforks, but even these simple tools are in short supply. Haystacking is done by the same method as a hundred years ago. Most haystacks and virtually all strawstacks are left in the fields. Roofed storage facilities with or without drying equipment are extremely rare. Because of these primitive conditions, the hay loses proteins, vitamins, and other elements. In some years the loss is as much as 50 percent.

The shortage of fodder made it necessary to consider using distant meadows in the basins of the great Siberian Ob, Yenesei, Lena, and Amur rivers in the sparsely populated areas of Siberia and the Far East for haymaking. This work was started at the end of the 1970s as an experiment, but it has been suggested that it needs to be developed as a specialized branch of the fodder industry.[29] Special mechanized fodder brigades prepare the hay in these areas in pressed brickettes, which are easy to transport by ship and barge along the rivers. Some of the ships are factories for making grass flour and grass vitamin granules. Similar fodder manufacturing flotillas are expected to appear in the European part of the Soviet Union and their products will be sold to other collective and state farms or to the state.

The main problem of animal feeding in the Soviet Union is the deficiency of proteins for pigs and poultry and of proteins and protein-producing nitrogen compounds in cattle fodder. According to scientific standards, each statistical feeding unit should contain 116 grams of protein, but often it only contains 80 to 90 grams and the rest consists of carbohydrates, fats, and other nutritional elements.[30] The effect of protein and nitrogen deficiency and a disproportionately high carbohydrate content is to delay growth and cause larger fat deposits in the cattle and poultry delivered for slaughter. It also means that livestock and poultry need more feed and fodder per unit of production of meat, milk, or eggs. The protein content of animal feed can be increased by simple agricultural methods or by more sophisticated industrial methods. Agricultural methods are cheaper, since all that is required is better planning and organization of all the elements of the agricultural cycle. The proportion of clover, alfalfa, and other leguminous grass crops in the sown grass and in the natural meadow plant population should be increased. There are several high-protein plants (like lupin, particularly the alkaloid-free forms) which can be specially selected for protein-rich fodder and silage crops. Increasing the cultivation of these plants will also improve soil fertility, since they fixate nitrogen from the atmosphere. But the simplest way to improve the protein content is to use correct methods of hay mowing and making. Hundreds of studies have been made to establish the stage of growth when plants contain the highest content of digestible protein and should be mowed. This is normally the blossoming period. Mowing, like almost all other seasonal agricultural work, should be done in the shortest possible time during this optimal period. However, it tends to be prolonged in the Soviet Union and to be dependent on poorly qualified urban workers and students.

Improving the protein balance by industrial methods involves adding nitrogen-containing chemicals (ammonium, urea, or carbamide) to coarse fodder and silage. The chemicals are assimilated by the microbial flora of the intestines of the cattle to syn-thesize proteins. Pigs and poultry cannot transform these chemicals into proteins and they would be toxic, but the diet can be enriched by adding protein made from yeasts or other microbial sources. The idea of using yeasts, algae, and other microorganisms (or single-cell organisms) emerged in the early 1960s. They could be grown from the by-products of the oil industry (hydrocarbons) or the cellulose and chemical industry, or be produced by pho-tosynthesis, like *Chlorella*. This source of protein was considered important for countries like Japan, which are heavily dependent on the import of food, but it is only in the Soviet Union that the industrial development has taken place of commercially viable plants for large-scale production of single-cell proteins (SCP). A special microbiological industry was established about twenty-five years ago and by 1963 the Soviet Union was producing 58,000 tons of yeast protein. In 1984 there were more than 110 large protein-producing plants in operation with an annual production of 1,420,000 tons of protein per year.[31] It forms part of the chem-ical industry rather than the agricultural industry. Many new plants are under construction. Western reviewers of Soviet bio-technology acknowledge that "the USSR is undoubtedly the world-leader in SCP production."[32]

The production of yeast protein for livestock by using waste sources of energy and waste chemicals seems eminently rational. This form of food does not depend on weather conditions or good transport facilities. However, the target of 10 to 12 million tons of yeast protein predicted by optimists (and it is almost certainly an unrealistic target to be achieved in ten years) will not solve the problem of feeding the livestock. Yeast protein is an enricher, not a food product. Single-cell proteins will only contribute to resolving the problem of livestock feeding if the many other prob-lems connected with traditional sources of animal food are also solved. Moreover, it should be stressed that single-cell proteins are not cheap. Economic considerations have delayed their large-scale production in many other countries. The technological pro-cesses include many stages of chemical and enzymological processing of raw materials (cellulose, by-products of the petrochemical industry, and wastes of the food industry) and the use of many different chemical and mineral components. In the United States the retail price of SCP from various types of yeast was much higher in 1982 than the price of protein products from soybeans or skim milk.[33]

It is difficult to justify the rapid growth of sophisticated industrial methods of protein enrichment when it would be much easier to prevent the loss of proteins in fodder products which are already available. The losses of nutritional elements are higher than the value of the industrial supplements. It is widely acknowledged that the nutritional quality of hay is lower now than in the 1930s, or even in the 1920s when about 80 percent of all haystacks were kept in sheds and barns during the winter. Most peasant households had barns. In the 1980s many *kolkhozy* and *sovkhozy* have built modern barns and equipped them with facilities and equipment for drying, pressing, loading, and unloading. Nonetheless, *90 percent* of all the hay in the Soviet Union is kept in the open, not even covered by plastic or other rain-resistant material.[34]

Many complaints are voiced about the quality of the silage and haylage which now forms the largest complement of coarse fodder. It has been admitted, for example, that about half the total fodder in the Soviet Union in 1979–1980 was classified as substandard, third-class quality (containing about 2.5 less feeding units per ton than first-class fodder).[35]

Conclusion

The principal conclusion of this chapter is obvious. Large-scale livestock projects of the industrial type have failed because they were constructed too fast and without reliable, well-tested mechanization or proper supplies of feed. At the same time individual, private ownership of farm animals has not increased even when restrictions were lifted. This is primarily because the number of rural households has fallen, but a contributory cause is the low productivity of the labor-intensive work involved in caring for animals and the difficulties of feeding them. Even the best *kolkhoz* and *sovkhoz* animal farms suffer from shortages of skilled and qualified labor, incomplete mechanization, shortages of meadows and pastures, and the high price of feed grain and fodder. Livestock farming has remained unprofitable despite artificially high procurement prices and large subsidies.

The government price policy for feed, food, and livestock production makes no sense. Food prices continue to be subsidized, while the price of animal food and fodder products are allowed to rise to reflect production costs. It is thus more profitable for individual households and many *kolkhozy* and *sovkhozy* to buy food grain and bread from the state to feed their livestock than to buy animal feed. Despite many attempts to prevent this, it has become so widespread that a special resolution was passed by the Politburo and Central Committee in 1985 which severely criticized the "mass use of food resources and the wholesale purchase of bread and other products from the urban and rural trade systems by *kolkhozy, sovkhozy,* and the population as a whole to feed livestock."[36] Until then it was only individuals who were criticized by the press and by government and Party organs for using bread to feed animals. Now for the first time the collective and state farms were held equally responsible. However, with the procurement price for "live weight" of pork at 1,500 percent of the retail price of wheat bread and the price of pork higher than the price of beef, it clearly made better sense for *kolkhozy* and *sovkhozy* to buy bread which is easily available than to produce their own high-cost fodder and feed grain. The 1985 resolution also criticized the state and party organizations of many districts which

> tolerate a wasteful attitude to bread . . . and conduct explanatory work amongst the population poorly. This causes great moral and material damage and does not correspond to the general tasks of developing livestock farming.[37]

The Five Year Plan (1981–1985) was not fulfilled and the actual output of meat and other livestock products fell far short of the targets in each annual plan of the period. Moreover, the performance during the first four years of the Food Program introduced in 1982 has also been well below expectations. The absence of any visible growth in livestock production per capita in the last decade has been a source of great frustration for the government and the Central Committee, which have invested enormous resources in this branch of agriculture. Direct investments into the livestock industry since 1965 (on the construction and reconstruction of livestock farms and the creation of farm-mechanization, microbiological, and complex fodder industries, etc.) have been at the level of 70 billion rubles (about 100 billion dollars). But these investments have merely succeeded in reversing negative trends. The rapid growth which, it was hoped, would be stimulated has not occurred.

Livestock agriculture would collapse if the enormous state subsidies were withdrawn. A rational price policy has been delayed for so long that any attempt to introduce it now and to make the retail price of meat, milk, eggs reflect production costs of feed grain, fodder, and pasture feeding would produce a shock effect far greater than that produced by the modest price rises for meat and butter imposed by Khrushchev in 1962. But it is inevitable that a rational pricing policy must come. It is simply impossible to develop livestock farming and to improve the quality of consumer products without a substantial increase in retail prices. Most of the current investments are used to keep the price of meat and milk at the 1962 level (the average retail price of beef and pork in the shops is about 2 rubles per kilogram, and the price of chicken is 50 percent higher), despite inflation and the significant increase in average incomes. As a result there are no government resources left to invest in improving the quality of the processing of meat, milk, and other products. The quality of meat sold in the shops has deteriorated markedly and the variety of meat products has declined. Many popular brands of sausages and processed meat have disappeared entirely. There has also been a decline in quality and variety of dairy products. Producing ordinary milk is unprofitable for the state and to convert it into yoghurt, cream, cheese, and to make skim milk proteins for animal food is far too expensive. As a result there is very little variety of food available in Soviet shops.

If the government wishes to stop the decline in private production of meat and milk (or to increase it) private households must be given additional allotments for making hay and fodder and some pastures and meadows must be divided into sectors and distributed amongst *kolkhoz* members and *sovkhoz* workers. This idea was mooted in *Pravda* in 1983,[38] but no practical measures have been taken to put it into effect. And if productivity is to be increased, *kolkhozy* and *sovkhozy* must be given production targets, rather than being told how many cattle and pigs to have. The only way to increase productivity is to reduce the number of livestock and make more economic use of the limited resources of feed grain and fodder.

The socialist state has not been able to solve a classical capitalist problem by socialist methods—to increase the production of a commodity which has been kept too cheap artificially and which is unprofitable. If consumers want to have more and better-quality meat and dairy produce, they must pay for this luxury. When the number of fish in the rivers and lakes of the Soviet Union declined, the government allowed the price of freshwater fish to rise proportionally. Unfortunately, overfishing reduced the catch so much that prices became prohibitively high and freshwater fish virtually disappeared from ordinary shops and became available only in the special closed shops for officials and for export. But the high prices finally halted the decline and, in some cases, made it possible to increase the population of valuable freshwater and Caspian species. There is a good lesson in this for the future production of meat. One would hope that the price of steak will not need to rise as high as the price of caviar or sturgeon. But at least it would mean that people who do not now know what good steak tastes like, because there is none in the shops, would be able to find out, even if they could only afford it once a week or once a month. If meat prices are not allowed to rise, animal fat, bones, and subproducts will continue to be used in increasing proportions to meet the target figures for meat in the Food Program.

Chapter 9

Mechanization
and Chemicalization

Mechanization and chemicalization are the main techniques available for intensifying agriculture. It was natural, therefore, that the post-Khrushchev leadership should concentrate on developing both sectors rapidly. As we have seen in Chapter 6, abolishing the Machine Tractor Stations in 1958 reduced the number of mechanics, drivers, combine operators, and other technically qualified workers directly involved in agricultural production. Moreover, the absence of a MTS network to take delivery of agricultural machinery inhibited production in this sector of industry. The *sovkhozy* had never used the MTS service and they continued operating normally, but the *kolkhozy* did not have the financial resources to afford complex machinery. The industry was decentralized, and after the economic reforms of 1958 many of the ministries were replaced by regional Councils of National Economy *(Sovnarkhozy)* operating under the supervision of State Committees. It was logistically difficult for the collective farms to shop around amongst the hundred or so *sovnarkhozy* for the plants which produced the equipment and fertilizer they required. After Khrushchev's fall from power, centralized ministries began to reappear, but the new governmental system under Kosygin was different from the one which had existed before 1957.

Until 1957 the Ministry of Agriculture had been responsible for the MTS system. The newly reestablished ministry did not wish to take over the network of repair and servicing stations, called *Selkhoztekhnika* (an acronym formed from the Russian words for "agricultural technology"), which had been set up in 1960–1962 to serve the *kolkhozy*. The Ministry of Agriculture was now responsible for the quality of the agricultural work on both *sovkhozy* and *kolkhozy*, as well for agricultural education and science, the specialized experimental stations, the specialized farms set up to produce high-quality seeds, and so on. *Selkhoztekhnika* was left to expand according to the demand for repairs and servicing. While the MTS had a direct interest in the best possible harvest (since their work was evaluated in kind), the *Selkhoztekhnika* stations were paid in cash. When the *kolkhoz* machinery was poor, the *Selkhoztekhnika* system earned more, easily overfulfilling their plans for repair. Thus the relationship between the technical services and the collective farms was based on the worst possible principles. But in the haste of recreating a ministerial form of government in 1965, no one could think of a better solution. No better system emerged for twenty years. Only in 1985 did the government finally replace the enormous number of agricultural ministeries and state committees with a gigantic, consolidated State Agro-Industrial Committee (*Gosagroprom*), which placed the various branches of agriculture under one administration.

Agricultural machinery had become slightly more sophisticated between 1957 and 1965. It was therefore thought appropriate to create a separate Ministry of Machine Building for Livestock Farming and Fodder Production to supervise the production of equipment for animal farms, in addition to the Ministry of Tractor and Agricultural Machine Building. A State Committee for Material and Technical Servicing of Agriculture was also set up to serve as the intermediary between the production industries, the *Selkhoztekhnika* system, and the *kolkhozy* and *sovkhozy*. An entirely separate ministry was created for the Production of Chemical Fertilizer, and the application of fertilizers on the *sovkhozy* and *kolkhozy* became the responsibility of *Soyuzselkhozkhimiya* (All-Union Agro-chemistry Service), a network similar to *Selkhoztekhnika*. It, too, was paid in cash and had no responsibility for the size or yields of the harvest. A fourth ministry dealt with irrigation and land reclamation, while construction works (including the assembly of systems of mechanization) was the responsibility of the Ministry of Agricultural Construction.

The post-Khrushchev reorganization thus created a complex administrative system for the intensification of agriculture. It would be an impossible task to examine the performance of all the separate branches of this cumbersome apparatus. This chapter will concentrate on some key sectors of mechanization and chemicalization. It can be assumed that if the performance of key sectors has improved, the improvement would be reflected in the efficiency of the other branches of this giant "agro-industrial complex," and vice versa.

1. Tractors and Tractor-Related Machinery

A major reason for the significant increase of investments into agriculture after 1964 was the need for the technical reconstruction of the agricultural machinery industry. Output needed to be increased and modernization was required. The shortage of mechanics and tractor drivers made it seem sensible to design new, more powerful, multipurpose machinery. Previously trailer machines, drawn by tractors and requiring various trailer operators, had predominated. Tractors had been introduced in the 1930s when there was an abundance of labor in the countryside. When the industry began to modernize in the 1950s, foreign agricultural equipment was bought as models to copy and there was an increasing tendency to build complex aggregates in which hitching was used to give the tractor driver control over the attached equipment. Trailer operators were no longer required for most types of agricultural work because the tractor drivers could plough, cultivate, or sow using one-axis, two-axis, or multiple hitches of

TABLE 37
Tractor Power in Agriculture
and Annual Deliveries of Tractors

	1960	1970	1975	1980	1982	1985
Physical units (thousands)	1,122	1,977	2,334	2,562	2,649	2,798
Average power per tractor (horsepower)	42.7	56.6	65.2	74.5	78.8	80.9
Annual deliveries from industry (thousands)	157	309	370	348	350	393

Source: Nar. khoz., 1984, pp. 216, 240; 1985, p. 268.

a vertical or horizontal type. Soviet planners realized how advantageous this was and decided that if the tractors were made more powerful, the productivity of the tractor drivers could be increased. As Table 37 indicates, the number of tractors grew steadily from 1960 to 1985 and there was an accompanying increase in power per tractor.

The figures in Table 37 give no indication whether there were sufficient tractors to satisfy requirements. In most industrial countries agriculture was mechanized very rapidly after the war. A comparison of the level of "tractorization" in Europe, North America, and the Soviet Union was made by Davydov.[1] He found that in 1970 the Soviet Union was well behind the United States and most European countries in total tractor power expressed as horsepower units per 100 hectares of arable land and orchards (the figures were 49.0 in the Soviet Union, 109.0 in the United States, 125 in East Germany, 216 in France, 220 in Britain, and 430 in West Germany). The only European countries which were below the Soviet Union in Davydov's list were Yugoslavia, Romania, and Poland. In terms of physical units the United States had 4,562,000 tractors for agricultural use in 1970. Thirteen years later, in 1983, the Soviet Union was still far from reaching this number.

It could be argued that it is natural for countries where farming is a private enterprise to have more tractors, each with a smaller work load. It is certainly true that a tractor in West Germany does not work as many hours as a tractor in the Soviet Union. This should imply that Soviet tractors are more productive, given a similar tractor life-span in both countries. In fact, one of the most serious problems of mechanization in the Soviet Union is the short active life-span of tractors and other machinery. This explains why the number of tractors produced annually in the Soviet Union is approximately the same as in the United States, while the number of tractors working in Soviet agriculture is far below the American level. It also explains why the total number of tractors working in the fields increased by only *0.8 million* between 1970 and 1985, while about *6 million* tractors were delivered from industry to agriculture in the same period. The brevity of the life-span of Soviet tractors has become more obvious in the last few years. It is clear from the figures in Table 37 that the growth in the number of physical units slowed down after 1975 (an increase of 40,000 to 50,000 per year). At the same time, the tractor industry delivered an average of 360,000 tractors to *kolkhozy* and *sovkhozy* per year (the actual production was about 550,000 per annum, but a significant number went to other branches of the economy).

One possible explanation of why the average life-span of Soviet tractors is four times shorter than that of Western European tractors could be higher productivity per tractor in the Soviet Union. In fact, the actual acreage of work per tractor power unit has declined since the abolition of the MTS in 1958. *Narodonoye khozyaistvo* used to give productivity figures per one tractor unit (15 horsepower) calculated as "hectare ploughing units per annum." In 1940, when most tractors were small 15-horsepower machines, the figure was 411. It rose to 532 in 1955, but then fell to 508 in 1953 and 470 in 1965. Later figures have not been given, but other studies, which explain it by an increase in the number of tractors per 100 hectares, confirm a continuation of the decline.[2] Moreover the total life-span of each tractor has not grown. From the figures in Table 37 it can be seen that in 1970–1985 about 85 percent of all tractor deliveries replaced machines that had contributed to the growth of the total number of tractors employed in agriculture. Before the abolition of the MTS the rate of growth was the same (50,000 per annum between 1950 and 1958), but only 40 percent of newly delivered tractors replaced old ones, while 60 percent contributed to annual growth.[3] The more powerful and sophisticated tractors produced in the 1970s and 1980s were less reliable and less durable.

The shorter life-span of tractors also reflected the poor quality of the repair and service facilities and a comparative reduction in the number of qualified mechanics and engineers on the *sovkhozy* and *kolkhozy* or working in the repair shops and factories of *Selkhoztekhnika*. In 1965 there were 2,304,000 tractor drivers, mechanics, and combine operators for the 1,613,000 tractors and 520,000 combine-harvesters used in agriculture. By 1985 the number of tractors had risen to 2,800,000 and that of combines to 847,000, but only 3,031,000 drivers and mechanics, almost the same number as in 1979 (3,018,000), were available.[4] This means that there was an average of 1.0 qualified people to operate or service each machine in 1963–1965, but only 0.8 qualified people to do the same job on each much more sophisticated and powerful machine in 1984–1985. Since a driver can only work one machine at a time, this does not indicate higher productivity, but a shortage of qualified personnel. The situation is particularly serious on the *kolkhozy*, where the number of mechanics, tractor drivers, and combine operators has not risen since 1970. The shortages began after the abolition of the MTS in 1958. In 1957 there had been 150 drivers and combine operators in the MTS and *sovkhozy* per 100 machines and the 1:1 ratio of worker to machine in 1965 already indicated a decline. In the late 1960s many experts were expressing disquiet about the reduction, forecasting that it would lead to a deterioration in the quality of mechanization and the durability of the machinery.[5] But the trend became even worse in the 1970s and 1980s.

A similar situation has affected the number of truck drivers. The ratio of drivers to trucks was 0.9 in 1970 and 0.8 in 1983, while the number of trucks used in agriculture grew slowly from 1.4 million in 1975 to 1.7 million in 1982. Although the production of cars rose steeply in the Soviet Union in the 1970s, the number of passenger cars grew much more rapidly than the number of trucks (in 1970 the annual production of passenger cars was 344,248 and of trucks 524,507; the numbers rose to 1,327,000 and 787,000 respectively in 1980[6]). The agricultural sector received about a third of all the trucks produced in 1980 (270,000), but the number of trucks working in agriculture has been growing very slowly, from 1.4 million in 1975 to 1.6 million in 1980. Neither *Narodonoye khozyaistvo* nor the CMEA statistical yearbooks published the number of trucks produced or the number delivered to agriculture from 1981 to 1985. Withholding statistical data usually indicates a negative trend. The acute shortage of trucks in agriculture is demonstrated by the fact that during the harvesting season and each time there is a major agricultural campaign tens of thousands of drivers are drafted from the cities and industrial centers with their trucks. Every spring the government passes a resolution empowering local executive councils to mobilize urban drivers as a temporary measure.

The shortage of qualified personnel was recognized early in the 1960s and an attempt was made to increase the admission of students to the mechanization faculties and departments of the agricultural institutes and technical colleges. However, the number of engineers and mechanics who graduate annually is normally three or four times higher than the annual increase of engineers and mechanics working in agriculture. Many students prefer to find work in the new industrial centers rather than returning to the villages and working in agriculture.

A serious error was made in choosing the type of tractor which would be most useful for agricultural work. In 1965 it was decided that more powerful tractors were required. The deliveries of caterpillar tractors for agricultural work increased from 85,600 in 1965 to 148,200 in 1975, while the number of smaller wheeled tractors rose by only 30 percent, from 153,000 to 222,200.[7] Caterpillar tractors, however, proved to be too slow, heavy, and cumbersome for most normal field work (except for ploughing virgin lands) and it was difficult to repair and service them locally. Moreover, their technical quality was poor. By 1976 it was finally realized that they were unsuitable, and the number delivered to agriculture began to decline (to 125,300 in 1984). The most popular tractor was the "Belarus," produced by the Minsk Tractor Plant. But this model was also suitable for export and although the volume of production increased, the number available for Soviet agriculture fell from 56,800 in 1965 to 49,200 in 1984. In 1982 the value of exported tractors was 252 million rubles.[8] The quality of export machinery is much higher than the quality of tractors produced for internal consumption. Many plants have special facilities to improve the performance and durability of export machinery.[9]

Although the impracticality of caterpillar tractors was finally recognized, the tendency to increase the power and size of wheeled tractors continued. It was equally misguided. The initial intention was to compensate for the shortage of tractor drivers and mechanics. Before the war the most widely used tractor was a wheeled 15-horsepower model with iron wheels without tires (there was an acute shortage of rubber products in the Soviet Union). It was suitable for almost every soil and for the unsurfaced roads which were to be found in the Russian countryside. It was probably natural that larger and more powerful tractors began to be produced when the industry was reconstructed after the war. The rapid increase in average power per tractor in the last twenty years can be seen in Table 37. But the trend has gone too far. In 1981 the Cheliabinsk tractor plant began the mass production of 160-horsepower tractors and the Leningrad Kirov plant began to produce a 300-horsepower K-701 model with very large wheels and huge tires, as well as a special 500-horsepower model for the virgin lands. It was soon found that these models were too large.

Heavy tractors are, in general, too unwieldy for agricultural use. The heavy wheels damage the soil structure and the tractors cannot be used when the soil is even slightly wet. The optimal time for spring sowing is when the soil is moist, but heavy tractors cannot be used until it dries out. Even the 150-horsepower T-150 tractor produced by the Kharkov plant, considered the best of the high-power tractors, can only be used for spring and autumn ploughing if the soil is not too wet. A modernized version has recently been designed, with double wheels to reduce the pressure on the soil. This model is more suitable, but the modernization of old models was delegated to the local mechanics of the *Selkhoztekhnika* stations and they have not been able to cope with the task.

An analysis of tractor productivity in several regions of the Ukraine in 1981 indicated that the highest index of use was registered for smaller tractors of the Belarus type.[10] They could be used in local conditions for 260 out of 365 days, whereas the less maneuverable tracked models could only be used for 200 days per year. The index of use was lowest for the powerful wheeled tractors of the T-150 type, which, ironically, is the model which is growing fastest. Although their technical design and reliability are better, they are simply too heavy and they cannot operate on clay or wet soil. In 1984 the Central Committee adopted a resolution to increase the production of 150-horsepower tractors specially designed for agriculture.[11] There is a project to build new tractor plants for this purpose. It was a surprising decision, since the real need is for small or very small, (called "mini-tractors") tractors. There are no tractors small enough to be used on the very small fields which are common in the central and northern areas. The shortage of small tractors has led to a revival of propaganda about the need to reintroduce "real horsepower."

Powerful, heavy tractors are often used for minor transport work. This is not only uneconomical from the point of view of fuel; it also often damages rural roads beyond repair. The problems that are caused have been vividly described in a recent article by Yuri Gribov.

The old folk say that there used to be an ordinary road here and people usually travelled in carts. Next to the track there was a narrow path for pedestrians and the whole thing was about 4 metres wide. The fields stretched out on either side and in the summer, before the harvest, heavy ears of rye caressed the arms of the pedestrians. This quiet, pensive country road joined two ancient Kostroma villages, Borisoglebskoye and Zavrazhye . . .

About fifteen years ago I counted six or seven roads here, one next to the other, broken and ruined. And on my last visit, I was really upset by the place. It was the second half of April, the snow had completely melted and the larks were singing incessantly in the pure, blue sky over the fields. But this vernal paradise did not please or move one. And the reason was that the road along which we were making our way, the whole terrestial vista before us, was disfigured, scarred by caterpillar tractor tracks, by the wheels of machines and tip-up trucks, by deep chasms filled with muddy, stagnant water. I couldn't make out which of the dozen roads in a band no less than about 200 metres wide was considered the main road. It was a wound on the body of the earth, on its fertile soil, pitylessly trampled down with the stalks of the winter wheat . . .

"How much earth has been spoilt here?"

"You calculate," said my companion, a teacher I knew from Zavrazhye. "It's about 10 kilometers from village to village. You multiply. I can't bear to say the amount."[12]

This is not a unique case. Thousands of fields and unpaved roads have been destroyed in this way. As a result many rural villages have become even more isolated from the district center and from one another. The roads are unpassable for buses and passenger cars. They would be almost unpassable for horse-driven carriages, if there were any left to use.

2. Combine-Harvesters

The most crucial work of the entire agricultural season is harvesting of the grain crops. It must be done swiftly. The timing of sowing is also important since it requires a combination of moist soil and warm weather, so that the seeds germinate quickly and their roots reach deep into the topsoil. But sowing is not labor-intensive and most *kolkhozy* and *sovkhozy* can manage without any extra assistance. Harvesting, on the other hand, always requires the mass mobilization of additional manpower. Industrial workers, students, schoolchildren, soldiers, clerks, and drivers together with their trucks are drafted for the harvest. If the eastern regions expect a good harvest (it is usually gathered in September), combine-harvesters and operators often have to be transferred from the Ukraine and North Caucasus after they have gathered the harvest there in August. Weekly statistical reports of the harvesting campaign are published in *Pravda, Izvestiya, Sel'skaya zhizn'*, and other newspapers, giving the acreage and percentage of harvested fields, local conditions, problems, and comparisons with the previous season. By following the reports for the last few years, it becomes apparent that some fields in Siberia, the Altai, and parts of the Urals are not harvested until the beginning of winter. It is also clear that 100 percent of the sown area of spring crops is never harvested— this is the rule rather than an exception for grain and silage crops, sugar beets, and potatoes. In the cotton fields the special cotton combine-harvesters cannot work late in the autumn and a significant proportion of the cotton crop is collected by schoolchildren and students late in October, November, and even December, if the autumn is warm enough, in Uzbekistan and the other cotton-growing areas.

The harvesting season is a strain for the whole country. Efforts to avoid the mass mobilization of the urban population by more efficient mechanization have not yet produced visible results, although there have been significant increases in the number of combine-harvesters for grain and other crops. Table 38 shows the growth in the number of harvesting machines in the last two decades. The figures in Table 38 explain some of the main problems. The mechanization of corn and sugar beet harvesting is poorly developed and the number of harvesting machines for these crops has declined in the last decade. The number of grain

TABLE 38
Number of Harvesting Machines, 1965–1984
(Thousands of Physical Units)

	1965	1970	1975	1980	1985
Grain combines	520	623	680	722	832
Corn combines	60	34	47	52	33
Beet combines	64	57	68	62	53
Potato combines	19	36	62	70	63
Cotton combines	33	39	44	55	63
Silage and fodder combines	191	139	252	269	257

Source: *Nar. khoz.*, 1965, pp. 395, 399; 1985, pp. 268–269.

harvesters rose between 1975 and 1985, but not fast enough when the increases in yields are taken into account. The daily acreage worked by a combine-harvester depends on the harvest. If the yields are high, it works more slowly since it not only mows, but also threshes the grain and loads it into trucks. The official plans envisaged a substantial growth in the harvest in the 1980s and the production plans for combine-harvesters were revised accordingly. In fact, the harvests in 1979–1985 were not as high as expected, but this was partly caused by the shortage of combines which prevented the harvest being gathered as quickly as necessary. As a result some of the harvest was lost.

The reason it is so vital that harvesting take place quickly is that once maturation ends, the grain and other seeds are no longer firmly attached to the main body of the plant. In the normal reproductive cycle of the plant the grain or seed will drop to the ground and either begin growing immediately (winter crops which can survive the frost during vegetation germinate immediately), or after a dormant period (spring crops survive the winter in the form of dry seed).

Harvesting is an art. Cereals must be cut when their grain

seeds are almost mature—still attached to the plant, but no longer strongly enough to resist being separated by the threshing process (this is called the wax stage of maturity). When the grain is fully mature (the hard stage), the seeds are so fragile that they can be blown off the plants by wind or knocked off by the process of mowing. In the days before combine-harvesters, farmers preferred taller cereals and the harvest was done in two stages. The first stage of mowing with sickles (or mowing machines or sheafers) was done a few days before the end of the wax maturation stage. The farmer could harvest different sections of the fields selectively, as the cereals matured. The final stage of maturation took place with the cereal already in sheafs and the sheafs were then threshed. With the advent of the combine-harvester the system changed. Short varieties of cereal with simultaneous maturation are now more convenient, since the most economical way of harvesting is to combine the mowing and threshing process. But because of the fear that the work cannot be completed quickly enough, most farms in the Soviet Union now use what is called *separated* harvesting. In the first stage the harvesters work as mowing machines only, cutting the cereals during or immediately after the wax stage of maturation, when the grain is still too soft for threshing. After cutting, straight rows of plants (called *valki*) continue to mature. A few days later the combines return to collect the *valki* or mature cereals and do the threshing. This method would make economic sense if the first step were done by simple mowing harvesters, (rather than by heavy and sophisticated combine-harvesters), and if the two stages followed one another in quick succession (if the interval is too long, grain can be lost) and without any intervening rain. As it is, the total harvest is probably increased slightly (because of lower losses), but at a heavy cost due to greater use of fuel, machinery, and the work force.

Although the planning of the combine industry provided for increased production to keep pace with increased yields, low quality and poor servicing slowed down the growth. The number of working combine-harvesters grew only by 167,000 between 1975 and 1985. Annual production was at an average level of 130,000, which means that of the 1,300,000 combines produced from 1975 to 1985, 1,133,000 replaced worn-out machines. The entire stock of combine-harvesters is replaced every six to seven years. (In the United States the average life of a combine-harvester is about twenty years.) Combines are used for a very short period of time each year, often as little as two or three weeks. The technical quality of many types of Soviet harvesters is very low. Chernichenko, a serious, critical commentator of Soviet agriculture, has recently published an excellent analytical discussion of the problems of the quality of the combines produced by the giant agricultural machinery plant in Rostov-on-Don for the Ukraine and other main grain regions of the south (see note 9). However, the "Sibiryak" combines, specially designed for the eastern parts of the country and produced by the Krasnoyarsk plant, are even worse than the Rostov type. Many complaints of their poor performance have been published. One Siberian combine operator published the following letter in *Pravda* in 1981:

> I have been working as a combine operator for many years and I must say that there is no reliable, high quality grain harvester for Siberian agriculture. The "Sibiryak" combine, produced by the Krasnoyarsk plant, gives rise to a great deal of criticism. It is inefficient, losing large quantities of grain while harvesting. And how much time the mechanic has to waste on checking a new combine when it arrives from the factory! The quality of the blocks and components of the "Sibiryak" is very low. A machine off the assembly line cannot even complete a single harvest season (which only lasts a month in Siberia) without requiring repairs. As a result, many operators refuse to work with the "Sibiryak."
>
> I would like to know whether the managers of the Krasnoyarsk combine plant are thinking of cardinally modernizing their harvester and seriously improving its quality and reliability in the new five year plan?[13]

This very critical letter was published to enable relevant officials to reply. Readers were told that a new and better-designed model was undergoing field tests. However, the previous model had been in the production line for more than ten years. It takes years for old models to be replaced and it is clear from some reports that the new models were not yet in use in Siberia by 1985.[14]

Combine-harvesters are usually given attractive names. The 1970 generation was called "Niva" ("large field"), "Kolos" ("cereal head"), and "Sibiryak" ("Siberian"). For the 1980s the designers came up with a more modern machine, called "Don," which was expected to be in mass production from 1986. The production date has now been postponed to 1987. But the new model has proved unsuitable for Siberian conditions. It is too sophisticated, and other defects have been discovered. The combine operator mentioned above who complained about grain losses in Altai because of faulty combines was sceptical about the future of the new model. He described how the forty best combine operators from different parts of the Soviet Union were invited to test the new machine at the Rostov plant and give their opinion about its operational quality.

I saw this mass—a gigantic machine. Powerful . . . But for some reason all the forty notable combine operators of the country who had been invited to "Rostselmash" (we were separated when we filled in the forms so that we could not discuss them) favoured, as it turned out later, more or less the same thing—simplification . . . the "Don" needs a not inconsiderable capital expenditure for maintenance, technical servicing and storage.[15]

The "Don" has been designed as a new family of modern combines. The "Don-1200" and "Don-1500" are designed for the *chernozem* grain-producing regions, and modified models should be suitable for non-*chernozem* regions. The new design is expected to reduce the loss and damage of grain during threshing which was endemic in previous models. Several hundred different industrial plants and design bureaux belonging to thirty different ministerial networks took part in the design and testing of various components of this machine.[16] The design stage lasted more than seven years. It takes more time and effort to design a new combine-harvester in the Soviet Union than to design and put into operation a new battle tank or a new aircraft. Brezhnev, Andropov, Chernenko, and Gorbachev are on record as saying that the "Don" combine-harvester is an extremely important machine and that the whole country is waiting for it. Many government and Party resolutions have emphasized that mass production must start in 1986. However, it has been acknowledged that the test models of the "Don" do not yet fulfill the expected technical requirements or operational reliability.[17] Efforts were made in 1985 and 1986 to reduce the number of technical and operational problems related to the very heavy weight of the "Don," which could damage the topsoil.

These problems are all too familiar in a new technology. It is quite certain that the impact of the new combine on grain production will be minimal in 1987 and 1988. The new machine is too sophisticated and expensive, and the combine operators will have to be retrained to work it. It is also still too heavy for some soils, particularly wet soils. The adaptation period will continue for several years. It is too early to predict the final performance of the "Don," but it is unlikely that it will make the difference which is expected (reduction of grain losses by 10 to 13 million tons). Even if the design is perfect, complex machines require repairs and service. And it just these two basic conditions of successful mechanization, currently the obligation of *Selkhoztekhnika*, which represent the weakest sector of the Soviet agricultural system.

3. The Problems of Servicing and Repairs

All machinery requires regular servicing and repairs. Qualified engineers and mechanics are needed, as well as spare parts, workshops, and other facilities. The greater the variety and generations of machines, the more problems that occur. There are thirty different tractor models in the Soviet Union, a dozen different kinds of truck, several grain and other combines, mowers, drying equipment, ploughs, cultivators, sowing and fertilizing machines, and many others. Each requires different spare parts and properly qualified mechanics. Most industrial plants deliver machinery, even sophisticated models, in kits, and the machines have to be assembled and tested on the spot. Before 1958 all this was the responsibility of the MTS and the machinery belonged to the state. Hence the state had to take care of service and repair. The *kolkhozy* paid the MTS for field work, but had no responsibility for repairs. The MTS had a direct interest in the final results of the harvest since their work has evaluated and they were paid in produce. It was in the interests of the MTS that the machinery should arrive from industry in the best possible condition and be reliable and durable. In any case, it was not in the interests of the state for the MTS to receive faulty machinery, since the state had to cover the costs of assembly and repair.

The abolition of the MTS and the creation of *Selkhoztekhnika* changed these relations completely. The machinery now belonged to the *kolkhozy*, and they had to pay for repairs. *Selkhoztekhnika* was not directly involved in the agricultural process and was run on commercial principles. There was a scale of repair payments which the *kolkhozy* paid from the money they earned from procurements and other sales. Since repairs were expensive and often of poor quality, most collective farms set up their own small workshops for minor repairs and service. This was often sensible because of the vast distances between the farm and the nearest *Selkhoztekhnika* station. However, few *kolkhozy* had proper equipment or spare parts and the standard of their repairs was not very high. It was at this point that the useful life-span of complex machinery began to decline. Even in rather good agricultural areas like the North Caucasus, where the *kolkhozy* were prosperous and there was an extensive network of *Selkhoztekhnika* stations, the durability of machinery (expressed, for example, in the total acreage of work done or the hours of work done before repairs were necessary) had declined by 30 percent in 1966 compared to the durability of similar machinery in the MTS prior to their abolition.[18] Repairs became a real burden and often consumed about 35 percent of *kolkhoz* funds. An attempt was made to set certain standards of repair (for example, a guarantee of 2,500 hours of work for a tractor engine after repair). However, transporting heavy machinery to the repair shops remained a major problem, particularly for *kolkhozy* situated far from the district or regional center where the *Selkhoztekhnika* facilities were usually located. The *Selkhoztekhnika* stations had to be situated near the main tarred roads or the railway stations. It was decided to differentiate between larger *Selkhoztekhnika* stations which would deal with major repairs and smaller stations which could be established in a denser network to undertake minor repairs and servicing. A third set of more sophisticated, larger facilities would be established to undertake the kind of rebuilding or "rejuvenation repairs" which often required industrial technology. However, this latter project is still at the discussion stage.

A constant problem in providing a good repair service is the shortage of spare parts. This is a chronic disease of the Soviet economy as a whole and many branches of industry simply ignore the production of spare parts. Over the years thousands of articles have been published in the Soviet press describing the plight of agricultural machinery, often stranded in the fields for days or weeks with a minor fault which cannot be repaired for lack of spare parts. Another problem is caused by the expectation that an increase in production can take place without reconstruction or modernization of industrial plants. Attempts to increase productivity without modernization often have adverse effects on the quality of the product. Moreover, *Selkhoztekhnika* can no longer send faulty machines back to the production plants. Its brief is not only to deal with running repairs, but also to correct the faults caused by poor manufacture. It was thought that this would be economical, because the transport system is already overloaded. In fact, it has made industrial plants even more careless about the quality of the machinery they produce. Many plants no longer assemble or test machinery before delivery. As a result, the productivity of the plants has increased, but the final cost of the machinery has risen and the work of *Selkhoztekhnika* has become far more complex.

By 1981 *Selkhoztekhnika* had overtaken the MTS system in financial terms with only a fraction of the MTS obligations. In 1958 there were 8,800 MTS stations employing 2,953,000 workers. Of these, 1,696,000 worked directly in agriculture as tractor drivers, combine operators, or brigade chairmen. The number of engineers and mechanics engaged in repair work was no more than 500,000. In 1981 *Selkhoztekhnika* consisted of 8,000 stations with a work force of 1,700,000, all of whom were involved in repairs and servicing. The annual payments by *kolkhozy* to *Selkhoztekhnika* in 1976–1981 for repairs and servicing was in excess of 10 billion rubles and the sale of machines and spare parts through the *Selkhoztekhnika* system amounted to 20 billion rubles per year.[19] This was more than the profit that the *kolkhozy* could possibly earn from procurements and other sales. In the same period the total agricultural GNP from *kolkhozy, sovkhozy,* and private households was 120 billion rubles per year. The *kolkhoz* share was probably about 30 percent. For *Selkhoztekhnika* high capital turnover is a matter of pride, since their plan is formulated in rubles of turnover. But when *Selkhoztekhnika* makes a profit, the *kolkhoz* system must be suffering a net loss.

The general consensus amongst agricultural experts is that the *Selkhoztekhnika* system needs complete reorganization. There has even been some discussion about the possibility of reestablishing the MTS, at least for more sophisticated machinery. However, if *Selkhoztekhnika* survives it is not because it is important to the *kolkhozy,* but because it is vital to the industry which has benefited from abolishing individual testing and quality control of machinery and from being able to distribute it without having to do the final job of assembly. If *Selkhoztekhnika* were to lose its function of taking care of this final stage, the agricultural machine building industry would be unable to meet its planned production levels. In 1981, about 50 percent and in 1982, 65 percent of all the machinery which arrived at the *Selkhoztekhnika* stations had to be assembled and tested.[20] Moreover, the stations' functions include the installation, repair, and service of equipment used on animal farms. Thus it is clear that *Selkhoztekhnika* has developed into an extension of the machine building industry and the cost of transforming it has been paid by *kolkhoz* funds.

In the last ten years *Selkhoztekhnika* has been directly responsible for the financial collapse of many small *kolkhozy*. But the logic of the relationship is such that it is easier for *Selkhoztekhnika* to take over all the mechanized work required on the *kolkhoz* (on the same principle as the MTS used to do this work) than for the bankrupt *kolkhoz* to be transformed into a *sovkhoz*. All the machinery of the insolvent *kolkhoz* is transferred to *Selkhoztekhnika* on a lend-lease basis. *Selkhoztekhnika* operates it and is entitled to part of the *kolkhoz* production in return. Another form in which the MTS have been resurrected is under the name "interfarm mechanization stations" (*mezhkhozyaistvennye predpriyatiya po mekhanizatsii*, or MPM for short). In this case several small, weak *kolkhozy* combine their machinery and repair facilities and attach them to the nearest *Selkhoztekhnika* station. In effect there is no difference between the MPM and the old MTS.

In the end it will be necessary to admit that the 1958 reform was wrong and reestablish the MTS. It does not make economic sense to have an expensive *Selkhoztekhnika* network whose profit increases in direct proportion to the number of defective machines and faulty spare parts supplied by industry. The growth of production in the agricultural machine building industry is at about the same level now as the growth of extra work necessary to make these machines usable. Indeed, there is little economic sense in the relationship between any of the sectors of agriculture. It has been calculated that the total amount of time and funds spent every year on repairs in the *Selkhoztekhnika* system alone would be sufficient to produce 1,500,000 tractors.[21] This is three times greater than the number of tractors actually produced in the Soviet Union in 1982 and about the same as the entire number of tractors produced in the world in a year. Many people are now ready to admit that the MTS served the purposes of mechanization much better. They also admit that the MPM experiments look very much like the resurrection of the MTS and that the MPM could break the present vicious circle. But acknowledging past errors and mismanagement on such an enormous scale is not easy for the Soviet leadership. Even if Khrushchev can be blamed for the original error, the subsequent twenty-nine years of continuing waste and bad management can scarcely be attributed to him.

4. The Chemicalization of Agriculture

As a graduate of the College of Agro-chemistry of the Moscow Agricultural Academy I have always firmly believed that proper fertilization plays a crucial role in successful agriculture. Plants need certain chemical elements. The ability of plants to use light to make sugars from atmospheric carbon dioxide and water is the main source of life on earth. But plants take most of their nitrogen, and all their potassium, phosphorus, sulphur, iron, copper, and many other elements and microelements, from the topsoil. These elements must be returned to the topsoil if the earth is to remain fertile. The amount that is returned must be increased if the harvest is to increase. Organic material or humus must also be returned to the soil, so that the soil structure remains in a state of reasonable repair. These are laws of nature and laws of agriculture. If they are followed, the quality of cultivated soil will improve. If agriculture is to be scientifically based, it must improve the value of the soil, increase the amount of topsoil and humus, and prevent erosion. In the final analysis, it is chemistry that determines the amount of food available for humankind. What has been called the "Green Revolution" in the Third World is the introduction over the past twenty years of special varieties of cereals which are responsive to fertilizer and which convert a higher proportion of their photosynthate into proteins, carbohydrates, and grain oil. But without fertilizers these new crops (which are short-statured with upright leaves and can resist flattening) have no advantages over traditional varieties.

In 1973 (my first year in Britain) it seemed that Soviet agriculture was doing very well. The grain harvest was a remarkable 222.5 million metric tons. The average yield was 17.6 centners per hectare, almost double the 1965 level. The success seemed mostly to be due to an increase in the use of chemical fertilizers. The amount of chemical fertilizer delivered to agriculture had increased in direct proportion to the increase in the harvest, from

6.3 million tons of "pure" nutritional elements in 1965 to 13.7 million in 1973. In terms of tonnage of actual fertilizer (which often contained only 14 to 15 percent of "active" substance) an enormous amount of work had been done. More than 60 million tons of different mineral salts had had to be delivered to the farms. It had required more railroad cars than were used for the entire evacuation program of people, industry, farm animals, and the like from West to East in 1941–1942.

The amount of chemical fertilizer delivered to agriculture continued to rise during the next decade. But the harvests began to decline. As Table 39 shows, the growth in production of fertilizers was very impressive. In 1981–1985 the amount of fertilizer delivered to agriculture was double the 1973 level. The amount used on grain crops had trebled (previously they had been used more for technical crops). Nonetheless, the harvests were static in 1979–1985, remaining at an average level of about 180 million metric tons, well below the 1973 level. The amount of fertilizer applied per hectare was higher than in the United States, where 100 kilograms of nitrogen, phosphorus, and potassium was used per hectare.[22] In Byelorussia and the Baltic states the amount of fertilizer used per hectare has been higher than in Western Europe and Japan. Why does it not have the same effect? There is no simple answer.

The first problem noticeable from the figures in Table 39 is disproportion. In 1960 and before there was more phosphorus per hectare of arable land than nitrogen and potassium. From 1965 onward nitrogen dominated the other elements. There is more nitrogen than phosphorus in the body of a plant, but a significant part of it comes from bacterial nitrogen fixation from the atmosphere. The process takes place not only in bacterial symbiosis with leguminous plants, but also in the topsoil. The content of usable phosphorus in the topsoil is a crucial indicator of fertility. If there is a deficiency, increasing the amount of nitrogen or potassium fertilizer will be futile. Scientifically, the best ratio of nitrogen (as N_2) to phosphorus (as P_2O_5) is close to 1:1 (0.9 is considered acceptable for many soils). In the Soviet

TABLE 39

Deliveries of Chemical Fertilizer to Agriculture, 1965–1984[a]

(Million tons of active substance)[b]

	1965	1970	1975	1980	1982	1985
Total	6.3	10.3	17.2	18.8	20.1	25.4
Nitrogen	2.3	4.6	7.3	8.3	9.0	10.9
Phosphorus	1.5	2.1	3.8	4.8	5.3	6.8
Phosphorus (as phosphorite powder)[c]	0.6	1.0	0.9	0.8	0.8	0.7
Potassium	1.9	2.6	5.2	4.9	5.0	6.8

(Kilograms of active substance per hectare of cultivated land)[d]

	1965	1970	1975	1980	1982	1985
Total	28.4	46.8	77.5	83.9	90.0	113.2
Nitrogen	10.3	20.9	33.0	36.9	40.3	48.8
Phosphorus	6.7	9.8	17.2	21.3	24.0	30.5
Phosphorus (as phosphorite powder)	2.8	4.4	4.0	3.7	3.4	3.5
Potassium	8.6	11.7	23.3	21.9	22.3	30.4

Source: Nar. khoz., 1979, pp. 261, 262; 1985, pp. 270–271.

[a] The total production of fertilizer grew more rapidly, but exports of fertilizer were increasing.

[b] Until 1981 Soviet statistics not only gave the figures for active substance, but also a higher figure for "conditional units." This corresponded to the new weight of the most usual mineral salts. This double figure often gave rise to misunderstandings. Sometimes there was a third figure indicating the real weight of individual fertilizers.

[c] Phosphorite powder is listed separately in Soviet statistics because it is a poor source of phosphorus in an insoluble form.

[d] Pastures and meadows are not included.

Union the ratio is still only 0.6. This is too low and it reduces the effectiveness of the fertilizers.

Among the East European countries, the highest level of fertilization occurs in Czechoslovakia (344 kilograms of active substance per hectare), Hungary (300 kilograms per hectare), and

East Germany (314 kilograms per hectare). The levels are lower in Poland and Romania (231 kilograms and 122 kilogram respectively) than in Byelorussia (287 kilograms per hectare), the Baltic states (266 kilograms per hectare), and in Soviet Central Asia where the cotton crop has always been given priority. However, in the East European countries the proportion of nitrogen to phosphorus (approximately 1:0.8) is better than in the Soviet Union,[23] and there is a better balance of potassium. None of these countries are self-sufficient in chemical fertilizers and they import large amounts from the Soviet Union and other countries. Consequently, they can obtain a better balance.

Most of the arable land in the Soviet Union is deficient in phosphorus.[24] Acid soils assimilate phosphorus fertilizers with difficulty and the phosphorus in ground phosphorite powder is practically insoluble in such soils. The use of phosphorite powder (which is merely the milled mineral) rather than superphosphate (or double superphosphate) is uneconomical and a sign of backwardness. The ground powder contains a very low percentage of active substance in an insoluble form. It probably costs more to transport the powder than is gained by the marginal improvements obtained by using it. In general, the Soviet Union lags well behind most other countries in the industrial production of the most effective forms of chemical fertilizer containing high percentages of active substance per ton of manufactured product. To deliver 25.0 million tons of active substance in 1985, it was actually necessary to move more than 100 million tons of manufactured products (superphosphate, phosphate powder, potash, potassium chloride, ammonium solutions, and other substances) to the farms. There are no statistics available for the production of the individual salts and products which are used for fertilization, but from the complaints of the agrochemical stations, it is clear that many fertilizers are still used in physiologically inbalanced forms, like potassium chloride (KCl), which leaves chloric ions in the soil, or sodium nitrate ($NaNO_3$), which leaves the sodium unused. Mixed together they increase the concentration of sodium chloride (NaCl) in the soil, or create salination.

Amongst the fertilizers, phosphorus is probably the most problematic substance over the long term. Mineral deposits of phosphorus (as rock phosphate and apatite) are not abundant and there are no alternative sources. Nitrogen can be produced not only from mineral resources, but also from atmospheric nitrogen (although the process consumes significant amounts of energy). Potassium is usually produced from minerals, but it can also be extracted from the salt in ocean water (although this is an expensive method). The best Soviet phosphate deposits are very far from the main agricultural areas (there are rich apatite deposits in the Kola peninsula in the Arctic). The richest potash deposits (crude potassium carbonate) are on the western slopes of the Urals and in western Byelorussia. There are other potassium and phosphate deposits, but, with the exception of some phosphate deposits in Kazakhstan, they are lower grade and equally far from the main centers of agriculture. However, the Soviet Union does not have good deposits of nitrates, and like most other industrial nations, has to rely on a synthetic ammonia process which combines the nitrogen of the air with hydrogen (hydrogen is a by-product of coke ovens and is also available from natural gas).

In countries which import most of their mineral fertilizers, the chemical industry can be suitably located and can specialize in producing complex fertilizer granules containing different proportions of individual chemicals or mixing them with compost. Granulating the fertilizer is extremely beneficial. It prevents the fertilizer being leached, absorbed, or fixated in the soil and makes some fertilizers safe enough to be introduced into the soil together with seeds. Moreover, it is easier to transport and convenient for storage and mechanized application. In the Soviet Union both the granulation process and the production of complex granules (containing specific proportions of elements and microelements for different crops) are at an early stage of development. The main deposits of phosphates and potash are separated by long distances. Ammonia is usually produced close to the sources of hydrogen (the metallurgical industry) and energy (gas and oil). With a poor and overloaded transport system, it is no easy task to arrange the transportation of nitrogen, phosphates, and potassium salts from different parts of the country to special plants located in the centers of agricultural production where they can be mixed into granulated fertilizers. As a result, the normal practice is to deliver the individual fertilizers separately to the *kolkhozy* and *sovkhozy* and mix them locally. Many types are still transported unpackaged in metal railway cars, even though this makes them prone to damage. At the rural railroad stations they are simply unloaded onto the ground, without cover or protection from rain. In 1982 the chairman of the agrochemistry network, V. P. Nikonov, reported that as much as 10 percent of Soviet fertilizer is lost during transportation. He also said that the fertilizer was unloaded onto the ground at 603 railway stations and that only 45 percent of it was kept in storage.[25] Loading and unloading is poorly mechanized. About 10 million tons of fertilizer (in salt form) arrives at the local agrochemical centers in solidified form as a result of poor storage or transport conditions. Solidified fertilizers are almost impossible to use, and some of them (for example, potassium nitrate and ammonium nitrate) become explosive when they are solidified, and too dangerous to handle (potassium nitrate is the main component of gunpowder and ammonium nitrate is widely used as a nondetonating explosive for "soft" blasts in mining and other work). Losses during transport can be roughly estimated, but the losses in the *sovkhozy* and *kolkhozy* are not registered. The ammonia is usually delivered in a liquid solution with a very low concentration of ammonia (about 20.5 percent). This makes it difficult to distribute. In the United States and Western Europe there are techniques for making dry ammonia, with 82 percent concentration of actual fertilizer. This is much more suitable for transport, packaging, and application.

Although these problems are serious, an even more acute problem is organization. The use of chemicals in agriculture is complex and difficult. Apart from the major fertilizers, the chemical industry also produces hundreds of other chemicals which are necessary for modern agriculture. These include various microelements, herbicides, pesticides, and fungicides. Many types of soil require periodic applications of lime to reduce acidity (more than 40 million tons of lime is produced annually). Manure, compost, and peat constitute the major part of normal fertilization and about half of the total plant part of normal fertilization and about half of the total plant nutrient elements is supplied via these organic fertilizers. They cannot be replaced by less bulky chemicals, because the organic mass is essential to the soil structure, to restore the loss of humus and for the bacterial processes which restore the fertility of the soil and are essential for the better use of chemical fertilizers.

Official statistics on the use of organic fertilizer are unreliable because the fertilizers are produced and used locally and the figures given are based on reports from *kolkhozy* and *sovkhozy* which cannot be verified. The total weight of all concentrated and coarse animal feed (hay, silage, haylage, feed beet and feed potato, pasture grass, feed grain, etc.) climbs to 1,500 million tons annually. Together with different forms of compost, some based on peat, this amount of fodder makes possible the production of approximately the same amount of organic fertilizer. The use of organic fertilizer has improved during the last decade. In 1970 only 468 million tons were distributed on the fields. In 1980 the figure rose to 803 million tons, and in 1984 to 983 million tons.[26] However, this is still considered well below the amount required and the application varies from area to area. In Byelorussia 15.4 tons were used per hectare of cultivated land in 1984, for example, while in the Ukraine only about half this amount was applied (8.7 tons per hectare), and in the RSFSR the amount was 3.7 tons per hectare. It has been calculated that in the North Caucasus much more soil humus is lost each year through soil erosion than can be formed from organic fertilizers. Soil erosion also removes more mineral elements than are added via mineral fertilization.[27] The preparation and application of organic fertilizers is unpopular work, and it is poorly mechanized. Moreover, organic fertilizer is rarely applied at the ideal time (before the autumn ploughing or in fallow fields). It is frequently applied at the worst possible time, during the winter, because that is when both the transport system and the farm workers are not engaged in the urgent tasks of the agricultural season.

The organizational problems date back to 1958 and the abolition of the MTS. When the decision was made to abolish the

MTS, Khrushchev and his advisors only considered the problem of machinery, ignoring the fact that the MTS were also responsible for the storage and distribution of chemical fertilizers and that they owned the specialized machinery which was required to distribute it. Each MTS had an agrochemical laboratory which identified the fields in the area which were most deficient in particular nutrients and then supervised the proper application of chemical and organic fertilizer. This highly specialized work was done by graduates of the agrochemical colleges, soil scientists, or agronomist-agrochemists. Agrochemical colleges and faculties were created in several institutes in the 1930s when it was decided to set up a network of agrochemical laboratories associated with the MTS. The experts who worked in these laboratories classified local soils according to their acidity and prepared local soil charts with characteristics of fertility, humus content, proportion of nitrogen, phosphorus, potassium, and other elements. They advised on the most rational use of the limited local resources of lime, chemical, and organic fertilizer. The laboratories represented the interface of agronomical science and practice, with mutual benefit to both.

The abolition of the MTS in 1958 left the agrochemical service in disarray. Individual *kolkhozy* could not take care of them. Some of the laboratories were later attached to local general experimental stations and others were included in the district departments of the Ministry of Agriculture. But many were simply closed down. Direct contact and interaction between agrochemistry and agriculture was seriously reduced. The laboratories which remained confined themselves to advisory functions. The machinery for applying the fertilizers was sold to the *kolkhozy*. It was only twenty years later that it began to be realized that the increasing production and delivery of chemical fertilizer needed more serious supervision of the way it was used. It was clear that the increase in production of fertilizers was far greater than the increase in crop yields. Finally, a Central Committee Plenum issued a directive in July 1978 ordering the establishment of a specialized agrochemical network, modelled on *Selkhoztekhnika*. It was called the All-Union Agrochemistry Service, or *Soyuz-*

selkhozkhimiya, and within two years it consisted of 150 regional and 3,000 district departments. It incorporated into one complex the agrochemical laboratories, plant protection stations, research institutes, design bureaux, and many other organizations which had been linked with the *kolkhozy* and *sovkhozy* on the one hand, and the Ministry of the Chemical Industry on the other. In 1981 a Ministry of Chemical Fertilizers was separated from the Ministry of the Chemical Industry.

The creation of the *Soyuzselkhozkhimiya* network was extremely rapid and efficient. It now employs about 500,000 people and deals with a great number of different tasks. It owns an impressive amount of machinery for various chemicals, storage facilities, analytical laboratories, and it even has a fleet of airplanes and helicopters which have been specially designed for spraying fertilizers, herbicides, or pesticides from the air. It publishes a great deal of literature and the amount of chemicals, organic fertilizer, and minerals it handles each year is growing. Yet the harvest has not grown since 1979, when *Soyuzselhozkhimiya* was established. Again, as in the case of *Selkhoztekhnika*, the relations which had previously existed between the MTS and the *kolkhozy* served the purpose better. The MTS were materially interested in the final harvest. Although *Soyuzselkhozkhimiya* has to fulfill plans for the various work which needs to be done and is paid for its services, it is not really dependent on the final harvest. It is reponsible for its professional work, but not for the results. The reports issued by *Soyuzselkhozkhimiya* indicate how much work has been done in financial terms (the total turnover in 1981 was 6.8 billion rubles), the tonnage of the various fertilizers it has handled, and what the complaints are against the transport system and the Ministry of Chemical Fertilizer, the Ministry of the Chemical Industry, and the dozen other ministries that produce chemicals for agricultural use. However, they do not mention the effectiveness of fertilization for the various crops in the different agricultural zones. Yields and crops are beyond the responsibility of *Soyuzselkhozkhimiya*. Here again is a vicious circle. Those who are most interested in the harvest and whose incomes depend on its level (the *kolkhozy* and *kolkhoz* brigades) are not masters, but dependents of *Selkhoztekhnika* and *Soyuzselkhozkhimiya*.

Cooperation between the two networks was not very good. Repairing *Soyuzselkhozkhimiya* machinery became a problem, for example. The agrochemical network now uses about 150,000 trucks, many thousands of various types of tractor, machinery for applying fertilizer, and so on. The *kolkhozy* pay for their repair, but *Soyuzselkhozkhimiya*, like *Selkhoztekhnika*, belongs to the state. Moreover, it does not want to pay exorbitant prices for the poor quality of *Selkhoztekhnika* work. As a result the Central Commitee and Council of Ministers passed a resolution in 1981 allowing *Soyuzselkhozkhimiya* to establish its own repair stations and garages. However, the creation of a combined state Agro-Industrial Committee at the end of 1985 changed the relations between the two services. It will take several years to establish proper coordination and cooperation between different sectors of the agricultural complex.

In discussing mechanization and chemicalization, I have not tried to give a comprehensive picture of all the achievements, problems, and failures. Only the major problems and a few of the hundreds of ways in which chemistry is used in agriculture nowadays have been mentioned. Improving the fertility of the soil, controlling soil acidity, preserving or improving the humus, improving salinated soils, fighting weeds, parasites, and fungi, improving fodder, and using hormones for controlling livestock growth all depend upon chemistry. The Soviet Union exports vast quantities of fertilizer (to the value of more than a billion rubles in 1982 and 1983), and many types of complex chemical compounds, pesticides, and herbicides are imported. The problems in such a complex endeavour are legion. But the main difficulty is clear: the volume of production and delivery of fertilizers and chemicals for agricultural use is growing very rapidly and is already well above the level in the United States, but the practical agronomic effects of this massive production are, at best, modest. Indeed, they could be said to have been invisible in 1979–1985 since they were reflected in higher production costs, but not in higher crop yields.

Conclusion

Population growth (not just in the Soviet Union, but in the world as a whole) has made it impossible to feed people with the output of crops which can be achieved using traditional agricultural systems. Moreover, the rapid decline of the rural population and the population of draft animals, together with the growth of towns and cities which need to be fed, have made it necessary to introduce comprehensive mechanization of all aspects of agricultural work. Mechanization in itself does not increase crop yields, but it makes the work of farmers far more productive. In countries like the United States, Canada, or West Germany, the amount of energy which is consumed per worker is higher in agriculture now than it is in industry. The Soviet Union is moving in this direction, but not in a well-coordinated fashion. Shortages in mechanization create annual emergencies which necessitate the mass mobilization of millions of people from urban areas for temporary seasonal work on the farms. Indeed, all of Soviet agriculture has been in a permanent state of emergency in the last decade. Seasonal agricultural works become major national campaigns and affect the lives of every social group in the country, from schoolchildren and students to industrial workers, soldiers, scientists, and government and Party officials. This abnormal situation is a clear manifestation of the inability of the government and Party apparatus to solve the problems of comprehensive mechanization, despite vast investments. It also reflects the asymmetrical, and often contradictory, relationships between the main partners in what has become known as the "agro-industrial complex"—the planning services, industry, *Selkhoztekhnika*, the *kolkhozy* and *sovkhozy*, the land reclamation network, the system of construction work, the research system, and so on. The formation of the "agro-industrial complex" was intended to reduce disharmony and disproportions between the various constituent parts. In fact, it has only crystallized the problem. The most important participant in the complex is the actual farmer, the man or woman who works in the field. Yet the farmer is the least influential member of the whole system. He is the most dependent member, whereas in a properly organized system of cooperation he would be the master, the central figure, who would be served by the rest as assistants, collaborators, and advisors.

In summarizing the situation in the mechanization of Soviet agriculture, it is impossible to pinpoint a single factor which explains the poor record and inadequate performance. There are technical, planning, and organizational errors. The relationships between the various bodies which are concerned in the mechanization and chemicalization process represent a bureaucratic nightmare. Research institutes are fragmented and serve different ministries. Design bureaux are linked to industrial plants and not to farmers. There appears to be a drift towards a kind of anarchy in which important sectors of agriculture are entirely neglected. In Chapter 7 it was seen that the steadily declining acreage of rye was due to the inability of planners and designers to produce combine-harvesters which are adapted to this crop. For identical reasons the acreage of buckwheat, sorghum, peas, and other valuable crops has declined. The cultivation of flax has also become difficult because suitable specialized machinery does not exist. The same is true for many other crops which are now only produced on private plots without any mechanization. Centralized planning results in concentration on the most important machinery, for example, combine-harvesters for wheat, tractors, cotton combines, silage towers, elevators, and the like. A bureaucratic system cannot take care of every crop or every aspect of livestock farming, and it cannot take local conditions and traditions into consideration.

If mechanization is crucial for replacing a shrinking rural population, chemicalization is essential for increasing the output of each cultivated hectare. The population increase and the particularly rapid growth of urban population has made it essential that farmers double or treble the amount of food they produce from each hectare. This cannot be done without chemicalization. More than 60 percent of the increases in yields in the postwar period has been due to chemicalization, fertilization, and control of weeds and pests. The remaining 40 percent is due to improvement in crop varieties (to make them more responsive to fertilizers and resistant to infections, insects, and parasites) and in irrigation. In the Soviet Union, for the same increase in chemicalization made by most other industrial countries there has been a much lower growth in yields. And there has been no growth at all since 1979. There are many "objective" factors to explain this, like the cold climate in the north and the dry climate in the south and east. But climatic conditions are only partly to blame. There are many other economic, organizational, technical, and historical factors which the government has been unable to handle properly and efficiently. In essence, they should not be dealt with at government or Central Committee level. It would be far better if the central planners took responsibility for general strategy and decided about really crucial issues, but did not try to pass resolutions to cope with every single minor problem.

According to the plan, the production of mineral fertilizer should have reached a level of 36 million tons of active substance in 1985. This target has not been met, but this is not a failure. The increase would have required moving 115 million tons of chemicals to the villages, when it is acknowledged that 10 percent of them would have been lost during transport. Reducing losses would make much more sense than increasing deliveries. According to the plan, there was particularly to have been an increase in the production of nitrogen. But why increase the production of nitrogen when the ratio of nitrogen to phosphorus and potassium is already too high? Priority should be given to phosphates and potassium to reduce the imbalance. This would make better use of investments, even if the total volume of fertilizer was less impressive than the planned targets. But it would make little sense to increase the production of phosphates and potassium salts without making storage facilities available on the farms. It would be far more sensible to invest in developing the industry to make granulated complex fertilizers, which are more easily assimilated and which reduce the substantial losses in the soil. If it is clear that the continuing growth in production of fertilizer has not had any effect on the harvest over a period of ten years (the harvests at the beginning of the 1970s were the same or higher than those in 1980–1985), it would be more rational to find out how to improve the effectiveness of the available fertilizer, rather than to concentrate on increasing production still further. Moreover, there is no point to increasing the production of mineral fertilizer without increasing the application of organic fertilizer as well. Organic fertilizers are essential if chemical fertilizers are to have the proper effect. To make this balanced approach possible, more power and influence must be given to local farmers and agronomists, rather than to Moscow bureaucrats.

Chapter 10

Organization and Economy

Agriculture is probably the only branch of the national economy of all countries, rich and poor alike, which produces essentially the same products as it did one hundred, two hundred, or even three hundred years ago, and which will continue to do so in future centuries. Modern science, technology, and organizational structure have influenced agriculture mainly by raising its productivity (increasing the yields, or the output of crops and animal produce per acre), and by decreasing the amount of human labor, particularly rural labor, required to produce a unit of food. A larger proportion of the agricultural economy (food processing, research, the manufacture of agricultural machinery, the production of energy and fertilizers) has become part of industry and moved from the villages to the towns.

There are certain natural limits to increasing agricultural productivity. By the end of the nineteenth century, the limits of extensive development had been reached in Europe, North America, and many Asian countries. The Soviet Union reached this limit in the 1950s and there has been no substantial increase in cultivated acreage since the end of the Virgin Land Program. In Africa and South America extensive development continues because of rapid population growth. But the ecological cost is high and greater problems are created than those resolved. The limits to the intensive development of agriculture vary, depending on climate and soil. Selection, chemicalization, soil improvement, mechanization, and irrigation can raise yields substantially, but not infinitely. The number of warm days per year, the intensity of sunlight, the ability of technology to return all the elements of fertility to the soil, and the amount of renewable water create natural limits of intensive development, which can be predicted for different geographical zones.

The Soviet Union does not have the best geographical conditions for very high levels of productivity. The cold climate and the long winter make only one harvest of main crops possible per year (in some tropical countries, three harvests of cereals are possible per year). The shortage of water is a second important obstacle. However, despite these drawbacks, a very substantial increase of agricultural production is possible. The average grain yield, for example, could be increased from the prerevolutionary level of 7 to 8 centners per hectare to 15 to 16 centners per hectare merely by introducing an improved rotation system and by other simple methods that do not require heavy financial investments. However, it would require reducing the acreage under cereals, something the Soviet government has been unable to contemplate. Between 1970 and 1981 the acreage under grain crops rose from 119.3 to 125.5 million hectares, while the acreage under technical crops, potato, and vegetables declined by 2 million hectares. The acreage of clear, fallow fields also declined (from 28.9 million hectares in 1940, to 18.4 million hectares in 1970 and 16.4 million hectares in 1981). In 1982–1985 the cereal acreage was slightly reduced and the acreage of fallow lands increased by 4 million hectares. This was not the result of proper planning, however, but merely a failure to meet the planned targets of winter crop sowing.

After the 1950s an increase in agricultural production and a simultaneous increase in the productivity of rural labor could only be achieved by the intensification of agriculture. Two key factors of intensification, mechanization and chemicalization, were discussed in the last chapter. But there are many other factors—for example, land reclamation, irrigation, the selection of crops best suited to local conditions—all of which require vast investments, the involvement of industry, and proper coordination between the industrial and agricultural sectors of the economy. They also demand a serious evaluation of the agronomical, ecological, and economic factors that contribute to making renewable performance possible while preserving a balance of the factors that contribute to soil fertility.

The subject matter of agricultural economy includes (among others) planning, the analysis of performance in different sectors of agriculture, the statistics of income of farms and farmers in different parts of the country, the dynamics of procurement, market, and retail prices, the correlations between productivity, and the organization of agricultural work of various types. In other words, it is a vast subject. Many Western analyses of the Soviet agricultural economy concentrate on the poor harvests in comparison to other countries, the enormous shortfall between the plans and the real level of production, and the main trouble spots.[1] Soviet books on the economy and organizaton of agriculture, on the other hand, usually present an optimistic picture of the successful development of all branches, concentrating on particular successes, for example, the increase in the number of machines or in the production of fertilizer or cotton.[2] They also invariably pay tribute to the CPSU's correct agrarian policy. In reality this policy represents a long history of crises and mismanagement. It is true that there were no mistakes between 1965–1985 of the magnitude of the requisitioning policy of War Communism in 1918–1921, of the forced collectivization and de-kulakization of 1930–1932, or of the aboliton of the MTS in 1958. This explains the growth of production between 1965 and 1978. On the other hand, the decline in agriculture from 1979 to 1986 indicates the limits of Brezhnev's agro-industrial approach. The post-Brezhnev leadership has tried various new methods (Andropov's campaign for strict discipline, Chernenko's program of irrigation and land reclamation, and Gorbachev's plans for intensification and administrative reorganization) to reverse the decline. But their effects have been minimal and the decline continues.

If vast new investments do not produce returns, if the increased use of mineral fertilizer does not raise yields, if intensive mechanization does not resolve labor shortages, and if the annual massive mobilization of the urban population to work in agriculture is still required, there must be something wrong in the overall organization of the agro-industrial complex and in the agricultural economy. This chapter will analyze this organization and economy. It seems natural to begin with a brief review of the human resources of agriculture, that is, the men and women on whom all current and future programs ultimately depend.

1. Social and Demographic Changes in Rural Areas, 1965–1985

Neither the creation of agro-industrial complexes nor massive investments in agriculture reversed a trend which had become very obvious after the abolition of the MTS in 1958—the increased incidence of *kolkhoz* bankruptcies, the decline of small village settlements, particularly in the non-*chernozem* areas, and the decrease in the size of the farming population. The practice of paying stable monthly salaries (rather than paying in kind for *trudodni*) improved the income of individual *kolkhozniki*, but it also created insoluble financial problems for weak *kolkhozy*. They often had to borrow money from the bank to cover salaries and if the harvest was poor they were frequently unable to repay the loans. When their debts became too large, the state was finally forced to intervene and transform the *kolkhoz* into a *sovkhoz*. In some regions the process reached epidemic proportions. In the Leningrad region, for example, there was not a single *kolkhoz* left by 1983. Table 40 indicates how the transformation proceeded in the country as a whole. In addition to the growth of the number of *sovkhozy*, there was also a rapid increase in the number of agricultural production units (battery chicken farms, specialized farms attached to food-processing plants for meat, milk, fruit, vegetables, oil, sugar, wine, etc.), which were called "interfarm

TABLE 40

Transformation of *Kolkhozy* into *Sovkhozy*

	1956	1960	1970	1980	1984
Number of *kolkhozy*[a]	83,000	44,000	33,000	25,900	26,200
Acreage of cultivated land (millions of hectares)	179.0	115.9	99.1	95.2	92.0
Number of *sovkhozy*	5,099	7,375	14,994	21,057	22,500
Acreage of cultivated land (millions of hectares)	31.5	67.2	91.7	111.8	109.3
Interfarm enterprises[b]	—	—	4,580	9,638	10,100
Cultivated land and pastures (millions of hectares)	—	—	NA	4.0	3.9

Source: Nar. khoz., 1956, pp. 106, 109, 147; 1965, pp. 257, 277; 1980, p. 219; 1984, pp. 223, 294, 304.

[a] A record number of 5,068 *kolkhoz* bankruptcies was registered in 1960. In 1961 there were 2,906, in 1965 1,865, and in 1969 1,192. After 1970 the rate declined to 300 to 400 per year.[3]

[b] There figures refer only to the enterprises which are located in rural settlements.

enterprises" *(mezhkhozyaistvennye predpriyatiya)*. They often also served neighboring *kolkhozy* and *sovkhozy*, taking in their state procurements to process them. A number of interfarm service institutions were set up (for land reclamation and irrigation, electrification, artificial insemination of farm animals, complex fodder, building materials, forestry, etc.), as well as recreation and social facilities for the rural population (sports facilities, recreation and holiday facilities, houses of culture, old-age homes, etc.), and education and medical facilities. The poor condition of the rural roads and of rural trade have made it necessary for each of these institutions to undertake some agricultural production. Part of the attached land is divided into individual plots and the rest is called an auxillary farm and has to supply food for the workers and for schools, hospital canteens, and kitchens.

Financial insolvency was the main, but not the sole, reason for turning *kolkhozy* into *sovkhozy*. In some cases the process was connected to attempts to create specialized farms. It was explained as a progressive symptom of the change from a cooperative form of production (*kolkhozy*) to a higher, socialist form of production (*sovkhozy*). However, at the same time it was admitted that the transformation did not in itself cause an improvement in economic performance or level of production.[4] The cost to the state (to cover *kolkhoz* debts and other payments) was substantial, but there was seldom any compensatory improvement in production. At the Twenty-third Congress of the CPSU in 1966 the practice was criticized and as a result the pace declined.[5] But it proved impossible to halt the process.

The formal decision to allow the transformation of a *kolkhoz* into a *sovkhoz* is made by the government following a recommendation by the All-Union *Kolkhoz* Council, the body created in Stalin's time to represent collective farms. The recommendation is usually initiated by the local regional administration and the Ministry of Agriculture through the government of the republic. In 1975–1980 the *Kolkhoz* Council refused 589 applications because the *kolkhozy* concerned were considered cconomically viable.[6] Often the decision is made to combine several neighboring poor *kolkhozy* into one large *sovkhoz*. Occasionally, if the poor *kolkhoz* has a more successful neighbor, the two are amalgamated into a larger *kolkhoz*, despite the natural reservation of the more successful collective farm. This is why the average *kolkhoz* size has increased from 2,700 hectares of cultivated land in 1960 to 3,000 in 1970 and 3,600 in 1983.

In general, as the figures in Table 41 demonstrate, the total number of people engaged in agricultural work has remained static. However, there has been in substantial decline in the

TABLE 41
Rural Population by Profession
(Millions)

	1960	1970	1980	1985
Total	108.2	105.7	98.3	95.9
Kolkhozniki	22.3	17.0	13.5	12.6
Sovkhoz workers	0.0	10.0	12.0	11.9
Interfarm enterprise workers	—	—	0.5	0.5

Source: Nar. khoz., 1984, pp. 5, 326; *SSSR v Tsifrakh v 1985*, pp. 5, 134–137.

number of *kolkhozniki*. Moreover, the young adult rural population has migrated to the towns and cities in large numbers. As
a result the proportion of elderly people in the rural population
has grown faster than the proportion in the urban population.

The migration of young people (sixteen to thirty-five years of
age) from rural to urban areas in the 1959–1970 period is obvious
from the figures in Table 42, which also reflect the decline of
the birthrate during the war and postwar period and wartime
losses. Migration was more widespread in the RSFSR than in
Central Asia and the Transcaucasian republics. The tendency
certainly continued in the period after 1970 and many articles
are published in newspapers and magazines decrying the movement of young people from the villages. The government has
tried to prevent them from migrating, but with negligible results.
The increase in the incomes of *kolkhozniki* and *sovkhoz* workers,
the introduction of pension schemes for the rural population and,
finally, the abolition in 1976–1980 of the legal discrimination
against the rural population which prevented *kolkhozniki* and
sovkhoz workers from having internal passports, leaving the villages, or changing their jobs without the permission of the rural

TABLE 42
Rural and Urban
Demographic Changes, 1959–1970
(All-Union Censuses)*

Age group	1970 population as a percentage of 1959 population	
	Rural	Urban
10–14	154	173
14–19	98	170
20–24	55	109
25–29	57	93
30–34	89	131
35–39	123	162
40–44	155	207
45–49	85	114
50–54	71	104
55–59	113	170
60–69	125	186
70–79	109	165
80–99	140	201

Source:[7].
* Figures demonstrating the age distribution of the population were not published in the one-volume selective results of the 1979 census. This was partly because the negative trends in life expectancy would have become obvious and, particularly, the evident decrease in the life expectancy of the rural male population.[8]

Soviets slowed the process down a little. Passport restrictions had been introduced after collectivization in 1932 as a measure to keep the peasants in the villages for as long as the government wanted them to work there. It was this more than anything else which discouraged young people from joining *kolkhozy* or becoming *sovkhoz* workers when they left school, or reached the passport age of sixteen, or when the boys had completed their two-year compulsory military service at age eighteen/nineteen. Fear of the irreversible loss of the right to an internal passport (which in legal terms meant the loss of freedom to travel within the Soviet Union—for foreign travel a special foreign passport is necessary, a privilege which few achieve) thus produced the very reverse of what had been intended and militated against the rejuvenation of the rural working population. The staged introduction of internal passports for the rural population in 1976 (extended over a period of four years) certainly made it easier for some villagers to leave and take up industrial employment. But it also removed the fear of entering a serf-like dependence and some school-leavers and demobilized soldiers became more willing to stay in or return to their villages for a while, before selecting their future employment or education. A proportion of these young people settle in the villages permanently.

The introduction of internal passports for the rural population was the single most important social reform during Brezhnev's tenure of office. It made the rural population more mobile and increased the pressure that it could exert for an improvement of the quality of rural life. Until recently, industrial development has created many vacancies in the towns and cities, and there is always a demand for unskilled labor. But the current approach towards modernizing industry may reduce the need for manual labor and serve to reverse the unfavorable demographic changes in rural areas and to improve the quality of *kolkhoz* and *sovkhoz* labor resources.

2. The Agro-Industrial Complex: An Attempt to Integrate Agriculture into a Modern National Economy

Traditionally industry and agriculture were considered independent branches of the Soviet economy, administered in different ways and kept separate. There was a political reason for the separation. Workers and peasants belonged to different social classes with different class interests and different psychology. According to Marxist-Leninist theory, peasants belong to the petite bourgeoisie and their ultimate dream is private ownership of the land and the means of production. However, by the 1970s, when both *kolkhozniki* and *sovkhoz* workers were paid salaries, the distinction between industrial workers and rural peasant workers became irrelevant. Agricultural work came to be considered as part of a more complex agro-industrial cycle. On the production side, the complex consisted of the manufacture of agricultural machinery, fertilizers and other chemicals, fodder and feed, and included a complex system of transport and a network of educational and scientific establishments, all necessary for the satisfactory completion of the various kinds of work involved in the agricultural cycle. On the distribution side, the complex comprised storage facilities, food-processing plants, procurement and purchase agencies, transport facilities, and a network for distributing food products to the population. It was decided that it would be an advantage to administer this cycle as a whole. Although the term "agro-industrial complex" had been used in the 1960s (it was included in Khrushchev's 1961 Party Program), it was at the July Central Committee Plenum in 1978 that final arrangements were made to delineate the agro-industrial complex as a distinctive branch of the national economy and to establish joint governmental and Party administration.

In my opinion it is no accident that agricultural performance actually began to decline after this administrative reform. The reorganization, like the abolition of the MTS in 1958, was well intended. It was declared to be a new step in the development of Soviet agriculture. However, the implementation and the creation of a joint administration had far-reaching negative consequences which would have been entirely predictable had the reform been based on real economic principles rather than carried out by an incompetent bureaucracy guarding its own interests. It became evident in the next few years that the agricultural machine building and fertilizer industries became less responsible for the quality of their products, while their consumers lost any power of rejection and control as well as their independence. Previously they had been the *market* for machinery and chemicals. Now they became an integral part of a huge, unified system in which the production of food and machinery was lumped together in financial terms as "the overall production of the agro-industrial complex" with a separate section in the national economic statistics. Similarly, the recipients of agricultural production—the procurement agencies, processing plants, and food industry—ceased to be the market for *kolkhoz* and *sovkhoz* products. Instead they became partners with the producers, under joint administration. The formal amalgamation of the agro-industrial complex into a single budgetary unit for expenses and profits reduced the effects of the economic factors which should have influenced the performance of individual plants, factories, *kolkhozy*, and *sovkhozy*. The result was the paradoxical situation that all the economic indicators of the performance of the *kolkhozy*, *sovkhozy*, and agricultural industries began to decline, while the overall value of the agro-industrial complex grew. An attempt is currently being made to reintroduce economic factors by making changes at the bottom rather than at the top, and creating economic incentives for small agricultural units (brigades and *zveno*). It is too early to judge the effects of this new experiment, but it will become clear from the following discussion that it is unlikely to make much difference in the long run unless there are other changes.

The development of the agro-industrial complex was the result of slow bureaucratic processes related to the intensification of agriculture and the significant increase in central investments in agriculture. In 1965, when the Central Committee dismantled Khrushchev's decentralized regional administration and restored the traditional ministerial system, it was decided to combine the Ministry of Agriculture and the Ministry of *Sovkhozy* into a more powerful single ministry and to supplement it with ministries responsible for mechanization and chemicalization and an additional system to take care of the agricultural produce. The agricultural sector of the government now included the enlarged Ministry of Agriculture, the Ministry of Tractor and Agricultural Machine Building, some departments of the Ministry of the Chemical Industry, the Ministry of Procurements, and the Ministry of the Food Industry. The All-Union network of *Selkhoztekhnika* did not fit into the ministerial structure, but it was included in the government via the State Committee for Material and Technical Servicing of Agriculture. These six branches of government had independent budgets and appropriate networks of industrial or service facilities. Only the Ministry of Agriculture, the Ministry of Procurements, and *Selkhoztekhnika* were represented at the regional or district levels and they had well-differentiated tasks and responsibilities. In 1965 the chairman of the Council of Ministers of the USSR, Alexei Kosygin, started to implement his well-publicized economic reform, which was intended to give individual branches of industry and plants more independence and to create some elements of a market economy and real competition for consumers. Economic independence (using the power of industrial and trade profit and the right of consumers to reject low-quality manufactured products) included removing the system of dual management (by both government and Party apparatus) of industry. Kosygin wanted to curtail the Party industrial apparatus and its interference with the work of the government.

Before the war, the economic apparatus of the Party had consisted of two main Central Committee departments, industrial and agricultural. Later it had burgeoned into a duplicate of the government system. The hypertrophy had been most rapid during Khrushchev's decade in office, when the Party apparatus had become a substitute for the decentralized governmental economic system. The Central Committee acquired departments of energy, machine building, chemical industry, high technology and instruments, heavy and military industry, and transport. Finally for every government ministry there was a parallel department or sector in the Central Committee with veto powers. Any important governmental decision or appointment had to be approved by the appropriate Central Committee department. This dual management impeded economic reform, but neither the Party bureaucracy in Moscow, nor in the national and regional capitals, favored any limitation of their semi-executive powers.

When Brezhnev became chairman of the Presidium of the Supreme Soviet in 1977, the supremacy of the Party system over the government became complete. Ministries and other governmental networks could be created with ease by a decree of the Presidium of the Supreme Soviet. Between 1977 and 1981 several

new ministries and state committees were added to the administration of agriculture and agriculture-related industries. They
included the Ministry of Chemical Fertilizers, the Ministry of
Agricultural Construction, the Ministry of Machine Building for
Livestock Farming and Fodder Production, the Ministry of Land
Reclamation and Irrigation, the Ministry of Meat and Milk Production, and the Ministry of Fruit and Vegetable Production. In
addition to the six new ministries, *Soyuzselkhozkhimiya* was
formed with a network of agrochemical stations. New, independent industrial and agricultural organizations were also set up
on the model of *Ptitseprom* (the poultry industry factories). The
largest one was a network for the microbiological industry,
Glavmikrobioprom SSR. Other ministries contained departments which dealt with agriculture (for example, chemical and
light industry), and new departments were created (for example,
a department within the Ministry of the Automobile Industry for
the production of trucks and lorries for milk and cattle, and a
department in the Ministry of Aviation to produce special planes
for spraying fertilizers and chemicals. Many of these new ministries had representatives at the regional and district levels.

The administrative system for agriculture became enormously
complex. *Kolkhoz* chairmen and *sovkhoz* directors had the greatest difficulty in dealing with each individual ministerial or state
committee network separately. But they had no choice. If they
needed fertilizers, they could only be obtained from *Soyuzselkhozkhimiya.* If they wanted to purchase or repair machinery,
they could only do so through *Selkhoztekhnika.* If they wanted
to build a new animal farm, they needed the plans and cooperation of the Ministry of Agricultural Construction and the Ministry of Livestock and Fodder Machine Building. They could not
carry out land reclamation or irrigation works without the Ministry of Land Reclamation and Irrigation. Moreover, they had to
deliver their produce to different procurement systems: meat and
milk had to be delivered to the plants belonging to the Ministry
of the Meat and Milk Industry, grain to the Ministry of Procurement, potato and cabbage to the trade network of the Consumer
and Trade Society, sugar beets and oilseeds to the plants of the

Ministry of the Food Industry, and fruit and vegetables to the plants belonging to the Ministry of Fruit and Vegetables. The forests were supervised by the State Committee of Forestry. Their plans were coordinated by the Central Planning Committee and they had to send weekly or monthly production reports to the Central Statistical Bureau. The local Party committee supervised their performance and the local Soviet managed local finances, roads, hospitals, schools, and other facilities. Clearly, the system was far too cumbersome and complex to be efficient. It was called the agro-industrial complex, but it was more a set of competing hierarchies than an organization with a rational bureaucratic structure.

Difficulties of administration and coordination were a constant subject of discussion in the press and at Party and government meetings. Finally the problem was raised at the Twenty-sixth Party Congress in February 1981. There were two possible solutions: simplification, or the creation of an organizational superstructure to coordinate the various components. The state and collective farm representatives were naturally in favor of simplification, on the grounds that "land needs one boss." Brezhnev and the Central Committee apparatus were in favor of an additional superstructure, believing that the agro-industrial complex represented progress. Their view prevailed and the agro-industrial complex was given legal status. It was to operate at district, regional, republican, and All-Union levels. However, the relations between the top and lower levels remained very loose. One republic, Georgia, was allowed to simplify the system. The Georgian Supreme Soviet passed a decree replacing the different agricultural ministries with a joint Committee on Agriculture in which the former ministries were represented by sectors and departments. This solution simplified financial and organizational relations at the lower levels.

In the rest of the country, the representatives of the different ministries and networks were united at district level into a district agro-industrial unit (called *raionnoye agro-promyshlennoye ob'edineniye*, or RAPO for short) and became members of the RAPO Council. At higher levels, similar, larger units were established (with the *R* in RAPO replaced by the name of the region or republic, for example, Smolensk APO, Stavropol APO, etc.). At the highest level a Commission of the Council of Ministers on Matters of the Agro-industrial Complex (Commission of *Agroprom*) was established which was, in effect, a separate agricultural government with limited powers. It united all the ministries and state committees which had anything to do with agriculture and it was chaired by the first deputy prime minister in charge of agriculture. The meetings of *Agroprom* were reported in the press and its decisions on current problems (supervision of procurements, construction projects, transport, sowing, harvesting, etc.) had the power of government decisions. The actual composition of the commission is not fixed and it appears to include representatives of the Party apparatus. However, major decisions involving economic measures (changes in procurement prices, economic incentives, mobilizing the urban population for seasonal work, changes in procurement quotas, etc.) still remain the joint responsibility of the Central Committee and the Council of Ministers. There were many variations of this new administrative superstructure at local and regional levels. An active exchange of experience took place between the different districts and regions about the best way of distributing responsibility, financial, and material resources. The Council of Ministers of the USSR tried to unify the structure of RAPO and the regional APO's, and in December 1982 "Model Statutes" were approved for district and regional agro-industrial complexes.[9]

District agro-industrial units (RAPO) were established by decision of the district Soviet and its Executive Committee. They united the *kolkhozy* and *sovkhozy* and all interfarm production units, the district units and organizations of the ministries of Agriculture, Fruit and Vegetable Production, Procurements, Meat and Milk Industry, Food Industry, Land Reclamation and Irrigation, Agricultural Construction, Forestry, and local *Selkhoztekhnika* stations. Their main task was to coordinate work on increasing agricultural production, improving the soil, using funds rationally, and improving the mechanization and technical services. They also supervised the transformation of some farms into specialized farms, and gave the necessary economic and technical support for individual plots. RAPO operated through a council on which the individual branches and units were represented, as well as the *kolkhoz* chairmen and *sovkhoz* directors.

The structure and tasks of the regional APOs were very similar, but they could also decide on prices and salary scales and they included some units which did not exist at a lower level (for example, large meat-, milk-, or food-processing plants which absorb produce from a number of districts). The higher-level APOs resembled Khrushchev's short-lived regional agricultural Party committees except that this time the split was in the government hierarchy and the regional Soviets rather than in the Party. The representatives in RAPO or APO of the various ministries and committees continued to be employed by these ministries and committees.

RAPO was partly created as a result of pressure from below. The multiplication of agriculture-related ministries and committees, each with their local network, had created a bureaucratic nightmare. There were endless complaints in the press about the difficulties of the multiple dependence of the *kolkhozy* and *sovkhozy*. A typical article was published in *Izvestiya* a year before the creation of RAPO. It described the plight of the *sovkhozy* in the small Zhivilsk district in the upper Volga basin.[10] The fact that there are only *sovkhozy* and no *kolkhozy* in the area is an indication that the local agriculture is poor. However, the *sovkhozy* were under the administration of eleven different state organizations and departments, all of which were represented at the district level. The agricultural department of the local Soviets only had advisory functions and had no control over the ministerial networks. The local bureaucracy had increased threefold since 1966—in the regional center, Cherboksary, the number of officials in the local Soviet system alone concerned with agriculture had grown from 84 in 1966 to 304 in 1981. Several hundred other officials worked in *Selkhoztekhnika, Soyuzselkhozkhimiya*, the agricultural construction department, the land reclamation department, and the other organizations with local offices. The result of this bureaucratic proliferation had been reduced efficiency. Understandably, this led to the demand for a more unified administration. RAPO and APO were an attempt to solve the problem without reducing the local bureaucracy.

One of the negative effects of RAPO and APO, however, was to reduce the responsibility of the *kolkhoz* and *sovkhoz* management for agricultural production. Previously they were held directly responsible for the poor performance of their farms. Now there was collective responsibility and collective leadership. The financial success of RAPO was measured not only by the value of crops and livestock, but also by the value of the machinery which was delivered or repaired, the amount of fertilizer, and the evaluation of the land reclamation or construction work done. Thus the value of agricultural production could decline, while "the overall value of production" might be seen to be growing. From 1983 *Narodnoye khozyaistvo* began to give figures for the overall production of the agro-industrial complex calculated in rubles.[11] The 1984 figures were compared to specially calculated figures for 1975 and 1980. During this period the overall value of the production funds grew from 258 billion rubles in 1975, to 366 billion rubles in 1980 and 497 billion rubles in 1985. At the same time the value of agricultural production (crops and livestock, including the private sector) increased from 113 billion rubles in 1975, to 122 billion rubles in 1980 and 135 billion rubles in 1985.[12] In other words, for a rather modest increase of agricultural production of 22 billion rubles (in fact, it was rather less because there was a poor grain harvest in 1975—in 1976 and 1977 the value of agricultural production was 123 billion rubles), the total investments into the agro-industrial complex grew by 239 billion rubles.

Since the July Plenum of the Central Committee of the CPSU in 1978, all rural capital construction work has been carried out by the state free of charge. Large modern animal farms are built on *kolkhozy* and *sovkhozy* on the same principles as industrial factories, mines, or plants in the Urals or Siberia, or the Amur-Baikal railroad. The *kolkhozy* and *sovkhozy* may complain later about the quality of the work, the technical parts, or the failure of designers to take local conditions into account. But they do not complain about the practice, because they do not pay the cost. It is better to get something as a gift from the state, even if it is useless, than to get nothing.

It is clear that the agro-industrial complex, in its initial form, has improved neither the quality nor the productivity of agricultural work; but it has made it much more expensive. The RAPO-APO system was created to improve coordination and to bring *kolkhozy* and *sovkhozy* into the decision-making process. But the economic implications were not tested before implementation. The idea of an agro-industrial complex was by no means new. The concept had been introduced into the 1961 Party Program by Khrushchev. Nor were RAPO and APO new. The first RAPO had been created as an experiment in local initiative in the Viliandski district of Estonia in 1975,[13] and a second was created in 1979, also in Estonia. The experiment was successful and in 1980 RAPO were created in other districts in Estonia. The subject was raised at the Twenty-sixth Party Congress in 1981, and again during the discussion of the Food Program at the May Plenum in 1982, when RAPO and APO were recommended for the Soviet Union as a whole without any analysis of the differences between conditions in Estonia (which has an extremely well organized agricultural infrastructure, high levels of productivity, and a very high cultural level of work) and conditions elsewhere. In Estonia the RAPO were intended to accelerate a development which was already successful. In other parts of the Soviet Union they were expected to raise the level of development of backward districts. It was to be a cure for the sick, not a stimulus for the healthy. Not surprisingly, the new administrative system could not work the same miracle that it had in Estonia.

In the discussion of the results of three years of the new form of administration (1983–1985) more attention was paid to its shortcomings, failures, and the continuation of bureaucratic proliferation than to its successes and achievements. The agro-industrial councils did not acquire more power. Nor was any real consolidation of the different branches of the agricultural economy achieved. In the end the RAPOs and APOs developed into a new, very heavy bureaucratic superstructure in which discussion and debate took place, but where rapid and flexible decision-making was impossible. The negative effects became obvious in 1985 when a comparatively good maturing harvest suffered significant losses due to the poor and uncoordinated work of the different sectors of rural administration. The initial American estimates during the summer put the grain harvest at the level of 200 million tons. But only 191.7 million tons were harvested and the total value of agricultural production in 1985 was the same as in 1984, a very poor year. Radical and rapid reorganization was necessary.

It was carried out on November 22, 1985, by a joint decision of the Central Committee and the Council of Ministers of the USSR. A "super-committee" was established to absorb and replace most of the ministries and committees which had previously been responsible for different branches of agriculture. The ministries of Agriculture, Fruit and Vegetables, Meat and Milk Production, Rural Construction, Procurement, and the State Committee on Industrial and Technical Work in Agriculture (with its *Selkhoztekhnika* network) were simply abolished and merged into a consolidated State Agro-Industrial Committee, or *Gosagroprom SSSR*. Departments relating to agriculture in other ministries were also transferred to it (from the ministries of Light Industry, Irrigation, and Land Reclamation). Although the technical agricultural ministries (Tractor, Combine and Agricultural Machinery, Mineral Fertilizer, Livestock Farm Machinery, etc.) were not merged with *Gosagroprom SSSR*, they were put under its control. All the ministers with agricultural sectors and the chairman of the agricultural sector of Gosplan were included in the *Gosagroprom* collegium, and so were the agricultural bureaucrats from the Ministry of Finance, the State Bank, *Tsentrosoyuz* (the rural trade organization), the Central Statistical Bureau, and many others.

In effect, a separate agricultural government has been organized which can operate separately from the government responsible for the heavy, machine tool, and defense industries. This is the most radical reorganization of the Soviet economic administration since Khrushchev's decentralization of the economy in 1957 and the creation of separate industrial and agricultural Party and local Soviet networks in 1962 (both of which were considered serious errors which contributed to Khrushchev's downfall and which were abolished in 1965). The chairman of *Gosagroprom SSSR* was appointed that day by decree of the Presidium of the Supreme Soviet. He was to be Vsevolod Murakhovsky, first deputy prime minister and Gorbachev's close friend. It seems obvious that Gorbachev himself will be in charge of the system and that Murakhovsky will act as his deputy.

The replacement of more than a dozen independent administrative networks with one consolidated committee (the system which had previously been tested successfully in Georgia) certainly simplified the chain of command. It also made many thousands of officials and experts redundant. They could now be employed in more direct practical work. But *Gosagroprom SSSR* was created in haste without any preliminary discussion. There seems to be considerable confusion at the local level. The functions of the RAPOs have changed, but press reports indicate that no one quite knows what they are. In fact, the new administration is, apparently, more efficient than the previous, very fragmented system. The decision-making process has been simplified and the enormous bureaucratic apparatus has been reduced. But the problems of Soviet agriculture require something more substantial than administrative reorganization. This was the tenth time agriculture had been reorganized since the war. Each time the same pattern has been followed—fragmentation, followed by consolidation. There were no visible practical improvements in agricultural performance in 1986. Clearly it was not only the administrative superstructure that was responsible, but also some basic elements of the system.

3. *Problems of the Agricultural Economy*

What are the economic aspects of agriculture? The very subject seems to have changed over the years. In the 1940s and 1950s, for example, courses on the economy of agriculture covered topics like profitability, increase of productivity, and the relationship between the income of the *kolkhozniki* and that of the *kolkhozy*.[14] Modern textbooks on the agricultural economy, on the other hand, discuss quite different sets of problems: state planning, state investments, scientific and technical progress, the industrial base of agriculture, the agro-industrial complex, and so on. As soon as procurement prices became higher than retail prices for many food products, the whole problem of the profitability of agriculture became irrelevant. Production costs also grew dramatically and they are often higher now than procurement prices. The state not only subsidizes the price of food, but also most construction works, land reclamation, irrigation, and mechanization. Since profitability has become impossible, books on agricultural economy stress the importance of efficiency, or how to produce more food at any cost, because food is an essential commodity and society needs it.

There are many uneconomical situations in Soviet agriculture which seem rather absurd. The space for one cow in a modern, purpose-built animal farm, for example, cost 1,724 rubles in 1980.[15] The cost of producing milk is growing steadily and is often higher than the procurement price (see Table 43). No profit from the sale of milk could be large enough to cover the cost of constructing new farm buildings, even if the payments were extended over thirty or forty years. The government, therefore, has only two alternatives: to build new, more mechanized farms free, or to increase procurement prices so that the *kolkhoz* or *sovkhoz* can return the investment. The first alternative has been chosen, so that new funds can be invested in reconstruction rather than used to pay old debts.

In fact, the public pays for either alternative. The budget consists of taxes and money which is created by workers in other branches of the economy. It is, therefore, the population itself which pays to keep agriculture alive and food prices low. This irrational state of affairs could probably be justified if it was efficient. In fact, it causes inefficiency, as well as many other problems. When economic principles are ignored, the production of the same amount of food tends to cost more, not less, because no one cares about expenses. Thus the population enjoys artificially low prices for food, but pays for the privilege in other ways: by having low salaries and pensions, a poor national health service, poor-quality food, and having to tolerate losses and inefficiency. It would make far better sense to give subsidies to lower-paid groups of the population to buy food rather than to the procurement and trade networks which sell it. The present system has led to a situation in which large groups of the population have significant amounts of unspent income and savings. Their demand for high-quality food, particularly food of animal origin, is unsatisfied, and the shortage of food is rapidly becoming chronic.

In a world in which about two billion people suffer from malnutrition, large industrial countries should develop economies which make them self-sufficient in food, or give them disposable excesses for export. There is general agreement that food is the most essential commodity, and that it must receive priority in national economic planning. Food must be produced, even if the cost of producing it is high. However, if the production costs are not reflected in the prices paid by the consumer, normal planning becomes very difficult. It is certainly not very rational to import food from other countries by selling nonrenewable resources.

In considering the problems of the Soviet agricultural economy in an historical perspective, it will be seen that a comparatively rational approach was tried only once, during the brief 1953–1957 period. The increase in procurement prices was entirely justified and it was natural to invest in exploiting new land. Until 1953 the agricultural sector had been considered purely as a source of direct and indirect profit for the development of industry. Procurement prices for most agricultural products were artificially low and retail food prices were reasonably high. At least 60 to 70 percent of the income of most families was normally spent on food. Nevertheless, the resulting diet was rather poor. At the same time, the prices paid for manufactured goods were much higher than their production costs. Therefore peasants who spent their modest incomes on consumer goods rather than on food were also creating profits for the state. For a poor country (which is what the Soviet Union was at least until 1955), this policy was wrong in that it discriminated heavily against the peasantry, whose income and standard of living were much lower than that of the workers. The national product was not divided fairly amongst the various groups of society and this retarded the development of agriculture. Khrushchev began to deal with this economic injustice and the situation improved. But the same method of improvement cannot be repeated over and over again and still have the same effect. When procurement prices continued growing and rose to well above retail prices, many food products began to be used in a wasteful way. The widespread use of bread to replace fodder is only one example of this abnormal state of affairs.

As we have seen in Chapter 6, procurement prices for the main agricultural products were raised in 1953–1963. By 1962 the prices paid by the state for livestock and dairy products had reached a level which made it impossible for the state to make any profit. Khrushchev decided to raise the retail price of meat and milk, but his decision aroused discontent in provincial industrial centers. The average industrial salary doubled between 1963 and 1983, from 102 to 210 rubles per month,[16] while retail food prices remained unchanged. At the same time, as can be seen in Table 43, procurement prices continued to rise. Subsidies were required to cover the high procurement prices, the full cost of food processing, and the expenses of the food trade.

The 1983 average procurement prices are not yet available—the prices have been listed by region and according to quality, but the economists have not yet calculated an average figure which could be compared with the 1980 figure. The figures which have been published so far have indicated the percentage increase rather than the amount in rubles. There was a special additional 50 percent increase for products delivered above the average procurements for 1976–1980,[17] which was offered as an incentive. The practice of paying higher prices for procurements in excess of the official plan was not new, but usually the plans were so high that few *sovkhozy* and *kolkhozy* could fulfill them, far less exceed them. What was innovative about the new offer was that it was not based on the target figures, but on average deliveries from that particular farm in 1976–1980. Thus pay-

TABLE 43

Procurement Prices
for Compulsory Deliveries by *Kolkhozy*[a]
(Rubles per Metric Ton, Except for Eggs)

	1964	1966–1969	1971–1975	1976–1979	1980	1985
Grain	86	104	101	103	110	130–150[b]
Potato	67	66	75	78	108	NA
Vegetables	79	92	115	118	128	NA
Sugar beets	27	26	30	31	34	NA
Cotton	341	463	566	601	—	
Milk	122	151	199	234	266	
Meat						
(live weight)[c]						
Cattle	805	1,244	1,612	1,735	1,900	2,000
Pigs	1,160	1,465	1,554	1,649	NA	NA
Sheep	556	851	1,008	1,122	1,245	
Eggs	20	65	72	85	89	
(per 1,000)						
Wool	3,906	4,213	5,114	5,390	6,360	NA

Source:[19].

[a] Procurement and retail prices vary a little from region to region in the Soviet Union. The figures in Table 43 represent the average for the country as a whole of the prices paid to *kolkhozy*. The prices paid to *sovkhozy* are slightly lower, although the difference has become much narrower since 1965.[20]

[b] In July 1985 the USSR Council of Ministers introduced a new system of evaluating wheat based on its protein content. The procurement price for "hard wheat," which was 150 rubles per ton, could rise to as much as 300 rubles for hard wheat of the highest quality. There are now four different procurement classes of soft and four of hard wheat, each with its own procurement price. However, when this system was first applied in 1986 many farms and procurement centers complained that it was too difficult to sort the wheat into classes in the haste of the harvesting season. A small quantity of rain during harvesting can change the quality of the grain in a field.

[c] Live weight is the weight of the animals delivered to the slaughterhouses or collected from the *kolkhozy*. It is usually 40 percent higher than the slaughter weight, for which figures are given in Table 44.

ments were made, even if target quotas were not met. In fact, the incentive did not prove to be too expensive. The harvests were so high in 1976 and 1978 that the average level for 1976–1980 was well above the previous five-year average and it was difficult to exceed. Agricultural production in 1981–1984 was lower than the average 1976–1980 level, particularly for field crops. There was some increase in livestock production, but this occurred mainly in the chicken and cattle farms which were outside the collective and state farm system. Despite the very high procurement prices paid for livestock products, *kolkhoz* animal farming usually operated at a loss, since production costs grew more steeply than procurement prices. The production of a ton of milk, for example, cost the *kolkhozy* 177 rubles in 1970, 217 rubles in 1975, and 235 rubles in 1977. The production costs per ton of live weight of cattle in the same years were 1,166 rubles, 1,574 rubles, and 1,639 rubles.[18] Eggs cost 76 rubles per 1,000 to produce in 1977, slightly higher than the procurement price for that year. The only product which earned a small profit from sales to the state was grain, which cost 65 rubles per ton to produce in *kolkhozy* and 82 rubles in *sovkhozy* in 1977. However, the production costs of grain rose sharply in 1979–1984, when investments and expenses were higher, but harvests were lower than in 1977.

By 1966 to 1969 procurement prices for livestock products were higher than retail prices. In 1980–1983 each kilogram of beef, mutton, and butter sold to the consumer cost the state more than it cost the consumer, an abnormal situation by any reckoning, which may perhaps have made sense in a very poor country with a primitive food industry. In the Soviet Union, however, where a considerable part of the meat purchased by the public has traditionally been processed meat (sausages, *pel'meni*, minced meat, smoked meat, etc.), high subsidies have inhibited meat processing (the price of processed meat has also not risen since 1962), since it would merely add to the expenses and require even higher subsidies. The production of cheese has grown more slowly than the production of milk for the same reason.

Another consequence of subsidizing retail prices has been to delay the introduction of modern technology for packaging, refrigerating, and so on. In most food shops butter is not pre-packed—it is cut into pieces from boxes or barrels and sold by weight. Eggs are sold loose. It is the consumer's problem to provide suitable containers. This probably reduces the state's expenses, but is also increases the losses of food products. In Leningrad, a city which has a privileged status for food supplies and high-quality products (both because it is the "cradle of the revolution" and because it is a hero city and a tourist center), only 40 percent of the food on sale is packaged, and the packaging is usually done by the shops.[22] This particular feature of the food trade has delayed the introduction of supermarkets and other forms of self-service.

Initially, procurement prices were increased in an attempt to stimulate certain branches of agricultural production. But each further increase has meant that the state spends billions of rubles just to keep things moving. There is no question of either the state or the farms making a profit. In 1975 state subsidies for food were at the level of 25 billion rubles. Two further increases in 1976–1979 made an additional allocation of 5.3 billion rubles per year necessary.[23] But at the end of the 1970s more than half of the state and collective farms were registered as operating at a financial loss. The salaries of the *kolkhozniki* and *sovkhoz* workers, the cost of machinery, the cost of services provided by *Selkhoztekhniki* and *Soyuzselkhozkhimiya*, and other expenses, were growing faster than the increase in procurement prices. Moreover, all the measures which were intended to raise productivity, increase the harvests, and improve the efficiency of agricultural production had very little effect.

The disproportion shown in Table 44 between retail prices and production costs of livestock products is clearly far too great. In both economic and practical terms, it would be an error to allow the disproportion to grow. Since 1970 the state has also subsidized the production of grain, potatoes, and vegetables. Although production costs are still lower than the retail prices of these goods, the difference is too small for a profit to be made from their commercial sale. The retail price of potatoes is 0.10 rubles per kilogram, of cabbages and beets, 0.14 rubles per kilogram, of rye

TABLE 44
Production Costs of Agricultural Products in *Kolkhozy* and State Subsidies for Some Food Products in the RSFSR[a]
(Rubles per Kilogram)

	Production cost 1965–1983 (rubles per ton)		Retail price 1963–1983 (rubles per kg)		State subsidy of retail price 1983 (rubles per kg)	
Meat (live weight)[b]			Meat products		Meat products	
Cattle	1,010	2,468	Beef	1.9	Beef	2.99
Pigs	1,183	2,393	Pork	2.1	Pork	1.55
Sheep	741	1,736	Mutton	2.0	Mutton	2.77
Milk	163	340	Milk	0.36	Milk	0.17
Butter	NA	4,800	Butter	3.6	Butter	4.36
Grain	53	86	Bread	0.25[c]	Bread	NA
Potatoes	45	144	Potatoes	0.10[d]	Potatoes	0.30
Eggs (per 1,000)	75	116	Eggs (per 10)	0.10	Eggs (per 10)	0.15

Sources: State subsidies, [21]; production costs, *Nar khoz.*, 1965, p. 409; 1983, p. 278; retail prices are for average quality products in Moscow food shops in 1983.

[a] Production costs in the RSFSR are higher than for the Soviet Union as a whole. They are slightly lower in the Ukraine and Byelorussia, but higher in Central Asia and Transcaucasia. There are slight zonal variations in retail prices as well.

[b] Live weight is normally 30 to 40 percent higher than carcass (slaughter) weight. Prices of retail meat are average for meat of different quality.

[c] Rye bread costs from 0.16 to 0.22 rubles, wheat bread from 0.28 to 0.50 rubles.

[d] The retail price for potatoes is seasonal, ranging from 0.10 in October–April to about 0.4 to 0.5 for new potatoes in June–July.

bread from 0.16 rubles to 0.22 rubles per kilogram, and of wheat bread from 0.26 rubles to 0.40 rubles per kilogram. These prices have remained constant since 1953, despite the fact that procurement, transport, storage, milling, processing, and marketing have all become more expensive.

Procurement prices were increased once again from January 1983 as part of the Food Program. As a result 16 billion rubles per annum had to be added to the agricultural budget.[24] However, the new increases have failed to stimulate an overall increase in agricultural production (with the exception of a modest increase in livestock and milk, too small to make any difference to the population as a whole). The gap between procurement prices for meat and retail prices has become so great that it makes economic sense for rural households to sell their own livestock to the state and to buy meat for their own consumption from the state trading system. Many cases of corruption have been reported in which meat and butter have changed hands several times with a large profit to people working in the trading system. For example, the same carcass of cattle can be sold to the state, delivered to the wholesale storage system, be registered as sold, and then start the circle again. In the process, local officials can make large illegal profits, while reporting an increase in procurement. This misguided policy resulted in acute shortages of meat and dairy products in 1980–1982. There was some improvement in 1983–1985, but it was the result of the anticorruption campaign and the wide publicity given to the trials and the penalties paid by corrupt officials in the trade system and the ministries of trade of the RSFSR and other republics. In 1983–1985 many regional and district officials were dismissed for falsifying the procurement statistics. From 1986 the regional branches of *Gosagroprom SSSR* were given the power to raise retail prices for fruit and vegetables but the structure of the new regional prices of these perishable goods is not yet known.

The integration of numerous industries which are only indirectly related to agricultural production (rural road construction, building of agro-towns, etc.) into the agro-industrial complex has made it difficult to make sense of the real volume of investment in agriculture. Since 1965 investments have usually been divided into two main groups: agricultural development and agricultural production. The latter includes financing the production and repair of machinery, fertilizers, land reclamation work, the construction of farm buildings, and other activities that are directly involved in generating agricultural products. It also includes state subsidies of retail food prices and the cost of agricultural administration. Investments into agricultural development include financing the development of related industries, constructing new plants to produce agricultural machinery or chemicals and fertilizers, paying for the network of research and educational establishments, and investing into the processing of food products (sugar plants, fruit- and vegetable-processing plants, slaughterhouses, meat combines, etc.). Investments in the agro-industrial complex as a whole include all the foregoing, as well as investment related to the production or consumption of food. Since 1983 the official investment figures have included the light industries which use agricultural produce to make commercial food and consumer goods (sausages, sweets, shoes, sheepskin, textiles, etc.), the bread and fish industries, and the food trade. Thus the larger part of investments in the agro-industrial complex is spent on urban workers. In 1984 the number of people employed by the agro-industrial complex was 45.4 million, only about half of which were *kolkhozniki* or *sovkhoz* workers.[25]

Economists vary in the figures they give for investment in agriculture. However, it is clear that in 1965–1985 the growth of investments in development was more rapid than in production. Nonetheless, the growth of investments in production was greater than the increase in agricultural production. The average annual total value of agricultural produce from all types of farms (including private plots) was 100.4 billion rubles in 1966–1970, and 131 billion rubles (in comparable prices) in 1981–1985, an increase of 30 percent.[26] But investments increased by 280 percent in the same period.[27] In 1982–1985 they formed about 30 to 32 percent of all capital investments in the national economy. The growth of the overall agricultural budget also grew more rapidly than agricultural production. For every billion rubles spent on agriculture during the last decade the value of agricultural production has increased by only 0.1 billion rubles, and the increase has come almost entirely from the livestock sector (it is partly due to the import of feed grain which is neither included in the expenses nor considered an investment). Investments into field crops has not brought any visible growth in products. Until 1975 long-term (up to twenty years) and short-term (up to one year) bank credits to industry were much higher than credits to *kolkhozy* and *sovkhozy*. The situation has changed since 1978. In 1984 the value of short-term credits to agriculture was 75.8 billion rubles (of which 34.6 billion went to *kolkhozy*) and the value of long-term credits was 45.5 billion rubles to *kolkhozy* and 9.7 billion rubles to *sovkhozy*. The value of both long- and short-term credits to industry in that year was about 101 billion rubles.[28] The total amount of credits to agriculture in 1984 was more than 130 billion rubles, while the total value of agricultural production in that year was 135.0 billion rubles, about 20 percent of which came from private agriculture. Even if one takes half of all agricultural products to be marketable (in fact, the amount is well below 50 percent for field crops), the value is well below the value of the annual credits.

The credits extended to agriculture are actually grants to cover expenses and losses, rather than money to stimulate production. *Kolkhozy* and *sovkhozy* have been less and less able to meet their financial obligations and they have had to use bank credits to pay monthly advances and salaries. Almost every agricultural Plenum of the Central Committee has had to pass a decree writing off their increasing debts, in the hope of giving agriculture the chance to make a new start. The last such gesture was made at the Food Program Plenum in May 1982, when Brezhnev reported:

> To improve the financial position of *kolkhozy* and *sovkhozy*, it has been decided to write off their debts on loans from the bank to the value of 9.7 billion rubles and extend the repayment periods of other loans to the value of more than 11 billion rubles. This will enable *kolkhozy* and *sovkhozy* to direct the funds which have thus been released towards further extending production.[29]

It is interesting to note that at the July 1978 Plenum on agriculture a similar decision was made—7.3 billion rubles of debt were written off and 4 billion rubles of credits were rescheduled over twelve years.[30] The total value of the debts was not reported, but since the writing off did not improve the financial situation of the *kolkhozy* and *sovkhozy*, 11.3 billion rubles must have represented only a fraction of their total debt. In 1982 more than 20 billion rubles of debt were written off and rescheduled, but short- and long-term borrowing from the banks was not reduced. One can therefore assume that the farms did not benefit from the funds released through Brezhnev's generosity. It should also be remembered that *kolkhozy* and *sovkhozy* which do not make a profit are exempt from paying tax on their financial turnover. The collective and state farms received at least 600 billion rubles of credits in 1978–1984. Their current debts therefore probably amount to 150 to 200 billion rubles, or 8,000 rubles for each *kolkhoz* member and *sovkhoz* worker. This is equal to their salaries for the last five to six years.

If the annual borrowing by *kolkhozy* and *sovkhozy* is much higher than their total product, the agricultural branch of the economy can be considered virtually bankrupt if it is judged by the principles of a capitalist market economy. The bankruptcy is not, however, caused by high floating interest rates, the usual cause in capitalist economies. The interest rate on credits from the State Bank is only 1 percent per annum for short-term credits and 0.75 percent for long-term credits (up to twenty years).[31] The interest paid on credits is much lower than the rate of inflation for manufactured goods, machinery, and other industrial products. If the credits are not repaid in time, the annual rate of interest rises to 3 percent. Any Western bank which charged so little interest and wrote off bad debts so often would not be able to survive for very long. The Soviet socialist economy, however, has no choice but to write off the debts and cover up mismanagement. The losses on agriculture are covered by other branches of the economy. However, the generally poor state of affairs in the consumer sector makes it more and more difficult to continue the practice without making a serious attempt to introduce radical reforms.

Many Soviet economists understand the problem, but are simply unable to influence events or even to express their views openly and clearly. They write about their ideas in the academic economic literature, usually in the form of tentative suggestions rather than outspoken criticism. The problems created by the misuse of bank credits have produced the reasonable suggestion that a separate bank should be created to serve the agro-industrial complex and that it should be based on the principle of balancing income and investment.[32] This would certainly make it more difficult to use other sectors of the economy to cover the losses. But as the situation stands at present, the government is unlikely to follow this advice. There have been many other suggestions about ways to reduce production costs, about connecting production costs to retail prices, and so on. One thing must be clear to everyone: the methods by which the *kolkhozy* and *sovkhozy* currently operate do not work.

4. Material Incentives: Guaranteed Payments versus Contract Brigades

Lenin, Stalin, and Khrushchev all recognized the importance of material incentives and tried to use them in the development of agriculture. In 1921, for example, material incentives were the main argument for introducing the New Economic Policy. Peasants were taxed on the basis of acreage of cultivated land and any surplus after paying this tax could be sold or consumed. After collectivization, material incentives were included in Stalin's main *kolkhoz* law: after fulfilling state procurements, paying the MTS and creating a seed reserve, the remaining produce was to be divided up between households. The idea was simple—if the *kolkhoznik* knew that he would receive the residue of the harvest as payment in kind, he would try to make the residue as large as possible. But whereas NEP succeeded in acting as a material incentive, the residue principle failed. Khrushchev did not change the system entirely, but he supplemented it with advance payments in kind and in cash. At the end of the season *trudodni* were calculated and advances were deducted from the annual total earned by the *kolkhozniki*. The frequency and size of advance payments rose during Khrushchev's decade in power and this improved conditions for the *kolkhozniki*. However, by 1964 their incomes were still below the average income of *sovkhoz* workers and only about half the average income of industrial or office workers.

In 1966 Brezhnev abolished residual payments and introduced new ideas about material incentives. The Central Committee and Council of Ministers of the USSR passed a decree on May 16, 1966, "On increasing the material incentives of *kolkhozniki* and developing co-operative agriculture."[33] Guaranteed cash payments were introduced for the work done by *kolkhozniki* and it was hoped that this would both improve their standard of living and give them an incentive to increase their productivity. The guaranteed payments were calculated on the basis of the scale of payments for similar work on the *sovkhozy*. The *kolkhoz* management (chairman, accountant, agronomist, etc.) were paid on the same salary scale as similar employees on the *sovkhozy*. Moreover, members of poor *kolkhozy* received exactly the same advance as those of wealthy *kolkhozy*. However, the final calculations at the end of the year depended on the harvest and what was left of it after all other obligations had been met.

The system of guaranteed payments certainly increased the incomes of the *kolkhozniki*. Increased production was also rewarded, but usually as a bonus over and above the guaranteed payment. Final payments also reflected higher harvests in the form of bonuses, but these tended to be small. When procurement prices for all agricultural products were increased substantially in 1966, the government expected that the *kolkhozy* would have enough money to pay the monthly advances. In books on agriculture written after 1966 this particular reform was praised as the most important and effective change since collectivization. In the standard textbook for secondary school teachers on the history of Soviet agriculture, for example, the following assessment of the reform is given:

By introducing guaranteed payment for the work of *kolkhozniki* the manner of distributing income was fundamentally changed. Salary funds began to be divided monthly at a guaranteed level, not, as was the case previously, from the residue. In this way the principle of the "residual" formation of a salary fund for *kolkhozniki* which had existed in the *kolkhozy* was overcome. According to that principle the salary fund consisted only of the money that was left over after the payment of all obligatory payments and the deduction of money for the *kolkhoz* social fund. Now the strict rule functions in *kolkhozy* that a fund for the payment of guaranteed salaries is formed first from the income which is received.

The payment of guaranteed salaries is one of the most important measures directed towards resolving one of the fundamental social tasks of society, bringing the standard of living of the *kolkhoz* peasantry closer to the standard of living of the working class. As a result of moving to guaranteed payments for work, the material interest of the *kolkhozniki* in the development of social production and in the growth of productivity has become stronger. This is the basis of the appreciable increase in the income of *kolkhozniki*.[34]

But where are the real material incentives in this reform? In 1967 the experienced and serious agricultural economist, G. Lisichkin, popular for his thoughtful, often brilliant essays on agricultural problems published in the literary magazine *Novyi mir*, tried to explain that the 10 percent increase in agricultural production in 1966 was the result of the new system of payments.

So what is so special about what has happened in this sphere of the national economy that it should give rise to such a significant increase in production? Perhaps the *kolkhozy* and *sovkhozy* have received a lot of new technology in this time? Perhaps they've been given twice or three times more fertilizer? Perhaps a lot of specialists have been replaced and they have begun to manage things on a scientific basis? Neither the first, nor the second, nor the third. . . . It has been achieved not by some kind of technological miracle, but by much simpler, but reliable means. The payment of *kolkhozniki* and specialists was increased—and their productive activity rose. This is what has guaranteed the growth of production. Until recently many *kolkhozy* could not make monthly payments for the labour of their members, but since the move in 1966 to a system of guaranteed payments there has been a great improvement in the situation. People have begun to live better, and this has told on production.

People began to be paid more and the number of hands grew. The number of hands grew and they managed to take the fertilizer out on tractors in two shifts. The same machines, but they worked at double the productivity, the same cattle and the same earth, but the new attitude to them gives completely different results.[35]

In fact, the new system of payments was an attempt to prevent the virtual collapse of the *kolkhozy*. As we saw at the beginning of the chapter, bankruptcies had accelerated during Khrushchev's tenure and many *kolkhozy* were turned into *sovkhozy*. The process did not stop after the March 1965 Central Committee Plenum. At the end of 1965, 1,865 *kolkhozy* disappeared, more than in 1964 (705) or 1963 (271). The leadership began to realize that the process would destroy the whole *kolkhoz* system unless something was done to remove the social and material differences between *kolkhozy* and *sovkhozy*. Their assessment was correct. The peasants were well aware that the economic collapse of a *kolkhoz* merely meant that it would be transformed into a *sovkhoz* and they had no reason for trying to prevent this, since they knew it would be a change for the better for them. Although the *kolkhoz* system offered them slightly larger private plots, the active campaign against private agriculture in 1961–1964 had made this advantage irrelevant.

It became clear later that the reform of the payment system was as misguided as the abolition of the MTS in 1958. It is true that agricultural performance was better in 1966 than in 1965, but this is not very surprising. Nineteen sixty-five was an extremely poor year and the grain harvest was 30 million tons below the 1964 level. At 171.2 million tons, the 1966 harvest was a record for the 1960s. But the amount was much lower in 1967, 1968, and 1969 (148, 169, and 162 million tons) and there was no growth in the overall value of agricultural produce. Between

1966 and 1969 the annual growth of agriculture was only 0.8 percent.[36] Whereas the incomes of the *kolkhozniki* grew substantially, the incomes of the *kolkhozy* declined. The reason was simple—increased production costs. The new salaries were reflected in the production costs, which rose so sharply that the 1966 procurement price increases were absorbed. The production costs of potatoes, for example, increased from 46 rubles per ton in 1965 to 74 rubles in 1970, of live weight of cattle from 1,017 rubles to 1,373 rubles. The procurement prices for these products were 66 rubles per ton for potatoes and 1,244 rubles for live weight of cattle.

Moreover, the *kolkhozy* did not have ready cash available to make the guaranteed monthly advances, so they borrowed from the banks. In 1965 the short-term credits of the *kolkhozy* were at the modest level of 0.4 billion rubles and the long-term credits were 3.9 billion rubles. They had tripled by 1970, to 2.5 billion rubles and 10.3 billion rubles respectively, despite the reduction in the number of *kolkhozy*.[37] In 1966–1970, 3184 *kolkhozy* became bankrupt and were transformed into *sovkhozy* (the bankruptcies accelerated towards the end of the period).

An attempt was made to solve the problem by raising procurement prices yet again in 1971 (see Table 44). In the case of many products the increase was so substantial that procurement prices rose to a level well above retail prices (the procurement price for live weight of cattle, for example, rose to 1,612 rubles per ton, while the retail price of meat remained 1.9 rubles per kilogram). This created a problem for the state, of course, but it also created difficulties for the *kolkhozy*. Although they were paid more, they also found it uneconomical to continue making payments in kind. Whereas previously payments in kind had been considered a primitive method of renumeration, *kolkhozniki* could now earn more from them than from cash payments. It had previously been normal practice for *kolkhozy* to sell various products to the local population at production cost, which was below the retail price. Now there was no interest in selling produce locally, since state procurements offered a much better price. The agricultural economist quoted before, Lisichkin, published an essay a few years later about the plight of rural intellectuals and professionals entitled "The Rural Paradox: How to Get Food in the Village."[38] Local rural shops ceased selling meat, milk, cheese, and other local products because retail prices were fixed by law and procurement prices were higher. It was much easier to sell to the state than to worry about local food processing. While the *kolkhozniki* could feed themselves from their private plots, local teachers, doctors, nurses, social workers, engineers, and others did not have this option. This became one of the factors which made it so difficult to develop the rural areas.

The creation of the agro-industrial complex added to the problems of rising production cost. Payments to *Selkhoztekhnika*, *Soyuzselkhozhimiya*, the land reclamation system, and so on, were reflected in the production costs. As a result, production costs increased; however, there was no concomitant increase in volume of production, and the number of *kolkhozy* and *sovkhozy* operating at a financial loss rose every year in the 1970s. The service and industrial sectors of the agro-industrial complex were operating at a profit, while the debts of the *kolkhozy* and *sovkhozy* were mounting and salaries were being paid from new bank credits. Although it was clear that continued guaranteed monthly payments to the *kolkhozniki* would only be tenable if there was a complete change in the system of service charges and in retail prices, the government merely continued increasing procurement prices. Prices rose again in 1981, 1983, and 1985. More and more money was poured into agriculture without any visible effect on the volume of production. This was a very misguided policy, but the government perceived very few options to improve the situation.

The most obvious solution would have been to increase retail prices. But this was a difficult choice to make. It would have been an acknowledgment of defeat for Brezhnev, and he had no wish to make that kind of admission towards the end of his life. Andropov and Chernenko were each only in charge of the country for a year and neither of them had time to deal with the problem. Gorbachev presumably has more time and more understanding, but it will be a difficult choice for him, too. To some extent he is responsible for the present state of affairs: he was Central Committee secretary in charge of agriculture from 1978. But there is a more intractable problem. Food prices have been kept low for so long (since 1953 for cereals and bread and since 1962 for livestock and dairy products) that the disparity between them and the cost of production has become enormous. Any increase in retail prices designed to improve the discrepancy would have to be huge. It would almost certainly be extremely unpopular.

A second option would be to decrease production costs, so that *kolkhozy* and *sovkhozy* would have more cash available and could begin to repay their huge debts. Although this would mean that the government would continue making vast payments for procurements, part of the money would return to the state treasury in repayments and reductions of annual credits. The collective and state farms would also have more money available to invest in development. Not surprisingly, this is the option which has been chosen. Efforts have previously been made to find ways to reduce production costs, but the problem has only been recognized as urgent in the 1980s. There have been a number of local experiments, with research groups and institutes offering solutions and local *kolkhozy* and *sovkhozy* testing them. At the end of 1980 the Central Committee and Council of Ministers of the USSR passed a comprehensive decree, "On improving planning and economic stimulation of production and the procurement of agricultural products." Procurement prices were increased yet again.[39] But the decree also contained some elements of material stimulation for brigades and the smaller *zveno*. (A brigade normally consists of five to ten *zveno* of about ten people each. For smaller tasks a *zveno* can consist of three to five people only, sometimes members of a single family, and can operate as an independent working unit). The final harvest was to play a larger role in determining the annual income of members. The decree was ineffectual, however, and agricultural performance was even worse in 1981 than in 1980. The new system of payments was enormously complicated, since account was to be taken of the performance of individual members of the brigade or *zveno*, their professional level, the result of "socialist competition" within brigades, and many other factors difficult to assess. Finally the government decided to simplify the whole system.

There had already been signs that there was one particular form of organization and payment which seemed to be popular with *kolkhozniki* and *sovkhoz* workers, as well as with their chairmen—the system of contract brigades or *zveno*. Originally called *beznaryadnaya brigada* ("a brigade which makes its own plans") and later, *brigadnyi podryad* ("a brigade with its own contract"), the method seemed to be successful although it had not been designed with agriculture in mind. Indeed, it had not really been designed: it had sprung up spontaneously in industry on the workers' own initiative. It had been used in agriculture as a temporary measure for specific tasks. The principle was simple. Brigades of various sizes (the size depended on the task, size of field, etc.) or smaller *zveno* are given full responsibility for one full cycle of agricultural work (usually one rotation system of four, five, or six fields). The members of the brigade or the *zveno* cannot be transferred by the *kolkhoz* management to other work. The brigade makes a contract with the *kolkhoz* or *sovkhoz* management which indicates the volume of production and the payment. Payment depends not on individual operations (which was how the previous system worked), but entirely on final results. It is up to the brigade members to decide how their money is to be advanced and what pattern of work to adopt. If it produces more than the contract specifies, the money earned from the higher procurement prices paid for excess production is divided amongst all the members. If the brigade can manage with fewer members, each member receives more money. Thus within the brigade real economic principles rule—higher harvests produce higher incomes, and hard and efficient work earns material results.

In his report to the May 1982 Food Program Plenum, Brezhnev advocated that contract brigades should be introduced as widely as possible. The press praised the efficiency of the method. In addition to brigades for the full agricultural cycle (which needs rather large brigades with their own machinery and drivers), attempts were made to use a similar arrangement for smaller works, for example, using *zveno* for cultivating potatoes, producing fodder, taking care of animals, and so on. The hope was that a sense of mutual responsibility would be created, since everyone in the brigade or *zveno* would be interested in the final results. At the same time the task of the agricultural administrative system would be simplified: the *kolkhoz* and *sovkhoz* management would not have to inspect and evaluate each individual operation. The result would be higher productivity, and higher incomes for brigade members if they managed their task with fewer workers. Brigades were given the right to decide about the quality of all specialized work (the use of fertilizers, repairs, etc.) and to reject any work if the standard did not conform to the original contract. In March 1983 the system was approved by the Politburo, which called it a system "which gives higher results in agricultural production with smaller expenditure on labor and funds."[40] It was recommended that the method should receive wider application, but that brigades should only be formed in *kolkhozy, sovkhozy*, and other agricultural units on a voluntary basis. The Ministry of Agriculture offered a model contract for brigades or *zveno*.[41] In fact, although it is easy to see that the system successfully stimulates productivity and improves efficiency, it is not immediately self-evident how it achieves the reduction in production costs which its proponents claim.

The success of the contract brigades depends entirely upon cooperation between members and whether they are prepared to work hard. The final income depends upon everyone's work, since there is no special tariff for particular operations. Extra work caused by factors like the weather and weed contamination must be done without extra pay, merely because the final harvest depends upon it being done. The final reward may be much higher than under the previous system, but an element of risk does exist. The system has proved more popular for some crops than for others (for example, it is popular for vegetables because surpluses can be sold through the open market, and less popular for grain crops or fodder). Brigades are also more suitable for young farmers than for old, and for men rather than for women who have children to care for. For this reason the method cannot be recommended for universal use. At a special conference on the economic problems of the agro-industrial complex held under the auspices of the Central Committee in March 1984 (Chernenko and Gorbachev were the main speakers), contract brigades were called the most progressive form of agricultural organization.[42]

While it is certain that the contract brigade system has great potential and creates material incentives, the method is still experimental and controversial. In 1983 only about 10 percent of the *kolkhoz* and *sovkhoz* work force was united into contract brigades (1.9 million people). In 1984 the figure rose to 23 percent (4.3 million).[43] By 1985 about 30 percent of the agricultural work force belonged to contract brigades. Between 1982 and 1985 the average monthly income of a *kolkhoznik* rose from 129 to 153 rubles and of a *sovkhoz* worker from 159 to 180 rubles. The general statistics do not indicate the difference between the incomes of members and nonmembers of contract brigades. But most of the increase must be due to the brigades and it reflects a growing differentiation between more and less profitable works.

The system has been most popular in the regions suitable for technical crops, fruit, and vegetables (Central Asia), and much less popular in Estonia and Latvia (where it includes only 2 to 5 percent of the work force). There are drawbacks to the system and they are difficult to resolve. First of all, brigades require a stable personnel. Secondly, their output has to be assessed separately and cannot be mixed with the general production of the *kolkhoz* or *sovkhoz*. This creates logistic problems. Thirdly, the power of the brigade chairman during the contract period is considerable, comparable to the power of the farm director or chairman. In fact, since the brigade extends over a fixed area, it acts like a miniature *kolkhoz*, although with more flexible rules. Fourthly, the method of payment introduces economic differentiation into rural life. If the brigade is successful, the income of its members may be three or four times higher than average. Indeed, some brigades report their members' incomes to be 400 to 500 rubles per month, higher than the salary of a qualified industrial worker and the equivalent of a lecturer's or university professor's salary.[44] Given the method of payment, it is not surprising that the system is more popular in fertile areas that enjoy a good climate. Within those areas, it is more favored for well-situated than for far-flung fields. It is also easier to stimulate the productivity of field workers in this way than of those who work on animal farms.

In 1984 contract brigades represented 23 percent of the agricultural work force and produced 47.6 percent of cultivated crops, 18.5 percent of cattle, and 40 percent of other livestock (pigs, sheep, poultry). Despite the increased income earned by contract brigade members and their increased productivity, the system appears, however, to have had little effect on the overall performance of Soviet agriculture. The total agricultural output (in volume and in value) was practically the same in 1982–1985. The fact that contract brigades have had no visible economic impact on the total production figures indicates the main problem. Because they are based on the voluntary principle, they have turned out to be feasible for lucrative crops in favorably situated areas. The richer *kolkhozy* may become even richer, while the poor become increasingly impoverished as they lose their more active and able workers, who migrate to other areas.

Within *kolkhozy* and *sovkhozy* the differentiation between more and less profitable areas of work has also become more clearly fixed. Agricultural work is often attractive to the traditional rural population because of the diverse skills required and the absence of monotony. The individual farmer takes care of a variety of crops and animals, needs to know the machinery, the problems of fertilizers, and so on. The contract brigades, however, became more specialized. They naturally first took over mostly "cash" technical crops like sugar beets, sunflower, corn, vegetables, and "intensive" fields for high-quality wheat. Growing feed and fodder crops; making hay, silage, and haylage; working on potato fields; transporting fodder to livestock farms: all these require a great deal of manual labor and were less popular with the contract brigades. It was difficult to evaluate the results of these operations in financial terms based on the cost of the final product. These essential, but less profitable, works were thus left to older people (usually women) and to temporarily mobilized urban workers.

In the discussion on contract brigades there were many arguments pointing out their high productivity, efficiency, and the high incomes they generated. Little was said about their limitations, however. As things stood in 1986, the system looked like a perverted Stolypin reform. The Stolypin reforms made it possible for more active and able peasants to separate from the rest of the communal peasantry and to do better for themselves. In the contract brigades, the same thing appeared to be happening not on the basis of the segregation of the land, but of the type of work. The Stolypin reforms could proceed to their logical end— the creation of a class of independent, prosperous family farmers. The contract brigade system also stimulated the appearance of brigades based on families or relatives which did particularly well. They were called "contract collectives on a family basis."[45] But by the 1980s rural families were too small for this form to have much future. Nineteen eighty-four was the last year in Soviet rural history in which the official number of *kolkhoz* households (12.6 million) was lower than the number of *kolkhozniki* (12.8 million). By 1985 the number of *kolkhozniki* had dropped to 12.6 million, the same number as of households.[46]

There were only two ways in which the "Stolypin factor," which was dividing villages and creating social tension, could be removed. One was to return to the old-fashioned system of guaranteed cash payments on the basis of individual performance and quotas. The other was to make the contract brigade system compulsory for all agricultural workers and to devise a payment scale which would be acceptable for all types of work. Gorbachev could not return to Brezhnev's old system. On March 28, 1986, therefore, the Central Committee and Council of Ministers of the USSR passed a comprehensive decree, "On the further improvement of economic mechanisms in the agro-industrial complex of the USSR." The decree instructed *Gosagroprom SSSR* to devise a new system of payment and higher productivity quotas (which were intended to reduce the high cash incomes of existing contract brigades). "Family and individual contracts" were legalized as one of a number of forms of "collective contract," providing that the family income would be no higher than the income of members of other contract brigades for the same work. However, it was now considered essential to transfer all agricultural, food-processing, and other agro-industrial work to the system of contract brigades and *khozyaistvennyi raschet* (balancing salaries, expenses, and the value of the final product).[47] From 1987 all agricultural work was expected to be organized on the basis of contract brigades. The freedom of choice between the brigades and the less demanding guaranteed monthly payments had ended. Whether the new system will have any influence on the general performance of Soviet agriculture remains to be seen. But the general aim of reducing production costs in all parts of the agro-industrial complex cannot be achieved without an initial decline in all forms of rural income.

Conclusion

It is clear that the post-Khrushchev leaders have not found any easier or better solutions to the problems of agriculture than Khrushchev did. Agricultural production has increased only marginally if it is calculated on a per capita basis, and the economic cost has been inordinately large. The organization of local, regional, and central administrative bodies became extremely complex, contradictory, and even more bureaucratic than under Khrushchev. The creation of a united agro-industrial complex made the crucial members of the complex, the *kolkhozy* and *sovkhozy*, less responsible for their own work. The relationship between production costs, procurement, and retail prices has become even more irrational. The government has no choice but to cover agricultural expenses and losses and to subsidize retail food prices, all rural construction and modernization programs, and higher rural salaries. By the 1980s agriculture had begun to consume about 27 to 30 percent of the annual budget and more than 100 billion rubles annually of long- and short-term bank credits. *Kolkhoz* and *sovkhoz* debts have become so high that the whole relationship between the socialist sector of agriculture and the national economy has become difficult. Moreover, the high cost of agriculture has made it difficult to find financial resources to invest in industrial modernization and development. Agricul-

ture, more than anything else, has been responsible for the slow-
ing down of the entire Soviet economy in 1975–1985 and the
increasing signs of incipient economic crisis. Moreover, the increased mobility of the rural population has created zones with
different levels of development. The climatically less favorable
non-*chernozem* areas of the eastern, western, and central regions
of the RSFSR and Byelorussia have almost become disaster areas
in comparison with the Ukraine, the Baltic republics, the North
Caucasus, and Central Asia.

The general decline in all economic indicators in agriculture
in 1979–1985 has led the government to support less orthodox
systems of economic incentive and more flexible forms of organization which reward a kind of private initiative based on the
common interests of the brigade or *zveno*. If it is given a chance
to develop, this new form of organization will begin to contradict
the interests of the intermediate state and Party bureaucracy and
it will require more liberal legislation. The appearance of finan-
cially more independent, flexible contract brigades will cause
economic and "professional" differentiation in rural areas and
hard-working, active, and wealthy farmers (or kulaks) will emerge,
as the Stolypin reforms intended. Although this development is
economically viable, it will contradict both the traditional principles of *kolkhoz* and *sovkhoz* agriculture and the Soviet system
of bureaucratic administration.

There are already signs of attempts to prevent the preferential
development of contract brigades in selected "profit-oriented"
branches of agriculture and to reduce agricultural production
costs by accelerating productivity more than incomes. The failure
of Stalin's system of *trudoden* payments, of Khrushchev's combined system of *trudoden* payments plus cash advances, and of
Brezhnev's system of guaranteed monthly salaries have led to
the newly designed, very complex method of payment based on
the volume and value of the final product. However, the enormous
subsidies paid to keep the retail prices of agricultural produce
low have made it impossible to achieve the intention of increasing
agricultural production and improving the food balance of the
population's diet. It has become essential to reduce production

costs and increase retail prices. The former will cause an inevitable decline in rural incomes and the latter will lead to a higher cost of living for the urban population. However, the government would be able to release the funds which are now wastefully absorbed in food subsidies and use them to raise the income of those groups of the population (the low paid and the pensioners) which would suffer from higher food prices. The wasteful system of centralized investment in agricultural development should also be replaced by sounder economic arrangements based on local initiative. Essentially what Soviet agriculture requires is a kind of "deregulation" and more freedom of choice between different economic and organizational models.

Chapter 11

Private Agriculture

The first decision Brezhnev and Kosygin made about agriculture, in November 1964, just one month after Khrushchev's dismissal, was embodied in the decree, "On the elimination of unjustified restrictions on the subsidiary household plots of *kolkhozniki, sovkhoz* workers and employees."[1] Khrushchev had also begun by relaxing restrictions on private agriculture, but had reversed this policy later to force peasants to devote more of their time to working on the *kolkhoz*. Brezhnev, however, supported private agriculture steadily until the end of his life and his successors have continued to do so. The Party and government finally began to realize the vital importance to Soviet agriculture of these small privately cultivated plots, not only because of the disproportionate amount of food produced on them (about 30 percent of the total national agricultural output), but also because the *kolkhozy* and *sovkhozy* are simply unable to cultivate the many labor-intensive crops for which there are no proper means of mechanization. It was also clear that if the exodus of the rural population was to be limited, the possession of private plots and the right to work on them without outside interference was crucial.

All land was nationalized in the Soviet Union at the time of the Revolution and the private plots are not private property in the real sense of the term. The state leases small plots for private cultivation directly, or through the *kolkhozy* and *sovkhozy*. Article 13 of the constitution guarantees the right to this kind of cultivation.

Citizens may be granted the use of plots of land, in the manner prescribed by law, for a subsidiary small-holding (including the keeping of livestock and poultry), for fruit and vegetable growing or for building an individual dwelling. Citizens are required to make rational use of the land allotted to them. The state, and collective farms provide assistance to citizens in working their small-holdings.

Property owned or used by citizens shall not serve as a means of deriving unearned income or be employed to the detriment of the interests of society.[2]

Traditionally there have been several forms of private agriculture in the Soviet Union, each with a separate set of laws and regulations specifying the size of the plot and the recommended type of cultivation. The predominant form, and economically the most important, is represented by the personal plots cultivated by *kolkhozniki* and *sovkhoz* workers. In the former case the plot is leased by the *kolkhoz*. A family has a right to a plot as long as at least one member of the family is a *kolkhoznik*. The days when all the adult members of a rural family worked on the *kolkhoz* are long since over. The number of family members working as *kolkhozniki* has declined steadily since the war. In 1940 the number was 2.2, in 1950, 1.5, in 1963, 1.2, and in 1982, 1.03.[3] However, by 1985 there were 12.6 million households living on *kolkhozy* and exactly 12.6 million *kolkhozniki*[4]: in other words, in all families only one member of the household worked on the *kolkhoz*. There is no discrimination on grounds of sex and no compulsory retirement on the *kolkhozy*. Young people can join from the age of sixteen. The constitution declares that it is

. . . the duty of, and a matter of honour for, every able-bodied citizen of the USSR to work conscientiously in his chosen, socially useful occupation and strictly to observe labour discipline.[5]

In urban families it is customary for both able-bodied adult members of a family to work, although each of them will receive a higher salary than the income of a *kolkhoznik*. In rural families, on the other hand, this is the exception rather than the rule. As a result there is a reserve labor pool which chooses to be "socially useful" and "work conscientiously" only in private agriculture. Soviet statistics give the total number of *sovkhoz* workers (11.9 million in 1985), but do not list the number of independent households. Private *kolkhoz* plots cover a larger acreage than private *sovkhoz* plots (see Table 45) and the average size of each plot is slightly larger: 0.30 hectares per *kolkhoznik* and 0.20 hectares per *sovkhoz* worker. The third group of the rural population which needs subsidiary plots for economic reasons consists of those who live in the village but do not work on the land—such as old-age pensioners, teachers, medical personnel, employees of *Selkhoztekhnika* and *Soyuzselkhozkhimiya*, local officials, and those who commute to the towns to work (about 10 million families). Each such group has different legal arrangements and a different size of plot. Finally, current legislation gives urban families the right to cultivate small allotments in the country not because they need to, but because it is considered a useful form of leisure activity. The size of these allotments varies from 0.04 to 0.06 hectares and they number over 6 million and are increasing. Thus the total number of privately cultivated plots, 39 to 40 million in 1986, is well above the total number of peasant *nadely* before 1913 and in the 1920s. Clearly collectivization did not eliminate the private sector, despite Stalin's strenuous efforts to bring this about.

In fact, private agriculture occupies only 1.6 percent of the total arable land in the Soviet Union. Nonetheless, in the 1980s

TABLE 45

Distribution of Arable Land

(Sown Land, Fallow Land, Meadows, Pastures,
Orchards, and Vineyards, in Million Hectares)

	1965	1975	1985
Collective farms	228.6	189.0	173.9
Leased to *kolkhozniki* and other villagers for private agriculture	4.98	4.42	4.16
State farms	311.6	356.2	378.7
Leased to *sovkhoz* workers for private agriculture and as allotments to urban families	2.6	3.6	3.9

Source: Nar. khoz., 1965, p. 257; 1975, p. 343; 1985, p. 202.

it produces more meat, milk, and eggs annually than the total annual amount of these products produced by all sectors (private, collective, and state farms) in 1933–1939. Moreover, it does this without any mechanization and virtually without horses. Indeed, the techniques and methods used in private agriculture today are more backward and primitive than those used by the peasant to cultivate his *nadel* a hundred years ago. Nonetheless, private agriculture has become vitally important, and the decline in private production which became apparent in the 1970s and 1980s provoked intensive efforts by the government to improve the situation.

The fact that about 1.6 percent of the arable land produces about 30 percent of the national agricultural product in the Soviet Union (35 percent in 1960 and about 40 percent in the 1950s) often leads Western analysts to compare the seemingly good prospects for the private sector with the low productivity of the socialist sector. In fact, neither sector is doing well. It is true that the *kolkhoz* and *sovkhoz* sector shows a poor use of arable land for the production of field crops and livestock products, while the private sector uses its land in a much better way. Nonetheless, it has a very low productivity per unit of labor. This is due to the almost complete absence of mechanization suitable for small plots. The cultivation by urban families of vegetables and fruit on small allotments can be found in many countries of the Western world. There, too, the plots are small and very little mechanization is used. However, in Western countries the allotments have little economic importance to the country as a whole. It is only in the Soviet Union and in those Eastern European countries which have adopted the Soviet model of agriculture that "subsidiary" or "auxiliary" private plots are of vital importance to the national economy and more particularly, to the rural population. More than half of all the food consumed by the rural population is privately produced and this includes about 90 percent of all high-quality food (meat, milk, eggs, vegetables, and fruit). The abolition of payments in kind for *trudodni* in 1966 and the universal introduction of cash payments for all work has increased the importance of private plots in the rural economy. But private agriculture also makes a vital contribution to producing a balanced diet for the population as a whole.

Soviet authors often stress the dominance of the socialist sector to indicate how successful collectivization has been. But in so doing they ignore the essential fact that there are a number of important crops which are either entirely, or almost entirely, produced by the private sector, without mechanization and without any of the advantages of "scientific agriculture." For millennia, agriculture has been concerned not only with the production of food, but also with the spontaneous selection of the best and most productive varieties of crops and livestock for particular conditions. Millions of people cultivating small Soviet plots also practice selection, but not in a way that will help the future, more productive, use of these crops. Official statistics indicate that more than 60 percent of all potatoes, more than 30 percent of vegetables, more than 50 percent of all fruit, and about 30 percent of

TABLE 46
Proportion of Crops Produced
from Privately Cultivated Plots
(as a Percentage of the Total National Output)[a]

	1960	1965	1975	1980	1985
Grain crops[b]	2	2	1	1	1
Potato	63	63	59	64	60
Vegetables	44	41	34	33	29
Meat	41	40	31	31	28
Milk	47	39	31	30	29
Eggs	80	67	39	32	28
Wool	22	20	20	22	26

Source: Nar. khoz., 1965, p. 265; 1985, p. 185.

[a] The official statistics give the percentage of the production in *kolkhozy* and *sovkhozy*. The percentage produced by private plots can be calculated by subtracting the production of the socialized sector from 100.

[b] This mostly consists of corn produced in the North Caucasus and Transcaucasia. No cereals are produced privately.

meat, milk, and eggs are produced by private agriculture (see Table 46). But it also has the virtual monopoly of production of such important crops as carrots, onions, garlic and other spice crops, tomatoes, beets, soft fruits, honey, rabbit meat, and flowers. About half of the country's much famed fur trade depends not on hunting in the woods and the taiga, but on the private sector.

Some Soviet authors and politicians are now making a concerted effort to portray private agriculture as a special form of socialist agriculture and an integral part of the agro-industrial complex. One group of experts has produced political, economic, and even cultural arguments to prove that "subsidiary private agriculture" is a perfectly logical supplement to the dominant socialist sector. The economist, V. Nefedov, for example, explains:

Subsidiary private agriculture (SPA) occupies a particular place in socialist agriculture and is an integral part and special form of socialist property. The socialist nature of SPA is determined by socialist productive relations and by the part played by the farming of the population in the reproduction of the vital means and incomes of the toilers of social production and in the creation of general state food reserves. . . .

In analyzing the functioning of subsidiary private agriculture and working out measures to regulate its development, it is important to take account of the social aspects. SPA plays an important role in the work education of children and this was mentioned at the June 1983 Plenum of the CC of the CPSU as one of its most important tasks. The work of adolescents in SPA implies more than pretending to work. It instils diligence, influences the development of a sense of values, predetermines their interests and choice of profession and strengthens their preference for a rural way of life. Being a supplementary source of income, SPA guarantees a higher level of welfare to its owners and to a certain extent it consolidates the rural population.[6]

In other words, private agriculture enriches the peasants and turns their children into farmers. The author does not deny that there are some negative aspects to private agriculture.

At the same time there are negative aspects to the influence of SPA on the life of the population. Since it is basically confined to the family, private agriculture to some extent weakens the interest of the family in the productive collective. Taking up much free time, SPA retards the growth of culture and education in its owners. It remains one of the significant factors in the social differences in labour between the town and the countryside, since it preserves routine, heavy manual labour and the most patriarchal form of peasant land cultivation and animal farming in an almost inviolable form.[7]

Other Soviet experts pay more attention to the limitations of private plots, their incompatibility with socialist principles, and the way in which they contradict the cultural development of a modern industrial society.

Any specialist or worker who is going to live and work in the country has, without fail, to acquire a subsidiary private plot, his own cattle and a kitchen garden. As you know, lately this is not only not forbidden, it is encouraged in every way possible. "Do I really have to?" asks the matriculant finishing his schooling at a village school . . . the prospect by no means suits all those who have grown up in a village. And young specialists, completing their courses at the technical college or institute in the town also do not rush off to move to the countryside, since they know what daily difficulties await them, first and foremost with food. And the local inhabitant begins to wonder whether it's worth it. . . . The conditions for cultivating a private plot have become immeasurably more difficult than they used to be. The pasture land has been ploughed up, payment in kind has been abolished and one used to be able to use it to feed the cattle and poultry much more easily. One used even to be able to borrow a horse from the *kolkhoz* to transport a sack or two of bran home, or a sack of hay and some straw. The problem is there aren't any horses now on the *kolkhoz* or *sovkhoz*. And one can't always get a K-700 tractor to work on a peasant homestead. It's not that the chairman or the director resents lending the machine to a person now and then. It's just that the peasant thinks that when it turns the machine will smash everything around.

People in the village want to live and work decently . . . The archaic conditions of the *kolkhoz* homestead have begun to contradict the life-style and education of people, their dress, furniture, etc.[8]

As we have seen in the previous chapter, the abolition of payments in kind based on the size of the harvest, and the introduction instead of monthly cash payments initiated uncontrollable economic processes which increased production costs. This, in turn, led to higher procurement prices, which rose above town retail prices. The result was that the sale of food in rural shops was inhibited. The cultivation of private plots became vital for providing a normal diet for the rural population. This was deliberate government policy in the expectation that the overall economy would be stimulated. Abolishing payments in kind made it possible to increase the proportion of marketable grain and other crops procured by the state. It also meant that more feed grain and fodder for *kolkhoz* and *sovkhoz* farm animals could be provided. Peasants, who now received only cash, were expected to take care of the intensive cultivation of their own private plots and to use their cash reserves to buy manufactured goods. There was an overabundance of goods in the shops which were of such poor quality that the more sophisticated urban population did not buy them. It had already become a tradition to send them to the village shops to be sold to the less discriminating rural population. But the peasants chose to spend their cash on food rather than on manufactured goods. What is more, they purchased food in the towns and cities not only for their own consumption, but also to feed their livestock.

As Table 47 and 48 indicate, production from the private plots did not increase vastly, despite official encouragement and permission to double the size of *kolkhoznik* plots form 0.25 to 0.5 hectares. The absence of small-scale mechanization and of horses made it difficult to use the auxiliary plots more efficiently and the modest increase in production which occurred in the 1980s was not related to special measures of support, but to the shortages of food products in the towns and cities and the restrictions which were placed on the amount of food which individuals could purchase in the shops. Food shortages also caused the market price of privately produced food to rise steeply and this, too, stimulated private agriculture. Like any other private business, agriculture can be stimulated by market demand. However, the five- to tenfold difference between the state retail price in shops and the market price of many products, particularly early fruit and vegetables, became a source of embarrassment to the government. In 1986 attempts were made to reduce market prices by intro-

TABLE 47

Total Value of Production
from the Socialized and Private Sectors
(Calculated in Comparable 1973 Prices)*

	Percentage of value of overall national agricultural output	
	Kolkhozy, sovkhozy, and interfarm units	Individual households
1960	64.4	35.6
1965	67.5	32.5
1970	70.3	29.7
1975	71.7	28.3
1979	73.5	26.5
1982	71.2	28.8

Source: Nar. khoz., 1982, p. 193 and [9].

* The comparison is made on the basis of procurement prices in 1973. In fact the value of products in the private sector is higher than indicated because of their higher quality, diversity, and sales through the private market, where prices are higher. The official statistics omit some products (berries, flowers, etc.) and list only traditional crops.

ducing legal restrictions and repressing "intermediate" traders (speculators).

As is the case in any open market, small farmers prefer selling their products to intermediate wholesale traders to travelling long distances to towns and cities themselves. It is rare for a rural family to own a car. If a car owner (often from the same village) collects produce from a number of farmers and delivers it to be sold on the market, he naturally hopes to make a profit. Since 1986, however, people who sell produce on the market have to be in possession of a temporary permit which certifies that they themselves grew the products. The system was designed to reduce prices and eliminate the middleman and his unearned income. Instead it has reduced the amount of produce available in the markets throughout the country and almost doubled the price of market fruit and vegetables. For most farmers it is simply not

TABLE 48

Rate of Growth of Production
in Socialized and Private Sectors
(Calculated in Comparable Prices)

Percentage, 1965 level taken as 100

	1958	1965	1970	1975	1980	1983	1985
Kolkhozy, sovkhozy, & interfarm units	86	100	128	133	150	165	166
Individual households	101	100	111	110	107	119	116

Source: Nar. khoz., 1965, p. 260; 1984, p. 229; *SSSR v Tsifrakh v 1985,* p. 121.

worth the effort to travel to the nearest (far less to a distant) town to sell a bucketfull of cherries or young cucumbers. The market sale of products from small allotments and from the forests (wild cherries, mushrooms) has also declined. At the same time, the state agencies have neither the facilities nor the personnel to make small-scale procurements of easily perishable produce. Moreover, they are unwilling to pay proper prices. Large industrial cities in the north, the Urals, and Siberia have been particularly hard hit by shortages of fresh fruit and vegetables and there have been reports of vitamin deficiencies in areas which are heavily dependent upon private wholesale deliveries of produce from Central Asia and the Caucasus. Soviet newspapers have been full of complaints about the empty markets and the astronomic prices. This is a good practical illustration of the inability of socialist agriculture to replace the private sector. If the new legislation is not lifted or changed, private agriculture could be inhibited in future years.

It is obvious from Table 46 that private plots have remained an important source of potatoes and vegetables, but the proportion of meat, milk, and eggs produced has declined. The government

TABLE 49

Comparison of the Production of Potato,
Vegetables, Meat, Milk, and Eggs in 1909–1913
and by Individual Households 1973–1976*
(Million Tons)

Annual average	Potato	Vegetables	Meat	Milk	Eggs
1909–1913 (total production)	30.6	5.0	4.8	28.8	11.2
1973–1976 (private plots only)	58.5	8.0	4.6	29.4	27.7

Source: Calculated on the basis of *Nar. khoz.*, 1975, pp. 310–311; 1982, p. 169.
* The rural population was 130.7 million in 1913 and 98.8 million in 1976.

has tried hard to reverse this trend, but the number of privately owned cattle, and particularly cows, has continued to decline (from 18.5 million in 1960 to 13.1 million in 1985) because of the difficulties of feeding the animals and the time that is required to take care of them. Field crops are seasonal, whereas livestock requires even more labor in winter than in summer. As the comparison of the amount of meat, milk, and eggs produced privately in 1909–1913 and in 1973–1976 suggests (Table 49), the rural population now produces sufficient high-quality products for its own consumption. Indeed, Soviet *kolkhozniki* enjoy a better and healthier diet than prerevolutionary peasants did. Their average income would put almost all of them into the kulak class by the standards of the 1920s. They have probably reached the limit of the productivity of their small household plots, but in any case, they are reluctant to increase their production of meat, milk, and poultry for the market because in purely financial terms, the free market offers higher profits for crops like carrots, lettuce, onions, tomatoes, and fruit. They also prefer to sell less, but for higher prices, and the state shops cannot compete with the private market.

In comparing the production from private plots in the 1970s with the agricultural level of the whole of Russia in 1909–1913 it should be kept in mind that peasants no longer need to cultivate grain or technical crops on their plots, nor do they need to supply fodder for working horses. On the other hand, the productivity level (the number of working hours per unit of production) is probably lower now than it was in 1909–1913, when horses were used to plough and cultivate the land. Manual labor plays a larger role in private agriculture now than it played in the peasant communes in 1913. The transportation of fodder from the fields to the villages, which is the main problem now, was done by horse and cart fifty or sixty years ago.

The state has tried to make private households contribute to the centralized procurements of meat, milk, and eggs. However, despite increases in procurement prices, state purchases from private households declined more sharply in 1965–1985 than did total output from private plots. This decline was most visible between 1975 and 1982. In 1975 the state purchased 1.8 million tons of meat, 2.6 million tons of milk, and 2 billion eggs from individual households. In 1982 the figures were 0.4, 0.1, and 1.2 respectively. The *kolkhozniki* and *sovkhoz* workers clearly preferred to sell their surpluses for higher prices through the free market. The government offered generous assistance, including bank credits, to stimulate private agriculture and encourage the sale of surpluses to the state. The press actively attempted to create a favorable climate, making special heroes of the peasants who did well. A typical hero, for example, who would have been treated as a dangerous kulak in 1929–1931, was described as follows:

Kholyusha is a typical villager of a particular time. It doesn't even enter his head to be anyone else and that someone else ought to supply him with the necessities of life. Therefore he uses his kitchen garden and his entire plot to make sure he has enough of everything. This is what his domestic ag-

riculture looks like: In front from the red porch and at the
back from the store rooms, cook-houses, barns and other
buildings are piled one behind another. . . . [the] good milk
cow has a two year old heifer and the calf, born in the summer, has fattened up over the winter. In the goat barn a
dozen goats and the billy-goat, Yeryoma, are munching straw
together with six sheep. The little piglets are grunting peace-
fully and two dozen geese waddle around the yard or lie on
the dirty snow like grey boulders. Two turkeys spread their
strong tails and wings . . . from time to time lazily beating
them before a good flock of well-fed little turkeys. Here the
ducks are making a racket and the chickens are pecking,
guarded by two cocks, one white and one red. Down below
is the kitchen garden, probably the largest in the village.[10]

A decree of the Central Committee and the Council of Ministers
on September 14, 1977, legalized an increase in size of subsidiary
household plots from 0.25 hectares to 0.5 hectares.[11] After the
granting of internal passports to peasants in 1976, this was the
most important decision that had been taken about rural life since
1932. However, a few households availed themselves of the increase and the average size of household plot had only risen to
0.32 hectares by 1985. Without mechanization it was too difficult
to cultivate a larger plot. A new decree was passed on January
8, 1981, "On additional measures for increasing the production
of agricultural products from the subsidiary household plots of
citizens."[12] The term "citizen" was used to indicate that the law
covered not only the plots cultivated by peasants, but all others,
including urban allotments. The decree made it clear that the
decline in level of production from private plots was a negative
trend which increased consumer pressure on the state trading
system at a time when food supplies were not very high.

The most important of the measures to encourage private agriculture was the abolition of the strict limit on the number of
livestock which could be privately owned. The limits had existed
since collectivization and had been formalized in the basic *kolkhoz* statute of 1935. Peasant families could own no more than
one cow, one heifer, and one calf, a sow, and a few piglets. The

new law permitted each household to own more animals, but the extra livestock was to be shared with the collective or state farm through special contracts. Peasants could raise more pigs or cattle, but they had to sell them to the state, not on the private market. The *kolkhoz* would pay over the procurement price obtained from the state. Fodder and feed grain could be obtained from the *kolkhoz*, *sovkhoz*, or from the state, but it would have to be paid for. *Kolkhoz* and *sovkhoz* meadows and pastures could be used. Because of the very high procurement prices for meat and milk and the comparatively low price for feed grain and fodder, peasants could make a profit from raising extra livestock. At the same time the milk or meat they delivered to the state would be registered as part of the delivery quota of the *kolkhoz* or *sovkhoz*. The intention was to tap some of the reserves of unused labor in rural areas. The decree was warmly welcomed by traditional peasants of the Kholyusha type. But the problem was that there were very few peasants of that type left. The author quoted above gives a vivid description of daily life in the Kholyusha household.

> Even on holidays, Kholyusha does not go into the clean half of the house, where, like in other people's houses, there is a television set on a polished table, a large bed with a bedspread, a settee covered with red velvet. He huddles in the hall or in the kitchen, together with the little calves, lambs, goslings, chicks and turkeys which he hatches here by the hundred, ceaselessly, like on a good conveyor. The atmosphere in the hut is such that even the village women who are used to everything shy away.[13]

The 1981 decree also gave individual households the right to lease extra land from the *kolkhoz* or *sovkhoz* to grow fodder crops, in addition to the traditional plot which is normally used for potatoes, vegetables, and fruit. A peasant family can now cultivate as much as one hectare of land privately, half for food and half for fodder, free of tax.

The legislation on urban allotments was also liberalized and the allotments virtually became private property which could be inherited by other members of the family on the death of the "owner." It was thought that the right to bequeath a garden plot would have a significant influence on the kind of investment that people would make in the land and property. Previously plots could not be inherited, although they could be sold to other members of the cooperative on the basis of the value of the fruit trees, the house, and other items on the land itself. The new law, it was hoped, would make allotments even more popular. The wish to have a small plot of land with a house was still alive in millions of urban men and women who had been born in the countryside. Many workers and intellectuals who had never lived in the village would also love to have a small country house—ownership of a *dacha* is the dream of many families. Treating these urban allotments as private property was an important factor in encouraging the development of "garden co-operatives." However, the size of the allotments remained rather small (0.04 to 0.06 hectares) and there were restrictions on the type of house which could be built. It could only have one room, for example, and it could not exceed 25 square meters. This is too small to be a real *dacha*. A person or a couple could stay for a weekend, but it would not be suitable for a family with children. Soviet law does not permit an ordinary family to own two dwelling houses or apartments, even if one of them is a *dacha*. The ownership of a proper *dacha* suitable for habitation is permitted only for creative purposes—for writers, musicians, composers, academics—or it is given as a state honor to retired generals, distinguished personalities, and government and Party officials.

Despite the restrictions, the number of allotments rose in 1981 and 1982. In 1982 about half a million tons of fruit and 2 million tons of potatoes were produced on these allotments, which occupied only a quarter of a million hectares. These statistics are very approximate, however, since the plots are not taxed and their products do not enter any sales. The figures come entirely from selective surveys and questionnaires. But it is likely that the produce from these plots has gone a little way towards reducing the demand and pressure on the state trading system for potatoes, vegetables, and fruit. On the other hand, the hope that rural households would increase the number of livestock they owned has not been fulfilled. Part of the problem is that the decree stops short of allowing really private ownership. Peasant families can earn extra income from owning more livestock, but the income comes from the *kolkhoz* rather than from free enterprise. The amount of work involved and the fact that the peasant is still working for the *kolkhoz* makes the idea unattractive. On the one hand, rural families tend to be smaller now than they were in the 1920s and 1930s and on the other, their children go to school for as many years as urban children. As a result, there are fewer people available in the households to look after extra livestock. In the description quoted, we have seen how difficult Kholyusha's life must be, even through the number of animals and poultry he owns is entirely within the limit prescribed by the *kolkhoz* law.

Peasants can own up to ten sheep in the black-earth regions of the Soviet Union. The rules about how many goats can be owned are purposely ambiguous. When collectivization began in 1930, goats were the first animals to be sacrificed and their number fell sharply from 10 million in 1929 to 3 million in 1933 (the number of cows fell from 29 million to 19 million in the same period). Goats have therefore never been considered *kolkhoz* farm animals. In the effort to restore the loss as quickly as possible, the government never regulated how many goats could be kept. There are also no restrictions on the number of poultry that can be raised privately. Peasants like Kholyusha are not universally praised in the Soviet Union. Lisichkin, for example, is critical of Kholyusha's way of life. Instead he praises the seventy-year-old retired agronomist and his wife who decided to raise some pigs in their household for the *kolkhoz*. He also raises the problem which is probably the most important factor militating against an efficient private livestock industry: the absence of any form of small mechanization for small farms based on family work.[14]

Although there is a vast variety of equipment available for large farms, no implements or machinery are produced by state industry which would be suitable for individuals. All kinds of traditional and hand implements must be made by local industry. But the production of these items is not specified in the state plans. They have to be specially ordered and, since they are not in the official plan, they have a very low priority for managers who must make sure of fulfilling their plans. A related problem is the absence of suitable transport and facilities. The *kolkhoz* is now obliged to provide fodder, but there are no means available of delivering small amounts. There is no suitable cutting equipment, and no kitchens to prepare proper swill for the extra pigs. Moreover, the increase in the number of private animals has produced a demand for new buildings attached to individual households.

Individual household plots have always been clearly oriented towards the market, and that situation has not changed. In regions where the *kolkhozy* and *sovkhozy* have their own large fruit farms (Moldavia and the Crimea) and the market price for fruit is low, for example, private agriculture concentrates on livestock and on fruit for export to Siberia and the arctic region. In the Baltic states and Byelorussia, on the other hand, 90 percent of the locally produced fruit comes from private plots. In Uzbekistan 73 percent of meat is produced privately. The annual value of all the products sold on the free markets in Soviet towns in 1980 was 7.4 billion rubles, while the value of the products from private plots sold to the *kolkhozy* was only 0.36 million rubles.[15] Some products are sold in the villages without going through the markets, although by law all animals have to be examined by a veterinary surgeon before slaughter (there have been individual cases of anthrax and small epidemics of other infectious diseases linked to uncontrolled sales of infected meat in the Urals, Central Asia, Moldavia, and Siberia).

Despite encouragement, support, and intensive propaganda, the production of private agriculture has grown only modestly, by 16 percent from 1958 to 1985. Most of this growth is from the cultivation of early vegetables and other "cash" crops. The amount of milk and meat produced privately has declined. The number of private cattle (including cows) has fallen from 31 million in 1940, to 29.2 million in 1959, 28 million in 1966, and

24.0 million in 1985. The number of pigs has also declined (around 16 million from 1941 to 1983, but only 13.9 million in 1986, having risen to a maximum of 18.2 million in 1966 and fallen to a minimum of 13 million in 1973). The number of privately owned sheep and goats also decreased between 1960 and 1986. If private agriculture had been encouraged as part of collectivization, it might have produced better results. It could probably also have been stimulated in the late 1940s and 1950s, when traditional peasants who remembered the famines were still alive. But by the 1970s and 1980s the rural population had changed. People in the villages are better educated now, and they receive salaries, holidays, and pensions. They watch television and read books. They require a more sophisticated approach than the one tried by the government. They would work more productively if they were provided not only with targets and financial incentives, but also with the proper means of production.

To some extent the message has been understood by the government. In 1979–1980 a small 5-horsepower tractor, weighing only 300 kilograms and suitable for use by individual households, was designed and tested by the Minsk tractor plant. However, the number produced annually, 1,200 in 1983 and 3,000 in 1984,[16] is still too low to make any difference. The problem is that there is no state plan for the production of this model tractor, and therefore, no target to reach. Orders have been placed with other tractor plants for small tractors, but there, too, only a few thousand have been manufactured. Moreover, tractors alone cannot solve all the problems. Special attachments are required for ploughing, cultivating, transport, and so on. A new branch of the agricultural machine building industry is required to serve the 25 to 30 million individual households. But Soviet industry is simply not ready for this task. The government has always found individual households useful because they have been cheap and have not required any substantial financial investment. It has been calculated that in the RSFSR alone, which produces about 50 percent of the total national agricultural product, the replacement of privately produced food by the *kolkhoz* or *sovkhoz* sector would require 40 billion rubles of investment and the additional employment of 3 or 4 million full-time workers.[17] But even this is an underestimate, because the *kolkhozy* simply would not be able to do the job properly. Soviet industry finds it easier to make thousands of very powerful tractors than millions of small ones. The same is true of other kinds of machinery. If private agricul-ture is really to be encouraged, then what is required is the development of small-scale private or semiprivate industry or a new "New Economic Policy." Another factor which has militated against the production of small-scale mechanization is the policy of economizing on gasoline and diesel fuel. Most of the oil in the Soviet Union now comes from Siberia. As a result it is very expensive and the government wishes to reduce the consumption of oil products. The production of millions of small tractors or multipurpose engines does not fit into this fuel austerity program.

It was therefore inevitable that the possibility of removing restrictions on the private ownership of horses would be seriously considered. The entire horse population was expropriated in 1930–1933 (with a resulting enormous loss in the number of horses) and ever since then, it has been illegal for *kolkhozniki* to own horses or other draft animals. The only exceptions have been in areas where horses are absolutely essential for transport (for example, in nomadic agriculture) and in some Moslem areas, where horses were permitted instead of pigs (because the Moslem population does not usually consume pork, whereas it does consume horse milk and horse meat). It began to seem that the ban on the private ownership of horses would be relaxed in the late 1970s and early 1980s. By the 1970s the horse population had fallen to 5.6 million (fewer than in Mexico) and a large proportion of them were used for sport and for the army. The ban had always been insensitive to peasant traditions—horses traditionally link the peasant to the land, and in the Cossack areas the traditional culture was closely tied to equestrian prowess. The government has been discussing the abolition of the old laws, but there is considerable reluctance to pass the necessary legislation. The expropriation of horses was the central and most controversial part of collectivization. Cancelling it now would call into question the wisdom of collectivization and the way in which it was carried out. In the official histories, the collectivization of horses as a means of production is considered correct. And if the horse was not considered essential for individual households in 1930, the public might well ask why it should be so important in the 1980s when there is comprehensive mechanization and the existence of an agro-industrial complex.

However, economic necessity and common sense may prove stronger than political prejudice. In the last version of the model *kolkhoz ustav*, adopted by the *Kolkhoz* Congress on November 27, 1969, and approved by the government a day later, *kolkhozniki* were not given the right to own a horse. If a peasant family needed a horse for a valid reason (such as living in an isolated house in an area where there were no roads), permission had to be given in each individual case by the Council of Ministers of the particular republic. There were cases in 1970 when various Councils of Ministers granted permission for the inhabitants of some villages in the Altai and Tuva areas (mountainous regions of Siberia), in Yakutiya, and in the mountain areas of the North Caucasus and the Urals to own one horse per household. But these decisions were the result of transport problems and the need to produce horse milk. In some areas of Siberia the climate is so severe that cows cannot survive. Similar permission was granted in 1970–1979 in the Central Asian and Caucasian republics. But in no case was permission given to a *kolkhoz* family to own a draft horse for working purposes, since this would contravene the general *kolkhoz* laws. There is, however, no restriction about state farm workers and other citizens owning horses and this is the loophole which has been used by local government. The Supreme Soviet of the RSFSR passed a law on August 6, 1982, allowing citizens (with consideration for local conditions and traditions) to own one draft animal (horse, mule, donkey, camel, ox, or buffalo).[18] This was a breakthrough. The Supreme Soviets of other republics had passed similar decrees even earlier, but they had specified that citizens who had the right to own a working horse should not be members of a *kolkhoz*. Now practically all rural families except *kolkhozniki* have the legal right to own a horse and one foal. This discrimination is totally illogical and will probably be lifted in due course. *Kolkhozniki* have the largest household plots and the greatest need for working horses. It would be inordinately strange if rural families who do not work on the *kolkhozy* retain the right to own horses, while *kolkhozniki* continue to be denied the possibility.

It will take some time for the new legislation to make a difference to the extremely low number of working horses in the country. It takes about three years to raise a working horse and each mare cannot produce more than one foal per year. At the moment, the reproductive capacities of the horse population are very low and the existing studs produce horses for sport rather than work. Horses bred for sport are unsuitable (and too expensive) as draft animals. The total number of horses in private ownership was 667,900 in 1985, and this is registered as a 30 percent increase since 1970.[19] The rate of increase of privately owned horses was about 4 percent per year between 1980–1985. This is very low when one bears in mind the many millions of people who would like to have a horse. Moreover, most of the 667,900 horses are not draft animals, but are used for transport and milk. More than half of them are in Kazakhstan and Central Asia. The use of draft animals is becoming more common in the Baltic republics. The governments of Estonia and Latvia seem to have found a way around the ban on *kolkhozniki* owning horses. One way around the law is for *kolkhoz* pensioners to acquire a horse and lend it to their children to help with the work. There is no law against lending horses. This has been described in an article which considers the social benefits of the practice.

In the Baltic republics horses are usually owned by people of pensionable age. But when there is a horse even adolescents still at high school will work on household plots with pleasure. This has a positive influence on the work education of young people. In such families young boys quickly acquire the skills of independently cultivating a personal plot, transporting loads, pasturing cattle on horseback and other horse-related work. And the pensioners have the opportunity to do as much work as they can manage to produce food and improve the standard of living of the family. The absence of horses for use in subsidiary agriculture means that tractors and unnecessary fuel have to be used.[20]

The problem of using horses for agricultural work is not confined to the very limited numbers available of suitable breeds. There is also an acute shortage of all horse-drawn implements and industry no longer manufactures this kind of equipment. Even horse-drawn ploughs have to be made locally. But the reentry of the horse into Soviet agriculture has begun. It will take about a decade before there are any economic effects. When horses become as common in rural areas as they were before collectivization, Soviet agriculture will have come full circle.

Chapter 12

Problems and Prospects

It is common, in the West, to consider the crisis in Soviet agriculture as part of the more general crisis of the Soviet and East European (with the exception of the Hungarian) economies. Although this is a valid approach for the light and consumer-oriented industries, the link between agriculture and industry as a whole does not work in quite this way. Soviet industry certainly has many problems, but they are neither as deep nor as serious as the problems in agriculture.

In 1929–1941 Soviet industrial development was the most rapid in the world and the technical level was rather high. Agriculture, however, was not doing well and could not provide the rapidly growing urban population with adequate supplies of food. Soviet industry performed very well during the war. In the postwar period of reconstruction the disproportion between industry and agriculture became even wider. If all the funds in industry and construction in 1928 are taken as 100 percent, they grew to 852 percent in 1940 and to 1,257 percent in 1950. The growth of funds in agriculture over this period, on the other hand, was insignificant: from 100 percent in 1928 to 123 percent in 1940 and 117 percent in 1950.[1] In the next decade agriculture was slightly more successful, but it still lagged well behind industry. Industrial production tripled between 1950 and 1960, whereas agricultural production grew by only 61 percent. In 1960–1970 industrial production more than doubled, while agricultural production grew by 37 percent. Although industrial growth slowed down in 1970–1985, there was still an impressive 104 percent increase, while the growth of agriculture was only 22 percent.[2] Moreover, the cost of this 22 percent increase was enormous. In 1970 all the funds in agriculture (including those for buildings, machinery, fertilizers, etc.) were valued at 106 billion rubles (in 1973 prices). By 1984 they had reached 306 billion rubles.[3] For each 10 rubles of new funds, less than one ruble's worth of food was produced. The growth of funds in industry was also higher than the increase in production, but the difference was more modest.

The main problems in industry have to do with quality. The primary concern of the government is to raise the level of technology. Improvement and modernization are required, rather than emergency aid. The problems in agriculture, on the other hand, are far deeper and they concern both quality and quantity. Food supplies have been growing more slowly than the growth of the urban population (and more slowly than the total population growth in 1976–1986). It has become necessary to import increasingly large quantities of food to avert serious shortages.

Soviet agricultural development lagged behind agricultural development in the rest of the world in 1960–1986. Agricultural performance in Africa was worse on a per capita basis (but not in absolute figures). Between 1970 and 1981 food supplies in Africa grew by 25 percent, while the population increased by 35 percent. The continuation of this disproportion between food production and population growth in 1982–1985 together with a drought produced the worst famine in recent history and millions of deaths from starvation in Ethiopia, Sudan, Somalia, Chad, and Uganda. In the same period South American food supplies grew by 49 percent, North American by 36 percent, Asian by 37 percent, European by 21 percent, and Oceanian by 32 percent. In the Soviet Union the total population growth in 1970–1986 was 12 percent, whereas the production of food crops (grain, potatoes, vegetables, etc.) rose by only 2 to 3 percent. Although the total value of agricultural production increased by 12 percent, the rise was mostly due to an increase in cotton production (30 percent) and in livestock and poultry products based partly on substantial imports of feed grain and other animal food.

Except in Africa, the amount of food per capita increased throughout the world (the highest increase was 14 percent in Europe, and the lowest was 9 percent in Asia). In Africa, per capita production declined by 8 percent.[4] The situation in the Soviet Union was practically the same at the end of the last decade as at the beginning, but if substantial amounts of grain and oilseed had not been imported, there would have been a decline. The food balance in the Soviet Union has begun to depend far too heavily upon imports. In the 1970s and 1980s more than 30 percent of all marketable grain was imported. Soviet purchases (about 40 million metric tons annually, the largest in the world) account for more than 20 percent of the world grain trade. Domestically, the *kolkhozy* and *sovkhozy* are far too dependent upon multibillion nonreturnable credits from the state bank (which represent de facto grants and subsidized construction works) and on the mobilization of workers and students at crucial times. If this emergency support were withdrawn, the agricultural sector would be unable to function.

The official statistics which have been used in this book are freely available for research, but Soviet planners, Central Committee *apparatchiki*, and government officials have access to a more comprehensive set of figures, published separately for official use only. The open statistics only list how much grain has been produced and procured, for example, while the restricted access statistics include how much grain has been lost or wasted and how much has been absorbed by the nonfood branches of the food industry (for example, by beer and vodka production). Similarly, the open statistics give the number of *kolkhozniki* and *sovkhoz* workers, while those for restricted access analyze age and other variables of the work force. From 1981 to 1986 all information about the grain harvest has been removed from the open statistics, but one can be sure that it is available in the closed records. This is only one example of a general tendency to reduce the amount of information which is openly available.

The volume of published economic statistics grew steadily from 1956 to 1975 and then went into reverse. In 1975 *Narodnoe khozyaistvo* presented the results of the agricultural year in 218 tables. In 1984 the number was reduced to 170 tables, many of them less informative than in previous years. The shrinkage continues. There seems to be a third set of statistics available only to a select few which explains how reliable and honest the information in the first two sets is. It also assesses the black market economy in industry and agriculture and the proportion of the harvest which has been invented by falsifying the figures. This kind of authorized fraud (known as *pripiski*) has been common since Stalin's time and is natural in a command economy where the fate of both local and central officials depends on economic performance. Andropov's anticorruption campaign in 1983 was partly necessary because of the impossibility of normal planning without proper information about the volume of nonexistent products and the size of the black market economy. If the seriousness of the agricultural situation is apparent from analyzing the open stastistics, it can be assumed that the two additional sources of statistical information do not make it look any better. It has been reported, for example, that while the production of "statistical" milk grew in the RSFSR in 1981–1985 by 8 percent, the actual sale of many dairy products, such as yoghurt, cottage cheese, and cheese, has declined sharply even in Moscow.[5] The Soviet leadership cannot but know that something must be done to improve the situation.

While there have been food shortages in the Soviet Union, there has been no shortage of plans and programs. However, none of them have been fulfilled and none of their targets have been met. The solution to each successive failure is a new, more comprehensive, longer-term program, rather than a radical new approach. In this concluding chapter the material presented in the earlier chapters will not merely be summarized. Instead, Soviet agriculture will be examined from a slightly different angle to illuminate some aspects which are not normally considered. I shall begin by considering the current long-term programs of development and assessing their chance of success. In the final section I shall speculate about the future and about possible alternatives.

I started this book without preconceptions. I had begun the research out of interest and I had no idea what my final conclusions would be. I knew, of course, that the situation was difficult, but I did not suspect just how serious it was. Many of the results of my analysis have surprised me. The same thing is true of the long-term programs. Previous programs had clearly not worked. Some were counterproductive, others simply ill-conceived, and still others produced limited results at very high cost. I believed that previous mistakes were taken into account in devising new programs. After all, to learn from mistakes is a declared principle of Soviet policy. Unfortunately, it is a principle that has all too often been forgotten. Acknowledging mistakes is a painful process in the Soviet system of government.

Western analyses of the Soviet economic system are often deterministic, assuming that many of the developments have been inevitable. Even Alec Nove, one of the most competent Western experts on the Soviet economy, believes that individual leaders cannot be held responsible for economic failures. Firstly, as Bolsheviks there were certain policies they could not follow. Secondly, they could not escape the consequences of Russian history and climate. However, he insists that

. . . this is *not* intended to imply that whatever happened *had* to happen, by a sort of historic necessity or inevitability. There were choices. But a number of developments *could not* have occurred in the USSR, and it is pointless to "blame" Stalin or Brezhnev for not doing that which they could not do.[6]

I cannot agree with this view. The New Economic Policy in the early 1920s showed that there was a range of possible choices, including market-oriented farming. Later developments have shown that Stalin, Khrushchev, and Brezhnev did not choose the best of the alternatives which were available. In criticizing them, their mistakes and miscalculations become apparent. Blaming Russian "history and climate" is pointless. For one thing, the history of Russia and the Soviet Union in the twentieth century has been strongly influenced by the human factor. For another, agriculture is the natural link between climate, environment, and human society. If agriculture does not fit well into the ecological balance, we must blame people, not nature. The conflict with the environment is due to human error. It may well lead to the catastrophe which the doctrine of scientific socialism claims to be better equipped to avoid than any other social system.

1. *Some Critical Factors of Current Development*

To assess the outlook for the current long-term programs, it is useful first to examine the general conditions in which they need to operate. Clearly, food is the most essential commodity and has absolute priority over all other products. Investing to increase the amount produced has been an important goal of Soviet agriculture. The problem has been that investments in agriculture have proved progressively less effective and the cost of producing more food from the same area has risen enormously. While Soviet books on the agricultural economy do not acknowledge this, the regular increases in procurement prices and, in particular, in the amount paid for crops and livestock products delivered in excess of the average level for the past few years reflect the implicit acceptance of the fact. For many years now it has been easier for the Soviet Union to purchase food abroad to satisfy growing demands than to increase domestic production by additional investments. At the same time there has been no effort to restrict demand by discouraging population growth. Moreover, the attempts which have been made to increase domestic production have entailed severe environmental consequences. These factors create the general conditions in which the current programs operate.

FOOD IMPORTS

Food imports have grown faster over the last fifteen years than domestic food production. Soviet economists usually indicate agricultural growth by giving the overall value of the gross agricultural product. This figure is highly artificial. It includes very approximate assessments of individual production and of the residue of the harvest which has been left in the rural areas for local consumption, animal feed, seed, and other purposes. This part of the harvest is often inflated by means of *pripiski* to claim fulfillment or overfulfillment of the plan. It makes far more sense to look at the amount of marketable food available to the population and examine how much of it has been purchased abroad. It is, of course, natural to purchase products which cannot be cultivated in the Soviet climate (exotic fruit, coffee beans, olive oil, etc.). But the Soviet government also buys more than two million tons of oilseed, more than five million tons of sugar, more than one million tons of meat products, and large amounts of butter and other dairy products, eggs, vegetable oil, and vegetables.[7] If the amount of food purchased abroad is compared with the amount purchased from the *kolkhozy* and *sovkhozy* the seriousness of the situation becomes apparent. The figures shown in Table 50 explain far more vividly than the figures for total production why the government is so nervous about current trends.

Soviet import-export operations are growing very fast, and this is considered a positive phenomenon on the whole. In 1965 the total foreign trade turnover was only 14.6 billion "import" rubles (7.4 billion export and 7.2 billion import). By 1984 the turnover had reached 139.7 billion rubles.[8] The major export items were oil (41.6 percent) and gas (10.0 percent). The proportion of food products in the total amount of imports is very high (20.3 percent in 1973, 23.0 percent in 1976, 27.7 percent in 1981, and 22.5 percent in 1984[9]). It is more dominant in trade with the Western industrial countries. In financial terms, this means that the value

TABLE 50
Comparison of the Amount of
Marketable Grain Procured Domestically
and the Amount Imported in 1965–1985
(Million Tons)

	Domestic procurements	Imports*
1965	36.3	9.0
1966	75.0	3.9
1967	57.2	2.3
1968	69.0	1.2
1969	55.5	1.3
1970	73.3	2.2
1971	64.1	8.3
1972	60.0	22.8
1973	90.5	11.3
1974	73.3	5.7
1975	50.2	26.1
1976	92.1	11.0
1977	68.0	18.9
1978	95.9	15.6
1979	62.8	31.0
1980	69.4	34.8
1981	58.1	46.0
1982	69.7	37.0
1983	75.6	32.5
1984	56.2	55.5
1985	73.5	30.0

Sources: For domestic procurements, *Nar. khoz.*, 1975, p. 324; 1980, p. 209; 1985, p. 193 For imports[11].

* There are some minor variations amongst different sources of information about Soviet imports. The most accurate figures are given in the Foreign Agriculture Circulars of the U.S. Department of Agriculture. Normally the food import year runs from August to July of the next year. I indicated the beginning of this "double" year, which makes it easier to see that maximum purchases of foreign grain have been made in years of poor harvest (1965, 1972, 1975, 1981, 1984). In 1986, Soviet purchases of grain declined to 26 million tons because of serious reductions in oil sales due to the fall of the international oil prices. Oil is the main source of Soviet hard currency.

of food imports was 3.1 billion "import" rubles in 1973, 14.6 billion "import" rubles in 1981, and 16.1 billion "import" rubles in 1984 (about 25 billion U.S. dollars at the 1984 exchange rate). But the production of oil, the chief export commodity, has begun to decline over the last few years. The 1983 and 1984 plans were not met and the plan for 1985 was only 96 percent fulfilled. Moreover, world prices for oil and gas have declined sharply in 1986 and production costs have grown rapidly because of the shift of production to Siberia (in the statistics produced "for offical use only" Gorbachev has acknowledged that oil-production costs increased by 70 percent in 1975–1985[10]). As a result, in 1986 the foreign trade turnover dropped to 130 billion rubles. World food prices are growing faster than the price of energy and raw materials and there are no other funds available to pay for increased food imports. In 1972 the Soviet Union paid 46 "import" rubles for one metric ton of American grain. In 1984 the price was 118 "import" rubles. Expressed in dollars the price is even higher: the price of a ton of wheat was roughly 240 dollars in the United States in 1984 and the price of corn was 140 dollars. Ocean freight charges have also risen. In 1964–1980 state procurements of grain were about 40 percent of total production (in the poor years— 1967, 1979, 1980—the proportion dropped to 36 percent and in good years it rose to 40.7 and 40.4 percent in 1976 and 1978 respectively). The abolition of payments in kind to *kolkhozniki* in 1966 did not increase the proportion of marketable procurement grain as expected. Grain imports, which were low before 1972 (more grain was exported than imported except in 1963 and 1964), began to grow rapidly, reflecting the critical situation. A particulary dramatic increase occurred in 1979 (and later, although President Carter's grain embargo was in force). Some Western experts estimate that the level may reach an annual 50 million tons. Table 50 makes it clear that Soviet agriculture has been unable to feed the population, at least in 1979–1986. This situation has made Soviet planners and leaders desperate to raise the level of domestic production.

Demographic Policy

The need to import food to feed the population should have led to a reconsideration of the official demographic policy. For years the leadership has been worried by the very low birthrates in the European part of the Soviet Union. Attempts have been made to encourage a higher birthrate in the RSFSR, the Ukraine, Byelorussia, and the Baltic states. The birthrate in the RSFSR (only 15 per 1,000 in 1970), began to grow in the 1980s (to 16.9 per 1,000 in 1984), but in Soviet Central Asia it increased from 33 to 36 per 1,000.[12] In a large country which is so dependent on food imports this should be no cause for rejoicing. It was natural to encourage an increase in the birthrate in the postwar period, but once the domestic production of food ceased to keep pace with population growth, efforts to reverse the natural decline in the birthrate became counterproductive. Official demographic doctrine has always dismissed Malthusian theory (that world population will outgrow food supplies) as reactionary and a product of colonial imperialism. Soviet demographers have always insisted that the principle of "reproduction on a larger scale" will cope with the problems of population and agriculture. For political reasons it has been difficult to reverse this belief, but after criticism of the Soviet Union at the United Nations world conference on population problems in August 1984 for causing world food prices to rise and thereby making it difficult for poor countries to import food, the formula was marginally altered to "stable reproduction." In reporting the conference A. Isupov, chairman of the Census Department of the USSR Central Statistical Bureau, criticized the Malthusian approach, but admitted that demographic processes should depend on social and economic conditions. He insisted that the Soviet "stable reproduction" policy was correct.[13] What this meant in effect was an attempt to stimulate the birthrate selectively in the European parts of the country.

It is probably unnecessary to restrict the birthrate in the Soviet Union in the way it has been restricted in China (and, less successfully, in India), but official propaganda on increasing the birthrate should certainly be discontinued and family planning facilities should be improved, at least until the dependence on food imports has been reduced to an acceptable level.

ECOLOGICAL PROBLEMS

Soviet agricultural economists tend to ignore or criticize the "law of diminishing returns" which sets a finite limit to the way in which land can be exploited. In the 1940s and 1950s they argued that investing in the land would bring increasing returns. Since the level of real investments was very low, the figures they used were inconclusive. Now that the argument seems disproved, the subject has been dropped. Soviet economists are not yet ready to discuss the scientific limits of the productivity of land, despite the fact that the ecological processes resulting from overproduction and the decline in natural fertility seriously threaten the success of the long-term programs which have been launched to increase food production. The principle of diminishing returns on investments into agriculture was developed as long ago as the beginning of the nineteenth century, by David Ricardo. His argument is still considered valid, although scientific discoveries have caused it to be adapted. The principle is obviously valid when only quantitative increases of investment are made (for example, applying increasing amounts of the same fertilizer). If qualitative changes are made, comparatively small investments seem to bring disproportionally large returns. The discovery of herbicides and pesticides, for example, or the introduction of better crop varieties, raised the level productivity far above the cost of investment. However, the principle of diminishing returns still operates within these qualitatively new systems, particularly when the new system begins to disrupt the very fabric of the ecological system. Short-term experiments may seem to contradict the law, but long-term experiments usually confirm the natural limitations of the land.

As we have seen in Chapter 7, there was a significant growth in food crops, particularly grain, in the Soviet Union between 1954 and 1970. Grain production, which had fluctuated around 80 million metric tons before 1955, rose to 187 million tons, about

30 to 40 million tons of which was due to increased acreage rather than to improved methods of cultivation. Although there were several better harvests in the 1970s, the average harvest in the 1980s has been about 180 million metric tons. Compared to the standards of world agriculture, the progress in 1954 to 1970 was not really very dramatic: there was an unprecedented growth in food production in most countries of the world between 1950 and 1971. World grain production grew from 631 million metric tons to 1,237[14] without any particular expansion of cultivated land. Diets improved worldwide, and the consumption of livestock products increased sharply in the industrially developed countries. In the developing countries this period was known as the "Green Revolution." The turning point, according to Lester R. Brown, president of the Worldwatch Institute in Washington, D.C., was 1972.

> The years between mid-century and 1972 represented a unique period in the world's food economy. The excess production capacity that translated into surplus stocks and cropland idled under U.S. farm programs assured remarkably stable food prices. This period came to an abrupt end with the massive Soviet wheat purchase in 1972, when the decision was made to import grain rather than ask consumers to tighten their belts. Within months the world price of wheat had doubled and famine had returned to the Indian subcontinent, Africa, and elsewhere after an absence of a quarter-century.[15]

In the next decade growth continued, but it was slower and in Africa it was lower than the population growth. The rise of oil prices after 1973 made it more difficult for developing countries to buy food in cases of emergency. Countries began to borrow too much money and the accumulation of debts developed into a "debt crisis" which particularly affected South America, Asia, Africa, and Eastern Europe. The United States reduced its food aid, selling surplus grain to the Soviet Union instead. Countries which had previously relied on the United States now desperately tried to increase their harvests, often with resulting serious damage to the ecology. U.S. and Western European grain stocks had been rebuilt in the late 1970s and 1980s, but world food insecurity remained. Food supplies were transformed by the U.S. food embargo in the 1980s into "food power." The Soviet Union also tried desperately to increase its grain production and reduce its dependence on imports. Three very high harvests in 1973, 1976, and 1978 show the results of these efforts, but the resulting ecological damage to the topsoil was extremely serious and it has undermined future progress.

Topsoil is mankind's most essential and valuable asset. It is a biological formation, a carpet of life above the dead and infertile subsoil. If the pace of erosion exceeds the natural rate of soil formation, the topsoil thins and eventually disappears. This process has begun in both the United States and the Soviet Union: in the United States as a result of the farmers' response to export demands and high world prices, and in the Soviet Union as a result of excessive cultivation in the attempt to reduce imports and increase the livestock population.

There are two main types of soil in the Soviet Union, *podzol* (which is rather poor) and *chernozem* (the word comes from the Russian words for "black earth"). Russian and Ukrainian *chernozem* is the best soil in the world and it covers an area almost as large as that covered by *podzol*. It is a grassland soil with a black humic layer about 25 centimeters deep in the northern *chernozem* areas (Orel, Lipetsk, Kursk, Bryansk, and southern Byelorussia) and from 50 to 100 centimeters deep in many parts of the Ukraine, in the Voronezh and Belgorod regions of the central Volga basin, in Kazakhstan, and in the virgin lands of Siberia. In some parts of the North Caucasus it is as much as 150 to 200 centimeters deep. *Chernozem* is neutral and contains no clay. In the steppes it has remained very stable because there has been practically no leaching. In Canada, the United States, and Argentina there are also some areas of *chernozem*, but they are unstable and tend to accumulate clay when cultivated because of the higher level of leaching rainfall.

There has always been some erosion in *chernozem* areas, caused by the formation of ravines and gullies when sloping land was cultivated. However, the extensive use of chemicals, heavy machinery, and the reduction of the acreage of fallow land has made the problem far more serious. Some measures were taken in the 1960s, when the problem first became apparent, to improve soil protection. They were carried out energetically in the virgin land areas, where the monoculture system and the absence of protection from strong wind made erosion so serious that large tracts of land were completely destroyed. In January–February 1969 strong winds caused extensive damage to the topsoil of the North Caucasus. A law was passed in December 1968 to enforce soil protection and measures were enacted to increase soil fertility.[16] However, the law continues to be violated, not least by the government itself, particularly in areas of industrial development. Millions of hectares of arable land, for example, were flooded and destroyed on and around construction sites and hydroelectric projects. However, in retrospect and compared to what took place in the 1970s and 1980s, these problems seem minor. Most of the tractors working in the *chernozem* areas have been found to be too heavy (more than 2.5 tons). *Podzol* and light soils are even more vulnerable. The 12-ton "Kirovets" tractor leaves such deep tracks that it can cause ravines to develop. According to the official data of the Research Institute of Soil Protection there is an annual loss of 1,500,000,000 tons of topsoil due to erosion. Various kinds of erosion are taking place in 120 million hectares (53 percent) of cultivated land.[17] The annual loss of topsoil in the United States is about the same and it is considered a serious threat to American agriculture.[18] However, Soviet planners insist that the socialist system takes better care of its natural resources than the capitalist system, which is interested only in maximum short-term profits. The fact that heavy machines were causing erosion was first noted in the United States. Soviet specialists now admit that their attempt to copy the large, powerful American tractors was a mistake.

The loss of 1.5 billion tons of topsoil annually is serious, but other calculations and measurements suggest that this is probably an underestimation. Three prominent soil scientists have recently published an article in *Pravda*, for example, in which they state that the *chernozem* soils of the Russian plain have lost one-third of their humus in the last thirty years and become 10 to 15 centimeters thinner.[19] This means that 100 to 150 billion tons of topsoil has been lost from 100 million hectares, or 3 to 5 billion tons annually. It would take at least 200 to 300 annual harvests to do this amount of damage to soil fertility (unless fertility factors are renewed with organic and other fertilizers). The authors claim that at present the spring thaw and rain leach about 80 to 120 tons of loose soil annually from each hectare. Moreover, the loss of soil has accelerated in the last few years. For each 100 hectares of cultivated land in the *chernozem* areas there are 3 kilometers of ravines, and they grow each year. These figures were confirmed at a special conference of the Lenin Academy of Agricultural Sciences in 1985. The situation is particularly critical in the Volga basin, the central *chernozem* area. The local research institute has compared the amount of humus found in the soil by Dokuchayev in the nineteenth century (10 to 13 percent) with the amount found now. In most areas it has fallen to 4 to 7 percent, but in an increasing number of areas there is only 2 to 4 percent or 0.5 to 2 percent of humus.[20] A number of ideas have been suggested to make agriculture less destructive, but most of them require decades to introduce and the complete replacement of heavy machinery.

The obvious decline of agricultural production and productivity, the progressive severity of soil erosion, and the many other signs of severe practical and ecological problems are inconsistent with the continuing insistence by leading theoreticians of socialism that Soviet agriculture offers the best model of combining the needs of production with the preservation of the environment. Shakhnazarov, for example, a prominent ideologist and writer on political, economic, and futurological themes, blames the United States for disrupting the environment and reducing the planet's biological potential. His solution is simple:

> Clearly, a socialist transformation of industrial and agricultural production and the adoption of socialist methods of planning and regulating economic growth are required to

resolve the ecological problem. But bourgeois authors cannot come to this particular conclusion, although to some extent they recognize that a socialist system has advantages in matters of environmental protection.[21]

I personally have not come across the "bourgeois authors" who express such views. In one of the best-documented comparisons of U.S. and Soviet agriculture, Lester R. Brown accepts that American overproduction damages the soil. However, he also indicates that the Soviet type of agriculture makes the environment more vulnerable, and that large, heavy equipment and vast fields "eliminate some of the natural boundary constraints on soil erosion by both wind and water." He concludes that "production quotas can apparently be at least as destructive to soil as the profit motive."[22]

These are not the only serious general problems facing Soviet agriculture, but the discussion so far is sufficient to illustrate my argument that the Soviet Union has little chance of solving its food problems by increasing imports, and that increasing domestic production by the use of purely quantitative methods of more intensive cultivation also has natural limits.

2. The Long-Term Programs

Although five year economic plans are a long-standing and famous Soviet tradition, five years is not a particularly convenient period for a branch of the economy as unpredictable as agriculture. There are frequently, therefore, both longer- and shorter-term plans for agriculture which are independent of the five year plan. They vary in the geographic area and branch of agriculture to which they apply and some overlap with the five year plans (for example, the three and four year plans of livestock development in 1949–1951 and 1957–1961). The most extensive in terms of both geography and time was Stalin's plan for the afforestation of the steppes, designed initially for 1948–1968, but expected to continue for as long as it took to establish stable forest belts. The only one of these plans which was not only fulfilled, but was completed well ahead of time, was collectivization. All the others have either been abandoned or radically modified well short of their original targets. Nonetheless, the practice of making programs still continues. In addition to the Five Year Plan for 1981–1985 (which was not fulfilled), for example, and the plan for 1986–1990 currently in operation, there are several other plans currently in force, some designed to run until 1990, others to 2000. I shall analyze the three most important, which aim to make the Soviet Union self-sufficient in food by 1990 and to allow further progress beyond this date.

THE PLAN FOR DEVELOPING THE NON-*CHERNOZEM* ZONE OF THE RSFSR

The non-*chernozem* zone of the RSFSR (which includes Moscow, Smolensk, Kalinin, Leningrad, Novgorod, Kaluga, Tula, Ryazan, Yaroslavl, Vladimir, Gorky, Kostroma, Perm, Sverdlovsk, areas in the middle Volga, and near the Urals, etc.) produces more than 50 percent of the industrial output of the Soviet Union. Its agriculture, however, is backward. In 1970 more than 60 million people lived in this area, of whom more than 70 percent lived in towns in 1970. In the central Russian *chernozem* zone the urban population was only 40 percent and in the Ukraine it was 50 percent. Urbanization was particularly rapid between 1959 and 1970 and was unrelated to increased productivity. The exodus of the rural population from this area threatened the fabric of rural life, and the program of agricultural development was specially designed to reverse it. Although geographic and climatic factors indicated that investing in these *podzol* areas would give small returns, the government decided that the demographic problems were so serious that the balance of rural development should be redressed in favor of the Russian regions. In the spring of 1974 a decree of the Central Committee and Council of Ministers, "About measures for the further development of agriculture in the non-*chernozem* zone of the RSFSR," introduced a fifteen-year program to last until 1990.[23]

The program covers an area of 32 million hectares of culti-

vated land and 20 million hectares of good meadowland. However, the fields tend to be rather small and separated by forests.
The villages are as small as twenty to fifty households. Despite
this, for centuries the peasants in this area lived rather better
than those in the more prosperous central *chernozem* zone. Historically this was because the local *pomeshchiki* usually owned
small estates and found it uneconomical to use serf labor to cultivate their fields. Instead the peasants paid a levy to the *pomeshchiki* and used the long six- to seven-month winter to work
in local manufacture and trade to earn the money. As a result
they developed into more independent, better-off communities.
The striking difference between serfs who fulfilled their obligations by labor service and those who paid levies was observed by
Turgenev in 1847 in a story in which he compared a peasant
from Orel in the *chernozem* area to a levy-paying peasant from
Kaluga.

The Orel peasant is of short stature, round-shouldered, mo-
rose, with a sullen look. He lives in a wretched, aspen hut,
works on the *pomeshchik* land, does not trade, eats badly
and wears bast sandals. The Kaluga peasant pays tax and
lives in a spacious pine house. He is tall, with a bold and
cheerful mien and a clean, white face. He sells butter and
tar and on holidays he wears boots.[24]

Collectivization and the later development of towns in the non-
chernozem zone reversed the situation. Particular problems were
created by the restrictions on local village industry and trade,
which were systematically eradicated in the postwar period. Without local shops it became difficult to import food products from
the more prosperous south. The intention was to force the non-
chernozem area to become self-sufficient in food, but the effect
was to make it much poorer. Khrushchev hoped that amalgamating small *kolkhozy* into larger units would improve the situation, but it made little difference. In 1974 Brezhnev finally
decided to treat the non-*chernozem* area as a special problem,
offering emergency aid to prevent the further decline of the vil-

lages. By this time many villages were almost entirely deserted and a high proportion of the remaining population was old.

The fifteen-year program had the ambitious target of increasing agricultural production in the non-*chernozem* zone by 250 percent. Specific targets were set for the traditional crops of the area—rye, potatoes, vegetables, and flax—and for meat, milk, and eggs. A large amount of money was made available and a two-year period of grace was allowed to prepare local projects and estimates. Funds were provided for setting up agriculture-related industries (meat and milk factories, factories for tinning food, storage facilities, often with refrigerators). It was expected that the facilities would be required to deal with the 250 percent increase in agricultural production. The program became operational in 1976, but by the July Central Committee Plenum in 1978, local officials were already being criticized for making a slow beginning. Land reclamation proved to be more expensive than expected and many fields thought to be cultivated were found abandoned. They were either too small, or too far from the villages, to be amenable to mechanization. Roads were in ruins and about 10 million hectares which had been in use before the Revolution and in the 1920s and 1930s were abandoned bogs. A further 7 million hectares was overgrown with bushes. Acid rain had made the topsoil even more acid and large amounts of lime and chalk fertilizer were required before anything could be cultivated.

It was clear from the beginning that the rural infrastructure could not cope with the new tasks. A major part of the investments, therefore, was to be used for a resettlement program. Khrushchev's dream agro-towns were at last to become a reality. In 1974–1975 more than half the 142,000 villages in the area contained less than fifty inhabitants (ten to twenty families). Since it was impossible to provide satisfactory services and amenities to so many small, remote villages, radical solutions were proposed. Well-situated villages would receive special long-term construction credits to build schools, kindergartens, medical services, shops, clubs with cinema facilities, and so on. Collective or state farm workers who lived in small, less-advantaged villages would be resettled in new houses (for which they would receive long-term interest-free credits) in these selected villages. A crucial part of the program was to be the new road system. Between 1976 and 1981, 25,000 kilometers of hard-surface roads would be built to connect 4,000 *kolkhoz* and *sovkhoz* settlements with district or regional centers. Since the small outlying settlements would now be abandoned and crop rotation would have to be restructured, the land was to be zoned in a wide circle around the central village. Crops which require manual labor and animal farms were to be located, as is customary, close to the villages and the roads to the fields would be shorter and more convenient.

The program, however, increased the production costs for most crops to well above the costs for the Soviet Union as a whole and to more than procurement prices. One ton of potatoes, for example, cost 82 rubles to produce in a *kolkhoz* of the RSFSR in 1974 and in 1980 it cost 124 rubles. The cost of producing grain rose from 57 rubles to 76 rubles per ton and of live weight of cattle from 1,401 to 2,170 rubles.[25] The level of mechanization in the non-*chernozem* zone remained lower than for the RSFSR as a whole. The rural population continued to decline and the resettlement program and establishment of agro-towns did not stem the exodus. Between 1974 and 1980, for example, the proportion of rural inhabitants in the Vladimir region fell from 28 percent to 24 percent, in the Gorky region from 30 to 26 percent, and in Kalinin from 37 to 32 percent.[26] There were other signs that the program was failing. Deliveries of tractors, combines, and other machinery rose sharply, but repair and servicing facilities in the area were very poor and the rate at which equipment was lost was very high. The non-*chernozem* zone received 380,000 new tractors and 94,000 new combines in 1976–1980, for example, but 260,000 tractors and 62,000 combines were written off as unusable in the same period.[27] One of the causes was the poor roads.

Although the importance of the program was reaffirmed at the Twenty-sixth Party Congress in February 1981, the initial targets were scarcely credible any longer. The program was reviewed and relaunched within the new five year plan. A decree, "On the further development and the increased efficiency of agriculture in the non-*chernozem* zone of the RSFSR in 1981–1985," listed what had already been achieved in the 1976–1980 period. There had been 31.2 billion rubles of capital investments; 5.6 billion rubles had been spent on building schools for 490,000 children, hospitals with 15,000 beds, kindergartens and nurseries with 178,000 places, clubs, and 22.8 million square meters of new houses. Deliveries of mineral fertilizers had increased by 35 percent and 30,000 kilometers of hard-surface roads were being built. In terms of agriculture, however, the results were unimpressive, and republic and local officials were taken to task for not fulfilling the targets.[28] In fact, Solomentsev, chairman of the Council of Ministers of the RSFSR, admitted that the production figures for the non-*chernozem* zone were almost the same in 1976–1980 as in 1971–1975.[29] Procurements had increased slightly (by 4 percent for grain, 2 percent for potatoes, and 1 percent for milk), but this was probably due to reduced local consumption caused by the further decline in rural population. The actual production of potatoes, vegetables, flax, and wool declined (for flax by as much as 30 percent). The only success was an increase in the production of eggs. Gross agricultural output increased by only a third of the 9 percent increase registered for the Soviet Union as a whole in that period.

The new decree provided the area with 39.3 billion rubles for capital investments in 1981–1985. In that period 390,000 new tractors, 255,000 trucks, 104,000 combine-harvesters, and other machinery were to be delivered, as well as more fertilizers. There was to be more land reclamation work, more investment in local industry and the construction of more schools, hospitals, clubs, houses, and so on. To encourage people living in towns to move to the villages, they would now be allowed to keep their town apartments for up to five years. This was an important concession, because the law which prevented families from owning two dwellings was the most serious obstacle to recruiting young urban people to work even temporarily in the country. Production targets were reduced to a more realistic 30 percent increase in 1981–1985. Once again, it was hoped that the plan would transform the non-*chernozem* zone into a really successful agricultural area. The Central Committee made it clear that the program had priority.[30]

But even these modest targets proved impossible to attain and the decline of rural Russia continued. Available statistics indicate that the production targets have not been met in any year of the plan. Indeed, average procurements in some regions have been lower than in 1971–1975.[31] Instead of development, emergency aid has been required to prevent the total collapse of the rural community. Migration out of the area continued in 1981–1985. By 1984, 137 years after Turgenev described the Kaluga peasant, the villages in the area were kept alive by old women. *Izvestiya* described a typical *kolkhoz* in the Kaluga region:

Of the 483 members, 228 are pensioners, predominantly army widows. Almost everyone works, some part-time, others full-time. These women are the backbone of the *kolkhoz* because they work in it . . . the young people have dispersed and the plan must be fulfilled. . . . they work without complaining because their whole lives have been spent working.[32]

In 1985 the problems of the non-*chernozem* zone needed further attention. A new decree, "About the further development and increase of efficiency of agriculture and other branches of the agro-industrial complex of the non-*chernozem* zone of the RSFSR in 1986–1990,"[33] was an almost exact copy of the 1981 decree and it offered the same solutions: new investments, more machinery and fertilizers, and more land reclamation. Once again, it complained of poor returns on previous investments. To prevent any further migration of the rural population, restrictions were placed on the construction in the area of industrial facilities unrelated to the agro-industrial complex. Moreover, the number of new vacancies in the towns were frozen and urban industries were forbidden to employ people from rural areas. Since the previous hope of attracting urban dwellers back to the countryside had been disappointed, the freedom of movement of rural people was once again to be restricted. This was an acknowledgment of defeat. The issue of passports in 1976 had been intended to reduce the exodus of young people from the villages. When it failed to produce the expected result, the Gorbachev solution to the problem of rural demography was to remove freedom of movement. However, if Stalin's draconian measures failed to prevent rural depopulation, it is unlikely that Gorbachev's restrictions will work any better. The development of the Russian countryside is possible, but it will come about as a result of liberalization, not through a return to creating second-class citizens.

The "Food Program" for 1982–1990

The poor performance of agriculture in 1979–1981, the food shortages, and increasing food imports made it clear that radical improvements were required. In November 1981 Brezhnev blamed the adverse weather conditions, but said that the Central Committee was drawing up a food program in which

> . . . an important place should be assigned to such major problems as the improvement of the economic mechanism and system of management—the management of agriculture and of the agro-industrial complex as a whole . . . and, of course, local management. The collective and state farms themselves should have the final say in deciding what should be sown on each hectare and when one job or another should begin.[34]

This statement seemed to promise something more radical than just another set of target figures. Major reforms were expected. However, when the special Central Committee Plenum began to discuss the "Food Program" in May 1982, it turned out to offer no surprises. The full text was published on May 27, 1982[35]: it was merely yet another attempt to solve the agricultural crisis by means of more money, higher procurement prices, higher salaries for *kolkhozniki* and *sovkhoz* workers, more machinery, and more chemicals. The Brezhnev leadership not only seemed incapable of designing *reforms*, but also of analyzing the critical agricultural situation and defining it as a crisis. Weather conditions were still held responsible for the failures of the past few years.

The "Food Program" aimed for a reduction in food imports from capitalist countries and self-sufficiency in food resources. This would make the country less vulnerable to political pressure and guarantee its independence. Brezhnev explicitly referred to the grain embargo which had been imposed by President Carter in the wake of Soviet intervention in Afghanistan.[36] A substantial increase in the average production of the main crops was planned by 1990 and an improvement in the quality of the diet of the entire population. The production of grain was expected to rise to 250 to 255 million tons, of meat to 20 to 20.5 million tons, of milk to 104 to 106 million tons, of vegetables to 37 to 39 million tons, and of fruit to 14 to 15 million tons. The promised improvements of the "economic mechanism" and of "local management" were purely bureaucratic—the formation of the district and regional agro-industrial combined management committees (APOs and RAPOs) which were discussed in Chapter 10. It was extremely unlikely that this new, even more complex administrative infrastructure would bring about the rest of Brezhnev's initial promise: more leeway for independent decision-making by *kolkhozy* and *sovkhozy*. Brezhnev pointed out in his introductory speech that agricultural conditions within the Soviet Union varied so widely that there was no room for stereotypes. What was required instead was "managerial initiative, independence of decisions and enterprise," and he promised that the Central Committee would enhance the organizational and economic independence of the farms.[37] However, he also claimed that the APOs and RAPOs served this task perfectly well and were "fully-fledged and democratic management agencies." As we have already seen, all they really achieved was a growth of the bureaucratic apparatus and a reduction of the independence and responsibility of *kolkhozy* and *sovkhozy*.

The "Food Program" set specific goals for every branch of agriculture and every major food product, down to sweets, beer, drinks, and cheap fruit wines (Gorbachev later abolished the alcoholic part of the program and ordered that the production of cheap wines should cease). Enormous resources were promised for development. It was envisaged that about 33 to 35 percent of all centralized investments would be devoted to agriculture and the agro-industrial complex. By 1990, 3,780,000 tractors, 1,170,000 combine-harvesters, and vast numbers of other types of machinery would be delivered (40 billion rubles worth for field crops and 30 billions worth for the livestock sector). Specific targets were also given to each union republic for various crops. Each republic was to plan its own detailed "Food Program" on the basis of these targets, and each region and district was, similarly, to make a detailed program on the basis of the targets passed down by the union republican government. Regional and district authorities were then to present the *kolkhozy* and *sovkhozy* with their targets. Within these limits, the *kolkhozy* and *sovkhozy* were, of course, free to develop their own initiative.

As large and as comprehensive as the "Food Program" was, it did not cover all the necessary tasks. A series of supplementary programs, some introduced just before the "Food Program," others after it, were added. They included decrees like "Measures to increase the production of sunflower seeds, soyabeans and other oil crops" (March 27, 1982); "On the comprehensive development of agriculture in the regions of Siberia and the Far East" (April 21, 1982); "On measures to improve the economic mechanisms of collective and state farms" (May 28, 1982). Although they were not an integral part of the "Food Program," they were later published with it.[38] Never before had so many decisions and decrees about agriculture been made within a single year. None of them made much difference.

The results of the grain harvest in 1982 have not been officially reported, but unofficial estimates put it at 180 million tons, about 50 million tons short of the target. On the other hand, in 1982 the Soviet Union reached an all-time world record not only for the import of grain, but also of meat and sugar. About 40 percent of urban domestic consumption was now satisfied by imports.

The "Food Program" fared a little better in 1983, but the harvest declined again in 1984, and was well below the plan in 1985, and in 1986. The money has been spent, the machinery produced, and the bureaucratic changes launched. All parts of the "Food Program" are moving, except for the production of food. The program was the single largest, most expensive document ever produced on agriculture, but it was also the least imaginative. It has not worked because it is not a *reform*. It is merely a new directive, unremarkable in all its aspects, except for its cost. Officially the program is still in force. In practice it is dead.

THE LONG-TERM PROGRAM OF IRRIGATION AND RIVER DIVERSION

There are more than 3 million square kilometers of desert and semidesert around the Caspian and Aral Seas, more than the entire sown area in the country. Most of the low Volga and Ural areas, Kazakhstan, and Central Asia are either desert, or are covered with arid, salinated soil unsuitable for cultivation. The climate, however, is warmer than anywhere else in the Soviet Union and, with irrigation, the area can be productive. Most of the agriculture between the Volga and Ural rivers and in Central Asia depends on irrigation, but the use of water from the Kura, Terek, Volga, and Ural rivers (all of which flow into the Caspian) and from the Amu-Dar'ya and Syrdar'ya (which flow into the Aral Sea) has already caused severe environmental problems and the drying up of these two inland seas. The water problem is particularly acute in Soviet Central Asia, where the population has grown by 160 percent between 1940 and 1984 (population growth in the RSFSR in the same period was 29 percent). The population of Uzbekistan was 17.5 million in 1984, and together with the populations of Turkmenia, Tadzhikstan, Kirgizia, and Kazakhstan, 44.5 million people live in Soviet Central Asia. 22.5 million of them live in rural areas (the Ukraine has a population of 50.6 million, but the rural population is only 17.9 million).[39] Since 1960 the rural population of the European part of the Soviet Union has been falling rapidly, while the rural population of the Moslem areas has almost doubled. Since Central Asian agriculture specializes in cotton, grain and food have to be imported from other areas. Water shortages limit the development of the region and creates surplus labor, which tends to migrate to the towns. The need to employ local surplus labor and to reduce migration finally forced the government to think of ways of solving the water problem.

Two major projects have been under discussion and research for many years: diverting the Pechora River from its Barents Sea destination to the Volga basin and changing the course of the Irtysh, the great Siberian river which is closest to Central Asia. Using the waters of Siberian rivers was an attractive idea. An area of nearly 13 million square kilometers (58 percent of the territory of the Soviet Union) drains northward to the Arctic Ocean. Fourteen percent of Soviet territory (more than all the present cultivated land) is drained by the Irtysh-Ob rivers through the West Siberian lowlands. If this could be diverted to irrigate Central Asia, it would transform agriculture. Rice, maize, and other intensive crops could be cultivated in addition to cotton. Although both projects had been approved in principle, construction had never begun because of the enormous costs that were entailed. Diverting 25 cubic kilometers of water from the Irtysh annually requires a great canal about 200 meters wide, 12 meters deep, and 2,500 kilometers long. It would be the biggest single engineering project in the world and it has provoked worldwide discussion and the concern of environmentalists.

In October 1984 a regular Plenum of the Central Committee approved a long-term program of irrigation "to create a stable increase of the food funds of the country." The Central Committee had decided to introduce additional large-scale, long-term irrigation programs because other measures had failed to halt the stagnation of agricultural production. The new project was expected to give 12 million tons of extra grain in 1990 and 35 to 40 million tons in 2000 from arid regions. The increase would mainly consist of corn and rice, although more fodder crops would also be cultivated.[40]

The central part of the initial project (with a capital investment allocation of 50 billion rubles) involved transferring 5.8 cubic kilometers of water from the Pechora and Severnaya Dvina rivers to the Volga basin. This would also enable the Volga and Don basins to be irrigated. The second part of the project—the transfer of water from the Siberian rivers to the South Urals, Kazakhstan, and Central Asia—was also approved, although the details were not yet ready. It was expected that construction would be able to begin before 1990 and that the effects would be felt in 1990 to 2000. The Irtysh-Karaganda canal (about 400 kilometers long) was to be completed and operational before 1990 to irrigate some of the former virgin lands in Kazakhstan. The plans were rather modest compared to the earlier discussion about altering the whole course of rivers. Although ecologists had argued that this might change the world's weather pattern, the adoption of more modest plans was probably not caused by environmental concern, but by cost and other considerations.

Soviet experience with irrigation has not been without serious problems. Careless and incompetent irrigation can cause irreversible damage to the soil and there have been many complaints that the existing 33 million hectares of irrigated and reclaimed land are poorly used. In the Krasnodar area, where irrigation makes the production of about 200,000 tons of rice possible annually, more than 33,000 hectares of *chernozem* soil has been destroyed by excessive irrigation.[41] Irrigated lands have also caused contamination of the Azov, Caspian, and Aral seas with pesticides and other agricultural chemicals. Indeed, the Aral Sea is already so contaminated that it will probably remain unusable even when the injection of water from the Siberian rivers restores its level. Irrigated fields often stimulate the uncontrolled reproduction of parasites. In the cotton-growing areas, for example, insect parasites which had previously only reproduced a few times a year, now produce twenty-three to twenty-five generations annually. Only the substantial use of DDT (a highly toxic insecticide which accumulates in the environment and which, therefore, is now restricted in the United States and Europe) keeps the cotton fields in reasonable condition. But many cotton parasites rapidly develop a resistance to DDT and can accumulate large amounts of it. Instead, the birds and fish which feed off the insects suffer its effects. Irrigation, in other words, solves some problems, but creates many new ones, some of which have yet to be solved. The most serious problem which has arisen from the hydroelectric irrigation projects of the Volga, Don, and Dnieper is that the level of the water table has risen, and the ground water is often too saline in the steppe areas. One-fifth of the irrigated *chernozem* lands in the central *chernozem* zone and the North Caucasus have increased salination and hundreds of thousands of hectares of irrigated fields in other parts of the Soviet Union have been abandoned because of salinity or waterlogging.[42] Excessive irrigation also damages the soil structure.

Whether the potential ecological side effects began to be taken seriously or whether the prohibitive costs were the cause, the river diversion program which had been launched in 1984 was cancelled in 1986 when about 5 billion rubles were already wasted for initial works. In the Five Year Plan for 1986–1990, introduced at the Twenty-seventh Party Congress, the project was said to require further study and research.[43] The great new program was dead before it had actually been started.

Conclusion

The history of Russian and Soviet agriculture is a history of experimentation on a grand scale over a period of almost a century. It makes it possible to compare different methods, approaches, solutions, and programs both within Russia and the Soviet Union and between the Soviet style of agriculture and that of other countries. Although I shall not make a comparison myself, I have wanted to present the history of Soviet agriculture in such a way that a comparison could be made. Many Western scholars of agriculture make such comparisons. However, the main attempts to compare Soviet and American agriculture were stimulated by the massive Soviet imports of food in the 1970s and the authors tend to concentrate on the current Soviet system, without connecting the problems with historical processes in Russia and the Soviet Union from the beginning of the century onward.[44] Similarly, historians of the Russian Revolution, of Stalin's collectivization, or of postwar developments often do not consider current problems and their relationship to the past. Soviet authors and researchers, on the other hand, some of them with a much more intimate and direct knowledge of these events and problems, are severely restricted in the methods and approaches they can use and even in the way in which they can treat factual material. They often offer interesting discussions of individual problems, but they are not allowed to raise controversial issues or to give broad analyses in a historical perspective. They are also debarred from making comparisons with other countries or criticizing official programs.

The censorship restrictions which operate in Soviet science (both in terms of what can be published and in terms of access to foreign specialist literature) make the solution of economic, environmental, agricultural, and other problems much more difficult. When the problems of agriculture are seen in historical perspective it is clear that each country has to find its own way to solve food and agricultural problems. It was a mistake for Soviet leaders to emulate the American example and to try to reach the American level of consumption, and it had more to do with political rivalry than with economic necessity. But there were earlier, far more profound mistakes, the ill effects of which have not yet been overcome.

Collectivization, and the way in which it was carried out, was clearly an economic and political disaster. It changed the natural traditions of rural development far more profoundly than the Revolution did. The Revolution ended feudal and feudal-capitalist forms of agriculture, but it strengthened family-based agriculture. The primitive propaganda of Stalinism insisted that no future development was possible of family-based agriculture. But in most other countries of the world family-based agriculture developed successfully and proved highly productive. In Russia and the Soviet Union it would not have been an easy or rapid method of developing agriculture, but it was a possible way, as the Stolypin reforms had indicated.

Rural depopulation is a universal phenomenon, and it reached dramatic proportions in the United States, Canada, and Western Europe. It is not a conflict-free process. In capitalist countries it is caused by economic competition and provides a vivid example of a Darwinian "survival of the fittest." The farmers who are most productive, most hardworking, most inventive, most adaptive to new technology and methods, and most traditionally tied to the land survive and continue working the land. The total number of farmers of this caliber is declining, but their productivity is increasing. But in the Soviet Union collectivization has had the opposite effect. The most active and productive part of the rural population has been destroyed, first by de-kulakization, and later spontaneously. The nature of the work, the impossibility of individuality, the absence of responsibility, the inferior social position of farmers, the numerous restrictions on freedom and initiative, the discipline, the unpopular method of payment, the dependence on local bureaucracy, and often simply the utter dreariness of life in isolated villages have made the ablest, youngest, most active people strive to leave the *kolkhozy* and *sovkhozy* at all costs. Attempts to stop his exodus have had little success. Thus while only the most active, able, and devoted farmers remain on the land in the United States and Western Europe, in the Soviet Union it is the least able, the most passive, and the oldest who stay voluntarily. Others work on the land because they cannot leave for some reason or other, or because they have been mobilized and forced to work for a limited period. Few people have an organic, personal, material link with the land, because that kind of link can be forged only by private ownership and personal responsibility. Collectivization uprooted the rural population, and since then any serious trouble, drought, food shortage, organizational blunder, or resettlement campaign has led to millions more leaving the land. The nature, psychology, and traditon of a peasantry attached to the land has been destroyed, but the more sophisticated figure of a modern farmer has not emerged to replace it.

This is not to say that some level of collectivization would not have been acceptable (and probably beneficial) if the collective farms had remained just one of a number of forms of farming, and if they had continued to compete economically with the other forms. By now many of the changes which have taken place in

Soviet rural life are irreversible and it is practically impossible to
return to universal individual farming. However, in areas where
the local geography makes the fields very small and mechanization very difficult (in the mountain districts of Georgia, Ar-
menia, and other parts of Transcaucasia and the North Caucasus,
for example, or in the deserted small villages of the non-*chernozem* areas which are remote from central settlements) individual farming would make sense even now. It would also be sensible
in the sparsely populated areas of the Altai, Siberia, and the Far
East, where there are no villages to form *kolkhozy*. There is plenty
of land in the Soviet Union which is unsuitable for *kolkhozy* and
sovkhozy, but which could be used by individual farmers. In
terms of food production and the rural economy, individual farms
which supplemented the *kolkhozy* and *sovkhozy* would certainly
be beneficial.

The possibility of returning to family-based farms has ceased
to be unthinkable to some Soviet experts. It has been mentioned
as one possible economically viable measure by some competent
economists. It is not, of course, called a *return* to the past, but
something which has emerged as a logical development of socialist agriculture and which needs cooperation between personal
material interest and the interests of the socialist system. In an
interview with *Izvestiya*, for example, academician Zaslavskaya
acknowledged that there are already some independent family
working units which can sign contracts with *kolkhozy* or *sovkhozy*.

> It is not a traditional form, but it is economically very
> effective . . . with correct use, this form combines very well
> with social production.[45]

Lisichkin, whose "investigative" articles on Soviet agriculture
have been quoted several times already, recently published a book
of essays in which he considers the feasibility of family farms.[46]
As a result of the poor performance of agriculture in 1985, discussions about some kind of family farming were even more
audible in 1986. But the advocates of the idea argued in favor of

"contract family farms," where families would work within the traditional *kolkhoz* system as "family brigades." The mountain areas of the Caucasus, and far-flung farms in Lithuania and in the Briansk and Kirovsk regions were particularly mentioned in the press as being suitable for "family brigades."[47] In fact, in these areas the vast distances between the villages and the towns and the absence of proper roads would make it impossible for family farms to survive without *kolkhoz* assistance. Farmers would not, for example, be able to sell their products independently and would have to contribute them to the general *kolkhoz* production pool.

In his speech at the Twenty-seventh Party Congress, Murakhovsky, the chairman of *Gosagroprom*, supported the idea of contract family farms. Finally, the Central Committee and Council of Ministers of the USSR published a decision at the end of March 1986 making family contracts official.[48] *Kolkhozy* and *sovkhozy* were recommended to use family and individual contracts as "one of the forms of collective contract" on condition that their production would be delivered to the general pool and that their remuneration would not exceed the procurement prices paid for the products of other contract brigades. This is only halfway towards really independent family farms and it will probably prove unpopular and unsuccessful. All that has been granted is permission. There is no law or legal provision yet for family farms. Moreover, it is economically unjust. If family brigades are only tolerated in distant and inaccessible locations, their production costs will be higher and their manual labor greater. Farmers live and work in such locations without the benefits of social, medical and other services. The government has realized that the food balance of the country would benefit from tolerating family farms. But it wants to ensure that the people who live on those farms do not earn more than the rest of the rural population and do not make their enterprises really independent by having, for example, long-term leases. They can only obtain short-term contracts. As a result, this system is unlikely to attract many people, particulary young families.

It is clear that my assessment of the future prospects of the *kolkhozy* and *sovkhozy* is far from optimistic. In every branch of agriculture and for every crop there has been a peak and then a decline. This is hardly an accident nor is it related to the weather. The only growth (and it is very modest) which has continued is in the production of meat and poultry, but even this has only been possible because of enormous imports of feed grain. The domestic production of feed grain and fodder has also passed through a peak and entered a decline, and the reduction of meadows and pastures makes it impossible to retain livestock at the current level without imports. The peak in grain production occurred in 1976 and 1978. Other crops peaked earlier. The highest harvests of sugar beets were in 1968 and 1976 (94.3 and 99.9 million tons). By the 1980s the sugar beet harvest were 30 to 40 million tons short of the target. The peak oilseed harvest was 7.4 million tons in 1973, and by the 1980s production had fallen to 5 to 6 million tons. To satisfy domestic requirements 1.5 million tons had to be imported in 1981 and 2.1 million tons in 1982. The maximum production of potatoes was in 1968 and 1973 (103 and 108 million tons) and by the 1980s production was 30 to 40 million tons below target. The production of vegetables has been more stable, but mostly from private plots and at a level well below both target and demand. Milk production is at the same level now as it was in 1975–1980.

Soviet planners have made serious miscalculations. But a system which does not allow free discussion of past mistakes and current problems cannot avoid new errors. Too many promises of a better life have been made and the leadership has linked its own credibility and that of the Soviet system to these promises. An important way in which the Soviet leadership legitimizes itself is by claiming that there will be a better ecomomy, a better diet, and a better life in the foreseeable future. This makes it extremely difficult to introduce austerity measures, increase food prices, and reduce imports to make more money available for internal development.

There are serious organic deficiencies in *kolkhoz* and *sovkhoz* agriculture. The average farm is far larger than ideal. Some *sovkhozy* are so large that the director needs a helicopter to visit different sections. As part of a complex network under both Party and state control, *kolkhozy* and *sovkhozy* do not have free access to the scientific world. They can use new scientific methods only after they have passed through the filter of the bureaucracy. Bureaucratic delays sometimes mean that years pass before scientific discoveries are assimilated. Livestock and plant breeders have been incapable of serving the needs of agriculture in a flexible and efficient way. Agricultural science lags far behind that of the West, despite the larger network of research institutes and experimental stations. For decades Soviet science has copied some American or Western European methods without taking climatic differences into account, while ignoring other relevant and good techniques and discoveries.

The agricultural economy is so illogical that high harvests and high levels of meat and milk production are necessary, but economically bad both for producers and for the state. Production costs rose again in 1984–1986 to a higher level than procurement prices. *Kolkhozy* and *sovkhozy* which produce more may actually lose more, despite the extra payments for excess production. The state has to pay higher subsidies for good harvests than for poor. Thus when the harvest is good, as far larger proportion of the budget is spent on agriculture, leaving less funds for other branches of the economy. Moreover, the trade system usually loses money when it sells food. The whole food production system or agro-industrial complex works on the same principles as education, a national health service, or a social security system. If this continues, rationing should be introduced to ensure fair distribution. The present system, that is, selling food products as if they were consumer goods while subsidizing the whole production side, cannot be continued. The consumer appetitie always makes sure that demand is higher than the available supplies. Thus shortages are created, and shortages are often socially unjust.

The crisis in agriculture is having detrimental effects on other aspects of Soviet policy. Firstly, the commitment of 35 percent of the available investment budget to agriculture retards the development of many other important branches of the economy. It has recently been recognized that Soviet heavy industry (and the military industry) has probably been overdeveloped. Industry needs to be restructured so that the production of consumer goods can be improved and high technology adopted. The development of better communications, computerization, and high-quality consumer-oriented branches of the economy requires an increase in the service industry—the labor-consuming branch of the national economy. However, there are neither funds nor a pool of people for this kind of restructuring and modernization.

Secondly, food imports have become a serious and embarrassing international issue for Soviet leaders. It is not only that they make the Soviet Union vulnerable to external pressure. They also increase world food prices, thereby making life more difficult for poorer countries. In the 1970s Soviet officials used to insist that their food imports were part of a normal pattern of economic exchange: the Soviet Union not only imported food, but exported it to many countries as well. (This was true in the 1960s and early 1970s, when 2 to 5 million tons of food was exported annually to Cuba, Eastern Europe, and Vietnam, but since 1979 food exports have dropped to below a million tons annually.) Moreover, the inability of the Soviet Union to give food aid to starving African nations has been a blow to the credibility of the Soviet system and the myth of its economic success. But there are domestic opportunity costs as well. Food imports need at least 20 billion dollars annually, and this limits the amount of hard currency available for importing the high technology and other commodities required to modernize industry.

It is, in any case, an illusion to think that a real food balance can be maintained on the basis of internal subsidies and imports. The economic input into agriculture has been higher than the agricultural output in the form of food products for more than two decades. It may look as if this indicates giving priority to food and nutrition, but in general it is the public—the nation as a whole—which finally has to pay for poor management and bureaucratic inefficiency. Transferring capital from the industrial sector to agricultural subsidies and food imports makes it difficult to increase wages, pensions, and benefits, or to improve the health and education services. When profits generated in one, more successful, sector of the economy are absorbed by losses in other sectors, there are less funds for the overall improvement of the national economy and standard of living. A significant (although officially unrecognized) inflation has been eroding the living standards of many groups of the population over a number of years. It is not surprising that health, life-expectancy, and infant-mortality statistics have been classified in the Soviet Union since the early 1970s. They indicate that living standards have deteriorated. Protein deficiencies increased towards the end of the 1970s, and in the 1980s and there are certainly associated health problems.

It is clear that the agricultural crisis has generated many serious political problems. There are only two ways of dealing with them. The first is to reduce imports and introduce some form of rationing (this was done in some provincial areas in 1980–1985) and to repress the resultant inevitable discontent and dissent, reducing even further the freedoms of the rural population and any criticism which challenges the established system, while using coercion to raise the volume of agricultural production. This would be a modernized version of the Stalinist model of administration. It is very unlikely that it would be successful, but it is probable that this is the remedy that some conservative Soviet leaders would like to try.

The second option is liberalization, both political and economical. It would mean giving the public more freedom to discuss the crisis and to test various alternative solutions. There are numerous silly restrictions (on ownership of horses, size of allotments, possibilities of buying second houses, size of houses which rural families can own, internal travel and residence, renting deserted fields, free-lance work by individuals and small brigades, access of farmers to the free market, etc.) which could be reduced or removed. This would release a great deal of latent energy, and, because it would be popular, it could succeed. It would also reduce some of the tensions within society, while increasing the pressure of public opinion on the government and the Party leadership.

It is obvious from the controversial developments of 1986 that there are supporters of both alternatives in the current Soviet leadership, and that Gorbachev himself is behind the "progres-sive," if not the liberal, trend. (Gorbachev is the first Soviet leader with a real peasant's background. He already was frustrated with the previous failures of agriculture, and he probably understands that Soviet agriculture is now so weak that the *kolkhoz* and *sovkhoz* system could fall apart under a coercive policy.) In May 1986 the Gorbachev government restricted private food trade se-verely by legislation, and a steep rise in market prices resulted. The government retreated a few months later, enacting a decree that legalized "individual working activity" and the sale of pri-vately produced consumer goods. These events indicate the ab-sence of a proper strategy. The Gorbachev government also has tried unusual experiments in the form of "Food Fairs": during the winter of 1986–1987, the state encouraged and assisted *kol-khozy* and *sovkhozy* to bring produce to cities and sell directly from trucks, avoiding state shops and private markets. This at-tempt to bring market prices down was not very successful, but it shows that the state is trying to find new ways to remove the virtual monopoly private agriculture has over the production and sales of high-quality vegetables and fruits.

There seems to be a consensus in Gorbachev's Politburo that private initiative should be encouraged—but only within the tra-ditional *kolkhoz* and *sovkhoz* system, not outside it as before. Party leaders want the benefits of individual initiative without the chal-lenges of individual freedoms and real democratization. Half-measures, even in the right direction, hardly help Soviet agri-culture in any radical way. If no imaginative new strategy is found, the situation may get worse before it gets any better; and it may change only slowly.

But the processes that took place in the villages of Russia were crucially important causes of many of the social and political upheavals during this century and before. These upheavals fi-nally led to the destruction of all rural classes—the landlords first, then the kulaks, and finally the entire peasantry. The attempt to make the land productive with state-employed labor has failed. The resulting rural and food problems may well once again de-termine the history of Russia.

Terminology, Abbreviations, and Measurements

APO Abbreviation of *Agropromyshlennoye obyedineniye* (Agro-industrial complex) RAPO—district APO.

apparat, **apparatus** The machine, the organization of offices and officeholders (for example, the Party *apparat,* the state *apparat,* and so on). The English expression "political machine" would be an accurate translation, except that it is pejorative, while *apparat* is not.

apparatchik Familiar term for an official in the Party *apparat.*

batrak Agricultural laborer, usually employed by a kulak for payment in kind.

brigade Organized group of between thirty and one hundred workers.

centner 100 kilograms or 220.4 pounds. The same as quintal.

Central Committee or CC A high policy-making and administrative organization of the Communist Party, nominally elected by and responsible to the Party Congress. Directs the activities of the Party between Party Congresses. Each republic has its own CC.

chernozem Grassland soil with a dark humic horizon, from 25 centimeters to 2 meters thick. Usually neutral and considered to be the best agricultural soil.

CMEA The Council of Mutual Economic Assistance, the form of economic alliance of Soviet bloc countries.

Council of People's Commissars   The equivalent of today's Council of Ministers.

CPSU   Communist Party of the Soviet Union.

dacha   Holiday house, usually in the country or at a resort. For officials it usually means a special, state-owned villa, given either for a certain period or indefinitely as a property of a family.

desyatina   Unit of area, 2.7 acres.

gorkom   The Party committee in a town or city.

Gosagroprom   Abbreviation of *Gosudarstvennyi Agropromyshlennyi Komitet* (State Agro-Industrial Committee).

Gosplan   State Planning Committee.

gulag   The prison and labor camp network in the Soviet Union.

hectare, ha   A unit of land measure equivalent to 2.47 acres.

ispolkom   Executive committee. In districts, towns, or regions they are part of the local government networks.

Izvestiya   Central government newspaper, second in importance to *Pravda*.

khutor   Fully enclosed farm. Holding of a household outside the commune where land and house were consolidated on one piece of land.

kolkhoz   Collective farm, formed on the basis of common means of production and collective labor; an agrarian producers' cooperative which is obliged to make deliveries to the state at prices fixed by the state. Each member receives advance payments, checked later, as a share of the net income commensurate with the share of "labor days" he contributes to collective operations. Members also have private plots (up to 0.5 hectares) around their family homes.

kolkhoznik   Member of a collective farm.

kombedy   Committees of poor peasants and *batraks*. Organs of rural power during the "War Communism" period.

Kommunist   Main theoretical journal of the Central Committee of the CPSU.

Komsomol   Abbreviation of *Kommunisticheskoye Soyuz Molodezhi* (Young Communist League), the mass movement to which the majority of young people belong.

kopek   One-hundredth of a ruble.

krai   A large territorial subdivision of RSFSR, in which non-Russian ethnic minorities live in autonomous regions.

kraikom   The Party committee in a *krai*.

kulak   A Russian word meaning "fist." Before 1917 it was used for avaricious merchants or for peasants who had gained a hold over their fellows, for example, village usurers. After 1917 it was used to specify class differentiation in the countryside. The kulak was a well-to-do peasant, who rented land from others and produced on a relatively large scale for the market. The middle peasant (*serednyak*) had average-size holdings, mostly worked by family labor, and sold some surplus on the market. The *bednyak* (poor peasant) did not have enough land to feed his family and usually had to borrow or hire himself out. During collectivization the term *kulak* became a term of abuse for anyone refusing to join the collective farms.

MTS   Machine Tractor Station, a depot which serviced several collective farms with machines, drivers, and mechanics for many works (ploughing, sowing, harvesting, and so on).

MVD   Abbreviation of *Ministerstvo Vnutrennikh Del* (Ministry of Internal Affairs).

nadel   An allotment of arable land under any form of land holding.

Narkomprod   Abbreviation of *Narodnyi Komissariat Prodovolstviya* (People's Commissariat of Food Supply).

Narkomtorg   Abbreviation of *Narodnyi Komissariat Vneshnei i Vnutrennoi Torgovli* (People's Commissariat of External and Internal Trade).

Narkomzem   Abbreviation of *Narodnyi Komissariat Zemledeliya* (People's Commissariat of Agriculture).

Narodniks   Russian socialists who "went to the people," (the *narod*) in the 1870s, primarily to live among the peasants and spread socialist ideas in the hope of rousing them to overthrow the monarchy. Unlike the Marxists, the Narodniks held that Russia could go directly to a socialism based on communal land ownership without passing through an industrial capitalist stage. In the period from 1905 to 1917 the term was also used for parties and groups which generally identified with this tradition of peasant socialism, in particular the SRs, Trudoviks, and *Narodnye Sotsialisty* (People's Socialists).

New Economic Policy, NEP   Introduced by Lenin in 1921 in order to alleviate the heavy burden imposed by Civil War and the system of War Communism. It permitted private enterprise and was expected to last many years. It was terminated by Stalin at the end of the 1920s and replaced by collectivization and the five year plans.

NKVD   Abbreviation of *Narodnyi Komissariat Vnutrennikh Del* (People's Commissariat of Internal Affairs). Formed in 1934 to combine all internal security agencies. In 1946 it was divided into MVD (Ministry of Internal Affairs) and MGB (Ministry of State Security). The MGB was replaced by the KGB in 1954.

obkom   Abbreviation of *oblastnoi komitet* (regional Party committee).

oblast'   A major administrative subdivision of a Soviet republic, comparable to a province or state.

obshchina   Commune. Used both to denote the particular form of land holding, intermingled re-partitional strip farming, as well as the general village community which held the land in common.

OGPU (GPU)   Abbreviation of *Obyedinennoye Gosudarstvennoye Politicheskoye Upravleniye* (Unified State Political Administration), the name of the secret police when the Cheka was disbanded.

otrub   Farm with only fields enclosed. Holding of a household outside the commune where the land was consolidated in one place, but apart from the house.

podzol or *podsol*   Soil which forms in cold climates under coniferous forests. It is often acidic, with low humus content and poor fertility.

Politburo   The political bureau of the Central Committee of the CPSU. The top decision-making body in the Soviet political system. It was called the Presidium between 1952 and 1966. It consists of full members with voting rights and candidate members who attend meetings but cannot vote.

pomeshchik   From the Russian word *pomest'ye* ("estate"). A member of the gentry who owned land and usually lived on his rural estate.

Pravda   The national newspaper of the Central Committee of the CPSU.

pud   Old Russian measure of weight, equivalent to 16.38 kilograms.

raiispolkom   Executive committee in a *raion*.

raikom   Party committee in a *raion*.

raion   Administrative subdivision of an *oblast'* or of a city.

RSFSR   Russian Soviet Federated Socialist Republic, the official name of Soviet Russia from 1917 to 1922, when the USSR was formed. Now the name of the largest republic within the Soviet Union.

ruble   1.4 U.S. dollars, at the 1986 official exchange rate.

Selkhoztekhnika   An acronym formed from the Russian words for "agricultural technology."

Sel'skii Sovet or *Sel'sovet*   Rural soviet, the lowest level of local administration in the countryside, usually covering more than one village.

Soviet   The Russian word for "council," the basic governmental unit of the Soviet system.

Sovnarkhoz   Regional Economic Council. In 1957 Khrushchev set up 105 of them, but they were reduced to 47 in 1963 and were abolished in 1965.

Sovnarkom   Abbreviation of *Sovet Narodnykh Komissarov* (Council of People's Commissars).

Soyuzkhleb   An acronym formed from the Russian words for "All-Union association (*obyedineniye*) of grain"; part of *Narkomtorg*.

stanitsa   A large village in the North Caucasus.

state farm or *sovkhoz*   A state agricultural enterprise. *Sovkhoz* workers receive their wages in cash, whereas *kolkhozniki* are rewarded partly with money and partly with agricultural produce.

Supreme Soviet   The Soviet parliament, consisting of elected deputies in two chambers, one based on nationalities, the other on demographic electoral constituencies. Only one candidate, usually proposed by the local Party organization, stands for each seat.

ton, metric ton 1,000 kilograms, 2,200 pounds.

trudoden Workday unit, used to evaluate the work done by farmers. Different types of work have different *trudoden* values, unrelated to the number of working hours.

TsIK or VTsIK *Tsentral-nyi Ispolnitel'nyi Komitet* (Central Executive Committee of the Congress of Soviets, the supreme legislative organ of the Soviet Union until the 1936 constitution replaced it with the Supreme Soviet).

versta A unit of distance, 1.1 kilometers.

Union republics The Soviet Union is made up of fifteen republics which are called Union republics (or constituent or national republics). Where there are large and distinct national minorities, Union republics may be subdivided into autonomous republics and autonomous regions.

ustav A collection of rules and regulations for organizations.

War Communism The policy followed by the Soviet government during the Civil War (1918–1921), notably a ban on private trade, forcible requisitioning of grain, and centralization of economic institutions and activities.

Zemel'noye Obshchestvo Land society. The term used by the 1922 Land Code of the RSFSR to include land-users of all kinds, including communal, non-redistributable, and collective. In practice the term became equated in most Soviet discussion with the commune. Some Soviet commentators have suggested that the Soviet land society differed from the prerevolutionary commune, but in practice there were few differences.

zveno A small group of agricultural workers, a subdivision of a brigade.

References and Notes

The Cambridge University system of transliteration has been used except for the letter *e*, which has been transliterated as *ye-* at the beginning of words and after all vowels except ы. Proper names for which there is a conventional spelling in English have not been changed (e.g., Gorbachev).

CHAPTER 1

1. A. G. Rashin, *Naseleniye Rossii za 100 let, 1811–1913*. Moscow, Gosstatizdat, 1956.
2. A. M. Anfimov, *Krest'yanskoye khozyaistvo yevropeiskoi Rossii, 1881–1904*. Moscow, Nauka, 1980.
3. A. M. Anfimov, *Krupnoye pomeshchich'ye khozyaistvo yevropeiskoi Rossii (Konets XIX-go—nachala XX-go veka)*. Moscow, Nauka, 1969.
4. V. S. Nemchinov, *Sel'skokhozyaistvennaya statistika s osnovami obshchei teorii*. Moscow, Sel'khozgiz, 1945, p. 34.
5. Harrison E. Salisbury, *Russia in Revolution, 1900–1930*. London, André Deutsch, 1978, p. 113.
6. Leon Trotsky, *History of the Russian Revolution* (translated by Max Eastman), Vol. 3. London, Sphere Books, 1967, p. 37.
7. Ibid.

CHAPTER 2

1. G. A. Aksenenok and V. M. Chkhikvadze (eds.), *Leninsky dekret "o zemlye" i sovremennost'.* Moscow, Nauka, 1970.
2. *Izvestiya VTsIK* (Bulletin of the All-Russian Central Executive Committee), February 19, 1918.
3. *Istoriya sotsialisticheskoi ekonomiki SSSR,* Vol. 1. Moscow, Nauka, 1976.
4. *Dekrety sovetskoi vlasti,* Vol. 2. Moscow, Politizdat, 1959, pp. 261–262.
5. *Pravda* and other central newspapers, June 1, 1918.
6. H. H. Fisher, *The Famine in Soviet Russia, 1919–1923: The Operation of the American Relief Administration.* New York, Macmillan, 1927.
7. S. G. Wheatcroft, "Famine and factors affecting mortality in the USSR" and "The demographic crises of 1914–1922 and 1930–1932." Unpublished CREES Discussion Papers, University of Birmingham, SIPS No. 20, p. 5. (Received by courtesy of the author.)
8. *Narodnoye khozaistvo SSSR (Nar. khoz.) 1922–1982.* Moscow, Finansy i Statistika, 1982, p. 9.
9. *KPSS v rezolyutsiyakh i resheniyakh syezdov, konferentsii i plenumov TsK,* Vol. 2, *Sbornik dokumentov po zemel'nomu zakonodatel'stvu SSSR i RSFSR, 1917–1954.* Moscow, Politizdat, 1970.
10. V. P. Danilov, *Sovetskaya dokolkhoznaya derevnya: naseleniye, zemlepol'zovaniye, kozhyaistvo.* Moscow, Nauka, 1977, pp. 106–107.
11. *Sbornik statisticheskikh svedenii po Soyuzu SSR, 1918–1923.* Moscow, TsSU SSSR, 1924, p. 98.
12. V. P. Danilov, op cit., pp. 142–143.
13. Tsentral'noye Upravleniye Narodnokhozyaistvennogo Ucheta, (TsUNKhU) *Sotsialisticheskoye pereustroistvo sel'skogo khozyaistva SSSR mezhdu XV i XVI syezdami VKP(b).* Moscow, TsUNKhU Gosplana SSSR, 1932, p. 31.
14. *Tovarooboroty za gody rekonstruktivnogo perioda: Sbornik statisticheskikh materialov.* Moscow, TsUNKhU Gosplana SSSR, 1932.
15. V. P. Danilov, *Sovetskaya dokolkhoznaya derevnya: Sotsial'naya struktura, sotsialnye otnosheniya.* Moscow, Nauka, 1979, p. 325.
16. Ibid., pp. 319–320.
17. Ibid., p. 275.
18. J. V. Stalin, *Works,* Vol. 11. Moscow, Foreign Languages Publishing House, 1954, p. 215.
19. E. H. Carr and R. W. Davies, *Foundations of a Planned Economy, 1926–1929,* Vol. 1. Harmondsworth, Middlesex Penguin, 1974, pp. 74–75; R. W. Davies, *The Industrialization of Soviet Russia: 1, The Socialist Offensive: The Collectivization of Soviet Agriculture, 1929–1930.* London, Macmillan, 1980, pp. 42–43.
20. R. W. Davies, op cit., p. 42.

CHAPTER 3

1. Roy Medvedev (ed.), *Politichesky dnevnik, 1964–1970,* Vol. 1. Amsterdam, Alexander Herzen Foundation, pp. 121–123.
2. Editorial, *Pravda,* September 1, 1929.
3. R. W. Davies, *The Industrialization of Soviet Russia: 1. The Socialist Offensive: The Collectivization of Soviet Agriculture, 1929–1930.* London, Macmillan, 1980, p. 435.
4. A. F. Chmyga, "Kolkhoznoye dvizheniye v pervom desyatiletii sovetskoi vlasti," in *Oktyabr' i sovetskoye krest'yanstvo, 1917–1927,* Moscow, Nauka, 1977.

References and Notes 431

5. V. I. Lenin, *Collected Works*, Vol. 30. Moscow, Progress Publishers and London, Lawrence & Wishart, 1965, p. 196.
6. *Sobraniye zakonov*, 1929, No. 4, article 33.
7. *Kolkhozy v 1929 godu. Itogi sploshnogo obsledovaniya kolkhozov.* Moscow, Gosplan SSSR i RSFSR, 1931, pp. 1–4.
8. J. V. Stalin, *Works*, Vol. 12. Moscow, Foreign Languages Publishing House, 1955, p. 138.
9. V. I. Lenin, op cit., Vol. 29, pp. 265–266.
10. Ibid., Vol. 32, p. 484.
11. Ibid., Vol. 29, p. 178.
12. *Sel'skoye khozyaistvo SSSR, 1925–1928.* Moscow, TsU SSSR, 1929.
13. V. P. Danilov, *Sovetskaya dokolkhoznaya derevnya: Sotsial'naya struktura, sotsialnye otnosheniya.* Moscow, Nauka, 1979, p. 71.
14. J. V. Stalin, op cit., Vol. 12, p. 176.
15. V. P. Danilov, *Ocherki istorii kollektivizatsii sel'skogo khozyaistvo v soyuznykh respublikakh.* Moscow, Gospolitizdat, 1963, p. 105.
16. J. V. Stalin, op cit., Vol. 12, pp. 199, 201.
17. A. G. Doyarenko, *Iz agronomicheskogo proshlogo*, (2nd edition). Moscow, Kolos Publishing House, 1965; N. V. Orlovsky, *Aleksei Grigorievich Doyarenko.* Moscow, Nauka, 1980.
18. *Narodynoye khozyaistvo SSSR v 1956 godu. Statistichesky ezhegodnik. (Nar. khoz.)* Moscow, TsU SSSR. These collections of economic statistics are published annually and are the main official source of information about the Soviet economy in the past and present. They often, but not always, compare the figures for a given year with figures for prerevolutionary years (1909–1913, 1913 only, or 1916) and a period in the 1920s and 1930s. The information for the 1920s and 1930s covers the country within the borders which existed in those years. The figures for 1913 and for 1939 and 1940 sometimes show both the figures for the current borders and for the borders before September 1939 (when the Western Ukraine and Western Byelorussia were integrated into the Soviet Union). In 1956, when this new series of statistical yearbooks was launched, the figures given for agriculture, particularly for cereals and technical crops, were different from those available during Stalin's lifetime. At the Twentieth Party Congress in 1956 Khrushchev explained that the previously published figures for grain production after 1932 usually represented the "biological harvest" or the preliminary assessment for tax purposes. Khrushchev changed this practice and the figures for the actual harvest began to be given, i.e., the amount of grain which had actually been stored by the villages and in the state procurement system. The amount of information given in each year varies: the 1956 yearbook, for example, contains 296 pages of tables, while the 1963 yearbook has 759 pages. The maximum amount of information was released in 1965 (909 pages). Later less information began to be released (582 pages in 1980 and 560 in 1982). For this reason it is often necessary to collect information from several yearbooks to present a picture of the economy in the 1920s and 1930s.
19. In the official Soviet history of collectivization, Trapeznikov reports that in the North Caucasus only there were 2,895 harvest protection posts and 23,330 light cavalry groups manned by members of the Komsomol and the Pioneers to guard the fields. "These young patriots helped save 61,180 poods of grain," he states. See S. P. Trapeznikov, *Leninism and the Agrarian and Peasant Question.* Vol. 2: *The Historical Experience of the CPSU in Carrying Out Lenin's Cooperative Plan.* Moscow, Progress Publishers, 1981, p. 367. These protective measures were particularly common in 1933 in all the grain-

432   *References and Notes*

producing regions. In fact, this protection, which Trapeznikov describes as the "heroic" work of the Party, Komsomol, and Young Pioneers, was protection of the grain from the hungry peasants who had sown it. All the harvesting in 1933 was done under armed guard.
20. L. Kopelev, "Posledniye khlebozagotovki," in *I sotvoril sebye kumira*. Ann Arbor, Ardis, 1978, pp. 247–306.
21. J. V. Stalin, op cit., Vol. 13, p. 235.
22. *Sel'skoye khozyaistvo SSSR: Statistichesky ezhegodnik, 1935*. Moscow, Sel'khozgiz, 1936, p. 222.
23. V. Tendryakov, "Konchina," *Moskva*, No. 3, 1968, p. 37.
24. *Pravda*, December 4, 1935.
25. M. Maksudov, "Losses suffered by the population of the USSR, 1918–1958," in Roy Medvedev (ed.), *Samizdat Register 2*. London, Merlin Press and New York, Norton, 1981.
26. *Itogi vsesoyuznoi perepisi naseleniya 1970 goda. TsU SSSR*, Vol. 2. Moscow, Statistika, 1972, p. 20.
27. "Collective farm," *The New Columbia Encyclopedia*. New York, Columbia University Press, 1975, p. 597.

CHAPTER 4

1. *Svod zakonov SSSR*, No. 32, 1934.
2. *Kollektivizatsiya sel'skogo khozyaistvo. Vazhneishiye postanovleniya Kommunisisticheskoi partii i Sovetskogo pravitel'stva, 1927–1935*. Moscow, 1957. See also *Svod zakonov SSSR*, No. 49, 1934.
3. M. A. Vyzlan, *Zavershayushchy etap sozdaniya kolkhoznogo stroya*. Moscow, Nauka, 1978, p. 59.
4. Ibid., pp. 61–63.
5. V. P. Danilov, *Sovetskaya dokolkhoznaya derevnya: naseleniye, zemlepol'zovaniye, kozhyaistvo*. Moscow, Nauka, 1977, p. 221.
6. M. A. Vyzlan, op cit., p. 66.
7. *MTS vo vtoroi pyatiletkye*. Moscow-Leningrad, pp. 11–16, 47.
8. T. L. Basuk, *Organizatsiya sotsialisticheskogo sel'skokhozyaistvennogo proizvodstva*. Moscow, 1939, p. 212.
9. M. A. Vyzlan, op cit., p. 99.
10. Yu. V. Arutunyan, *Mekhanizatory sel'skogo khozyaistva SSSR v 1927–1957*. Moscow, 1960, p. 38.
11. Zh. A. Medvedev, *The Rise and Fall of T. D. Lysenko*. New York, Columbia University Press, 1969.
12. M. A. Vyzlan, op cit., p. 144.
13. This table was prepared on the basis of Table 5 and the population figures for those years. Production figures should not be confused with the level of consumption. The figures given for the production of grain include seed and feed grain, grain for industry (for example, for the vodka distilleries), and export grain. Note also that all dairy products are calculated as milk in the Soviet Union and that the statistics given for meat always include chicken and meat subproducts like lard.
14. M. A. Vyzlan, op cit., p. 208.
15. Ibid.
16. S. G. Wheatcroft, "Famine and factors affecting mortality in the USSR." and "The demograhpic crises of 1914–1922 and 1930–1932." Unpublished CREES Discussion Papers, University of Birmingham, SIPS No. 20, p. 24.

17. A. A. Tverdokhlebov, *Material'noye blagosostoyaniye rabochego klassa Moskvy v 1917–1937.* Moscow, 1970, p. 347.

CHAPTER 5

1. N. A. Voznesensky, *Voennaya ekonomika SSSR v period Velikoi Otechestvennoi voiny.* Moscow, Gospolitizdat, 1948, p. 42.
2. Ibid., pp. 92–93.
3. S. A. Vorkunov, *Leninsky kooperativny plan i ego osushchestvleniye v SSSR.* Moscow, Prosveshcheniye, 1980, p. 136.
4. I. V. Arutunyan, *Sovetskoye krest'yanstvo v gody Velikoi Otechestvennoi voiny.* Moscow, Izd-vo AN SSSR, 1970, p. 142.
5. *Nurenbergsky protsess.* Moscow, 1954, Vol. 1, p. 739, Vol. 2, p. 557. See also S. P. Trapeznikov, *Leninism and the Agrarian and Peasant Question.* Vol. 2: *The Historical Experience of the CPSU in Carrying Out Lenin's Cooperative Plan.* Moscow, Progress Publishers, 1981, Vol. 2, p. 481.
6. *Nar. khoz.*, 1963, op cit., p. 8.
7. *Sovetskaya ekonomika v period Velikoi Otechestvennoi voiny.* Moscow, Nauka, 1970, pp. 259–260.
8. S. I. Sdobnov, et al., (eds.), *Voprosy agrarnoi teorii i politiki SSSR.* Moscow, Politizdat, 1979, pp. 82–85.
9. Ibid.
10. N. S. Khrushchev, Chapter 7, "Famine in the Ukraine," *Khrushchev Remembers.* London, André Deutsch, New York, Little Brown, 1971, pp. 200–215.
11. Ibid., 203–205.
12. I. V. Arutunyan, op cit., pp. 323–324.
13. N. W. Bethell, *The Last Secret: Forcible Repatriation to Russia.* London, André Deutsch, 1974; N. Tolstoy, *Victims of Yalta.* London, Hodder and Stoughton, 1978.
14. I. M. Volkov, "Kolkhozy SSSR v gody chetvertoi pyatiletki," in I. M. Volkov (ed.), *Razvitiye sel'skogo khozyaistva SSSR v poslevoyennye gody, 1946–1970.* Moscow, Nauka, 1977. pp. 51–52.
15. Ibid., p. 60.
16. Ibid., p. 59.
17. Zh. A. Medvedev, *The Rise and Fall of T. D. Lysenko.* New York, Columbia University Press, 1969. The original title of this book was *The History of the Soviet Discussion on Biology and Agronomy in 1929–1966.* It contained an extensive discussion of Stalin's plan for transforming nature, its connections with the theories of Professor V. R. Williams, and the links between Williams and Lysenko. However, Professor I. M. Lerner, to whom I sent the manuscript in 1967 and who translated the book, omitted, abridged, or rearranged the sections relating to agriculture, soil science, and agrochemistry without my knowledge or consent. In the Notes (note 44, p. 270) to his translation, Lerner wrote:

> A chapter on the resurrection of Vil'yamsism in 1948 and the spread of the grassland system of agriculture throughout the nation is omitted. Its subsection titles are: "A theoretical analysis of soil formation concepts developed by Vil'yams," "The flowering of Vil'yamsism after the 1948 LAAAS session and the general adoption of the grassland system in the guise of the 'Stalin plan for tranforming nature'," "The new wave of persecution of the representatives of Pryanishnikov's school of agricul-

tural chemistry," "The role of Lysenko in the support and spread of Vil'yams' system."

Although Professor Lerner transliterates the name Vil'yams, it is, in fact, an American name. Williams's father, Robert Williams, was an American who went to work in Russia and settled there. The English title of the book was also Lerner's idea. We had met in Prague in 1965, where we discussed the possibility of publishing my book, which had been written in 1962. Although we were very good friends (he died in 1976), I was disappointed by his decision to remove the sections on agriculture and to concentrate solely on the genetic controversy.

18. B. A. Aleksandrov, *Stalinsky plan preobrazovaniya prirody v deistvii*. Moscow, Politizdat, 1952.
19. M. A. Vyzlan, "Plan polezashchitnykh lesonasazhdenii i bor'ba za ego osushchestvleniye." In I. M. Volkov (ed.), op cit., pp. 119–135.
20. *Nar. khoz.*, 1956, op cit., p. 128.
21. *Pravda*, October 6, 1952.
22. Published in *Pravda*, October 3 and 4, 1952. For an English translation, see B. Franklin (ed.), *The Essential Stalin*. London, Croom Helm, 1973, pp. 445–481.

CHAPTER 6

1. N. S. Khrushchev, *O merakh dal'neishego razvitiya sel'skogo khozyaistva SSSR*. Moscow, Politizdat, 1953, p. 28.
2. I. Lukinnov, "Sel'skogokhozyaistvennoye proizvodstvo i zeny," *Kommunist*, No. 4, 1968, p. 68. The financial expression of the different values in state-*kolkhoz* relations is extremely difficult because the prices of equipment considered to be the "means of production" and not available for retail sale are very arbitrary. Some economists have attempted to express them in "wheat equivalence," i.e., the amount of wheat which must be sold by a *kolkhoz* to obtain the equipment from the state. It was, for example, calculated that to obtain one small ZIS-5 truck, Ukrainian *kolkhozy* had to sell 99 tons of wheat to the state in 1940, 124 tons in 1948, and 239 tons in 1949. After the increase in procurement prices in 1953, the price of the same truck dropped to 53 tons of wheat.
3. A. M. Emel'yanov (ed.), *Kompleksnaya programma razvitya sel'skogo khozyaistva v deistvii*. Moscow, Ekonomika, 1980, p. 159; N. S. Khrushchev, *Stroitel'stvo kommunisma v SSSR i razvitiye sel'skogo khozyaistva* Moscow, Politizdat, 1964, p. 467.
4. V. J. Yushkov, *Zakupochnaya zena i rashirennoye vosproizvodstvo v sel'skom khozyaistvye*. Moscow, Ekonomika, 1980, p. 44.
5. L. I. Brezhnev, *Tselina*. Moscow, Politizdat, 1978, p. 4.
6. William Vogt, *Road to Survival*. London, Gollancz, 1949, pp. 230–231.
7. N. S. Khrushchev, Chapter 7, "Feeding the People," *Khrushchev Remembers*, London, André Deutsch, New York, Little, Brown, 1971, p. 121.
8. L. I. Brezhnev, op cit., p. 5.
9. R. A. Medvedev and Zh. A. Medvedev, *Khrushchev. The Years in Power*. New York, Columbia University Press and London, Oxford University Press, 1976.
10. N. S. Khrushchev, *Stroietl'stvo kommunisma v SSSR*, Vol. 3. Moscow, Politizdat, 1964, pp. 131–132.
11. *Nar. khoz.*, 1961, op cit., p. 291.

References and Notes   435

12. S. I. Sdobnov, et al., (eds.), *Voprosy agrarnoi teorii i politiki SSSR.* Moscow, Politizdat, 1979, p. 94.
13. M. P. Gubenko and G. K. Ol'shevskaya, "Nekotorye problemy razvitiya sel'skogo khozyaistva RSFSR," in I. M. Volkov, (ed.), *Razvitiye sel'skogo khozyaistva SSSR v poslevoyennye gody, 1946–1970.* Moscow, Nauka, 1977, pp. 336–339.
14. R. Medvedev, *Khrushchev.* Oxford, Blackwell and New York, Anchor Press/ Doubleday, 1982, pp. 116–117.
15. *Voprosy ekonomiki,* No. 9, 1963, p. 97 and *Nar. khoz.,* 1963, op cit., p. 337. *Nar. khoz.* gives the figures for mechanization in the various types of work concerning livestock production. In 1963 only 20 percent of milking was done by machine and only 2 percent of the fodder and animal feed distribution was mechanized in the *kolkhozy.* The figures for *sovkhozy* were only slightly higher.
16. R. A. Medvedev and Zh. A. Medvedev, op cit., pp. 94–101.
17. R. Medvedev, op cit., p. 171.
18. V. O. Morozov, "Sovershenstvovaniye oplaty truda kolkhoznikov (1953–1958)," in I. M. Volkov, (ed.), op cit., p. 293.
19. A. A. Konshin, (ed.), *Ekonomika sovkhozov i kolkhozov tselinnykh raionov.* Moscow-Tselinograd, p. 239.
20. *Nar. khoz.* op cit., 1963, pp. 312–313.
21. *Voprosy ekonomiki,* No. 8, 1965, p. 25.
22. A. P. Turina, "K voprosu o preobrazovanii kolkhozov v sovkhozy," *Istoriya SSSR,* No. 5, 1983, p. 7.
23. Martin McCauley, *Khrushchev and the Development of Soviet Agriculture.* London, Macmillan, 1976, pp. 217–218.

CHAPTER 7

1. Mal'tsev celebrated his ninetieth birthday in 1985. He is a practical agronomist who has never had any formal agronomical education. He achieved fame in 1946 when he was working as an agronomist in the Kurgan region in Eastern Siberia, and saved the harvest of his *kolkhoz* during a severe drought when most harvests in the area were lost. He was awarded a Stalin prize as a reward. In 1956 he was made an honorary member of the Lenin Academy of Agricultural Sciences of the USSR. His system was adapted to the geographic and ecological conditions of various eastern regions by the Kazakhstan (and later All-Union) Research Institute of Grain Production which had been established in 1956 to test and develop agro-technology methods for the virgin land areas. For details of the system, see the article by the director of this institute, A. I. Barayev, "Sovremennaya pochvozashchitnaya sistema zemledeliya," in P. P. Vavilov (ed.) *50 let Vsesoyuznoi Akademii Sel'skokhozyaistvennykh nauk imeni Lenina.* Moscow, Kolos, 1979, pp. 69–84.
2. U.S. Department of Agriculture. Foreign Agriculture Circular. Grains. *USSR Grain Situation and Outlook,* Washington, D.C., SG-7-86, July 1986.
3. See, for example, *Sel'skoye khozyaistvo SSSR: Tsifry i fakty.* Moscow, Kolos, 1972; *Sel'skoye khozyaistvo SSSR,* (assembled by G. M. Bogysh and V. G. Shaikin). Moscow, Kolos, 1977; *Sel'skoye khozyaistvo SSSR,* (assembled by G. M. Bogysh and V. G. Shaikin). Moscow, Kolos, 1982.
4. *Izvestiya,* September 20, 1984.
5. *Izvestiya,* October 4, 1984.
6. Yu. Chernichenko, "Rzhanoi khleb," *Novy mir,* No. 11, 1968, pp. 177–207.

7. *Vneshnyaya torgovlya SSSR v 1982 godu* (*Vnesh. torg.*: Statistical Yearbook). Moscow, Statistika, 1983, p. 261.
8. *Nar. khoz.*, 1980, op cit., p. 231.
9. Yu. Chernichenko, "Russkaya pshenitsa," *Novy mir*, No. 11, 1975, pp. 180–200.
10. P. M. Zhukovsky, *Kul'turnye rasteniya i ikh sorodichi*. Leningrad, Kolos, 1971, pp. 109–113.
11. A. Kostykov, "Glavny khleb," *Sel'skaya zhizn'*, July 3, 1984.
12. B. Archipenko, "Khleb i lyudi," *Kommunist*, No. 6, 1982, pp. 89–100.
13. O. Pavlov, "Polye grechishnoye," *Izvestiya*, March 7, 1985.
14. Yu. Chernichenko, "Pro kartoshku," *Sovetskii pisatel'*, 1982.
15. *Vneshnyaya torgovlya SSSR v 1982 godu*. Moscow, Statistika, 1983, p. 28.
16. P. M. Zhukovsky, op cit., pp. 414–418.
17. *Veshnyaya torgovlya SSSR v 1982 godu*, op cit., pp. 31, 41.
18. Ibid., p. 268.
19. *Statistichesky ezhegodnik stran-chlenov Soveta Ekonomicheskoi Vzaimopomoshchi: 1983 (CMEA Yearbook)*. Moscow, Finansy i Statistika, 1984, p. 200.
20. *Izvestiya*, July 6, 1985.
21. *Vneshnyaya torgovlya SSSR v 1984 godu*, Moscow, Statistika, 1985, pp. 259, 271.

CHAPTER 8

1. This table is based on a combination of Soviet and Western data. The Soviet sources were: "Belki," *Malaya Sovetskaya Meditsinskaya Entsiklopediya*, Vol. 1. Moscow, Sovetskaya Entsiklopediya, 1966, p. 907; A. A. Sozinov, "Problemy uluchsheniya kachestva zerna", in P. P. Vavilov (ed.), *50 let Vsesoyuznoi Akademii Sel'skokhozyaistvennykh nauk imeni Lenina*. Moscow, Kolos, 1979, p. 219. Western data on the amino acid composition of various foods are summarized in R. Block and D. Bolling, *The Amino Acid Composition of Proteins and Foods*. New York, Academic Press, 1947. Special tables of the amino acid composition of various food products are also published by the Food and Agricultural Organization (FAO) of the United Nations in Rome. Soviet and Western publications usually give slightly different figures for the amino acid composition of various grain and food products, probably because of different methods of analysis.
2. The initial estimation in this form for 1960–1964 was made by I. M. Lerner and H. P. Donald, *Modern Development in Animal Breeding*. London and New York, Academic Press, 1966, Table 2. I have updated the table for the period 1970–1980 on the basis of the growth of consumption reflected in the United Nations FAO yearbooks.
3. *Malaya Sovetskaya Meditsinskaya Entsiklopediya*, Vol. 1, op cit., p. 910.
4. *Nar. kozh. 1922–1982*, op cit., p. 447.
5. A. M. Emel'yanov (ed.), *Kompleksnaya programma razvitya sel'skogo khozyaistva v deistvii*. Moscow, Ekonomika, 1980, p. 159.
6. *Pravda*, January 5, 1977; *Ekonomicheskaya gazeta*, No. 6, February 1981.
7. *Production Yearbook, 1980*. Rome, FAO.
8. D. Bairamov, "Vernut' verbluda v pustynu," *Izvestiya*, April 12, 1983.
9. V. Vukovich, "Chem podoit' ovtsu?," *Izvestiya*, February 26, 1985.
10. *CMEA Yearbook 1985*, op cit., p. 66. These yearbooks usually give figures up to the year before the year indicated in the title. The *Narodnoye khozyaistvo* yearbooks include statistics for the year indicated in the title, and in

References and Notes   437

tables (demographic, livestock population, etc.) for the beginning of the subsequent year as well. Thus the 1984 *CMEA Yearbook* has figures up to 1983 only, while *Nar. khoz.*, 1983 includes some figures for 1984.
11. *CMEA Yearbook 1984*, op cit., p. 46.
12. *1984 Britannica Book of the Year*, Chicago, Encyclopedia Britannica, 1984, p. 697.
13. *Production Yearbook, 1980*, op cit.
14. *Nar. khoz.*, 1985, op cit.
15. *Ekonomicheskaya gazeta*, No. 50, December 1980.
16. *Izvestiya*, January 24, 1983.
17. *Pravda*, May 26, 1981.
18. V. P. Efimov and V. I. Manyakin, *Intensifikatsiya sel'skokhozyaistvennogo proizvodstva v SSSR*. Moscow, Statistika, 1980, p. 119.
19. *Nar. khoz.*, 1982, op cit., p. 384.
20. *CMEA Yearbook 1983*, op cit., p. 247.
21. *Nar. khoz.*, 1984, op cit., p. 312.
22. *Pravda*, January 21, 1984.
23. K. Vaino, "Zhivotnovodstvu osobuyu zabotu," *Kommunist*, No. 10, 1981, pp. 62–72.
24. *Ekonomicheskaya gazeta*, No. 31, July 1982.
25. *1984 Britannica Book of the Year*, op cit., p. 237.
26. Ibid., p. 697.
27. A. Amstislavsky, "Sgushcheniye zhizni," *Znaniye—Sila*, December 1984, pp. 7–9.
28. *Pravda*, January 16, 1982.
29. *Sel'skaya zhizn'*, August 31, 1982; *Izvestiya*, August 6, 1982.
30. G. Kovalenko, "Belok dlya zhivotnovodstva," *Izvestiya*, May 30, 1981.
31. *Nar. khoz.*, 1984, op cit., p. 174.
32. G. B. Carter, "Is biotechnology feeding the Russians?," *New Scientist*, April 23, 1981, pp. 216–218.
33. J. H. Lichfield, "Single-cell proteins," *Science*, Vol. 219, 1983, pp. 740–746.
34. *Sel'skaya zhizn'*, July 9, 1981.
35. *Sel'skaya zhizn'*, July 18, 1981.
36. *Pravda*, May 7, 1985.
37. Ibid.
38. V. Belov, "Trebuyetsya doyarka," *Pravda*, December 13, 1983.

CHAPTER 9

1. M. B. Davydov, "Comparative mechanization of agriculture in the USSR and other countries," in R. A. Medvedev (ed.), *Samizdat Register, 2*. New York, Norton and London, Merlin Press, 1981, pp. 210–219.
2. V. P. Efimov and V. I. Manyakin, *Intensifikatsiya sel'skokhozyaistvennogo proizvodstva v SSSR*. Moscow, Statistika, 1980, p. 113.
3. *Nar. khoz.*, 1963, op cit., p. 334.
4. *Nar. khoz.*, 1965, op cit., p. 444; 1979, p. 317; 1983, p. 312; 1984, p. 333.
5. I. Sal'nikov, "Nazrevshiye voprosy podgotovki sel'skokhozyaistvennykh kadrov," *Kommunist*, No. 4, 1968, pp. 53–62.
6. *CMEA Yearbook 1981*, op cit., p. 92.
7. *Nar. khoz.*, 1975, op cit., p. 335.
8. *Vneshnyaya torgovlya SSSR v 1983 godu*, Moscow, Statistika, 1984, p. 56.
9. Yu. Chernichenko, "Kombain kosit i molotit," *Novy mir*, No. 3, 1983.
10. *Pravda*, April 25, 1982.

11. *Pravda*, September 21, 1984.
12. Yu. Gribov, "Vstrechi v puti. Russkoye polye," in *Ocherk, 1981.* Moscow, Sovremennik, 1982, p. 42.
13. *Pravda*, January 15, 1981.
14. *Pravda*, May 12, 1985.
15. Ibid.
16. *Ekonomicheskaya gazeta*, No. 36, September 1983, p. 9.
17. *Izvestiya*, April 2, 1984.
18. *Pravda*, September 29, 1966.
19. *Ekonomicheskaya gazeta*, No. 4, January 1982.
20. P. Yakovlev, "Tekhnicheskoye obsluzhivaniye mashino-traktornogo parka," *Voprosy ekonomiki*, No. 8, 1982.
21. Yu. Chernichenko, op cit.
22. *FAO Fertilizer Yearbook 1980.* Rome, Food and Agricultural Organization, 1980.
23. *CMEA Yearbook 1984*, op cit., pp. 203–204.
24. V. D. Pannikov and V. G. Mineyev, "Khimizatsiya zemledeliya," in P. P. Vavilov (ed.), op cit., pp. 45–68.
25. V. P. Nikonov, "Agrokhimicheskaya sluzhba sela," *Ekonomicheskaya gazeta*, No. 11, March 1982, p. 2.
26. *Nar. khoz.*, 1984, op cit., p. 268.
27. *Sovetskaya Rossiya*, June 8, 1986.

CHAPTER 10

1. See, for example, A. Nove, *The Soviet Economic System*, London, Allen & Unwin, 1978; M. L. Goldman, *USSR in Crisis: The Failure of an Economic System*. New York, Norton, 1983.
2. For a few contemporary examples see I. A. Apal'kov and A. S. Smirnov, *Ekonomika, organizatsiya i planirovaniye sel'skokhozyaistvennogo proiz-vodstva.* Moscow, Kolos, 1980; A. G. Belozertsev, *Tekhnichesky progress i proizvoditel'nost' truda v zemledelii.* Moscow, Kolos, 1980; A. M. Emel'yanov and S. I. Polovenko, *Ekonomika sel'skogo khozyaistva na sovremennom etape.* Moscow, Moscow University, 1980; A. M. Emel'yanov (ed.), *Kompleksnaya programma razvitiya sel'skogo khozyaistva v deistvii.* Moscow, Ekonomika, 1980.
3. A. P. Turina,"K voprosu o preobrazovanii kolkhozov v sovkhozy," *Istoriya SSSR*, No. 5, 1983, pp. 6–7.
4. Ibid.
5. *XXIII Syezd KPSS. Stenograficheskiy otchet*, Vol. 1. Moscow, Politizdat, 1966, p. 67.
6. A. P. Turina, op cit., p. 13.
7. *Itogi Vsesoyuznoi perepisi naseleniya 1970 goda*, Vol. 2. Moscow, Statistika, 1972, p. 15.
8. Zh. A. Medvedev, "Negative trends in life expectancy in the USSR, 1964–1983," *The Gerontologist*, Vol. 25, 1985, pp. 201–208.
9. *Izvestiya*, December 9, 10, 1982.
10. *Izvestiya*, December 10, 1981.
11. *Nar. khoz.*, 1983, op cit., p. 196. Figures given in 1983 were reduced in 1984.
12. *SSSR v Tsifrakh v 1985 godu*, Moscow, Finansy i statistika, 1986, pp. 108, 116.
13. M. Bronshtein, "Problemy upravleniya regional'nymi APK," *Voprosy ekonomiki*, No. 6, 1984, p. 63.

14. N. K. Figurovskaya, *Razvitiye agrarnoi teorii v SSSR*. Moscow, Nauka, 1983.
15. A. M. Emel'yanov and S. I. Polovenko, op cit., p. 95.
16. *Nar. khoz.*, 1983, op cit., p. 411.
17. *Izvestiya*, December 17, 1980.
18. A. M. Emel'yanov (ed.), op cit., pp. 19, 159.
19. Ibid.; A. M. Emel'yanov and S. I. Polovenko, op cit., p. 221; V. Kim, "Zakupochnye zeny sel'skokhozyaistvennoi produktsii," *Voprosy ekonomiki*, No. 6, 1982, pp. 60–71; *Ekonomicheskaya gazeta*, No. 31, July 1981.
20. A. M. Emel'yanov (ed.) op cit., pp. 19, 159.
21. A. M. Emel'yanov and S. I. Polovenko, op cit., p. 222; *Ekonomicheskaya gazeta*, No. 33, August 1982.
22. *Izvestiya*, June 14, 1985.
23. *Ekonomicheskaya gazeta*, No. 31, July 1981.
24. *Kommunist*, No. 9, 1982, p. 13.
25. *Nar. khoz.*, 1984, op cit., p. 213.
26. Ibid., p. 207.
27. G. M. Bogush and V. G. Shaikin, *Sel'skoye khozyaistvo SSSR*. Moscow, Kolos, 1982, p. 207.
28. *Nar. khoz.*, 1984, op cit., p. 580.
29. L. I. Brezhnev, "O prodovol'stvennoi programme SSSR," *Kommunist*, No. 9, June 1982, p. 13.
30. L. I. Brezhnev, "O dal'neishem razvitii sel'skogo khozyaistva SSSR," *Pravda*, July 4, 1978.
31. I. A. Apal'kov and A. S. Smirnov, op cit., p. 424.
32. V. Tikhonov, "Kontseptsiya khozyaistvennogo mekhanizma APK," *Voprosy ekonomiki*, No. 8, 1984, p. 146.
33. "O povyshenii material'noi zainteresovannosti kolkhoznikov v razvitii obshchestvennogo proizvodstva. Postanovleniye Tsentral'nogo Komiteta KPSS i Soveta Ministrov SSSR," May 16, 1966.
34. S. A. Vorkunov, *Leninsky kooperativny plan i ego osushchestvleniye v SSSR*. Moscow, Prosveshcheniye, 1980, p. 177.
35. G. Lisichkin, "Spustya dva goda," *Novy mir*, No. 2, 1967, p. 162.
36. *Nar. khoz.*, 1974, op cit., p. 305.
37. Ibid., pp. 760–761.
38. G. Lisichkin, "Sel'sky paradoks. Kak prokormit'sya na sele," *Ocherk 1981*. Moscow, Sovremennik, 1982, pp. 172–187.
39. *Sobraniye postanovlenii pravitel'stva SSSR*, No. 1, 1981, pp. 4–21.
40. *Pravda*, March 11, 1985.
41. *Ekonomicheskaya gazeta*, No. 38, September 1983.
42. *Izvestiya*, March 27, 28, 1984.
43. V. Gayevskaya, 'Kollektivny (brigadny) podryad v sel'skom khozyaistve," *Voprosy statistiki*, No. 2, 1985, p. 38; *Nar. khoz.*, 1984, op cit., p. 327.
44. *Sel'skaya zhizn'*, May 20, 1983.
45. T. I. Zaslavskaya, "Vybor strategii," *Izvestiya*, June 1, 1985.
46. *SSSR v Tsifrakh v 1985 godu*, op cit., p. 134.
47. *Pravda*, March 29, 1986.

CHAPTER 11

1. "Ob otmene neobosnovannykh ogranichenii na priusadebnye uchastki kolkhoznikov, rabochikh i sluzhashchikh," Resolution of the CC CPSU and the Council of Ministers, November 13, 1964.

440   *References and Notes*

2. *Constitution of the USSR.* Moscow, Novosti Press Agency, 1980, p. 25.
3. *Nar. khoz.*, 1956, op cit., p. 140; 1963, pp. 341, 364; 1984, p. 276.
4. *SSSR v Tsifrakh v 1985 godu*, op cit., p. 134.
5. *Constitution of the USSR*, op cit., p. 50.
6. V. Nefedov, "Razvitiye podsobnykh khozyaistv," *Voprosy ekonomiki*, No. 11, p. 56.
7. Ibid.
8. G. Lisichkin, "Kak prokormitsya na sele," *Ocherk 1981.* Moscow, Sovremennik, 1982, pp. 175–176.
9. G. Shmelev, "Obshchestvennoye proizvodstvo i lichnoye podsobnoye khozyaistvo," *Voprosy ekonomiki*, No. 5, 1983, p. 69.
10. G. Lisichkin, op cit., p. 174.
11. "O lichnykh podsobnykh khozyaistvakh kolkhoznikov, rabochikh, sluzhashchikh i drugikh grazhdan," Resolution of the CC CPSU and Council of Ministers, September 14, 1977.
12. *Pravda*, January 18, 1981.
13. G. Lisichkin, op cit., p. 175.
14. Ibid., pp. 176–178.
15. G. I. Shmelev, *Lichnoye podsobnoye khozyaistvo. Vozmozhnosti i perspektivy.* Moscow, Gospolitizdat, 1983, pp. 81, 94.
16. *Izvestiya*, August 6, 1984.
17. V. Nefedov, op cit., p. 53.
18. See *Konevodstvo i konny sport*, No. 6, June 1985, p. 8.
19. Ibid., p. 7.
20. Ibid., p. 7.

Chapter 12

1. *Nar. khoz.*, 1963, op cit., p. 55.
2. *Nar. khoz.*, 1984, op cit., p. 36; *SSSR v Tsifrakh v 1985 godu*, op cit., p. 17.
3. *Nar. khoz.*, 1984, op cit., p. 59.
4. *World Statistics in Brief*, 7th edition. New York, United Nations Statistical Pocketbook, 1983.
5. *Izvestiya*, June 11, 1986.
6. Alec Nove, *The Soviet Economic System.* London, Allen & Unwin, 1978, p. 362.
7. *Vneshnyaya torgovlya SSSR v 1983 godu (Vnesh. torg.)*, Moscow, Statistika, 1984, p. 74.
8. *Vnesh. torg.*, 1983, op cit., pp. 6, 18; 1984. The term "import ruble" is used to define the ruble official equivalent of foreign hard currency which is actually used for food imports. However, the official exchange rate for rubles is artificial and does not reflect its value.
9. Ibid., p. 18; 1976, p. 18; 1974, p. 21.
10. *Kommunist*, No. 8, May 1985, p. 30.
11. U.S. Department of Agriculture. Foreign Agriculture Circular. Grains. *USSR Grain Situation and Outlook*, Washington, D.C., SG-7-86, July 1986; Lester R. Brown, *US and Soviet Agriculture: The Shifting Balance of Power.* Washington, D.C., Worldwatch Paper 51, 1982, p. 26; Robert L. Paarlberg, *Food Trade and Foreign Policy.* Ithaca, N.Y. and London, Cornell University Press, 1985, Table 6, p. 88.
12. *Nar. khoz.*, 1984, op cit., pp. 34–35.

13. A. Isupov, "Mirovye demograficheskiye protsessy i opredelyayushchiye ikh faktory," *Voprosy statistiki*, No. 2, 1985, p. 59.
14. Lester R. Brown, "World Population Growth, Soil Erosion and Food Security," *Science*, Vol. 214, 1981, p. 995.
15. Ibid.
16. *Pravda*, December 14, 1968.
17. *Izvestiya*, January 8, 1984.
18. *Soil Erosion: Quiet Crisis in the World Economy*. Washington, D.C., Worldwatch Institute, 1984.
19. A. Yanshin, V. Kovda and S. Zhukov, "Sud'ba chernozema," *Pravda*, May 31, 1984.
20. *Izvestiya*, December 5, 1984.
21. G. Shakhnazarov, *The Coming World Order*. Moscow, Progress Publishers, 1984, p. 147.
22. Lester R. Brown, *US and Soviet Agriculture: The Shifting Balance of Power*, op cit., p. 23.
23. "O merakh po dal'neishemu razvitiyu sel'skogo khozyaistva nechernozemnoi zony RSFSR," Resolution of the CC CPSU and Council of Ministers of the USSR, *Pravda*, April 3, 1974.
24. I. S. Turgenev, *Sobraniye sochinenii*, Vol. 1. Moscow, Khudozhestvennaya Literatura, 1954, p. 75.
25. *Nar. khoz.*, 1974, op cit., p. 425; 1980, p. 259.
26. *Nar. khoz.*, 1974, op cit., pp. 16–17; 1980, pp. 13–14.
27. M. I. Sinykov (ed.), *Nechernozemnaya zona RSFSR*. Moscow, Ekonomika, 1980, p. 11.
28. *Pravda*, April 15, 1981.
29. M. S. Solomentsev, "Nechernozem'e: novye gorizonty razvitiya," *Voprosy istorii KPSS*, No. 7, 1981, p. 6.
30. Ibid., p. 3.
31. *Pravda*, December 26, 1984.
32. L. Osheverova, "Sogret' odinokuyu starost'," *Izvestiya*, January 1, 1985.
33. *Pravda*, July 2, 1985.
34. *Pravda*, November 17, 1981.
35. *Kommunist*, No. 9, June 1982. This issue published the entire proceedings of the Food Program plenum.
36. Ibid., p. 10.
37. Ibid., p. 12.
38. Ibid., pp. 16–23. Published in 1982 as a separate booklet by Politizdat.
39. *Nar. khoz.*, 1983, op cit., pp. 8–9.
40. *Pravda*, October 24, 1984.
41. V. Velichko, "Sberech nashi chernozemy," *Izvestiya*, November 21, 1984.
42. *Pravda*, May 31, 1984.
43. *Pravda*, February 27–March 4, 1985.
44. See, for example, Lester R. Brown, op cit.; D. G. Johnson and K. M. Brooks, *Prospects for Soviet Agriculture in the 1980s*. Bloomington, Indiana University Press, 1983; Robert Paarlberg, op cit.; M. Goldman, *USSR in Crisis: The Failure of an Economic System*. New York, Norton, 1983.
45. *Izvestiya*, June 1, 1985.
46. G. Lisichkin, *Ternisty put' k izobiliyu*. Moscow, Sovetsky Pisatel', 1984.
47. *Izvestiya*, January 18, 1986; March 20, 1986.
48. *Izvestiya*, March 29, 1986.

MAPS

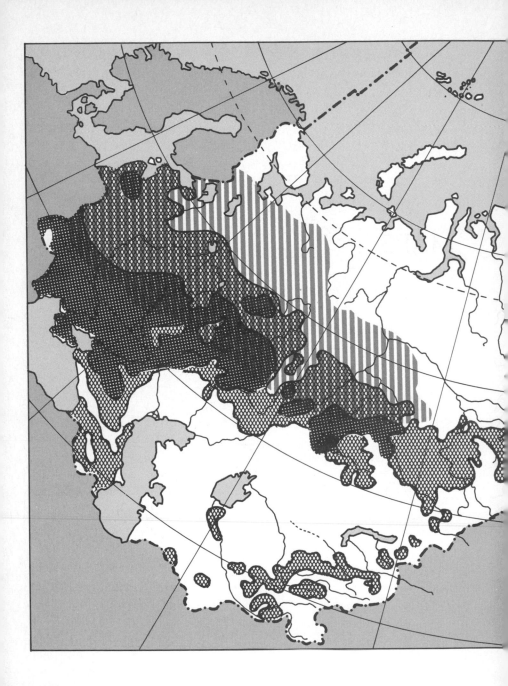

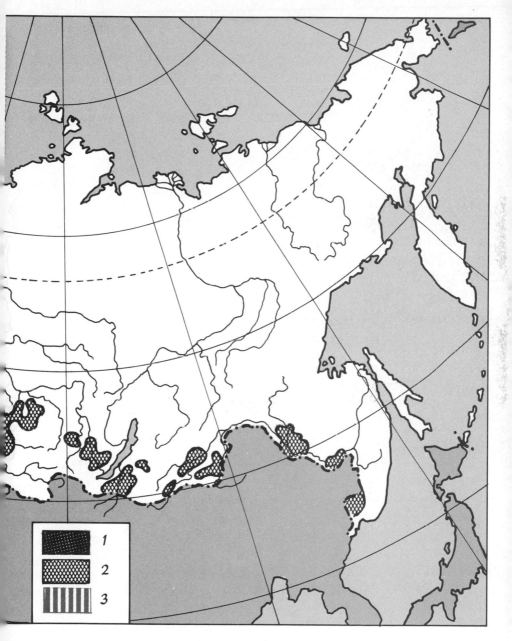

MAP 1. Agriculture in the Soviet Union
(Grain-growing Areas)

1—areas heavily sown to wheat;
2—areas less heavily sown to wheat, the main grain crop;
3—rye-growing areas

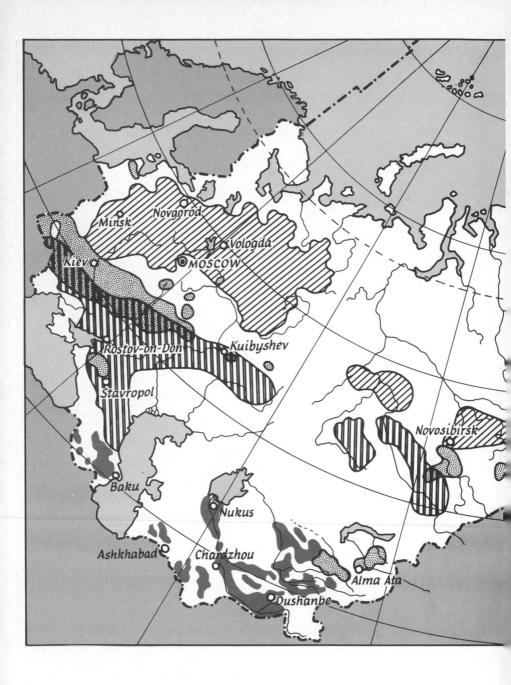

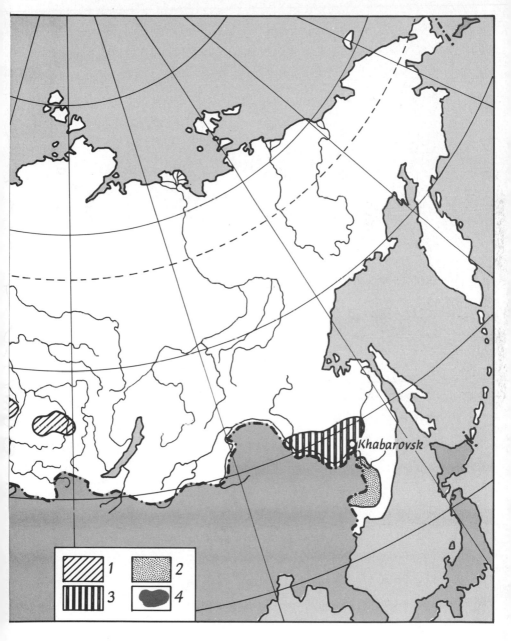

MAP 2. Basic Technical Crops

1— flax; 2—sugar beet; 3—sunflower; 4—cotton

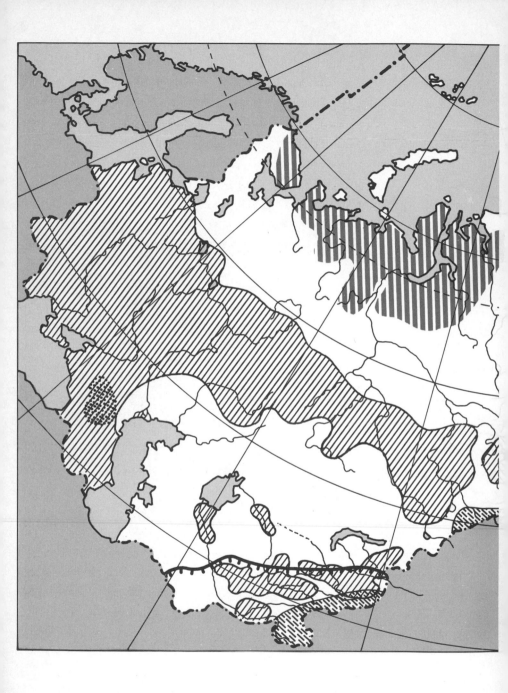

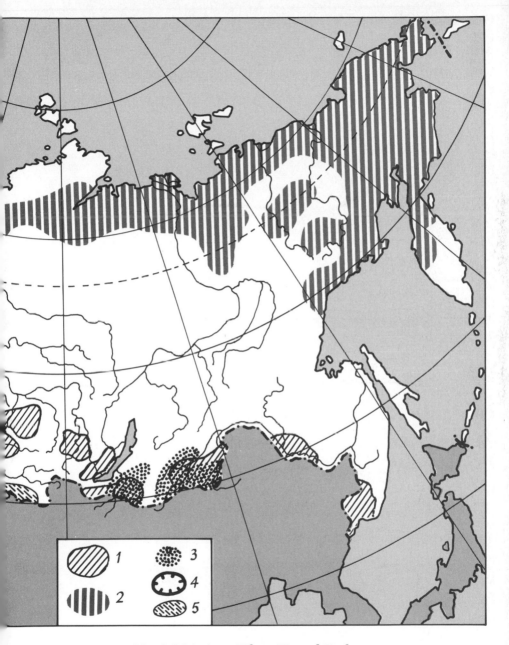

**MAP 3. Main Areas Where Horned Cattle,
Reindeer, Sheep, and Yaks Are Raised**

1—horned cattle; 2—reindeer; 3—fine-fleece sheep;
4—astrakhan sheep; 5—yaks

Index

451

456 *Index*

intensification of agriculture:
components of, 317
grain increase through, 210
limits to, 315–16
in livestock production, 243, 257,
264
see also chemicalization; mechanization
interfarm enterprises, 264, 318–20,
321
interfarm mechanization stations
(MPM), 300
investments in agriculture:
assessment of, 342–44
grain production and, 238
investment/production paradox,
325, 331, 343–44, 351, 389
livestock production and, 279
irrigation and river diversion program, 231, 270–71, 409–12
Isupov, A., 393
Ivan IV, Czar (Ivan the Terrible), 4

Kaganovich, L. M., 89, 90, 172
Kalinin, M. I., 37
Kamenev, L. B., 37
Karatygin, E. S., 84
Kazakhstan, Virgin Land Program in,
169–71
Kerensky, Alexander, 24
Khrushchev, Nikita S., 92
administrative and educational reforms, 186–90
agricultural expertise, 161–62
balance sheet of his agricultural
policies, 197–202
Exhibition of Achievements in Agriculture, 152
on famine of 1946–1947, 133–34
final harvest under, 207–8
final reorganization plans, 196
food shortage of 1963, 191, 193–96
impatience of, 185
kolkhozy amalgamation, 152–54
Lysenko's theories, support for,
162, 190
meat program, 180–83, 249
ministerial appointments and dismissals, 185–86
MTS, abolition of, 176–77, 308
New Pay policy, 184
openness about problems, 163

private agriculture, campaign
against, 193–95
procurement system reforms, 164–
67, 177–78
pronouncements, manner of, 204
retirement, 197
Virgin Land Program, 96, 167–68,
170–74, 192
"Khrushchev syndrome," 201–2
Kirichenko, 185–86
"Kirovets" tractor, 397
Kolkhoztsentr, 70, 73, 89, 320
kolkhozy (collective farms):
amalgamation of, 152–54, 320
bank credits for, 343–45, 350
capital construction work on, 331–
32
chemical fertilizer problems, 308,
309–10
financial problems, 154–55, 318,
344–45
guaranteed payments to members,
318
borrowings to cover, 350
calculation of, 347
economic collapse averted
through, 349
introduction of, 347
official praise for, 347–48
procurement prices and, 350–51
production costs and, 350
productivity and, 348–50, 351
solutions to problems generated
by, 351–52
livestock production, 182, 262–64,
265
machine operator shortage, 286
Machine Tractor Stations:
abolition, impact of, 178–80
mergers with, 176–78
members' desertion of, 156–57,
320–21
ministries, problems in dealing
with, 327–28, 330
mobility restrictions on members,
91–92, 95, 321–23
number of (1918–1929), 69–70
organic deficiencies of agriculture
in, 417–18
poultry production, 266
private agriculture:
current situation, 362–63, 364
postwar tax on, 155–56, 157, 162

462 *Index*

retail prices (*continued*)
  procurement prices, relation to,
    164–66, 337, 342, 350–51
  production costs and, 340–41
  strikes due to increases in, 183
  subsidies for, 250, 279, 335–36,
    337, 339–40, 341
Revolution of 1905, 13–14
Revolution of 1917:
  as agrarian revolution, xi
  commodity shortages, 26
  first Provisional Government, 21–
    23, 24, 25, 26–27, 28
  land redistribution failures, 22–23,
    24, 25
  nationalization of land, 28–29
  obshchiny, land confiscation by,
    23–24, 25–26, 28–29
  October Revolution, 26–28
  pomeshchik estates, destruction of,
    24, 25–26
  rural situation preceding, 20
  sowing season in spring, 22–23
  as spontaneous uprising, 20–21, 28
Ricardo, David, 394
rural depopulation, Soviet and western patterns of, 413–14
rutin (Vitamin P) production, 224
Ryasantsev, A. V., 84
Ryazan fiasco, 182
rye production, 215–18
Rykov, A. I., 72, 115

Salisbury, Harrison, 21
scientific advances, problems in as-
  similation of, 418
scientific approach to agriculture, introduction of, 205–6
SCP, *see* single-cell proteins
Selkhoztekhnika (repair and service
  stations), 325, 326
  creation of, 282
  differentiation of, 298
  failure of system, 300–301
  fault correction, responsibility for,
    298, 299
  kolkhozy, working relationship
    with, 282, 297–300
  personnel of, 298–99
  reorganization of, proposed, 299
  tractor facilities, 286
serfdom, 3–6
Shakhnazarov, G., 398

Shayakhmetov, Zh., 170, 171
sheep for milk production, 254
"Sibiryak" combines, 294–95
single-cell proteins (SCP), 276–77
Socialist Revolutionaries (SRs), xii, 6,
  14, 22, 31
soil erosion:
  collectivization and, 100
  excessive cultivation and, 396–97
  fertility, impact on, 307
  increases in, 397–98
  preventive measures, 397
  tractors as cause of, 397
  Virgin Land Program and, 192–93
soil types, 396
Solomentsev, M. S., 404
Soviets, 22, 46–47
sovkhozy (state farms), 70–71
  bank credits for, 343–45
  capital construction on, 331–32
  financial problems, 344–45
  gulag sovkhozy, 116
  kolkhozy transformed into, 96–97,
    155, 200–201, 318, 319, 320,
    349
  land regulations, 104
  livestock production, 262–64, 265
  ministries, problems in dealing
    with, 327–28, 330
  organic deficiencies of agriculture
    in, 417–18
  population patterns, 321
  as predominant form of agriculture,
    97
  private agriculture on, 363, 364
  see also contract brigades
Sovnarkhozy (Councils of National
  Economy), 281
Sovnarkom (Council of People's
  Commissars), 30, 57, 76, 102,
  109
Soyuzselkhozkhimiya (agrochemistry
  service), 283, 308–10, 327
speculators, restrictions on, 370–71
SRs, *see* Socialist Revolutionaries
"stable reproduction" policy, 393
Stalin, Josef, 37, 93, 94
  agricultural ministries, creation of,
    151
  collectivization, 46, 71–72, 76, 80,
    89
  CPSU, control of, 47
  death, 158